LYRIC SHAME

Lyric Shame

*The "Lyric" Subject
of Contemporary
American Poetry*

GILLIAN WHITE

Harvard University Press
Cambridge, Massachusetts
London, England
2014

Library of Congress Cataloging-in-Publication Data

White, Gillian C., 1968-
   Lyric shame : the "lyric" subject of contemporary American poetry /
Gillian White.
      pages cm
   Includes bibliographical references and index.
   ISBN 978-0-674-73439-5 (alk. paper)
  1. American poetry—20th century—History and criticism—
Theory, etc.   2. American poetry—21st century—History and
criticism—Theory, etc.   3. Emotions in literature   I. Title.
   PS325.W47 2014
   811'.5409—dc23

                                                    2014004433

FOR MY FAMILY

Contents

LYRIC SHAME

Introduction

His owner's voice arises, stern,
"You ought to be ashamed!"
What has he done?
He bounces cheerfully up and down;
he rushes in circles in the fallen leaves.

Obviously, he has no sense of shame.
—*Elizabeth Bishop, "Five Flights Up"*

ELIZABETH BISHOP'S 1974 poem "Five Flights Up" describes a dog owner's anthropomorphizing attempt to shame his pet.[1] The owner's statement "You ought to be ashamed!" works two ways—a speech act intended to produce the dog's shame, it also, paradoxically, would like to claim that that shame already should have originated with the dog. Shame involves thinking about what others think of you and, as the poem wryly suggests, knowing that "you" *are* a "you." The joke, that is, is that "obviously" the dog has "no sense of shame," or, anyway, it would be difficult to verify whether it has the complex self-awareness that could help us decide whether it is "shameless" or not. It becomes more and more difficult to decide whose shame is whose here. The line "What has he done?"—its pronoun hovering, undecided, over both dog and owner—makes it possible that the shame that the owner expects and projects onto his dog's submissive behaviors might in fact be his own.

Bishop's lines emphasize shame as an importantly mobile, intersubjective emotion, evident in the strange grammar it requires. Eve Kosofsky Sedgwick calls it a "transformational grammar," for "the absence of an explicit verb from 'Shame on you' records the place in which an I, in conferring shame, has effaced itself and its own agency."[2] Indeed, in Bishop's poem, the "I" is effaced, the poet's voice perhaps projected onto "his owner's," triangulating the dyad of dog and owner and subtly suggesting the possibility that *her* shame, along with his fantasy that he and his dog are watched, is also in question. After all, there are no quotation marks in the poem to mark the ownership of the statement, "Obviously, he has no sense of shame," another example of the strange "transformational grammar" of I and you, perhaps a suspension of Bishop's own agency (is she in or outside the poem?) and a gesture to shame's lightning-fast mobility. As Sedgwick theorizes it, "Shame . . . is not a discrete intrapsychic structure, but a kind of free radical that . . . attaches to and permanently intensifies or alters the meaning of—of almost anything," a "fleeting emotion" that is nevertheless capable of instituting "durable, structural changes in one's relational and interpretive strategies toward both self and others."[3]

The understanding of shame as a "free radical" that institutes changes in meaning has profound implications for a variety of interpretive situations: I am interested in the role of shame not only in instituting interpretive strategies toward self and others but also in institutions of literary interpretation. What if we interpret the dog that has no sense of shame, as he "rushes in circles in the fallen leaves," as a figure for what poems do in the current literary culture, circling about amid the question of shame? How does our reading of this poem (indeed, of post–World War II American poetry) produce a sense of shame, especially if the "owner's voice arises" (and here, we may read "owner" to include critics or the dominant interpretive culture) to call it a lyric poem, to make its I a "lyric I"?

This book revolves around a sense of shame involved in twentieth-century "lyric reading," producing and describing what I call lyric shame.[4] By "lyric shame," I mean primarily shame experienced in identifications with modes of reading and writing understood to be lyric, especially as these have been determined by a diffuse "New Critical" discourse by now so thoroughly absorbed as to seem natural. At the risk of oversimplifying the New Criticism, it is fair to say that the dominant conception of lyric, and of poetic interpretation, derived from New Critical theories and established in American universities in the late 1930s (and so influential, many poets and scholars argue, as to produce a "canon of taste" thereafter) contributed to a view of lyric poems as expressive objects that "speak" to the reader without, paradoxically, the reader's need to understand anything of the history of the work's production, reception, or circulation.[5] That understanding supposes lyric to be a genre transcending time and history, and the lyric poem, as one poet-critic recently put it, a "message in a bottle" that "speaks out of a solitude to a solitude," mastering the conditions of time and contingency.[6] Cleanth Brooks and Robert Penn Warren's *Understanding Poetry* (1938), widely distributed as a teaching tool that dominated poetic pedagogy for the next twenty-five years, also assumes natural connections between poetry, interpretive mastery, formal control, and a cure for existential dread, a cluster that has come to define both the ideal and anti-ideal of lyric in the twentieth and early twenty-first centuries. They write,

> For in so far as [the reader] appreciates the poem he has a sense of the conquest over the disorder and meaninglessness of experience. Perhaps this sense may be the very basis for his exhilaration in the poem—just as it may be the basis for the pleasure one takes in watching the clean drive of the expert golfer or the swoop of a bird in the air, as contrasted with the accidental tumbling of a stone down a hillside. It is this same sense of order and control given by a successful poem that confirms us in the faith that the experiences of life itself may have meaning.[7]

Brooks and Warren do not use the word "lyric" here, but as Steve Newman has argued, the Brooks/Warren close readings of even ballads in the opening section of *Understanding Poetry* seek to show a dramatic structure they assumed was inherent to "all poems," illustrating an interpretive mode that draws its premises from nineteenth-century lyric theory. Indeed, one could say, with Newman, that Brooks and Warren's readings of ballads, as of all poems, were instrumental to the making of "an American lyric subject."[8]

Even if one only dimly senses the values and politics that attach to the ideal of lyric that Brooks and Warren espoused (one so successful that it determines how most poetry is read in universities today), one might have encountered the "ambient shame" of lyric among academic readers and writers in the United States, especially as it attends the writing and reading of "first-person lyric," the Confessional, and "personal" poems.[9] "Lyric" is a charged word and concept: in poetry circles, it is a word and concept disparaged, defended, repurposed, and much discussed. Canadian poet and blogger Sina Queyras's recent call on her blog and on the Academy of American Poets blog for "New Lyric Manifestos" is characteristic of the lyric shame moment: despite many recent calls to hasten the "death of lyric," she argues, "what we appear to want is poetry that retains that y as in lyric poetry. We want a speaking subject, or we want to be spoken directly to, . . . to speak about something more pressing than what we think others are speaking about. What exactly is that? . . . We aren't about to move away from lyric, . . . but we can write to something else."[10]

Queyras's ambivalent call for a new lyric depends on a host of assumptions about a coherent "old lyric" that have been powerful in determining the discourses of contemporary poetry in North America and that *Lyric Shame* will historicize and question. The broadest aim of this book is to explore the sources, dynamics, and consequences of that ambience of lyric shame, then, especially as it circles about and gets projected onto the work, critical reception, and reputations of three twentieth-century American poets: Elizabeth Bishop, Anne Sexton, and Bernadette Mayer. Each of these authors' writing has been identified, by different audiences and in different spirits, with the expressive lyric (including that "speaking subject" to which Queyras refers). And given that "expressive lyric" is the chief abjection of a powerful and increasingly canonical avant-garde antilyricism now forty years in the making, it is an identification that opens these poets' work to shame. But thinking again of Bishop's little dog, whose shame is it?

Though poems "obviously" do not have selves, it is fair to say that in our tendency to anthropomorphize them (as happens if we think about their "speakers" or their "voice" or if we deem their supposed confessions shamefully narcissistic), they become subject to shame that is not, so to speak, theirs. The "lyric shame" of my title, that is, does not refer to expressions of shame in lyric or even shame about lyric. One of the broad premises of this book is that "expressive lyric" is an abstraction that gets projected onto some writing. More locally, my concern is the projection of "expressive lyric" onto some midcentury American work to produce its subjective voice. Such abstractions and projections can sometimes enable a positive identification, as when Helen Vendler imagines Robert Lowell to have been jealous of Elizabeth Bishop's "lyric transparency."[11] In the current academic climate, however, aspects of Bishop's identification with lyric, for one example of a broader trend, portray her as minor and conservative—articulating a form of public shaming. The lyric shame I wish to expose and explore here is that of poetry idealized as "lyric," or the lyric shamed—shame attributed to, projected onto, and produced by readings that anthropomorphize poems as "lyric."

The history of shame about lyric and (or as) poetry is long. For a brief example, the convention in Hellenistic poetry of *recusatio* (literally, "refusal"), by which a poet implicitly or explicitly refused a conventional subject or style, tended most often to entail the poet's halfhearted apology for his unwillingness (or purported inability) to write grand epic themes or meters, as opposed to lesser lyric or elegiac ones.[12] Poetry's regrettable marginality to public life is another ancient trope reasserted and historicized (as either a point of pride, a defense, shame, or a mix of these) by poets writing in English from at least the sixteenth century. Georgia Brown argues in her recent study of early modern poetics that English writers of the 1590s keen to imagine new political and literary subjects reference an ideal of lyric that is productive precisely for its "potentially shameful" associations "with the marginal experiences of privacy, and . . . distracting realms of emotionalism and desire."[13]

More relevant to this study is the present-day understanding of late-eighteenth-century "Romantic lyric," which, as Anne Janowitz has argued, has been shaped by a "lyric hegemony" evolved from the 1840s that flattens that era's idea of lyric into an image of a "secure poetic infrastructure for a transcendent self of lyric solitude." Scholars such as Janowitz have worked in the past ten years to recast Romantic lyric as a "theatre of engagement for competing and alternate versions of personal, political, and cultural identity" and to complicate the potent, monolithic myth of a Greater Romantic lyric mode by showing the period's varied and complex researches into identity as a mix of social determination and voluntaristic individualism.[14] Much of the modern and postmodern shame of lyric identification assumes the caricatured figure of the Romantic lyric that Janowitz and others seek to complicate, supposing "lyric" to be defined by unmitigated individualistic subjectivism, self-absorption, leisured privilege, and ahistoricism.

That said, it is not my intention to retell the history of the formation of a "lyric hegemony"; *Lyric Shame* rather explores one small chapter of the recent history of lyric reading in the United States to consider its influences on the reading, writing, and canonization of poetry and poetics in the U.S. academy. My object in *Lyric Shame* is to analyze the shame of "lyric" without attempting to turn it somewhere else; I locate its dynamics in modes of *reading* rather than in individual poems or authors' canons or in "bad" examples or phases of a genre. I do want to take stock of the canonical pressures that a New Critical characterization of "lyric," in its latest manifestations as Language and (more diffusely) post-Language antilyric discourse about "expressive" lyric, has exerted—hence my choice of authors here: each of the authors to whom I devote a chapter of this book—Bishop, Sexton, and Mayer—has been identified with (or, in the case of Sexton, asked to personify) the expressive "lyric" abjected by avant-garde antilyricism. What happens if we view that identification in terms of a history of lyric reading? What if instead of shaming their poems, we find the varied ways they register the pressure of midcentury literary norms, particularly the ideal of poetry's expressive privacy that New Critics claimed is inherent to all poetry? Critics have tended to read the figure of the speaker in these writers' works (even Mayer's, though to a lesser degree) in such a way that aligns them with the shame of expressive lyric. In what other ways could that figure be read? What new forms of lyric reading might their works provoke?

What *Lyric Shame* proposes is that these writers, conventionally thought to be "lyric" (whether defended or shamed for it), offer us new inroads through the problematic and interesting interpretive limit of the personal. They only awkwardly fit the "lyric" ideal abstracted and projected on them by both their fans and detractors, and they can even be read to foreground writing and discourse as these disrupt the figure of the poetic speaker that is so often assumed as quintessentially "lyric." Where does that get us? Even though Bishop and Sexton do not employ radically disjunctive techniques of avant-garde writing (and even though Mayer self-consciously tests the limits of disjunctive technique), we can identify, in heretofore-unimagined ways, their works' awarenesses of the shame an identification with lyric might entail. Might poems register resistances to lyricizing readings of them without taking on the premises of avant-garde antilyricism? I will read putatively mainstream, Confessional, and expressive works that exceed and test the limits of the New Critical conventions that they supposedly exemplify, a move that opens up new chapters in the history of what Virginia Jackson has called the "lyricization of poetry."[15]

Much of the work I read here, and whose shame I have often felt as my own, is self-consciously (even ashamedly) marked as "lyric"—overdeterminedly "overheard" and often perplexed, sometimes stranded—revolving around and even pushing against the impossibility of the speakers it has been held to embody. We can read this work to foreground canonical attachments to "personal" utterance as a critical problem full of possibility, and one that neither has to be read to shore up the ideal of lyric (as New Critical lyric-reading norms would dictate) nor (as avant-garde norms would counter) has to serve as antilyric lyric scapegoat. This work is ineluctably involved with and thus invites our awareness of the shame dynamics that enter lyric readings in the late twentieth and early twenty-first centuries. In this, I am arguing that lyric reading can be understood as, in its late-twentieth-century version, a kind of shaming. Poems are ashamed but have no sense of shame. What can we make of poetry if we try to unashame it, engaging (new? un-? something other than anti-) lyric readings of it?

READING FOR SHAME

In order to introduce some features of the poetic shame culture that this book explores and to preview the kinds of acute intersubjective critical problems that the idealization and anti-idealization of "lyric" raises within that culture, I would like to introduce you to a contemporary poem, "Anybody Can Write a Poem" (2010), by the young American poet Bradley Paul.[16] Like much of the most contemporary work that this study takes up, Paul's poem mobilizes the most ubiquitous, negative lyric stereotypes that get projected on some poems—solipsistic, rapacious ego, driven to mastery, narcissistic confessionalist, conservative both aesthetically and politically—that have made lyric a shameful identification in discourses of contemporary American poetics in recent decades. Paul's poem unfolds as a first-person past-tense narrative (that drifts in and out of "interior" meditation) of an online argument "I" has had with "an idiot" who "says anybody can write a poem." Here it is in full:

Anybody Can Write a Poem

I am arguing with an idiot online.
He says anybody can write a poem.
I say some people are afraid to speak.
I say some people are *ashamed* to speak.
If they said the pronoun "I"
they would find themselves floating
in the black Atlantic
and a woman would swim by, completely
dry, in a rose chiffon shirt,
until the ashamed person says her name
and the woman becomes wet and drowns
and her face turns to flayed ragged pulp,
white in the black water.
He says that he'd still write

even if someone cut off both his hands.
As if it were the hands that make a poem,
I say. I say what if someone cut out
whatever brain or gut or loin or heart
that lets you say hey, over here, listen,
I have something to tell you all,
I'm *different*.
As an example I mention my mother
who loved that I write poems
and am such a wonderful genius.
And then I delete the comment
because my mother wanted no part of this or any
argument, because "Who am I
to say whatever?"
Once on a grade school form
I entered her job as *hairwasher*.
She saw the form and was embarrassed and mad.
"You should have put *receptionist*."
But she didn't change it.
The last word she ever said was No.
And now here she is in my poem,
so proud of her idiot son,
who presumes to speak for a woman
who wants to tell him to shut up, but can't.

It is difficult not to notice how often the first thirteen lines figure poetic composition (anybody can write a poem) as *saying* and *speech* ("ashamed to speak"). This slip from writing to speech is most glaring in the awkward line, "If they said the pronoun 'I,'" for we would more commonly think of "saying I" or "*writing* the pronoun 'I.'" The line foregrounds the slippage between speech and writing, yet the poem as a whole can be read to proudly assert this idealization of poetry as "lyric"—as expressive speech. Statements by the author corroborate that reading: in an interview, Paul tells the poet Russell Bittner that the poem was "motivated" in part by his mother's death from pancreatic cancer in 2006, followed by the death of his grandmother three months later, events that turned his aesthetic toward the personal and expressive, we could say: "I found I could no longer write as hermetically and ironically as I had in my first book." Paul goes so far as to insist in the interview that "poetry is speech," invoking William Wordsworth (and thus an expressive theory of lyric often identified with Romanticism) to gloss Bittner's assumption that the poem is about how crisis can result in an aesthetic turn toward "lyric" virtues understood to be natural—chiefly, the personal and sincere—in spite of their potential embarrassments. Paul argues that his aesthetic shift might be described by the idea that "an undue emphasis on artifice is lost because 'a deep distress' humanizes your soul."[17]

As the comments about artifice, hermeticism, and irony suggest, the very emphasis in Paul's poem on the trope of poetic speech and its foregrounding of the identification of writing with speech is nevertheless not naïve: to the contrary, it seems knowingly informed by the understanding that first-person poetic modes can produce feelings of shame or the possibility of being shamed by others. It is no accident that this poem's occasion is an "online" argument: Paul is no doubt aware of the variety of weblogs, most notably *Harriet* and *Silliman's Blog*, on which, any day of the week in the past ten years, one could find invective-filled debates about "lyric" and "antilyric" poetics.[18] Nevertheless, one strong possible reading of the poem is that the author-I's argument with the "idiot" is that some people cannot write poems because they are too ashamed to engage expressive aesthetics: that is, to express themselves would be, in combination, so risky and self-indulgent as to result in something comparable to disaster.

However savvy the poem is to the lyric/antilyric debate, in this reading, its conclusion advocates a poetics of initially ashamed but finally triumphant self-expression; the impersonal, anonymous drowned woman transforms into the presumably dead mother because the opened floodgates of the personal have allowed such an imaginative transformation. Given what I know of Paul's biography, this renders his poem's "I" now not only genuine but autobiographical. The pathos of the poem in this expressive, psychological reading of it is that Paul is both the "I" who feels ashamed to write about his mother's death and the "idiot" who does it anyway.

However, what happens to the expressive reading if we take the slippage between writing and speech in the poem more literally; that is, what if we read it without identifying Paul with the speaker, the idiot, or "I" (in any combination)? Rather than accepting as rote the idea that "writing a poem" is the same thing as speech, in the more literal reading, we could take "writing a poem" and "speaking" as competing models for the production and interpretation of a poem. Then the poem reflects the late-twentieth-century concern about poetry's identification (as a genre) with "absorptive" first-person subjective expression and reflects on the shame of that inheritance of a "lyric" ideal for contemporary poets and critics. What is "ashamed to speak" is not a person ashamed to reveal himself—one repressed or shy or reluctant to engage the personal—but a poem ashamedly entangled in an identification of "writing" with "speech" that has described but also informed conventions of first-person poetic practice and lyric reading since the early nineteenth century.

Paul's poem suggests how fraught the taking on of tropes of the personal and "lyric" can feel at this historical moment—flagged by the grotesquely hyperbolized figuration of the consequences of "sa[ying] the pronoun 'I'": if the poem were to take on lyric-reading/writing norms, it would be *disastrous*—on par with a deadly shipwreck that is figured with connotations ("the black Atlantic") of a history of patriarchy and racial oppression.[19] Here, writerly acts of self-enunciation (saying "the pronoun 'I'") and acts of literary identification are not only personally shameful but figured as forms of culturally implicated violence: it is as though to say "I" and to "presume to speak" for this woman (indeed, to appropriate her as a Poe-like object for the expressive poem) will be to have caused her death.

That the hyperbole serves as more than a window into the psychology of Paul or a speaker is indicated, again, by what Charles Bernstein would call "antiabsorptive" effects, chiefly the foregrounding of poetry as *writing* to the point of ironizing what the poem "says":[20]

> He says that he'd still write
> even if someone cut off both his hands.
> As if it were the hands that make a poem,
> I say. I say what if someone cut out
> whatever brain or gut or loin or heart
> that lets you say hey, over here, listen,
> I have something to tell you all,
> I'm *different*.

Even as the semantic content of several lines encourages our identification of written poetry with expressive speech, they emphasize craft's artifice to the point of ironizing the illusion of poetry as spontaneous speech. The line "I have something to tell you all, / I'm *different*" depends on italics to make us "hear" (read) this "spoken" difference and only calls attention to the lexicality it suppresses by urging us to "listen." Furthermore, the specialness of "I" (its supposedly important difference from everyone else) is comically undermined by the fact that it wishes to make this claim on behalf of a universal "you." In only thirty-eight lines, the word "say" appears twelve times, along with "mention," "comment," "speak" (twice), and "tell" (a remarkable total of seventeen verbal-expression words that stand in for the act of writing a poem). Of course, it is the hands that (literally) make a poem, unless one truly does not have hands, at which point the need for scriptural technologies to mediate "voice" or other clichéd figures for poetic inspiration—gut, loin, and so on—that allow one to be (metonymically) "heard" by more than a live audience becomes pointedly apparent.

In this, the poem quietly complicates the very figures—of speech and hearing—that have been so instrumental to abstractions about "the lyric," figures that it nevertheless also seems (taken expressively) to advocate; "tone" is wayward at best through the next several lines, in which something that could be mocking irony (the mother's view of the son as such a "wonderful genius") gives way to a discursive oddity reminiscent of a John Ashbery poem ("Who am I to say whatever?"). Though messy in a way that mimics real speech, the poem nevertheless works against the ideal of "lyric" that the word "speech," conventionally, codes.[21] Indeed, despite Paul's claim that poems in his second book forfeit his earlier work's irony in favor of more straight communication, I have trouble seeing how "Anybody Can Write a Poem" evidences this turn. At the same time, given the revelation of pathos at the end, how can I not read the poem as sincere speech, given especially what I know of Paul's life?

As Paul's reader-interpreter, then, I am in an awkward and even uncomfortable position, one that mobilizes (and is mobilized by) the ambience of shame surrounding "lyric" as ideal and anti-ideal. At one level, Paul's poem seems informed by the knowledge that shame now attaches to the supposed politics of thinking of poetry as the "lyric" expression of a person. However, it also touches on and seems informed by the shame of thinking about poetry *without* using an expressive-interpretive lens. Should not Paul's testimony be proof enough that this is a personal poem?[22] Can I not hear Paul's voice urging me to "listen"?[23] At yet, at another level, avant-garde modes of lyric reading would take Paul's poem to be shamefully "lyric" or, in the words of the influential coauthored antilyric manifesto "Aesthetic Tendency and the Politics of Poetry," "a kind of metaphorized testimonial to the validity of one's life and moral choices," whose legibility at the level of the phrase and sentence, among other things, renders it shamefully "lyric."[24]

The background to this view is all too well known to those who are in
the academic poetry world, but it may warrant repetition here. In the 1970s
and 1980s, a group of poets now identified as Language poets brought
the concerns of poststructuralism to the poetics world, not least through
their critique of the "personal 'expressive' lyric."[25] Critiquing a form of isolated subjectivity that seemed to define the limits of both art and political
life in the United States, they turned against the assumed naturalness of
personal expression in a range of midcentury poetic modes: Beats, Confessionals, Deep Image, and New York School writing. As Craig Dworkin
historicizes it, Language poetry "stood in contrast" to both the "raw poetry
of the counterculture" and also "the cooked verse of the establishment," as
these depended on the understanding that "emotive expression was . . . the
basis for poetry." What they called for was "artifice" and "intellect" over
"nature" and "sentiment."[26] For one example, Charles Bernstein's seminal
lineated critical essay on the "new poetics"—the "Artifice of Absorption"
(1986–1987)—argues for "artifice" as a poetic and critical value by thinking through a dialectic (informed by poststructural theory) of "absorptive"
and "impermeable" qualities in texts. No poem is not a product of artifice,
Bernstein argues (with notable emphasis on punctuation marks that cannot be absorbed as "voice"), but "the artificiality of a poem may be more or
less / foregrounded," and though "absorption & antiabsorption are both
present / in any method of reading or writing . . . / one or the other may be
more obtrusive or evasive" (*Poetics,* 22). One way Bernstein describes the
difference between absorptive and antiabsorptive in his long "poem" is as
follows:

> By *absorption* I mean engrossing, engulfing
> completely, engaging, arresting attention, reverie,
> mesmerizing, hypnotic, total, riveting,
> enthralling: belief, conviction, silence.
>
> *Impermeability* suggests artifice, boredom,
> exaggeration, attention scattering, distraction,
> digression, interruptive, transgressive,
> undecorous, anticonventional, unintegrated, fractured,
> fragmented, fanciful, ornately stylized, rococo,
> baroque, structural, mannered, fanciful, ironic,
> iconic, schtick, camp, diffuse, decorative,
> repellent, inchoate, programmatic, didactic,

theatrical, background muzak, amusing: skepticism,
doubt, noise, resistance. (29–30)

For Bernstein, absorptive and antiabsorptive works "both require artifice, but the former may hide / this while the latter may flaunt / it" (30). And
though he imagines many paths to absorptive texts, he focuses heavily on
"realism" and techniques that promote an "illusionistic" reading. Quoting
Helen Vendler's claim that a poem is first read "illusionistically; later we may
see its art," Bernstein accuses her of being "very much under the spell of realist & mimetic ideas about poetry" (40). Related to Vendler's form of illusionistic absorptive realism is the version Bernstein attributes to Ford Madox
Ford, wherein

                                        the reader
(a.k.a. beholder) must be ignored, as in
the 'fourth wall' convention in theater, where what
takes place on the stage is assumed to be sealed
off from the audience. Nothing
in the text should cause self-consciousness
about the reading process: it should be as if
the writer & the reader are not present. (31)

With this reading of Ford, Bernstein overlays terms of nineteenth-century
lyric theory and lyric reading with his account of prose realist technique:
his "fourth wall" theatrical metaphor invokes the lyric theory of John Stuart Mill, a point made even clearer when Bernstein writes,

Many nineteenth-century lyric poems involve a self-
absorbed address to a beloved, the gods, or
the poet her/himself: an address that, because
it is *not* to the reader but to some presence
anterior or
interior to
the poem, induces readerly absorption
by creating an effect of overhearing in contrast to
confronting. (32)

Though Bernstein does not name Mill, his text draws on Mill's influential
lyric theory, as developed in the 1833 essay "What Is Poetry?" in which
Mill reads Wordsworth and Shelley in order to argue, famously, that all

14

poetry is "overheard" (in distinction to eloquence, which is "heard"). The figure has been central (if even only sometimes tacitly so) to much Anglo-American lyric theory after Mill. Indeed, as I will argue in detail later, it is the Mill-inspired abstracted version of poetry, which attempts to figure poetry's ideal existence as necessarily outside economies of "eloquence" and commerce (implied by the figure of the audience ideally ignored and ineffectual), that comes to be identified with modern lyric, largely in New Critical appropriations of it, and that a variety of poststructural literary theory identifies against. This Mill-inspired version of poetry, as I will go on to argue, greatly informs the Language critique of 1970s and 1980s expressive poetics, and both in turn contribute to the atmosphere of lyric shame in which Paul's poem and my reading of it cannot help but participate.

And yet I hope my reading of Paul's poem suggests some of the difficulty of locating its possible antilyric investments in its technical features, which Bernstein would probably find (to the contrary) primarily "absorptive," not unlike the lyric of the nineteenth century. It is an interpretive conundrum that Sianne Ngai also raises in her chapter on paranoia in *Ugly Feelings*, in which she thinks about the irony of the fact that Roland Barthes produces his idea of "writerliness" (formative for Bernstein's antiabsorptive category) from readings of the classic realist novel: even if the qualities of the writerly text "seem to describe twentieth-century avant-garde literature in its diverse entirety [this] still does not mean that concepts like writerliness can be used as criteria for distinguishing work produced in this cultural context from work that is not."[27]

One implication of Ngai's assertion is the possibility that *avant-garde* or antilyric is, like lyric, a way of reading: thus the problem, as Ngai puts it, of an "excessive reliance on concepts like 'writerliness' to account for the qualitative differences between works produced under the material conditions that give rise to an avant-garde and those that sustain an official verse culture."[28] This matters to my argument insofar as I read Bishop and Sexton as very much part of a broad cultural shift that the antilyric/"lyric" binary obscures: though their works are comparatively "absorptive," indeed self-conscious about their return to poetic techniques that resemble Victorian or Romantic verse more than modernist poems, they too were thinking both with and against the idealization of poetry as "lyric" in the Millean terms with which New Critics *and* Bernstein think. And this is a feature of their work that is less clearly seen if we incline to read it through either a lyric or antilyric reading paradigm. As my reading of Paul's poem proposes, I do not think we can resolve the question of my (or Paul's) or the poem's lyric shame except by turning to something *other* than the poem's words to aid us—to the interview, for instance, or to a theory of how to read poems. Put another way, the poem's words alone are not going to help determine where the shame of first-person "lyric" originates—with Paul? his poem? with myself as his post-Language reader?—for they participate in and perform a slippage between text and speech whose history and problems include Paul's poem and my reading of it but clearly do not begin there.

My own close readings of poems in *Lyric Shame* will often work against the assumptions of subjectivity and identity adhered to by the "lyric speaker" model (to which Paul's poem tacitly refers) that was consolidated and codified at midcentury by New Critics, particularly that the best interpretations of poems cohere around an identification with the image of a person divined through analytic interpretation. Nevertheless, those assumptions, or lyric-reading strategies, as recent work in historical poetics has theorized them, have been deeply ingrained by the New Critical pedagogical norms in place since the late 1930s. There can be pleasures that attend the entitlements native to old interpretive assumptions, which may explain why the exposure of those assumptions provokes shame. Glossing Silvan Tomkins's work on shame, Sedgwick goes so far as to claim that "without positive affect, there can be no shame: only a scene that offers you enjoyment or engages your interest can make you blush. Similarly, only something you thought might delight or satisfy can disgust."[29] As thinking on shame's affective dynamics since the mid-1950s has emphasized, shame involves the recognition that some aspect of the world or the self that one was not entirely aware of has been exposed not just to the world but also to oneself.[30]

Indeed, most interesting to me about Paul's poem is its invitation to think about not only his shame but my own shame about lyric reading as it is activated by (and activates) the texts I imagine to have been shamed or to be thought shameful by antilyric modes of lyric reading. What a loop! As Sedgwick writes, "Shame . . . seems to be uniquely contagious from one person to another. And the contagiousness of shame is only facilitated by its anamorphic, protean susceptibility to new expressive grammars."[31] The text construed as "ashamed" or "shamed," as Paul's poem seems to know, is a space of multiple reflections, and multiple projections, perhaps "the lyric's" last stand.

SHAMING THE LYRIC

Paul's poem provokes awareness that antilyric discourse dovetails with and depends on New Critical modes of lyric reading, in effect constituting one of its most current forms. Though contemporary poetry and criticism can seem aware of this, it is a fact so far undertheorized in the world of contemporary poetics. What Virginia Jackson describes as a late-twentieth-century avant-garde "reaction-formation for and against a version of the lyric that could exist only in theory" will be all too familiar to most working poets and critics of contemporary poetry.[32] What she gestures to is a decades-long discursive gridlock in the field of contemporary poetics, one in which, increasingly over the 1980s and 1990s, the call to account for oneself as either "for" or "against" "lyric," identified (by both its celebrators and its detractors) with interpretive mastery and the expressive speaking subject, felt almost inescapable.

From the perspective of contemporary North American poetics, theories of lyric reading are especially exciting for the promise they hold out to scholars to see what opens up in the realization that the "lyric" tradition against which an avant-garde antilyricism has posited itself (whether implicitly or explicitly) never existed in the first place—thus my sense that poet Lucas de Lima's phrase "ambient shame" is a fitting term for what I am describing: lyric shame floats free, everywhere and yet located nowhere, precisely because its cause célèbre is not a genre but an entrenched, common, perhaps inescapable way of reading.[33] To recognize this missing lyric object is to open the space to read in new lights a more varied and richer canon of twentieth- and twenty-first-century poetries, one too often parceled into "lyric" and "antilyric," or "avant-garde" and "mainstream." And yet, however helpfully theories of lyric reading encourage us to lay to rest that oppositional critical culture, three decades of a "reaction-formation" to the hegemony of lyric reading (a reaction-formation made legible only recently by work in lyric theory) has powerfully shaped how the field of twentieth-century poetry in the United States gets read. Antilyric reading, the latest form of lyric reading, has been one of the increasingly powerful lenses by which to map and historicize twentieth-century poetry and poetics, one that distorts by exerting (sometimes tacit) pressure to read some abjected texts lyrically and with shame.

I could reframe the above to say that both a poststructuralist critique of unified subjectivity and of expressive aesthetics generally, and also aspects of "Language poetics" specifically, inform my own approach to the work this book considers and (one even can suppose) the theory of lyric reading I draw on here.[34] The cultural turn after World War II that informs skepticism of the "lyric" subject—or of the expressive and humanistic subject that the word "lyric" metonymizes—can be located in myriad sources: in psychoanalytic theories about self and subject, the post–Judith Butler emphasis on the performativity of gender, among a range of theories informed by the poststructuralist turn. I focus on aspects of a diffused, diluted version of Language poetics here because, from Language's initial blend of poststructural theory, social critique, and an embattled advocacy of modernist poetic techniques, there emerged discourses with particular, local, and lasting influence on academic poetics in the United States that nevertheless cannot be located precisely in texts of Language writing or of poststructural theory.

Indeed, in invoking avant-garde antilyricism and Language, it becomes important to distinguish the discrete texts and concerns of various Language writers from the later, more diffuse critique of "lyric" that emerged, in part, in the wake of their initial oppositional writings. The oppositional discourse that emerged across the 1970s and 1980s in Language-oriented circles helped translate poststructuralism and other theoretical critiques of the cultural formation we call subjectivity into a form broadly, and pedagogically, useful to people thinking about poetry and poetics. Language critique of contemporary poetic tastes (largely focused on the "personal, expressive lyric") and of literary institutions first formed and spread in small circles—avant-garde discussion groups, workshops, listservs, and DYI small-press publications such as *L=A=N=G=U=A=G=E*, *Poetics Journal*, and *This*. Ideas circulated among small groups of writers such as Lyn Hejinian, Charles Bernstein, Carla Harryman, Ron Silliman, Barrett Watten, Bob Perelman, and Bruce Andrews (to name a few). Gradually, a critique first received (and positioned) as local, radical, and incendiary entered academic and poetic discourses in both MFA and PhD programs, as well as in undergraduate anthologies and curricula.[35] A process of gradual institutional dissemination and translation whose complex particulars are beyond the scope of this project saw aspects of that initial critique abstracted into a broad antilyricism that is now familiar in academic communities (some might even say it is passé) and that exceeds any particular Language texts. One somewhat-wearying result of the dilute antilyricism that has resulted is a set of weakly defended, widely circulated critical abstractions—"the

lyric 'I,'" "the expressive poem," "the voice poem," "the confessional poem"—
that serve for many people as shorthand for a range of concerns about poetic ethics, aesthetic politics, literary institutions, and subjectivity, and yet
that often function as distorting critical descriptions.

While the process of the Language critique's dissemination has helped
to make certain elements of poetic subject formation, reading strategies,
poetic institutionalization, poststructural and psychoanalytic theory, and
even lyric reading visible for poetics discussions, in its more diffuse forms,
the antilyric discourses that resulted tended to reinstall, in the abstract, the
very "lyric hegemony" (remembering Janowitz's phrase) that Language
writers seemed poised to denature and, in effect, to historicize. Silliman,
Hejinian, Harryman, Watten, and several others argued in 1988 that the
then-contemporary celebrated mode was a "lyric of fetishized personal experience," in which "experience is digested for its moral content and then
dramatized and framed."[36] They identify this lyric broadly as "New Critical,"
"voice" lyric, thus locating it in a set of institutions and historically located
tastes, and, in their descriptions, articulate aspects of a then-conventional
mode of writing that was all too visible at the time.[37] But in subsequent
historicizations of and elaborations on such arguments (some by Language
writers, some by their academic advocates), came the less trenchant claim
that this lyric mode is "traditional," previewed in the Confessional and a
major strain of post-Romantic lyric with origins in Romantic lyric. That is,
the argument lost its historical particularity, maintaining an abstraction of
"lyric" that unwittingly depends on modes of lyric reading.

Language writers were correct to recognize the interdependence of mainstream poetic production in the 1970s and 1980s and New Critical tastes,
as the New Critical pedagogical model of lyric reading did influence not
only the reading of poems as lyric but also the way poems were written
thereafter.[38] These pedagogical, interpretive modes were made broadly canonical in the midcentury in several widely distributed New Critical texts,
including Brooks and Warren's *Understanding Poetry*.[39] Brooks and Warren figured the poem as a "little drama" of a speaker whose features the
reader was charged with discerning as "value."[40] For Brooks and his later
collaborator W. K. Wimsatt, "the most fragile lyric has at least one character, that of the implied speaker himself, and it has a 'plot'—an arrangement of psychic incidents, with a development, at least of mood."[41] As
Scott Brewster points out, this was true also for Benedetto Croce in his
1937 definition of lyric for the *Encyclopedia Britannica,* in which Croce

defines the lyric as "an objectification in which the ego sees itself on the stage, narrates itself, and dramatizes itself."[42]

Yet in a way that resembles the New Critical tendency to assume these features as traditionally lyric, the antilyric readings that followed from Language critiques took those aspects of 1970s and 1980s poems that marked its embededness with New Critical interpretive strategies as endemic to a (bad) lyric tradition traceable in Confessional "voice lyric" and Romantic lyric.[43] As with Bernstein's "A Poetics," for instance, the manifesto of Silliman et al. subtly locates (whether self-consciously or not) the roots of "expressive" practice in John Stuart Mill's notion that lyric is private utterance "overheard," and reproduces Mill's assumptions.[44] Silliman et al. describe the canonical mode against which they stand as follows: "In such work, a compacted persona speaks a kind of metaphorized testimonial. . . . It is as if a distant judge were being appealed to in modest tones intended to argue one's case in a voice just loud enough to be overheard. Propriety is the rule."[45] Silliman and his co-writers' program for rejecting this Romantic / New Critical lyric inheritance involves advancing an alternative tradition marked primarily by "the use of a language that is not immediately identifiable as speech."[46] Indeed, in establishing the importance of the avant-garde tradition's emphasis on "the transformation of speech by writing" in binary opposition to canonical, New Critical "'expressivist' lyric" and its romantic tradition, they tacitly assume what this bad tradition is not: they intend to "lay bare language's inherent capacity to construct belief" by "disrupt[ing] its convention as communicative transparency."[47] The essay goes on to identify who is *in* that avant-garde tradition—Gertrude Stein and Louis Zukofsky; Frank O'Hara, John Ashbery, and Jackson Mac Low; and themselves), but only very weakly who is *out* of it (Howard Moss and William Stafford are the few named in this manifesto). The oppositional stance drawn around the question of "speech" in writing marks much Language and diffusely antilyric poetics of the time, work devoted not only to describing an alternative tradition but also to seeing it validated in institutions and through forms of social visibility— new anthologies, new channels of distribution, and university curricula.

As effective as this critique was in changing and sharpening discourse about politics and arts in the United States and shifting the way poems in the United States were read and written, the who is in / who is out critical mode that has persisted post-Language too often depends on a regrettable shaming rhetoric and, especially in its diffuse forms, on what are sometimes rather broad critical and historical brushstrokes. As Paul's poem suggests and as I will go on to explore in subsequent chapters, there is need to think further about which techniques and kinds of poem get read as "speech" (and as what kind of speech) and why. Furthermore, the bracing force of the early Language critique was propelled by a hyperbolic alignment of the "literary status quo" not just with tired conventionality, or the inert isolationism of suburban life, but also with (at one extreme) "the new right" of the Reagan era and (more pervasively) "a hysteria that is part of the dominant literary code; . . . a delimitation of the aesthetically possible that has political implications—in the exclusion of difference from normative forms of communication and action."[48] Since the late 1980s, for one aware of Language and later antilyric critiques and primarily sympathetic to their concerns about the politics and economics of art production and distribution in the United States, to feel interested in or identified with a writer deemed in its terms canonically "lyric" or "mainstream" foists on one an identification that is ashamed and shaming—driven by the not unreasonable, if sometimes bludgeoning, claim that one's poetic tastes and habits implicate political and ethical positions one has not consciously held. In short, to feel identified with a "personal, 'expressive' lyric" tradition (of murky origins) or poet might expose one, perhaps even to oneself, in ways that feel shameful and degrading.

One renowned and interesting instance of that enforced identification occurs with Ron Silliman's term "School of Quietude," perhaps the sine qua non of shaming critical terms in circulation and one that features prominently on his weblog (Silliman's Blog). Launched in 2002, it is one of the best-known blogs on contemporary poetry and poetics in the United States. Silliman's School of Quietude (SoQ) is always the ashamed other to his term "post-avant"—a mark of critical praise that bolsters the self-concept and self-esteem of any writer who feels comfortably identified with and by it. To be post-avant, in Silliman's terms, is to be in step with an aesthetic advance that indicates the individual poet's and reader's political progress and, implicitly, his or her psychological maturity. It describes work that evidences a clear commitment to the politics informing both avant-garde poetics from the 1960s and after and the radical Brechtian modernist poetic techniques he sees as their prefigure.

Though Silliman would argue that both the School of Quietude and the post-avant accommodate a great variety of work (in one post he asserts that there are thousands of working post-avant writers), the two are almost always invoked to advance an oppositional poetics and a history of "opposing poetries," as Hank Lazer has put it, whose boundaries are vigorously defended but difficult to determine.[49] Work in the SoQ, which Silliman defines loosely and with very little critical elaboration with reference to specific poems, is thought to be moribund in its faith in and emulation of "traditional" styles. The SoQ, as Silliman sees it, is marked by its claim that it is somehow more traditional than the "adjectival" poetry it takes as its other—that is, poetry that requires a qualifying adjective (avant-garde poetry, Beat poetry, New York School poetry, Language poetry, and so on). SoQ work conceives of itself, Silliman argues, as the "Unmarked Case," simply Poetry, or the "traditional" norm: "its most characteristic—even defining—feature," Silliman claims, "is the denial of its own existence. This in large part is because the phenomenon is invisible precisely to those who in turn are defined by it, just as the exclusionary maleness of 'men' was once invisible to guys."[50]

As correct as Silliman is to suggest the ubiquity of idealizations of "poetry" as such, his rhetoric in such statements, which abound in daily blog posts written over ten years, effectively negates possible dissent or even curiosity, rendering whatever difficulties might attend deciding what work qualifies as SoQ as the indicator that one's tastes or practices *are* SoQ. It is as though the one who asks, "What makes the School of Quietude a school?" automatically enrolls oneself. Silliman admits that he refuses to specify its particular features (because it is not his "school" after all), arguing that he has no "stomach" for the task of elaborating it, and he claims that, if the label rankles, the rankling itself is symptomatic of the SoQ's defensive unwillingness to admit its real features and its real tradition.[51] The SoQ is marked by an ahistoricist sense of "denial"—the "pathology at the heart of their poetry."[52] In Silliman's view, though SoQ writers try to claim Whitman and Dickinson as their heirs, the SoQ is in fact naïve to its *real* precursor or tradition, which is the genteel tradition of nineteenth-century American verse: "Whittier, Holmes, Bryant, Sidney Lanier & James Russell Lowell, for starters." Thus one of the few defining claims that Silliman makes about the SoQ is that it is antimodernist:

> What these poetries have in common, with a very few exceptions (virtually all from the vicinity of ellipticism), is consistency of viewpoint, narrative or expository lines that are treated as unproblematic, language that integrates upwards to meta-levels such as character, plot or theme.

Most of these poetries are set up to avoid at all costs that which the
Russian Formalists called *ostranenie* & Brecht later characterized as the
alienation- or A-effect, the admonition to *make it new, make it strange*.[53]

Silliman would have us see that, if the SoQ now attempts to claim affini-
ties with the avant-garde, it is because the avant-garde has now become
institutionally powerful. Which is to say, the SoQ is less a description than
an accusation, meant to catch out writers in their conservative assumptions
and in their unconscious pursuit of institutional favor. Silliman wants
to keep the SoQ and its "tradition" separate and thus, more or less, refuses
"third way" terms (such as Cole Swensen's "American Hybrid") as muddy-
ing the literary historical waters.[54] Silliman's anti-SoQ posts (and there are
many of them) thus seem not least intended to shame out of effectiveness
attempts to bring self-consciously "lyric" work under the umbrella of the
avant-garde. As the poet Ange Mlinko put it in her defense of the important
autonomy of "avant-garde" from "lyric," "I find a great many different kinds
of poems pleasing. But I don't insist they are 'innovative' when they're not,
or that they have some magical relationship to mid-century avant-gardes
when they do not."[55]

Mlinko's claim that third-way terms "insist" on "some magical relationship" to the innovative indicates how powerfully "the innovative" functions
in today's academic poetry culture, not just as an accolade of taste and potential success on the poetry market (which it is) but, moreover, as an index
of the poet's maturity and good politics. Conversely, to feel caught having
not known, and thus be identified by the term "School of Quietude," is
potentially shame inducing because the term is meant to implicate not just
one's literary tastes but one's politics and social attitudes. Though few other
poets or bloggers commit to this binary divide in poetics with quite Silliman's fervor, his rhetoric has been quite effective, baiting many poets and
critics into defensive postures and provoking years of debate, often vitriolic, on his blog's comments thread.[56] His willingness to assert categories
and evaluative critical comments returns questions of taste to the critical
agenda as politics, making its paranoia-inducing challenge all the more effective, for he knowingly "deploy[s]" it in a "strategic" and "tactical" manner; its shame-inducing qualities depend largely on hyperbole.[57] Take for
example Silliman's account of the SoQ's invisibility to itself in 2010: "[The
SoQ's] history & politics . . . should be apparent to anybody to the left of
Glenn Beck."[58] What if its history is not apparent to me? I might wonder.

The term induces a mix of anxiety, shame, and paranoia for those who feel implicated by it. Poet Daisy Fried, for instance, seems defensive when she writes to Silliman, after a post of his identifies her (with praise, as it turns out) among SoQ writers, "So do you think it's automatically conservative to value closure, to be generally accessible in traditional (which is different from conservative) ways, or to not be particularly interested in the opaque signifier? Is it automatically liberal on the other hand, to do the kinds of processes/practices/writings that are lately called experimental?"[59]

As Fried's question suggests, to be identified with or feel identified by the SoQ implicates more than behavior; it has bearing on the existential statements that make up one's self-concept (such as "I am a liberal," for instance, or "I am a great dancer"). To be challenged about the accuracy of the existential statements that make up one's self-concept is to be invited into the realm of shame—in which the self-as-object is judged according to one's internalized standards, or in which one's imagination of how others might judge one is activated.[60] For instance, if one believes, as Fried seems to do, that one is "a liberal," or even radically left politically, what happens when one discovers that a host of others would regard one's taste for a writer deemed SoQ as a decisive sign of just the opposite? Given that Silliman never clearly articulates a list of SoQ writers (indeed, he depends on the vagueness of the term's boundaries) and implies that the school is predicated on acts of unconscious affiliation, this leaves the question as to who falls under its Glenn Beck–like light unnervingly open. As Silliman knows, the SoQ label is magnetic to the extent that it is vague, and even if one chooses to ignore it, according to the logic of its definition, one is (especially) encompassed by it—cast in the sallow light of its accusation of political backwardness.

Silliman's inconsistency—he occasionally concedes to the possibilities of a "third way" in American poetics or the quality of this or that SoQ writer, only to reassert the importance of the post-avant/SoQ binary again—reiterates the extent to which the term's popularity depends on its confidence to bring the dizzying world of American poetics into some neatly legible system. It is powerful in large measure for its sheer assertiveness, as the terms of one blogger's skeptical willingness to take it on suggest:

OK, fine. I have mixed feelings about the "School of Quietude." I'm pretty sure that, if Ron Silliman ever deigned to notice me, he would

be very disapproving and would probably label me a "quietist" of the
worst and most shameful sort. But, it's clear that this meme has taken
hold. You could probably go on almost any lit blog you wanted, drop
the abbreviation "SoQ" and people will know what you're talking
about.[61]

This reader seems to appreciate the consensus (however problematic the
base for it) that SoQ builds. And this blogger is not alone in seeming to
long for an arbiter of the post-Language poetic-politics who might judge
them "in" or "out."[62] Why, otherwise, should writers who, it seems, have
little faith in the real value of Silliman's terms nevertheless engage him
either to clarify or to attempt to argue against him?[63] The poet Reginald
Shepherd accuses the idea of the School of Quietude (and thus inadver-
tently Silliman) of "petty viciousness" typical of personal attacks by avant-
gardes on anyone who "deviates from the party line," and yet Shepherd's
deep attachment to that line, in wanting to blur it, is clear: he edited a whole
anthology devoted to the concept of "lyric postmodernisms" and tried to
revamp the term "post-avant" as a hybrid term joining lyric and "antilyric,"
eliciting a record-breaking number of comments and a good deal of shaming vitriol in the process.[64] Silliman advances an oppositional discourse that
has radically changed canons, tastes, and the self-image of poetic practice in
the United States and whose critical consequences and meanings are still
being worked out.

Indeed, Silliman only represents one late and extreme example of oppositionality that has structured a good deal of academic journalism, reviewing, anthology making, and manifesto making about poetry, especially in the past fifteen years. The SoQ label is a marker meant to signal
a failure to be "innovative" or to be grown from an avant-garde tradition,
but it is just one late example of a rhetorical storm long in the making.
Though some observers might say that the poetry wars are over, attested
to by the presence of "hybrid" terms—including Shepherd's "lyric postmodernisms," Stephen Burt's "ellipticism," and the "third way" that Silliman himself both accepts and rejects—Silliman is still on the ground,
policing the border and reminding us that poetic tastes and affiliations are
not innocent and can be driven by often-unconscious allegiance to power
or the status quo.[65] This gives the lie to the frequent claim that the us-
versus-them animosity has passed and shows how tenacious is the binary
thinking of "outside" and "inside" that allowed the avant-garde to make

its position legible; the convention for many writers "in the field" is still to draw lines in the sand (it can feel impossible not to), if increasingly with an apology for rehearsing the oppositional terms. One might note the title of Craig Dworkin and Kenneth Goldsmith's new anthology of conceptual writing, *Against Expression,* which (for historically important reasons) asserts the history of that work's oppositions to "mainstream," "expressive" practice, even as the book itself, by its very nature as an anthology, seems geared for mainstream consumption and pedagogical absorption.[66]

More important, perhaps, we can see the idealization of lyric that incited that oppositional culture, kept in play (paradoxically) by the entrance of antilyric discourse into the mainstream. We can see how widely the issue of the "lyric I"—as problem, preoccupation, and source of shame—shapes thinking about poetry in the field: for one example, take the Academy of American Poets website's exhibit "Poetry Debates and Manifestos," in which, as the headnote tells us, "the Academy of American Poets presents thirty-one younger American poets writing about the great debates and manifestos that have shaped our poetry landscape."[67] Of the essays in the exhibit, at least half focus or touch on topics we could gather under the tent of lyric shame: speech-based poetics then (Wordsworth) and now (Tom Thompson); the "I" in poetry (Rachel Zucker); "First-Person Usage" (Cate Marvin); Romanticism's bequeathal of "inward-focused lyrics" (Rachel Galvin); "Language poetry," "self-as-speaker," and "Confessionalism's . . . tired modes" (Dana Levin); "personality" and "impersonality" (Geoffrey G. O'Brien, Joshua Corey, Stephen Burt); or, perhaps most revealing, the prohibitions against narrative "closure" and expression in the dominant contemporary lyric culture (Richard Tayson).

This is to say that we are still very much engaged with the problematics and shame dynamics of something we would like to sum up as "lyric." One consequence of this shame is how it perpetuates the tensions that created it: in the process of writing this book, I have found myself distracted by, and inexorably drawn into, rehearsals of what I risk reducing to "the Language critique" of lyric. I have become aware of how often I test poems, with interest but also too often with a sense of defensiveness, against those terms. This power of the ashamed or shaming mode of lyric reading has been productive, and yet there is an unwieldy pressure to defend writers abjected by those terms in those very terms.[68] Sedgwick's proposition that "political correctness" might be understood as a "highly politicized chain reaction of shame dynamics" may be apposite here, and now that the academy has fully absorbed the importance of Fredric Jameson's notion of the "political unconscious," it might be time to think about the complex shame dynamics that factor into the formation of not just this but a wider variety of literary debates and norms.[69] What productive possibilities come by reframing the antilyric aims of the avant-garde not as a formal accomplishment, or aesthetic-political progress out of the shame of "the lyric," but as an ashamed mode of lyric reading—the uneasy twin to the New Critical lyric reading it meant to cast aside?

WHY SHAME?

This book might have been called "The Poetics of Embarrassment." Recent research in psychology identifies both shame and embarrassment, along with guilt and humiliation, as subsets of what one researcher calls the "shame family," and all are categorized as "self-conscious emotions."[70] Self-conscious emotions are distinguished from the more "basic" emotions, such as fear or anger or sadness, for requiring from the subject self-awareness and the ability to self-represent and because they "facilitate the attainment of complex social goals."[71] Jeff Elison and Susan Harter locate the key distinction between shame and embarrassment in intensity, context, or both, suggesting that "in many Western cultures, everyday usage of *shame* denotes high intensity and a (usually) moral context (i.e., related to an offense, crime, sin, or harm to others)," whereas "embarrassment denotes low-intensity (even humorous) emotional reaction and a public context."[72]

In everyday usage, embarrassment and shame are used loosely to mean the same thing, and while in places I feel it more appropriate to use "embarrassment" rather than "shame" or to add "anxiety" to the mix, the intensity of affective response around the abjection of "lyric," and identification with that abject definition of "lyric," seems best described by shame and specifically by what Sedgwick calls "shame dynamics." Embarrassment's lightness seems inadequate, given the specifically ethical concerns driving poststructuralist critiques of subjectivity and lyric and their avant-garde instantiations. Researchers Brian Lickel et al. claim that "people feel embarrassed when they think that *others will see them as flawed*, but feel ashamed when they personally fear they *are flawed*"; shame arises

from an overstepping of moral proscriptions, whereas embarrassment
arises from a lapse in social conventions.[73] Of course, poetic choices *are*
social conventions, as Language poetry so smartly demonstrated: Language writing and its theorization brought to the poetics world the news
that form can be read as the "political unconscious" of poetry and that we
ought to be rethinking the institutionalization of some forms as "natural."
However, part of what interests me about the particular chapter of lyric
history that I am endeavoring to contribute to is how it emphasizes poetic
convention as involving, if not quite moral (if by "moral" we want to refer
to Judeo-Christian ethics that accord with modern written laws), then
ethical choices: it is precisely the *reading of those conventions as ethical
choices* that makes them "shameful," rather than just (as one can imagine
certain outdated poetic stylistics that are less intensely cathected might
seem) "embarrassing."[74] It is the weight of the assumption that to follow
the conventions of narratively legible, first-person expressive poems constitutes an ethical stance that makes it possible for a poet, when asked in
an interview if hers is a "narrative poem," to answer, "Totally. And I'm not
ashamed!"[75]

Shame's intensity is fitting for this study of modes of lyric reading, too,
given shame's psychological function not necessarily only to regulate but
also to raise awareness about the self's status in the minds of others. In an
article presenting research on "the evolution of shame," Paul Gilbert argues that "shame emerges from our complex evolved abilities to be aware
of 'how we exist for others.' . . . [It] is a response to feeling an unattractive
and undesired self."[76] And Jeffrey Stuewig and June Price Tangney argue
that shame is focused "less on specific behaviors and more on the evaluation
of the entire *self* against internalized standards."[77] Guilt, by contrast, Stuewig
and Tangney argue, "reflects feelings about *actions* that are inconsistent
with internalized standards. . . . When people feel guilt, they are motivated to make reparations for their *behavior*," but when they feel shame,
they want "to hide or disappear. . . . Shame emotions can act as warnings
that we 'live in the minds of others.' "[78] The earliest psychological interest
in shame's importance as an affect had to push against Sigmund Freud's
promotion of guilt as a primary affect for the supposed "civilized" (and
discontented) civilization and the mature subject. Gerhart Piers and Milton
B. Singer's groundbreaking 1953 "psychoanalytic and cultural study" of
shame (followed by work from Erik Erikson and Silvan Tomkins) paved

the way for new interest in the emotion and indicated that the key difference between guilt and shame involves what kind of transgression and self
structure precipitates the emotion: Piers and Singer argued that guilt occurs when a "boundary (set by the super-Ego) is transgressed," whereas
"shame occurs when a goal (presented by the Ego-Ideal) is not being
reached."[79] Thus, as object-relations theorist Charles Ashbach put it more
recently, with shame "the attack comes from the ego-ideal." This is significant because it is through our ego-ideal, supposedly, that we "maintain
our identities"; shame thus "threatens our very being."[80] As Sedgwick puts
it, glossing Silvan Tomkins, "shame attaches to and sharpens the sense of
what one is. . . . The implication remains that one *is something* in experiencing shame, though one may or may not have secure hypotheses about
what. . . . [Shame is not] the place where identity is most securely attached
to essences, but rather . . . it is the place where the *question* of identity most
originarily and most relationally arises."[81]

   That shame focuses one on, even alerts one to, the question of having a
self and of having one in the minds of others (not so intensely true in
experiences of embarrassment or guilt) makes it an especially apt and pro-
ductively complex term for the nature of the interpretive-affective dynamic I am trying to describe. From the perspective of the avant-garde
critique of "the personal, 'expressive' lyric," it is the supposed centrality and
authority given to "self" in conventional lyric writing (such as the "early
confessional 'voice' poem") that makes it shameful. If the point of the
shaming critique is to demote the prioritization of a too-stable image of
self, then it would seem right to charge the lyric with shame: to ask it to
stand down, to disappear. To be caught in and by a lyric reading intended
to shore up the figure of that too-aestheticized "I" subject indeed incites
for the writer/reader a desire to retreat from view. Put another way, exposing the priority given to self as shameful is meant as a check to the self's
priority in writing, so as to enable possible new ontologies. Thus, "shame"
seems the correct word to describe the dynamic tensions between the
critique of self and its hoped-for results: to say "shame on you" to a poet or
poem is in effect to command the problematic "person" of that poem, or
perhaps some claim for the self, to stand down.

   And yet, as Sedgwick's comments suggest, the shaming of a poem for
being too personal, too credulous of its "I" (its importance, its reality), can
seem in effect to *produce* the very "self" that the accusation of shame was

meant to identify and diminish—to construct, even in the hope of di-minishing or denying it, the idealized self or ego-ideal. In a 1958 essay on the "nature" of shame, Helen Merrell Lynd describes the experience as involving "astonishment at seeing different parts of ourselves, con-scious and unconscious, acknowledged and unacknowledged, suddenly coming together. . . . It is as if a self of which we were not aware" had asserted its power.[82] Without wanting to take Lynd's comments too far out of context, I would like to wonder to what extent shaming lyric read-ings of Confessional work such as Sexton's or of Bishop's might in fact be thought of as a kind of displaced shame.[83] We may call both the shaming of "lyric" and the shame of "lyric" forms of severed identification, at-tempts to pull away from the identification with an image of a person. Yet the process of identification with a person has been so long a part of our reading culture that it can seem a sort of horizon or limit, one that the shaming of lyric reproduces in negative form. To say "this poem should be ashamed of itself!" is to grant it a self, after all. In the shaming of a lyric text, we are asked to identify with a self, and a version of self-hood, that we are also supposed to be giving up. Obviously a text has no sense of shame.

What happens when we see the pleasures and shames of lyric readings as rather more broadly "ours" (that is, belonging to some readers) than something to abject, to project onto (some) poems? Might the attempt to disavow and project "lyric" as outside ourselves, out there in the poem, mask a more complex dynamic? What does the abject devouring ego, once a sign of the "poetic" (and now unsustainable and abject), have to do with reading? In trying to disavow it, do we fantasize a lyric that will always be suspended in its preinterpreted, contingent state? Is it possible that what is repressed in shaming lyric readings is a tenacious idealization of lyric? Put another way, could an identification with the ideal lyric subject, one we wish to project somewhere else, explain the idealizing shame about lyric? Even when most disavowed, the idea of a lyric subject reasserts itself as readings of "backward" "personal" lyrics that shore up a definition of avant-garde impersonality as progress. Lyric readings that privilege one interpre-tive destiny get confused with abstractions such as Victorian poetics, the Romantic or post-Romantic lyric, as "personal" poetry, the Confessional, or the "voice" poem. It is as if something once a pleasure—the illusion of writing's person—had returned, now in the guise of shame. And it is worth mentioning that the New Critical idealization of lyric was made possible by cultural privileges we all may still feel shamed by and yet are unwilling to acknowledge or give up.

My sense of "shame's" promise for opening up new thinking about the history of poetry writing and lyric reading has benefited from recent focus on the productive possibilities of shame and shame dynamics for queer and literary theory.[84] For many queer theorists, the concept of "gay shame" (the title of a recent collection of essays edited by David Halperin and Valerie Traub) has been instrumental in imagining "an affirmative queer future unrestricted by the increasingly exhausted and restrictive ethos of gay pride."[85] To think with (rather than against) gay shame has enabled a productive resistance to narratives of progress that have informed shaming (and ashamed) readings of texts once held to be "backward" by the standard of "pride"—ones marked by queerness or ambivalences toward modernism and thus unredeemable in a narrative of queer pride.[86] I am similarly interested in the potential value of allowing and exploring the shame of lyric reading, rather than repressing and projecting it elsewhere. What happens if we look at those midcentury texts deemed "lyric," and in some sense "backward" to the project of avant-garde modernist progress, to wonder why they have been asked to serve as repositories of our lyric shame? As Ruth Leys explains in her study of "survival guilt," the new prominence of shame as the "dominant emotional reference in the West" has involved its possibilities "as a site of resistance to cultural norms of identity," which speaks to a larger trend, helpful for my work here, to consider the potential good of examining once-neglected "ugly feelings" (as Sianne Ngai has put it) and the cultural forms and subject formations to which they give rise.[87]

According to Georgia Brown, theorists following Freud had tended to "ascribe shame to the public and external world, and guilt to the private and internal world."[88] Postmodern theorizations of literature as cultural form allow us to rethink those distinctions, as does new work theorizing the cultural forms and identity formations that shame depends on and produces.[89] Psychological theories of shame focus on its notably contagious qualities and on its importantly relational and intersubjective features. As Gilbert argues, intersubjectivity, an empathetic response "related to the moment-by-moment coregulation of participants as they experience the feelings of others directed at them," is the "key process in shame."[90] Gilbert, as a psychological researcher, is not theorizing the reading process or text, but we might extend his arguments to think about what part intersubjectivity plays in the shame dynamics of recent lyric and antilyric readings.

At the risk of being a bit plodding, let me say that reading can embroil one, to greater and lesser degrees, in moments of self-projection, fantasies about authorial intention, and ideations of the other and the self, whether one is figuring these as "speaker," author, implied audience, or "meaning" of a text. Reading importantly cannot be the site of "coregulation" that Gilbert describes; nevertheless, if in reading, I experience a sense of shame (either my own or on behalf of the text), have I not done so by mustering the image of another through whom to constitute that sense of shame? Given that shame depends on the actual or imagined presence of a witness, the shame that occurs in either reading or writing would seem to involve a conjuring of either an audience or a supposed writer or speaker. To read (or to figure someone as writing) a text *shamefully* is thus to socialize the reading process in ways that work against the supposedly private, isolated scenes of production and consumption normally associated with lyric as a genre. As I wrote earlier, to shame the lyric (either to charge it with shame or to feel shame by identification with it, either as a writer or reader) is perhaps to have always already rescued it from its supposed hermeticism and inwardness, even as it is also to produce the "I" who is shame's object.

What I am trying to formulate is that this often only internal conjuring of a witness that is so central to dynamics of shame and shaming suggest shame's rich resonances for concerns that, since at least the Romantic era, have been central to theories of the lyric. For those who think about how lyric has been constructed across the nineteenth and twentieth centuries, issues of audience and address have been paramount: Does lyric assume an audience for its supposedly private utterance? To whom (if anyone) is it addressed? Does it presume some distance from a social scene in which it might reasonably subject its supposedly "private" speech to shame?

SHAME CONFESSING ITSELF TO ITSELF

Here it may help to think in more detail about how the concept of American Confessional poetry has been constructed both to prefigure and in some sense to serve as the ultimate example of contemporary "expressive," lyric poetics often assumed to be rooted in Romantic practice.[91] This view in effect affirms M. L. Rosenthal's sense, in coining the idea of "poetry as confession" after he read Robert Lowell's *Life Studies* in 1959, that the Confessional took Romantic tendencies to new (shocking) heights.[92] What we have forgotten, of course, is that much of the work identified as Confessional by Rosenthal and A. Alvarez in the late 1950s and early 1960s seemed new and noteworthy for the fact that, in its apparent willingness to air "shameful" details of the author's personal life, it seemed to *challenge* certain modernist inheritances of Romantic ideas about lyric decorum.[93] Chiefly, the Confessional seemed to challenge the widely held assumption that what makes a lyric poem effective is its universal, impersonal, transcendent subject, an "I" whose expression of feeling is more than a discrete self and that we take to heart as "our own." This assumption had been promoted in the twentieth century, often with reference to John Stuart Mill's famous figure for lyric poetry from his 1833 "Thoughts on Poetry and Its Varieties": poetry is "feeling confessing itself to itself" that is yet "overheard" by an uncountenanced listener.[94] Still, the assumptions of this figure are worth drawing out in some detail, for if in some senses the Confessional seemed to challenge them, in other senses it has been credited—to its shame—with epitomizing them.

That for Mill lyric is "feeling" suggests its expressive and personal character as akin to Wordsworth's famous 1800 postulation, in the preface to the second edition of *Lyrical Ballads,* that poetry is "the spontaneous overflow of powerful feelings."[95] Mill's presumption that feeling in poetry "confesses" only to "itself" marked a notable demotion of the part that audience, verse culture, social mores, or economic pressures might play in the writing of lyric. Indeed twentieth-century uses of Mill, which are myriad if often tacit, have emphasized the idea that the effect of a lyric on its reader has little if anything to do with historical particulars such as its printing, circulation, performance, or address. Mill figures a peculiar space for poetry, as existing both in and out of the public world; though "printed on hot-pressed paper and sold at a bookseller's shop," poetry, if it wants to be *poetry,* nevertheless must aspire to an ideal disinterest, as if suspended in a radically private zone (Mill, "Thoughts," 97).

What Mill's figure wills away are the social contexts that might shape a piece of writing—both in its production and in its reception. The poet, ideally, should seem to address no one and yet affect "us." That is to say, Mill tries to imagine a privacy at once radically untouched by social concern and yet able to speak universally. If there is a sense of social directedness, even of particularity in the address in poetry, then the Poetry of the poetry is at risk: "But when [the poet] turns round and addresses himself to another person; when the act of utterance is not itself the end, but a means to an end, . . . when the expression of his emotions, or of his thoughts . . . is tinged also by . . . that desire of making an impression upon another mind, then it ceases to be poetry, and becomes eloquence" (98).

Still, the social world that Mill's figure separates out from "poetry" and that various twentieth-century critics deemphasize in reanimations of that figure keeps winking at the margins of Mill's page: again, poetry "is printed on hot-pressed paper, and sold at a bookseller's shop," which, if it is "a soliloquy," nevertheless is one that is produced "in full dress, and upon the stage" (97). He concedes that poetry might be written with publishing in view, even for money. So while he argues that poetry needs to conceal or eradicate "every vestige of such lookings-forth into the outward and everyday world," he nevertheless keeps having to admit the place of the social in the acts of writing and printing and circulating poetry (98).[96]

One underlying assumption of Mill's self-contradicting figure as it has been taken up and (mis)read by twentieth-century academic readers is that good lyric poems will be emotionally and culturally legible to anyone who encounters them; the experience of reading lyric will, ideally, take on the immediacy and privacy of "overhearing," so that lyric is, as Mill put it in an earlier version of the essay, "the lament of a prisoner in a solitary cell, ourselves listening, unseen, in the next."[97] Mill's image of prisoners side by side turns the particular audience member into "ourselves"—into a generalized "we" who listen(s)—for it collapses the mediations and distance inherent in acts of writing, printing, and book circulation into a spatiotemporal present tense: the poet speaks and we hear. It is a radically dehistoricizing figure, for it is as if to say that, when I read John Donne or Anne Sexton or Leslie Scalapino or a translation of Charles Baudelaire, the material and cultural particulars of my encounter—finding the poem printed on a broadside at a National Poetry Month event, in an anthology or collection (and what kind), in a classroom or at a bookshop or at a reading—hardly matter; in all cases, I would be "right there" "hearing" the speaker's "voice." The figure implies that the power of "lyric" inheres in its ability to reach an "us" spoken to (indeed constituted by) an unproblematic, uniform reception of the poem.

The Confessional seemed to turn away from the abstract universalism of this figure (and in this, it is like a wide range of midcentury poetic modes). It did so by (infamously) identifying the historical author and his or her personal experiences with the poem's supposed speaker—with the airing of personal shames understood as a breach of decorum. As Deborah Nelson puts it, writing of Robert Lowell (the poet whose radically "personal" work led Rosenthal to coin the term Confessional), "[Lowell's] innovation was to make himself . . . available . . . as a particular person in a particular place and time."[98]

If this was the radical force of the supposed airing of personal shame in the Confessional, the shame *of* the Confessional—its reputed emphasis on the figure of the speaking voice—is what makes it a magnified version of the "lyric shame" that this book identifies. Whether in Mill's claim (emphasized in misleading ways by later readers) that poetry is overheard or in Northrop Frye's famous rearticulation of Mill's idea of lyric as the genre in which "the poet, so to speak, turns his back on his listeners" or Helen Vendler's description of lyric as a genre whose purpose is to provide a vocal script for the reader and to assist in the reader's ability to "assum[e]" the represented "inner life" of an "abstract" consciousness "not engaged directly *in* social life" or Edward Hirsch's assumption that the "lyric poem [is] a special kind of communiqué . . . [that] speaks out of a solitude to a solitude," the prevailing assumption about lyric has been that it either blissfully leaves out or refuses the social sphere in which it might (or might not) come to shame.[99] If it is "overheard," the mode in which lyric is overheard is thought to effectively shield it from exposure to shame, for the reader's solitude is parallel to its own.[100]

This idealization of the lyric intersubjective space as paralleled forms of solitary confinement has been instrumental to both lyric and antilyric readings of poems and is what theorizing the shame of lyric reading might usefully help us revise. New questions arise, chiefly about ways in which we have underestimated the extent to which writers who get assigned to the lyric camp in fact struggled with twentieth-century Millean understandings of lyric and sought new forms of aesthetic and political agency in poetry in the age of high and late capitalism. If we neither attempt to rescue lyrics from themselves nor shame them out of the canon, we find new modes of lyric reading and writing available: What happens, for instance, when we put the lyric "solitary" prisoner in the panopticon, aware that his or her speaking will be witnessed by unseen others, aware that every private utterance is also constituted by its participation in discursive norms? What happens to the idea of lyric privacy when we can no longer idealize poetry as a form of human connection that rises above the conditions of capital? To the extent that the desire for and shame of audience are both part of our inheritance of the New Critical reading of Mill, shame is both a diagnosis and an attempt at a cure, a method and a mood in which to read. The avant-garde self-conscious refusal to "speak" in poems constitutes a refusal of forms of lyric isolation, but in what sense might it perpetuate those forms?[101]

However, with these new questions, we need to be cautious about reanimating and reprojecting shame. For instance, when Tiffany Atkinson (in an article subtitled "The Poetics of Embarrassment") proposes "to mount an argument to the effect that avant-garde poetry enacts a kind of aesthetic/political 'cringe' away from the apparent facility of lyric and post-Romantic poetry, and as such, does not quite exempt itself from the discourse of embarrassment," I am intrigued but long for more stress on "apparent."[102] Though Atkinson claims that she is interested in the productive possibilities of thinking about the embarrassments of lyric, I quarrel with how she also seems to want to reclaim her own lyric shame—outing herself as writing "narrative," "expressive" "lyric" in her own practice—as a badge of pride. Rather than claiming ourselves "lyric" or not, can we recognize ourselves as all in a lyric-reading culture together, one marked by shame?

Here we might invoke Bradley Paul's claim that his practice changed in part because he longed for an audience—"Once upon a time, I might've affected a pseudo-punk 'I don't care who reads it—it's about the poetry, man, not the audience.' But that's not true any longer—at least not for me," a point that his poem emphasizes, too ("listen" "I'm over here"). We need not read such gestures as either fully lyric or antilyric: Paul's poem can be read, rather, to foreground the economy of reading and writing that is so problematic for Mill and often suppressed in readings of him, even as it also foregrounds the desire to be *heard* as a shameful desire to enter into a "first person" tradition. The fact that both poets ("I" and the "idiot") are "online" is significant, for the Internet is a communicative medium that in many ways approximates the adjacent-cell metaphor so central for those who theorize lyric address through Mill, even as it constitutes a virtual verse community. Paul's poem defines poetry as a frustrated longing for an audience of hearers, a "whatever" that "lets you say . . . I'm *different*."

And yet, as Paul's turn to cliché to describe "whatever"—this supposedly "core" poetic impetus—suggests, even acts of positive differentiation turn, sometimes in complexly shameful and shaming ways, sometimes just in humorous ones, on forms of social normativity and conventions of verse culture. Indeed, "difference" is in Paul's poem identified with a clichéd drive to be heard.

And we might also invoke *The Trouble with Normal,* in which Michael Warner advocates the need for "an ethical response to the problem of shame," suggesting that "the difficult question is not: how do we get rid of our sexual shame?" but "what will we do with our shame?" The "usual response," he warns, "is: pin it on someone else."[103] As Douglas Crimp has pointed out, Sedgwick thinks through the psychological dynamics at work in such acts of "pinning," expressed (again) by "the grammatical truncation" of the phrase "Shame on you":

> The absence of an explicit verb from "Shame on you" records the place in which an I, in conferring shame, has effaced itself and its own agency. Of course the desire for self-effacement is the defining trait of—what else?—shame. So the very grammatical truncation of "Shame on you" marks it as a product of a history out of which an I, now withdrawn, is *projecting* shame—toward another I, an I deferred, that has yet and with difficulty to come into being, if at all, in the place of the shamed second person.[104]

What this suggests is that the purported shame of certain "lyric" modes (Confessional, voice poem, and so on) might be recast as a culture of lyric reading, more the "ambient shame" of poet Lucas de Lima's phrase. Thus, we might consider ways in which shame cannot be cast off but only reconfigured and, we hope, better understood. Though the "sexual shame" of queer theory cannot be made equal to the "lyric shame" I read here, it does seem broadly true, as Traub and Halperin suppose (also through Sedgwick) in their introduction to *Gay Shame,* that theorizations of shame have tended to imagine it as "something to 'work through' or 'move beyond'" rather than emphasizing the "project of analyzing it as an affective structure." The question of whether to make "transformative use" of shame or rather to "try to see what happens when we linger in untransformed experiences of it" is also my question: while I have wanted to rescue the poets I here engage from their, my, and their avant-garde readers' sense of shame (attributed to poems), I would like to consider what happens when we try to theorize more broadly the shame dynamics that neither party can quite escape.[105]

WHOSE SHAME? A CHAPTER SUMMARY

Though Elizabeth Bishop, the subject of Chapter 1, experienced considerable shame about identifying herself with poetry understood as Romantic and "lyric" throughout her career, I take her up not for the biographical implications of that shame but as a useful site through which to explore forms of lyric reading across the twentieth century as they have circled around the shame of "egotism" and lyric subjectivity. The chapter begins with a survey of the fact that Bishop's relatively small body of work has proved difficult to identify and place via the critical logics available for reading midcentury lyric. Indeed, her work can help to articulate the shifting roles that shame has played in critical attempts to make sense of revolutions of taste and shifting understandings about poetry's function in the midcentury. Turning to a reading of her late 1930s and early 1940s responses to the ethical poetics of William Carlos Williams (in such "known" poems as "Florida" and in a little-known fragmentary essay), I consider how deeply influenced she was by early modernist avant-garde concerns about the forms of subjectivity that "traditional" lyric principles were held to endorse. Lyric shame was in the air in the 1930s, and Bishop entertained its implications for both writing and interpretation through Williams's and Sigmund Freud's conceptions of modernity. The poems she wrote in response to that shame—explorations of subject formations that a "tradition of and reverence for likenesses"[106] (chiefly metaphor making and rhyme) problematically produce—were pivotal in forming her mature poetic and its concerns with the ethics of interpretation and forms of identification that occur in them.

Critics have struggled to read Bishop's turn toward a more "personal" poetics in the midcentury, in part because neither the pride nor the shame attributed to the Confessional seems to describe that work, and avant-garde lyric-reading strategies only exaggerate (with shame) its supposed investments in "voice" and managed tone. I focus on a range of "personal" poems in Bishop's 1950s work, collected in *Questions of Travel,* to argue that they are best read as her answer to the question of how to "revolt" at a point when every available form of poetic subjectivity (including those produced by Beats, "Confessionals," and midcentury teacher-poets) seemed to her

overinvested in expression and all too coincident with American wealth
and exceptionalism. These "personal" poems are neither suppressed expressions nor modest confessions but metadiscursive experiments whose assumptions (that discourse conditions the personal and expressive self) have
been obscured by available accounts of "personal" poetics at the midcentury. Though lyric readers and avant-garde antilyricists both have tried to
make Bishop into a poet of expressive "voice" and modulated tone, I find
that her mid-to-late work rather overturns the lyric-reading premises it
has been held to exemplify. In my reading, self-conscious about its own
shame of identification, Bishop has been easy to love but difficult to
read because she is a theorist of interpretation, particularly as it involves
what she took to be shameful, if culturally central, forms of projection
and displacement.

If we find that the work of one of our "most beloved" of contemporary
lyric poets ill fits the forms of lyric reading that have made sense of its
appeal, Chapter 2 finds that the work of our least-loved one—Anne
Sexton—ill fits her lyric reputation, too.[107] In the chapter, I take up this
culture more explicitly, thinking through how midcentury assumptions
about lyric and her Confessional reputation have ill served our ability to
read her. I wager that Sexton is the most shameful poet of the Confessional mode, contained by an abstracted lyric anti-ideal that, I argue, has
served as the scapegoat for the shame of lyric-reading practices and has
been caricatured as the perverse extreme of "lyric" premises by both "mainstream" and avant-garde readers. The story most often told about why Sexton represents "bad" lyric or "bad" confessionalism has had to do with her
own shameful "self-exposures" but also involves her seeming turn from an
ideal of interpretability (thought of as "craft"). I regard a range of her work,
across her career, as suggesting that, in a different critical climate, it might
have seemed avant-garde, given how it exposes and explodes lyric-reading
assumptions about poetic interpretability. Reading both her highly self-
conscious early work for its "antiabsorptive" qualities and also her late
poems' tendency to fly in the face of poetic decorum and ideals of lyric
"control," I find the work revolving around, even performing, the impossibility of the "speaker" that she understood it was supposed to produce. I
then turn to Sexton's fascination with forms of address as these expose the
suppressed, mediating figures of audience, intersubjectivity, and interpretation in the New Critical reading of Mill's lyric ideal. While we have
tended to denigrate the Confessional as inviting us to recognize the image of

a self-ashamed person who does not quite see us (heralding us with "shame on me!"), Sexton's work rather resists, or openly requires, our interpretation (exposing us with a "shame on you!"). It thus foregrounds and exaggerates the Millean theater of lyric, highlighting that figure's obsolescence and awkwardness as the metaphor for lyric production and interpretation at midcentury.[108]

In Chapter 3, I turn to Bernadette Mayer, an understudied living poet who was once strongly affiliated with avant-garde artists, performers, and poets of the Lower East Side and who is held to be a major influence on early Language practice and theory. I explore the sources and outcomes of Mayer's controversial turn, in the late 1970s, toward a practice that looks, on its surface, to be brazenly expressive, and one that led to her denunciation by her coterie as a "failed experimentalist" and an object of shame. Mayer's internalization of the shame with which Language poets in particular regarded her practice saw her produce a body of autobiographical poetry and prose that experiments with the figure of expressive "lyric" voice. Her late 1970s and early 1980s work constitutes a hybrid poetic-critical performance of "lyric shame" that is directly informed by the politics of the avant-garde and yet explores its unacknowledged shame of lyric reading. Since Mayer is largely unknown by academic readers, this chapter covers a range of her work produced from the 1960s to the 1980s but focuses on the long projects *Midwinter Day* (1978) and *The Desires of Mothers to Please Others in Letters* (1979), exploring how that work challenges our ability to read it lyrically, despite its self-conscious exploration of expressive tropes.

Mayer's theorization of "lyric shame" is consciously inspired by questions about gender and feminism that haunted avant-garde antilyricism, overshadowed by its antipersonal politics. Chapter 4 considers the hypermasculinization of lyric shame in a range of work by mainstream male poets who self-consciously flaunt a vexed performance of "lyric" at a point when avant-garde antilyric theory was first becoming institutionalized, widely read in academic settings, and understood as ethically important. I consider a variety of ashamed, self-conscious "epiphany" poems—by Robert Hass, Gerald Stern, Charles Wright, and James Tate—that self-consciously assume or address normative constructions of "lyric" in full and often glibly explicit awareness that they will be taken as suspect and even shameful. These poems, many of which appeared in the mid-1990s, help describe a pivotal moment in the history of contemporary poetics and lyric reading in the United States—that moment when avant-garde modes of reading and writing were becoming institutionally settled. These poems suggest a lyric mode whose sign is self-flagellation; one might say shame becomes the affective sign of subjectivity in this work—the only mode in which a particular kind of (interestingly male) "lyric" subject can persist. I end the chapter with a reading of Olena Kalytiak Davis's ironic meditative "The Lyric 'I' Drives to Pick Up Her Children from School" (2005), whose concern to evade the critical eye I consider, among other instances of postmillennial lyric shame, in a brief afterword. Self-conscious about the critical imperatives to write postsubjectively and revolving around a phantom, ashamed, or denuded subject that always already defines the interpretive horizons of contemporary American poetry, recent lyric shame poems and questions highlight the metapoetic and poeticritical self-consciousness of contemporary lyric (shame) practice. Davis's poem is hyperaware of the lyric-reading models (pro- and anti- represented by Helen Vendler and Marjorie Perloff) that define the horizons of the "lyric 'I,' " and it performs an oppressed hyperawareness of its participation in critical conceptions of the lyric subject. The poem closes with a longing for a poetic space that will remain untouched by critical interpretation and lyric reading. I close by suggesting some outstanding questions and further avenues for thinking with lyric shame, and by considering how lyric shame might complicate discussions of identity politics, race, and ethnicity in "the field," especially in lyric readings of poems by people of color.

Lyric Shame follows a historical trajectory through the twentieth century; starting in the 1930s with Bishop's responses to an early modernist avant-garde critique of lyric "traditions"; moving into the midcentury and the Confessional; turning to Mayer's late 1970s and early 1980s work and the responses it provoked; and closing by considering lyric shame as it might illuminate the interpretive questions and pressures that an unashamed postsubjective practice exerts for poets now. In each case, the quality of shame that attaches to lyric is somewhat different: for Bishop, the inheritor of early modernist ideals, traditional lyric bespoke forms of interpretive mastery that seemed inescapable despite the early modernist quest for an unmediated "reality" advanced by Williams; for the midcentury writer, lyric had become problematically identified with expressive practice and the solitary "speaker" (true for both Bishop and Sexton); for the late-twentieth-century Mayer, to return to the problems of lyric, audience, address, and technique that the avant-garde had theorized and to ask of it new questions made her an object of shame. However, hovering over all these readings is my own vexed, 1990s absorption of a critique of the expressive lyric. Many of the lyric shame poems I read in Chapter 4 seem at once to recognize the contours of that critique and to pursue modes that invite and deflect lyric readings at once. The poets seem to want to figure an (ashamed) self-awareness of the likelihood that their work will be read as lyric. It is a self-awareness that, by literalizing the anthropomorphism of poems as "lyric," collapses the space that once separated a poem and its interpretation, what we can read as a folding in (away) from lyric shame.

CHAPTER ONE

You Ought to Be Ashamed (but Aren't)

Elizabeth Bishop and the Subject of Lyric

AN EMBARRASSMENT OF LIKENESSES

In 1978, Elizabeth Bishop, in the full bloom of her public career, famously told interviewer Elizabeth Spires, "I never really sat down and said to myself, 'I'm going to be a poet.' Never in my life. I'm still surprised that people think I am. . . . There's nothing more embarrassing than being a poet, really."[1] While critics have tended to read Bishop's frequent references to the embarrassments of being (and becoming) a poet as personal—evidence of ego wounds from her stunning personal losses at an early age or a sign of the vexed "ambition and anxiety of the young writer"—we can understand such comments to illuminate a broader cultural shame surrounding poetic expression that arose and intensified over the course of her career.[2] Bishop's career, in fact, almost exactly spans the period in which a "lyric" model of poetic production and reception emphasized the personal expression of a fictional speaker as its norm, then as object of critique, and finally as object of shame. This makes Bishop a rich figure for this study, as the fates of her critical reception—both positive *and*, more recently, negative—have been decided, even when only tacitly, around the question of her poetry's "lyric" qualities and warrant rethinking.

In the mid-1930s, Bishop's political leanings made her feel embarrassed about the class implications and lack of social conscience that being a poet could be taken to imply (so that she felt she ought to "hold her tongue" about publishing poems in nationally known journals). By the time of her 1978 interview with Spires, Bishop's comments reprise an idea of "poetry" as a cartoon of the Romantic subjective "lyric." She tells Spires, "There must be an awful core of ego somewhere for you to set yourself up to write poetry. I've never *felt* it, but it must be there." Despite the disavowal, in several prose pieces that Bishop turned to in the 1930s to escape the anxiety about how, without shame, to write poems, she figures this "core of ego" in terms that critics, across the century, would increasingly associate (often negatively) with and even sum up as Romantic and "lyric." She lampoons the heroic, male authorial persona associated with Romanticism in one piece from the era, reducing him to a narcissistic "Byronic man" who admires himself in the mirror and spawns imitators left and right (without ever quite having to produce any actual poems).[3]

By the 1970s and the Spires interview, Bishop was a famous author herself, and her association of poetry with the "egotistical sublime" and "devouring egotism" that both John Keats and William Hazlitt had identified with William Wordsworth takes on a slightly new cast.[4] By 1978, the increasingly common identification of poetry with Romantic egotism was supported both by an established lyric-reading culture inclined to read most poetry expressively and as lyric and by a trend, since the midcentury, to associate poetry's potency and authenticity with the "personal" and the expressive, a turn commonly described as neo-Romantic.[5] It had been twenty years since New Critics such as W. K. Wimsatt and Monroe Beardsley, drawing on John Stuart Mill's readings of Romanticism, had declared the lyric a "verbal icon" best interpreted by "imput[ing] the thoughts and attitudes of the poem immediately to the dramatic *speaker*" and forty years since Cleanth Brooks and Robert Penn Warren had introduced similar lyric-reading practices to the university classroom.[6] By the late 1970s, as discussed earlier, a staunch antilyric discourse had emerged in reaction-formation to those New Critical and midcentury expressive lyric-reading practices and tastes. This antilyric response was most sharply articulated by Language writers, who, drawing on insights of poststructural theory, sought experimental forms that could decenter, demote, and deconstruct what more and more comes to be known as "the lyric I" and its "tradition." In a softer version of this position, many critics of the late 1960s and 1970s, also influenced by poststructuralist practice, held lyric (synonymous with poetry) to be a sign of rapacious ego and even a disrespectful use of others.[7] That neither the shameful expressive "lyric" nor its antilyric counterpart describes most of Bishop's poetry registers in her seeming to be caught, wavering, between what "being a poet" is thought to imply and what she herself has "felt" in writing poems, ample reason to look again at her already well-known work and the lyric shame it can be asked to bear.

Several of the critical modes regarding Bishop's work have, in moments, rendered her a shame-inducing love for me. I am inclined to moments of shame about loving Bishop's poems no doubt because my critical identification with her is strong. In one somewhat dated, if still influential, reading, Bishop is a modest, controlled and accurate, impersonal descriptive poet—a closeted miniaturist.[8] In another, one that loosely affiliates the idea of poetic "voice" with political agency, the "controlled tone" of Bishop's work is read as repression of the desire (belonging to the poet or her persona) to spill over into expression: in this reading, what Bishop's poems contrive and control are dramas of suppressed and released desires for self-knowledge through half-reluctant confession.[9] The line from her work that would metonymize this mode would be that in "At the Fishhouses," in which the sea swells "as if considering spilling over" but then does not.[10]

What induces shame in me about incorporating these Bishops into my canon is twofold: on the one hand, I resist the implication that she is minor (not worth the bother to read); and on the other, I resist the idea that she toes a repressive cultural line—shamefully ashamed as a political subject because stalled in a process of maturation that should see her progress toward frank expressions of gay pride or lyric experimentalism, self-centeredness, or free verse. This would accord with a Freudian repressive hypothesis that would read, for instance, the free-verse lines of a frank sexual nature in Confessional poems as a sign of their writers' liberations (rather than as a style and social norm that some writers adopted). In still another unsatisfying reading of Bishop (one implicit in the other two), her work is overrated and aesthetically conservative because, as Marjorie Perloff understands it, in its "orderly sequential-associative style," it is "drive[n] . . . to meaningful statement" and contrived to easy epiphany (as Frank O'Hara had argued in the 1960s about Robert Lowell's "Skunk Hour").[11] For Perloff, to be "drive[n] . . . to meaningful statement" marks a work's political conservatism because, in ascribing a great deal of authority to "voice," the "driven" poet controls the reader's experience and reaffirms "the lyric subject."[12]

What is a critic to do when faced with readings that intrude on the terms by which he or she identifies with an admired critical object? It is an affront to the fantasy of critical objectivity to ask such a question, of course, and a potential embarrassment. Nevertheless, it is an important question. Out of my own discomfort about accepting the Bishop that lyric and antilyric readings of her work propose, I have thought to recast the Bishop biographical paratext in order to affect our sense of what concerned Bishop as a writer. As Bonnie Costello has argued, the critical discourse around Bishop has tended to depend on biographical paratext: "Despite numerous citations of poststructuralist theory, recent Bishop critics retain a Romantic model of organic personhood in which the work is an uninterrupted extension of the poet, and the voice of the poem provides a path back to the life of the writer. . . . All these articles move from the biographical concrete to the metaphoric, often through wordplay."[13] This is true enough, and yet even Costello's brilliant reading of Bishop's work as "a configuration of various social impulses struggling toward transition, and as a meditation on the very problem of negotiating a relation between particular experience and the generalities of language," finds itself turning to biography at crucial moments to support itself: "perhaps it is time to put aside the idea of Bishop's art as the default or therapeutic position of an alcoholic-asthmatic-lesbian-homeless orphan cloaking and allegorizing personal experience, for an idea of art *she herself articulated*," she writes, turning then to quote the famous "Darwin Letter" that Bishop wrote to Anne Stevenson in 1964.[14] Espousing a Theodor Adorno–inflected way of reading Bishop's poems as (paraphrasing Adorno) "part of the larger contradictory wholeness of language," Costello then moves to locate this knowledge not in the poem itself or in herself, the critic, but in Bishop, via Bishop's reading of T. S. Eliot in the 1930s.[15] Biographical explanation of one kind (things that are private) is overthrown for biographical explanation of another (what Bishop read). I greatly admire Costello's reading of Bishop and frequently employ biographical readings myself. My point is not to shame Costello for her slip but rather to identify the moments when such slips occur with something that I believe Bishop understood and that is intricately enmeshed in the problem of the lyric shame situation I am addressing in this book: the anthropomorphic functions as a reading horizon, a structure so strong in shaping how we interpret text as to be nearly inescapable.

What I share with Costello is the wish to rescue Bishop from the lyric-reading models that "anthropomorphize the voice and absorb the author into it" and that have defined her work. Yet these seem tenacious, structuring principles for many (most) critics; there seems always the need for a writerly agent or intelligence outside the critic's, and outside the text's, to corroborate even such an argument as Costello's. I am (we are) in a lyric shame situation, then, with Bishop. What I find appealing about her poems is what they teach about how entangled with acts of projection and identification we become when interacting with art, and people, in moments of interpretation. Indeed, I cannot imagine a way to support that reading without turning to a construction of Bishop's lived intellectual life. Understanding that my will is to produce a Bishop who intended as much, I have wanted to turn to the paratext—to the biographical and critical field around Bishop. I am in a lyric shame situation, too, given the extent to which I find myself wanting to defend my interest in her work in the terms of Language-centered criticism. My work tries to be self-conscious about the lyric shame situation in which aspects of Bishop's practice fall into a kind of critical gap that has made it difficult to find terms for work that is neither lyric in the New Critical idiom nor antilyric in the post-Language idiom and that has made Bishop an object of defense among her best readers, particularly in the 1990s, as avant-garde lyric theory entered the academy, framing writers such as Bishop as conservative, and even reactionary, around the question of "lyric."[16]

Given Bishop's complex responses to her own embarrassment about writing under the sign of "poetry," responses fueled in part by her readings of William Carlos Williams in the 1930s, the reading of her work as operating in ignorance of the ethics animating the avant-garde suspicion of supposedly "lyric" subjectivity is not just wrong but symptomatic of a larger critical *aporia*. Indeed, the available terms for reading twentieth-century poetry have made it a defensive move to imagine Bishop's work as complexly shaped by concerns about not just the embarrassments but also the potential shame—ethical—of certain poetic-subjective stances. On the one hand, we have Helen Vendler's admiring assessment that Bishop is a paragon of the "lyric poet" serving (as all lyric poets "must" in Vendler's model) the "bizarre commandment to 'make it cohere,'" a vocation that "makes incoherence an anguish of peculiar magnitude for them."[17] On the other, we have Perloff's explicit dismissals of Bishop's work, made on the very same grounds; for her, Bishop's canon is marked by a "worried continuing" and by that aforementioned, unseemly "drive . . . to meaningful statement" that Perloff takes to be characteristic of the epiphanic, meditative lyrics of "late modernism."[18] Taken in Perloff's terms, which have so powerfully described and advocated the political force of a range of anti-expressive experimental work of the twentieth century, Bishop can seem to epitomize the key markers of "mainstream lyric practice" that avant-gardes have sought (and seek) to oppose. Indeed, recently, Perloff has been explicit in associating Bishop with the "expressivist paradigm of the 1960s" and, thus, the "mainstream" of the "Anglo-American" and "traditional lyric."[19] And Perloff is not the only one who singles Bishop out as exemplifying the "mainstream" for her supposed commitments to formal coherence and expressive poetics. For instance, poet Rae Armantrout (affiliated with Language writers) singles Bishop out to discuss the disappointing predominance of the "contemporary poetic convention of the unified Voice" in American poetry, which Armantrout claims supports an understanding of identity "based on identification" that compromises female empowerment: "American feminist critics such as Sandra Gilbert, Susan Gubar, and Alicia Ostriker . . . continue to valorize the poem dominated by a single image or trope and a trustworthy (authoritative) narrational voice. . . . [For instance,] Ostriker praises Elizabeth Bishop for her 'usual tone of trustworthy casualness.' "[20]

For another example, Ron Silliman, on his influential blog, has affiliated Bishop with the much-derided "School of Quietude," a designation that, for any writer or critic who cares about the political implications and effects of his or her writing or affiliations or who cares about the ethical-aesthetic questions that Silliman and his fellow Language-affiliated writers have advanced, is a shame-inducing brand.[21]

The expressive Bishop that all these writers—Ostriker (ostensibly), Armantrout, Vender, Perloff, and Silliman—share depends on an idea of lyric that, because it is an abstraction, has proved difficult to historicize, a difficulty most evident in Perloff's work. Perloff has, over the years, assigned the "lyric" qualities she opposes to Romantic aesthetics, to late modernism, and to early modernist lyric, always on the verge of realizing them as a set of interpretive paradigms or lyric-reading assumptions. In Perloff's particular reanimation of these assumptions, syntactically and narratively coherent work necessitates our identification with it and is taken to be more or less identical with the expressive speech of a speaking subject. Vendler shares these lyric-reading assumptions and, like Perloff, attributes them to the works themselves—thus my problem with reading Bishop lyrically: her concerns in her early career, and in her work of the midcentury, unsettle these very assumptions. Recognizing this does more than "save" Bishop's reputation in the eyes of her recent detractors or defend her as a Language poet. Instead, Bishop's work helps to show that a poem need not disrupt syntax or retreat from narrative forms to be read as multivalent and critical of normative language, a view that supposes that "traditional" techniques are static and to be read the same way across centuries. In other words, the lyric-reading premise in play even among avant-garde critics informing readings of poets such as Bishop (or whole eras or modes of poetic production, such as "the Confessional" or "Victorian poetry") dictates that the use of traditional forms, or narrative syntax, means closure and that forms of irony must always be read as "tone," which, of course, was one shared point among several New Critical pedagogical texts circulated in the 1950s and 1960s (that era when Ostriker, Perloff, Vendler, and Armantrout were students)—a mode of reading that informs their critical practices.[22]

This chapter focuses on readings of Bishop's mid- to late-twentieth-century experiments with, and *against,* premises of expressive speaker and tone, experiments whose origins I locate in her early encounters with the poetics and politics of William Carlos Williams. Bishop read Williams's ethical poetic of "reality" as addressing a problematic inheritance of a "tradition of and reverence for likenesses"—a "tradition" of attachment to formal mimetic orders such as rhyme but also to metaphor making and narrative.[23] Working with and beyond an initially somewhat simplified reading of Williams's early modernist poetics of "reality," Bishop considers the potential for forms of mimesis and metaphor making to produce problematic, even shamefully self-centered poetic subjects and forms of subjective experience. In several pieces from the late 1930s, she explores problematic acts of projection and identification as potential snares of "traditional" poetic thinking and looks in part to Williams for answers to this problem.

That Bishop arrived at concerns about what we now call "the lyric I" through thinking about mimesis and metaphor may seem surprising, since mimesis of this kind might not seem to involve questions of subjectivity. Yet in many important ways, Bishop's feeling, called to account by Williams's ethical poetics of "reality," led her to explore processes by which subjects stabilize their sense of themselves and the world, as well as the power of discourse and social forms to construct (and deconstruct) identity. Avant-garde discourses admiring of Williams's poems have, similarly, tended to assert Williams's early "disjunctive" styles (undertaken in the belief that "removing the aureoles" around words was an act "equivalent," as Perloff also supposes, "to removing the metaphoric or symbolic associations words have") as indicating a subjective stance markedly less anxious than for the Symboliste, metaphoric "tradition."[24] Perloff and others read disjunctive poetics as indicating a subjectivity that escapes turning the world into an occasion for the poet's self-report or self-stabilization and therefore as ethically advanced. In Williams's metonymic (as opposed to metaphoric) style, there is "no summing up, . . . no final epiphany that 'human voices wake us and we drown,'" Perloff writes.[25] Perloff praises Williams's "Improvisations" in contrast to Eliot's "The Love Song of J. Alfred Prufrock," the seemingly more cohesive, "planned" poem. Bishop's attraction to those very concerns of Williams that Perloff and other avant-gardes praise suggests how flimsy is the reputation for her supposed investment in "lyric" control.

The Bishop canon constructed by lyric- and antilyric-reading premises that take her as primarily anxious and invested in control becomes weirder and more interesting as we see her poems exceeding and testing the lyric readings they have been credited with producing. This in turn reveals an important, underserved prehistory to both New Critical lyric-reading and avant-garde antilyric-reading strategies, one that reminds us that many twentieth-century poets in the United States experimented with the subjective premises institutionally dominant from the 1930s forward by *reanimating* certain "traditional" techniques, such as rhyme. At the chapter's close, I briefly turn to poems by two poets roughly contemporary to Bishop, Gwendolyn Brooks and Countee Cullen. Their uses of rhyme in poems about childhood similarly ill fit the subjective premises that shame the personal lyric, asking us to read against the grain of lyric-reading conventions.

What follows, then, is an attempt to reframe Bishop's work and to explore its particular way of problematizing lyric-reading assumptions—often in what I call "metadiscursive" poems—about voice and expression. By "metadiscursive" I mean that, while all poems draw on and reanimate forms of discourse that link "personal" language to the social imaginary (and this, in a way, is what Costello argues in calling for more "rhetorical" readings of Bishop), I believe Bishop's work consciously amplifies and animates the discursive. Her exploration of scenes of discursive education, in such mid- to late-career poems as "Manners," "First Death in Nova Scotia," and "In the Waiting Room," provided her an answer for what form of poetic "revolt" she might engage at a mid-1950s moment of high capitalism that produced the conditions for poetry to court too-easy identification between author and poem, reader and author.

To see Bishop putting discourse near the center of her poetic practice, and to see this choice as her answer to concerns about "a tradition of likenesses" that she conceived, as a young writer, through readings of early modernist Williams and Sigmund Freud, helps show the inadequacy of the canonical sites for placing Bishop and may help open new conversations about the history of lyric reading in the twentieth century. Bishop finally does not choose the same methods of addressing problems of poetic subjectivity employed by avant-gardes in the United States; she does not go the way of concrete experiment and formal disruption, but her reasons, as her work with Williams shows, were considered and actually in keeping with other aspects of Williams's practice. While we might be tempted to say that her maintenance of narrative and rhyme suggests the endurance of nineteenth-century techniques and "traditions," it is important to specify that we cannot read Bishop (or Cullen or Brooks or anyone) using rhyme or narrative techniques after modernism in quite the way we would read those same techniques in nineteenth-century poems, given changes to the surrounding verse culture. I would propose to read Bishop neither as a Language poet nor as a Victorian.

After thinking about Williams's efforts to "escape" tradition and to demote the authority of the first-person subject, Bishop turns to poems that dramatize the making and consuming of art (typically as landscape), exploring those processes as they entangle the subject in forms of self-projection. Bishop turned the desire to *escape* forms of projection into dramatizations of that desire (and its inevitable failure). I read her as self-consciously motivated by an antisubjective ethical imperative that early modernist critiques of mimesis introduced. It was her identification with Williams's early modernist lyric shame that led her, in work thereafter, to present and explore the meditative "lyric" subject, rather than attempt to evade it.

"UNSUPERSTITIOUS DR. WILLIAMS": BISHOP IN THE 1930S

Much of Bishop's work of the 1930s can be read as exploring and sometimes parodying aspects of the literary culture to which she had dutifully apprenticed herself as a student and which had become a source of discomfort, and even embarrassment, for her. Bishop's prose fables of the late 1930s, for instance, test the idea of original and masterfully crafted work against a modernity that she imagines (and comes to embrace in imagination) as a diversity of potential readers. Some of her best poems of the era, such as "The Monument" (1939), can be read this way, too—as locating art's power in the contingency of its potential receptions. At this very same moment of her career, however, Bishop felt pressure to challenge her traditional understandings of what art *should* do in ways that, it appears, were acutely uncomfortable for her. The story of a young Bishop, recently graduated from Vassar, breaking down into tears and running out of a party in the midst of an argument about beauty (her opponents espoused the only ever relative value of beauty) suggests just such a conflict.[26] Bishop's removing herself from the conversation might be read as a shame response: passionate desire to defend an outmoded value leads to a personal discomfort so strong that she wishes to remove herself, effecting a kind of self-repression.

Another episode in this process, and one that has so far gone unmentioned in critical readings of Bishop's work, occurs in the late 1930s and early 1940s when, after reading several of William Carlos Williams's works, Bishop begins and abandons—again, a form of self-repression— "Unsuperstitious Dr. Williams," a review essay not intended, it seems, for any particular journal. Though Bishop's review was to be about Williams's prose fiction (*In the Money* most specifically), her draft begins with a curious comment about rhyme that touches on her ashamed wish to maintain a belief in beauty and enchantment and what she calls, somewhat mysteriously, a "tradition of likenesses." "To some extent," she writes,

> the idea of rhyme must be *or must be seen to be* superstitious—the idea that if two things sound alike they must be alike & that there is therefore some mysterious connection between them. . . . In his poetry, Dr. Williams has usually done without rhyme, & reading it, one . . . has the feeling of being in the presence of a free, enclosed, and self-sufficient soul.[27]

There is a clear ring of Freudian rhetoric in the passage (and there is evidence that Bishop was reading *Totem and Taboo* at the same time she undertook the review).[28] Bishop's seeming praise for Williams's having turned from the mystical power often ascribed to rhyme (especially in accounts of its origins) shows Williams to be "self-sufficient" and civilized. He is free from certain limiting dependencies; he has "done without rhyme"—a sign, she knows she ought to believe, of his maturity.

The assessment is not entirely genuine, however; Bishop goes on to forgive such beliefs as difficult to abandon (and puts in a pitch for rhyme's pleasures along the way): "It is all the more striking (valuable?) (pleasing to the reader)," Bishop hazards, "when one does find rhyme used, or internal rhyme, as if even [Williams] can't quite escape the older tradition of and reverence for likenesses." This tradition of likenesses also includes "plot": later in the review, Bishop writes that it is "delightful" to find Williams "breaking down once in a while" from his aspiration to "assiduously ignore[] exigencies of plot"—"superstitious correspondences" that, in Bishop's view, are the novel's version of the older, superstitious worldview that believes in rhyme.[29] Bishop understood that to be thought poetically hip meant accepting one's tradition as outdated, childish, and vaguely shameful.

The fact that Bishop engaged *Totem and Taboo* at the time is significant, for it suggests she read Williams's wish to escape a "tradition of likenesses" in its light, drawing on Freud's sense that to be modern, both individuals and society ought to dispense with "superstitious," religious worldviews and face what Freud called "reality," as I will discuss in the next section. Though evidently relieved (even delighted) to find that Williams in fact cannot "escape," Bishop here acknowledges what she knows a modern writer ought to understand—that, as a religious worldview does, a "tradition of likenesses" (more than just rhyme and plot) falsely enchants experience—thus her slight hesitation in saying that rhyme "must be, or *must be seen* to be superstitious" (my emphasis).[30] That Bishop cannot decide whether rhyme *is* or whether it just *ought to be* seen as "superstitious" is significant. It highlights a mix of assent and ambivalence toward the rejection of "tradition" framed as liberation, a rhetoric both she and Williams had been apprenticed to, one she both admired and questioned and finally doubted Williams was pulling off. In this, Bishop's comments also underscore her ambivalence toward Freud's "repressive hypothesis," ambivalence she extended to the poetic culture's emphasis on "voice" as self-realization in the 1960s. The repressive hypothesis informed early modernist rhetorics of form: for Freud, shame, like religion, is one force inhibiting drives such as sexuality (and thus is a childish or savage emotion). For early modernism, "rhyme" is a moribund nineteenth-century, paternalistic attachment inhibiting more authentic artistic (and truly American, modern) urges and expressions.[31] The terms of Bishop's skepticism and concern—recognizing that, despite Williams's claim to refuse rhyme and mature, rhyme reasserts itself—show that she believed one's entanglements in "old correspondences" (as she puts it in the late 1940s poem "The Bight") and traditional modes of reading and interpretation to be rather profound. Bishop understood this "tradition of likenesses" as a deeply grooved inheritance and a socially embedded historical burden, more powerful perhaps than one's will to dispense with it. At the same time, the passage suggests that she, like Williams, felt compelled to see the world in ways that would newly challenge the "tradition" she had inherited.

Of what consisted the "tradition of likenesses" that Bishop identifies? Bishop clearly means rhyme, but her inclusion of *plot* as well suggests that this "tradition" involves, more broadly, what Sir Philip Sidney called "figuring foorth" or artistic formation—formings and feignings of the mess of "reality" into likenesses and orderly shapes.[32] It is more than mimesis, if by mimesis we simply mean imitation: it is something more like coherence making and hermeneutics that Bishop invokes with her yoking of plot to rhyme, with a whiff of the Platonic tradition behind it, too. One more local text behind this late 1930s or early 1940s draft may very well be Brooks and Warren's *Understanding Poetry* (1938), whose claims for the successful poem's interpretable "unity"—wherein every "element" of a poem (rhyme, diction, meter, imagery) contributes to the unified expression—endorse the "tradition" that Bishop recognized as a source of concern for Williams. At stake in some of what Bishop explores in Williams, then, are idealized abstractions of poetry, such as those emphasized in lyric-reading pedagogies of the day, then being widely disseminated in universities.

It is no surprise that Bishop cared what Williams believed about that view of poetry, rhyme, and plot: in a letter to Anne Stevenson written on March 20, 1963 Bishop identifies Williams (along with e.e. cummings, Robert Frost, and Hart Crane, among others) as "Heroes" in her early experience of them (*PPL*, 845). That she associated Williams with an imperative understanding of rhyme as embarrassingly, or even shamefully, childish is also no surprise, given the sheer volume of Williams's comments on the issue, which have rendered him a synecdoche for the widespread suspicion of rhyme in the first half of the twentieth century. As John Malcolm Brinnin put it, Williams believed that traditional forms and prosodies "served only to falsify the experience it would transcribe."[33] As early as 1919 in *Poetry* magazine, Williams had claimed that "rhyme was a language once, but now . . . is a lie," a word whose ethical charge implicates rhyme in more than the failure to realize fresh perception. Indeed, in 1938 (though the quotation is difficult to source), Williams went so far, in his most overt politicization of form, as to call the sonnet a "fascistic form."[34] The year 1938 is also when Laura (Riding) Jackson renounced the writing of poetry in a series of polemical essays, a move perhaps anticipated by her poems of the mid-1930s, including the prose poem "Poet: A Lying Word," reprinted in her 1937 *Collected Poems;* the poem asks, "Does it seem I ring, I sing, I rhyme, I poet-wit?" and answers, "Shame on me then!"[35]

For (Riding) Jackson, the shame of rhyme involves its being a technique of an overemphasized subjectivity—"I . . . I . . . I . . . I poet-wit"; she extends early modernist faith that forms implied forms of subjectivity and thus ethics. One can wonder here whether New Critical lyric-reading methods, only then gaining popularity, informed this particular yoking of formal control (poet-wit) with the assumption of subjectivity. Brooks and Warren's emphasis on the "order and control" of the "successful poem" tended to be bound up with their claims about the controlled, achieved nature of the subjectivity on display as "drama" in "the successful" lyric poem.[36]

It is perhaps important to remember that it is also in the 1930s that more general conventional notions of poetry's ideal expressive lyricness, by and large assumed since the eighteenth century, came under suspicion in the United States. Milton Cohen explores the rising interest in leftist causes among writers in the United States in the 1930s that put conventional notions of lyric under suspicion, and he tracks a broadly felt pressure to find forms of literary art that, on the way to radicalizing readers and reflecting the plight of workers, could reform a bourgeois self-absorption that was also associated with poetry conceived as lyric.[37] Cohen describes this pressure effecting two broad, perhaps competing shifts, especially when taken from the vantage of current forms of antilyricism: first, a cultural suspicion about an aesthetics of difficulty (and thus of modernist technique); and second, a concern about the "self-absorption" of mainstream attitudes among leftist critics that was often voiced, implicitly or explicitly, as a critique of lyric. For one example, Cohen cites Malcolm Cowley's concern about a "desperate feeling of solitude and uniqueness" that he felt leftist literature should combat. Cowley singles out "lyric" as that feeling's sign and devalued remnant (15). Cowley called e.e. cummings "the last of the lyric poets" in his 1932 essay of that name, wondering, as Cohen puts it, whether "'lyricism' . . . was becoming irrelevant to the times" (93). For Cowley, the waning "vitality" of "lyric poetry" could be explained by a broad cultural shift in a whole verse culture, what he calls a new "lack of conviction on the part of [lyric's] friends" (93). Comments such as Josephine Herbst's that the "beauty of the thirties was its . . . chance to get out of the constricted *I* in what seemed a meaningful way" indirectly suggest that the failed lyric ideal in question involved the subjective first-person personal poem that, more and more across the century, had become identified with poetry as "lyric" (15).[38] And Genevieve Taggard, a "proletarian" American poet, published her *Collected Poems* with a manifesto that identified her work against the terms that came to be viewed as "lyric" in ensuing decades: "The reader will misunderstand my poems if he thinks I have been trying to write about myself (as if I were in any way unique) as a biographer might—or as a romantic poet would, to map his own individuality. Since the earliest attempts at verse I have tried to use the 'I' in a poem only as a means for transferring feeling to identification with anyone who takes the poem, momentarily for his own."[39]

This is just to say that it would have been clear to Bishop (though in part the terms are anachronistic to her moment) that the renunciation (or not) of formal choices could be held to indicate or implicate one's position in an ongoing debate about one's attachment to subjective norms associated even then with "lyric" and the forms of subjectivity they seemed to endorse—one's mode of approach both to the world and to others, or what Williams and others frequently called "reality." Critics have emphasized that early modernist Williams: the ethical poet who sought to represent "reality" more truly by freeing the poet's objects of attention, in effect, from that attention. This idealized Williams sought forms that could free reality from subjectivity and a worldview overinvested in the self's power, in imaginative solipsism, over "reality." This was a worldview whose agents included rhyme but also "the phrases words make" (rhetoric), as well as "poetical rhythms" and "grammar." These traditions, he felt, "stultif[y]," "bind[ing] us to our pet indolences and medievalisms."[40]

Despite the young Bishop's interest in what animated such early modernist rhetoric, nevertheless, she took Williams's rhetoric of "escape" to imply rather a disavowal of tendencies of perception and language (chiefly, of perception as ineluctably susceptible to cultural influence, and language as evolving and contingent in unpredictable ways) that she was then exploring in her prose work and went on to make one of her great, central subjects.[41] In wrestling with Williams as a metonymy for early modernist ethics, Bishop wrestles with the great weight of modernism's doubt (as Cary Nelson puts it) "about either the possibility or the political wisdom of identifying a single, unified speaking subject as the voice of a poem," as well as its rejection of narrative methods, and forms of coherence, in the process.[42]

To position Bishop in terms of Williams's early modernist ethical poetic (and a Freudian one at that) is important for understanding her place in a longer history of twentieth-century poetic-ethical culture in American criticism. Critics still praise Williams for avoiding what we could very well call a "tradition of likenesses"—not just rhyme but also (importantly) narrative, figures of speech, and metaphors most particularly—and take that avoidance to imply ethically advanced forms of poetic subjectivity. This discussion once turned on the ideal of egolessness, inflected by the image of Williams as realizing the "negative capability" of Keats. Later, and often with reference to Charles Olson's Williams-inspired "Objectism" of the late 1950s, writers explicitly or subtly influenced by poststructural critiques of the rational subject return to Williams as one beginning of an American avant-garde "line" of poets concerned to escape the worst shame of the subjective stance whose critical shorthand, across the twentieth century, became "the lyric I."[43] The understandable appeal of the fantasy that Williams did escape poetic figures of speech and thought is the vision of writing's release from the subject's controlling presence and, as a result, of the subject's release from the mess of self-involvement, inattention, and instrumental uses of the world in its alterity.[44] This positivist, constructivist note sounds in a variety of past and current critical claims about what poetry ought to do and be in order to respect alterity and to forfeit the worst forms of logos—the "lyric interference of the individual as ego" that Olson would excise with "Objectism"; in Albert Gelpi's praise of Williams's *Spring and All* for, purportedly, using "not a single figure of speech"; in J. Hillis Miller's claim that Williams's poetry is the paramount "poetry of reality" because it checks "the ego" and a "will to power over things"; or in the critic who, suggesting what Williams teaches us, summarizes as follows: "Good poems . . . will not use the . . . traditional poetic comparison 'is like' to join dissimilar things to express an idea. Instead, good poems will appear broken."[45]

This is to say that Bishop was not alone in turning Williams into an effigy of early modernist piety: the Williams by whom Bishop feels at first rebuked, like the one that Gelpi, Miller, and others advance, represents an oversimplified metonymy for early modernism's Freudian-inflected piety about the ethics of its new realism. Even by 1932, years before Bishop's review, Williams was critiquing the Imagist-Poundian claim that organic, antitraditional form represents an "escape" from the mess of figuration, a critique evident in the poem "This Florida," in which, if "we thought to escape rime / by imitation of the senseless / unarrangement of wild things," this project was "the stupidest rime of all."[46] Williams himself had already come to see the desire to escape "tradition" as another form of mystification. Bishop nevertheless feels called to account by a narrow version of early Williams, who, under Ezra Pound's Imagist dictums, views rhyme as not just a technique but a worldview that imposes a falsifying logic of sameness on what is wild, particular, and best represented in its "unarrangement."[47]

My eagerness to register Bishop's awareness of ethical formalisms is part of a lyric shame dynamic (one prefigured by Bishop's feeling called to account by a fantasied Williams)—an (ashamed) attempt to align her with the avant-garde who has dismissed her. Some critics—most notably Perloff—have read Bishop's disinterest in paratactic, disjunctive techniques as a failure that draws her into a "line" of Romantic and post-Romantic poets whose purported reverence for what we could call likenesses—"connections and continuities," metaphors and similes—is evidence of the (shamefully) high level of "authority" such poetry ascribes to its lyric speakers over the control of meaning.[48]

The shame of poetry's reputation as a form of privileged, leisured activity that endorsed and required the artist's seeming remove from a labor economy, a situation intensified through the 1930s, also operates in Bishop's lyric shame. The question of how poetic labor should be valued and how poets could or should express their concerns for the "actual world" was made ever more keen for left-leaning artists such as Bishop during that period.[49] By 1938 Bishop had spent several years exploring that problem in prose works, as well as testing and rejecting the idea that "form" and "tradition" are static entities that transcend contexts of their reception and articulation. In prose pieces from the late 1930s, she counters her fear of poetic escapism by challenging the idea that writers remain "self-sufficient" or "enclosed" apart from worldly and textual influences, including past traditions.[50] Work from this era also makes it clear that Bishop recognized but felt skeptical toward the idea that new forms and techniques represented epistemic advancement or could be taken, in themselves, as ensuring escape or progress. In a letter from 1940, she teases Marianne Moore for promoting radical technique as such: "I left off the outline of capitals [for the first word of each line] . . . and feel very ADVANCED."[51] (Notice how those "left off" capitals reassert themselves in the orthography of "advanced"). Her sense that meanings depend on contingencies of reception, the intellectual fruit of her 1930s prose experiments, would have tempered the belief that radical technique (or any technique, for that matter) opens a nondiscursive window onto material reality or allows a form of attention clean of subjective complication.

The epistemology of likeness making increasingly made Bishop uneasy, and she discovered in and through her engagement with her Williams-inspired shame a poetic that performs subjective intrusion and projection. This is not quite a new claim about Bishop.[52] And yet it is important to stress that missing this aspect of Bishop's work occurs when we identify her words with a rather narrowly conceived lyric speaker, a premise she rejected after reading Freud and Williams, in ways that both challenge the shameful Bishop of the lyric miniature, of repressed, modest self-expression, and help recast her reputation as the lyric writer of "worried continuing."[53] That she herself opted not to extend early modernist techniques in this process of wrestling with her lyric shame has tended of late to be read to indicate her disinterest in the ethics animating early modernist and objectivist techniques. Instead, Bishop opted for what I call a metadiscursive style, one in which ethical research and critique into poetic forms of attention depend on narrative and expressive modes whose subtly foregrounded discursive character tests most of the assumptions we tend, through Williams and Olson and certainly post-Language, to accord to those modes.

NOW I'M ADJUSTED TO REALITY

To see Freud animating Bishop's responses to Williams makes it clearer that in invoking "a tradition of likenesses," Bishop was thinking through a formidable ethical discourse about forms of attention and writing, and the subject positions they implied, inflected by the significant pathos with which she (among other poets) read Freud's claims for civilization's progress toward sociopolitical maturity. There is ample evidence that Bishop's association of rhyme and plot with this shamefully superstitious "tradition" emerged not just from her reading of Williams but also from her reading of Freud's *Totem and Taboo*—in particular, the third section of the chapter "Animism, Magic, and the Omnipotence of Thought."[54] It is a chapter that, among other things, lends itself to questions dear to modernist poets concerning the extent of the mental "control" one should or could exert over the world one sought to perceive and to honor "as it is." In Bishop's college writing, she had quarreled with what she took to be Freud's answer to that question, especially his assertion that the mature modern person should be able to resist a worldview that overvalues mental control. An essay she wrote as an undergraduate at Vassar, "Dimensions for a Novel" (1935), for instance, defends superstition and the omnipotence of thought (key subjects in *Totem*) as forms of cognition that the novel ought to *explore*. Novels thus far, she writes, have failed to capture "the interplay of influences between present and past," "cross references and echoes" that, she admits, might "in their lowest forms be called 'superstitious.'"[55] Low or not, Bishop goes on to defend superstition in that earliest work, nearly quoting (to different ends) the language of Freud's "Animism" chapter. Here is Freud:

> I have adopted the term ["omnipotence of thought"] from a highly intelligent man who . . . had coined the phrase as an explanation of all the strange and uncanny events by which he, like others afflicted by the same illness, seemed to be pursued. If he thought of someone, he would be sure to meet that very person immediately afterwards, as though by magic. . . . All obsessional neurotics are superstitious in this way, usually against their better judgment. (*Totem*, 107)

In "Dimensions for a Novel," Bishop explicitly positions herself against Freud's better judgment; rather than stop being "superstitious in this way," she insists that experience really *is* enchanted by such moments of coincidence and connection and proposes that novels should try to explore that enchantment. Though in doing so one might "be called either a primitive, or, worse still, a mystic," Bishop writes, echoing Freud, "I have always felt a certain amount of respect for superstitions . . . ; always I am startled when something I have dreamed of comes true, or someone I have

been thinking of arrives on the scene."[56] The reference to Freud is tacit but
clear: in maintaining her wonder at these situations, Bishop risks primitivity, refusing to distinguish between "real" coincidence and an "imaginary" projection of order and meaning, as Freud would have her do.

Five years later, Bishop is less defensive of superstition, with Freud's
chapter now informing the connection she makes in her review of Williams between forms of artistic control ("likeness" makings such as rhyme
and plot) and "superstition." One of Freud's central arguments in "Animism, Magic, and the Omnipotence of Thought" is that the magical thinking of both primitive men and neurotics follows from their reverence—
what he calls an "over-valuation"—for chance resemblances, particularly an
assumed likeness between wishes and actual events (*Totem,* 105–106). Indeed, the over-valuation of "all mental processes" (fictive power included)
defines the primitive's limited and problematic "attitude toward the world":
"Things become less important than the ideas of things. . . . Relations
which hold between the ideas of things are assumed to hold equally between the things themselves" (106). Freud is writing about delusions, but
Bishop very well may have heard in the passage an intertext of Williams's
early version of "Paterson" (1927), which substitutes the city of Paterson in
its thingness for the divine, the great origin of ideas—"Say it, No idea but
in things— / nothing but the blank faces of the houses" (*CP1,* 263). Freud
also argues that delusional, magical thinking is the result of "primitive"
man's "unshakeable confidence" in his mental "control" over phenomena,
a narcissism that remains in even scientific man's "faith in the power of
the human mind" (*Totem,* 110). Freud demands that society learn to face
"reality" (or existential contingency) without attempting to redeem it, recognizing that man is not the focal point of that reality (112). "Civilization
[must] acknowledge" human "smallness," Freud insists, for "the scientific
view of the universe no longer affords any room for human omnipotence;
men have . . . submitted resignedly to death and other necessities of
nature" (110).

Freud's sense that the "primitive belief in omnipotence" "still survives"
in men's faith in the power of the human mind would have been suggestive for Bishop, in her quandary about her attachments to "tradition."
Given moments in her writing after college that associate poetic choices
with superstition and primitivity, Bishop seems to have taken Freud's claim
to extend to specifically *poetic* or artistic forms of control, linking the
primitive's and neurotic's belief in "similarity" between seeming and being

to the poet's belief in the idea that if "two things sound alike they must be alike."[57] Freud himself suggests that "the omnipotence of thought" is "retained . . . in the field of art," though the "impulses" that first inspired art were religious and "are for the most part extinct today" (*Totem*, 113).

Bishop's draft on Williams is savvy in drawing the connection between Freud and Williams in their focus on mental and artistic attitudes as suggesting the subject's "adjustment" or not (as Freud would put it) to a "reality" inherently unredeemable either by traditional notions of transcendent art and beauty or by the religious worldviews that inform those notions (*Totem*, 112).[58] The suggestion is that an investment in artistic control could implicate one's subjective stance as "primitive," self-important, and ill adjusted to "reality." There are some echoes of this Freudian stance in moments of Williams's early writings, including Williams's view of Marianne Moore's originality and her "incomprehensibility" as "witness to the cost" of a laudable "escape from crude symbolism . . . and complicated ritualistic forms designed to separate work from 'reality'—such as rhyme [and] . . . meter" (*CP1*, 188–189). "Crude" and "ritualistic" and other such epithets in *Spring and All* reiterate Freud's dictums on how to be modern into advice for the modern reader of poetry. Promising a secular awakening delivered through technical novelty in *Spring and All*, Williams boasts that his poetry eschews the consolatory, refusing to "interpret our deepest promptings" (*CP1*, 177). Traditional poetic techniques, he goes on to assert, have only separated man from a "reality" ill served by the human forms imposed on it. Early Williams promises, in distinctly Freudian terms, that abandoning "ritualistic forms" will "civilize" modern poetry by freeing reality from human interference.[59]

Though, as Bonnie Costello has argued, Bishop admired but did not emulate Williams's "objectivism," she does explore the Freudian-Williams premise that poems need to become "adjusted to reality" (a phrase she picks up from Freud's *Totem and Taboo*) in a variety of late 1930s and early 1940s works—specifically, experimenting with poetic stances that demote the subject's authority.[60] "Florida" (1939), first published in *Partisan Review*, reads as an attempt to make poetic "adjustment" by refusing subjectivity: it is unrhymed, is written in free verse, and, true to Freud, describes a landscape awash with death and "necessities of nature" (*Totem*, 110). True to the Williams she feels rebuked by and quarrels with in her abandoned review draft, the poem suppresses—even tries to will away—its shaping intelligence. The poem's attention merely drifts amid visible

phenomena, accumulating images without quite framing them, forgoing
a linear course of thought—a stance quite unusual in Bishop's corpus.[61]

In the poem's first twenty-nine lines, it offers an impersonal, generalizing view of what "Florida" is, resisting expressive intrusion. There is no "I";
the poem's eye structures what we see without mooring itself in a specific
narrative or subjective point of view, a mode that few of Bishop's poems
had tried up to that point.[62] It begins as if occasioned by a command to list
notable facts about Florida:

> The state with the prettiest name,
> the state that floats in brackish water,
> held together by mangrove roots
> that bear while living oysters in clusters,
> and when dead strew white swamps with skeletons,
> dotted as if bombarded, with green hummocks
> like ancient cannon-balls sprouting grass. (*PPL*, 24, ll. 1–7)

Similes appear (suggesting description's never-neutral nature)—"dotted as
if bombarded," for instance—but as signature Williams poems of the era
do (for instance, "Nantucket," "View of a Lake," "Between Walls," "Sun,"
or "The Cod Head"—all from the mid-1930s), the poem dwells on this
landscape for no apparent reason. We are nowhere in particular in Florida;
animals are described in the plural, in terms of their general behaviors:

> Tanagers embarrassed by their flashiness,
> and pelicans whose delight it is to clown;
> who coast for fun on the strong tidal currents
> in and out among the mangrove islands
> and stand on the sand-bars drying their damp gold wings
> on sun-lit evenings. (24, ll. 11–16)

As though checking embarrassment at a lapse into anthropomorphism
(other "birds" are notably "hysterical" and unseen), what follows is another stated report—this time of the less human-like "enormous turtles," whose death comes as a rude shock across the line break, given
how little time we have been allotted to feel sympathy for their being
"helpless and mild":

> Enormous turtles, helpless and mild,
> die and leave their barnacled shells on the beaches,

and their large white skulls with round eye-sockets
twice the size of a man's. (24, ll. 17–20)

The birds have been invested with qualities special to humans—
embarrassment most particularly—but lines 17–20 undercut that specialness, with men and turtles merely mortal creatures with "eye-sockets."
"Florida" tries to stay adjusted to "necessities of nature," neither redeeming
them with nor imposing on them human paradigms. Even those isolated
images and "likenesses" that do burble up feel neither more nor less important than the turtles' instinctive progress toward the beach; both, the
poem suggests, merely happen.

However, the language's mix of idiosyncrasy and (expected) impersonality becomes odd at line 30, when the poem very nearly admits a "lyric I"
by specifying its temporal moment and thus (potentially) locating a seeing subject. At this point, we view not "the state," generally, but a specific
place: a mangrove swamp. After a verse paragraph break, the poem asserts
that events are happening "now," and though the gesture is still impersonal, things become less abstract and generalized:

Thirty or more buzzards are drifting down, down, down,
over something they have spotted in the swamp,
in circles like stirred-up flakes of sediment
sinking through water. (25, ll. 30–33)

Because of the participle and the attempt to number the buzzards, the
poem asserts more strongly that a seeing subject coordinates this set of
points; the moment suddenly verges on becoming a "drama," the term that
Brooks and Warren's college textbook claimed for "every poem," as that
would define both lyric reading (and the antilyric discourses they spawned)
for years to come: "Every poem implies a speaker of the poem, . . . and . . .
the poem represents the reaction of such a person to a situation, a scene, or
an idea. In this sense every poem can be—and in fact must be—regarded
as a little drama."[63] The poem veers toward satisfying such a lyric reading
and betraying Bishop's allegiance to a Williams-esque impersonality,
though only for a moment. In fact, the poem returns to the general perspective immediately, breaking the flow of lines with the two disjointed
observations offered in end-stopped lines that resignedly return to report-
age and quietly aestheticize death: "Smoke from wood-fires filters fine
blue solvents. / On stumps and dead trees the charring is like black velvet"

(25, ll. 34–35). Despite the high level of aestheticization (and we can note the alliteration and assonance), death and general report return.

Some critics have read "Florida" as a successful attempt to write a Williams-style descriptive poem, taking it as Bishop's turn from the "hermetic inwardness" of earlier poems such as "The Unbeliever" and "The Weed" or as an effort to "stick to the facts" of things or to turn humbly to the outside world and see it accurately, in imitation of her mentor, Marianne Moore.[64] The contemporaneous Williams review would support the assertion; however, the poem's nearness to the Brooks-Warren belief that all poems have a speaker, and its relation to later antilyric responses to that norm, seems rather more complex than critics have so far suggested. The poem's brief, late, almost guilty revelation of its own organizing eye, as well as its drift in and out of figuration and (notably pejorative) anthropomorphism, signals Bishop's ironization of the project of writing as if from no point of view, with no animating desire in play.

This is not to argue that the poem is a psychodrama of modesty toward or repressed desire for self-expression, as many of her 1940s poems of description have been read.[65] The humor (and sorrow) of the poem lies in the sudden admission that an ineluctably motivated attention arranges this view. The poem theorizes and dramatizes the desire and failure to "escape" lyric-reading norms involving the expectation of an organizing eye/I, much in the way Bishop's review describes the effort and amusing failure of Williams's attempt to escape the organizing "I" who makes rhyme. An implied author cannot help but be outed (wittingly or not) standing behind the curtain of the poem's impersonal, objectivist performance, a move that becomes funny when we notice that the exposure of this presence "behind" the scene occurs in the noting of a remarkable number of buzzards descending on "something they have spotted in the swamp." Quite suddenly, where and when things happen in this poem's space, questions the poem has thus far avoided by proceeding in the general, become important: What thing have the buzzards spotted? Is it the author herself? The lines draw description into the same terms as forms of predation, "ferocious obbligatos" (*PPL,* 25, l. 37).

In this, the poem also supposes that, however earnest about trying, one might fail to remain "adjusted" to what Freud would call "reality" (buzzards of course signaling death redeemed by something other than God or an afterlife). The sudden step out of adjustment into plot and subjectivity after this moment precipitates language more animated and judgmental, moralizing even, even if no subject appears to embody it: the coast is "monotonous" and "sagging" in line 28, and later, the moonlight is "Cold white, not bright, . . . coarse-meshed, / and the careless, corrupt state is all black specks / too far apart, and ugly whites; the poorest / post-card of itself" (25, ll. 40–43). The lines suggest disappointment and disenchantment; suddenly skies become "heavens"; a great effort to register an unenchanted Freudian landscape has failed.[66]

This turn is important, for the lines show the postcard ideal that has mediated this effort at antisubjective description all along. A historically contingent subjectivity (never mind if it is Bishop's) has, at the last, asserted a discourse of landscape through the disappointment that postcard and real do not match. The attention that at first let details stand as a list of unrelated phenomena has given in to a totalizing judgment and admits discourses of race and class; the "state is all black specks / . . . and ugly whites; the poorest / post-card of itself"—a sign of its being generally "careless" and "corrupt" (25, ll. 41–43). It is useful to remark the obvious here, that postcards are idealized, conventional views—titled framings of nature made often for commercial purposes. Furthermore, places cannot quite *be* postcards of themselves and remain themselves.

By invoking this contradiction, the poem points to the always already conventional nature of description, to a hermeneutic "tradition" of likenesses. Convention compromises both the effort to stay objective (for in what sense is language ever not touched by convention?) and the expressive possibilities of the poem taken as spoken (for what language is ever wholly personal?). This is reiterated by the ambiguity of the alligator call heard at poem's end. Though we "know" the alligator has "five distinct calls," named at the poem's end, in the poem, she "whimpers" (communicating with sound but not language) and generically "speaks," leaving us uncertain as to what has either been said or heard (25, ll. 45–47).

The force of convention on perception is even more obvious in Bishop's "Now I'm adjusted to reality," a Williams-Freud-inflected poem draft from the early 1940s. The phrase (which is the draft's first line and its refrain) also appears in part in several places in Freud's work, including his "Animism" chapter from *Totem and Taboo,* in the section that analogizes phases of "men's views of the universe" to the individual's phases of "libidinal maturation" and discusses the omnipotence of thought. Freud's passage implies that to do without the comforting sense of control over the world that magic and God (and art) provide is a mark of both an individual's and a culture's maturity:

> The animistic phase would correspond to narcissism both chronologically and in its content; the religious phase would correspond to the stage of object-choice of which the characteristic is the child's attachment to his parents; while the scientific phase would have an exact counterpart in the stage at which an individual has reached maturity, has renounced the pleasure principle, *adjusted himself to reality,* and turned to the external world for the objects of his desires. (*Totem,* 112, my emphasis)

In a move that reiterates Bishop's interest in Williams's slips (or are they hers?) into plot and rhyme, and the power of conventional understandings, "Now I'm adjusted to reality" portrays a consciously "adjusted" speaker who nevertheless cannot escape seeing the world in terms of the abandoned religious paradigm: "Now I'm adjusted to reality," the poem's refrain begins, "but oh! Mount Ararat, I long for thee!"[67] If the "I" in this poem has read Freud, adjustment has been unsuccessful: the refrain repeats and repeats, suggesting a melancholic resistance to change or the folly of thinking to rid oneself of old worldviews simply by virtue of will. In the draft, it is the gap between conscious disillusionment, on the one hand, and the remnants of belief, on the other (between different ways of seeing Mt. Ararat—at once a real place, an enchanted place, and a metonymy for the religious story), that reiterates the skepticism of the response to Williams (and perhaps to a certain Freudian therapeutic resolve). Bishop suggests that, even for those who are ideologically "adjusted to reality," conscious will to mature may not dislodge deep-seated cultural and discursive norms and inheritances: "God gave it first to Noah gave it to my father / And he gave it first to me." Even if Ararat's symbolic function is now empty—"My father gave me Mt. Ararat, Mt. Ararat. / In the days when that was that"—nevertheless, it is "given."[68]

"Now I'm adjusted to reality" is just one example of work that evidences the enduring influence of Bishop's engagements with Williams's ethical poetics and Freud's ideas about modern maturity, engagements that see her concern about the subject's stance toward reality move toward loosely articulated psychological epistemology. For Bishop the problem with achieving Freud's or Williams's program is the force of language to work against one's conscious intentions. Versions of this idea appear as thoughts about the intersubjectivity of language use, as early as 1935. Just before Bishop discusses her interest in "superstition" in "Dimensions for a Novel," for instance, she wonders about our unconscious parroting of others' language:

> In conversation we notice how, often, the other person will repeat some word or phrase of ours, perhaps with a quite different meaning, and we in turn will pick up some adjective or adverb of theirs, or even some pun on their words, all unconsciously. This trick of echoes and re-echoes, references and cross-references [effects a] . . . conformity between the old and the new.[69]

Not only can what shapes language use be unconscious, but Bishop regards the "conformity between the old and the new," one way of describing the persistence of "tradition," as a "trick" managed by language, for even phrases used with a "quite different meaning" will bear the "old" meaning along.

We might say that thinking about Williams helped Bishop to realize the power of discourse; she was exploring the difficulty of stepping outside discursive formations. Increasingly, over the next fifteen years, Bishop would pursue the force of language's "trick of echoes and re-echoes," more explicitly, as metadiscursive experiments. I use "discourse" and "discursive" here in the by-now-familiar Foucauldian sense, to mean, as Stuart Hall describes it, language that "governs the way a topic can be meaningfully talked about and reasoned about. . . . Discourse [both] 'rules in' certain ways of talking about a topic, defining an acceptable and intelligible way to talk, write, or conduct oneself, [and also] by definition . . . 'rules out,' limits and restricts other ways of talking, of conducting ourselves in relation to the topic or constructing knowledge about it."[70] There is ample evidence in Bishop's archive that the effort to train herself away from construing the world through "traditional," religious discourses (she was an unbeliever) alerted her to the power of discourse in ways that both are vital to understandings of her midcareer work and yet upset the lyric paradigms through which it has so often been read.

For instance, in an early draft of "The Bight" (begun in 1945) that clearly shows the poem's interest in describing a desecularized landscape, Bishop struggles to make the poem an "adjusted" description of landscape. The draft shows that the bight was chosen as a place lacking heavenly accompaniment, that she wanted to be seen (and to be presented) as Williams-esque, undesigned. It is as if the poem were trying to state this but quickly becomes entangled in old poetic tropes that persist even at the level of the word:

> No heavenly voice, no organ music plays
> Behind this scene

> World
> No soprano voices shrill (no organ music plays)
> Behind this world[71]

The seeming correction from "scene" to "world" suggests the challenge, even at the level of the word, to escape the residue of subjective, traditional, Christian interpretive and descriptive paradigms informing a "tradition of likenesses": "scene" invokes theatrics or painting (and thus a directorial, artistic presence), clashing with the poem's effort; Bishop opts instead for "world," somewhat less humanizing.[72] Notably, Charles Darwin (whom Bishop read very carefully throughout her adult life) had difficulty finding a language adequate to describe the contingency of the forces producing evolutionary change, a point he acknowledged in the third edition of *The Origin of Species* (1861). He apologizes for his phrase "natural selection," a metaphor that had been taken as implying God's active involvement "behind" random mutations and their success: "It has been said that I speak of natural selection as an active power or Deity. . . . Every one knows what is meant and is implied by such metaphorical expressions; they are almost necessary for brevity. So again it is difficult to avoid personifying the word Nature," which he goes on to define as "only the aggregate action and product of many natural laws, and by laws the sequence of events as ascertained by us."[73]

As Williams himself admits, in *Spring and All,* how "easy to slip / into the old mode, how hard to / cling firmly to the advance," all the while looking for a technical "advance" away from tradition, hermeneutics, and subjective self-centeredness (*CP1,* 191–193).[74] In Bishop's experiments, she seems to have appreciated a Williams whose call for mere seeing is nevertheless often elaborately *figured,* a performance of his own failure, as in the claim in an essay on Charles Sheeler "to pull out, transubstantiate, boil, unglue, hammer, melt, digest and psychoanalyze, not even to distill but to see and keep what the understanding touches intact—as grapes are round and come in bunches."[75] In contrast to his idealization by later critics as eschewing figuration, Williams rather performed the failure of the desire for the poet to be unashamed by the deforming power of human consciousness on things. Bishop was troubled by the possibility that, in the call to so radically demote subjectivity (contrary to what Brooks and Warren claimed "every poem" should do), poems would have to resist enchanting or even praising the world. And yet Williams's performances of this problem preview Bishop's practices in ways so far underexplored, perhaps because of his later idealization as the original proponent of lyric shame.

Here we could linger on Williams's performance of the problems of a meditative-subjective praise poetry in his 1935 poem "To a Wood Thrush." The poem draws on and critiques a Keatsian praise tradition in a parody of "Ode to a Nightingale." The poem's articulation of the shame of poetry (which became an even more explicit theme in his work of the 1950s) predates the lyric discourses of New Criticism and helps to clarify what Bishop also would have understood as the important challenge to traditions of poetic subjectivity in the 1930s, as well as the possibilities for ethical practice.

In the "Ode," Keats's speaker longs to achieve the thoughtless ease of the nightingale he praises, which "hast never known, / the weariness, the fever, and the fret" of human life. Human life is unlike the bird's, that is, because consciousness places on humans the burden to be "full of sorrow," to feel the passage of time. The darkling poet briefly asserts that he can achieve the bird's unconscious happiness "on the wings of Poesy" but, by the end, accepts his exile from the state of nature. Consciousness—the "dull brain" that "perplexes and retards," keeping him out of time with the flow of experience—inexorably separates the poet from what he loves about the object of his praise.[76]

In Williams's version of the ode, the poet's exile from the state of nature is not (as in Keats) an ineluctable consequence of consciousness but—importantly and inspired by Freud, perhaps—the result of "conventions" that have overvalued consciousness. This is the "tradition of likenesses" that concerned Bishop, it would seem:

> Singing across the orchard
> before night, answered

from the depths
of the wood, inversely
and in a lower key—

First I tried to write
conventionally praising you
but found it no more
than my own thoughts
that I was giving. No.

What can I say?
                         Vistas
of delight waking suddenly
before a cheated world. (*CP1,* 405)

"Cheated" makes the Keats "Ode" intertext especially clear. After praising the nightingale in high-flown poesy, Keats's subject is shocked into
self-consciousness, reminded by the word "forlorn" that he is no "immortal bird." The poem regrets that "fancy cannot cheat so well"—that one
cannot lose consciousness and dwell in the bird's immortal, natural state.
In this sense, both Williams and Keats share the complaint that poetic
language affords us only a fleeting sense of connection to the bird's song.

Despite this similarity, the important difference is that Williams prefers his world to be cheated, because the conventions of specifically Keatsian Romantic praise (a youthful, shameful love for Williams) promise
"no more / than my own thoughts"—thus Williams's stark dash after his
first few lines and the sudden, emphatic "No." His poem expresses a more
emphatic doubt about poesy's power than "do I wake or sleep?" (the closing question of the "Ode"). Williams's question, "What can I say?" raises
the shamed impasse (rather than mere confusion and disappointment)
that the desire for self-presence represented for him (and many later poets), a ratcheting up of Keats's uncertainty about the difference between
his poem and the bird's song.

If in asking, "What can I say?" Williams's work follows from and intensifies "a pressure to avoid or camouflage statement and abstraction"
that Robert Pinsky identifies with the Keatsian tradition, his early-twentieth-
century poetic also expressed the desire to escape statement and abstraction
altogether—to discover in formal experiment a way to bypass the Keats-

ian conundrum and thus demote the "tradition of likenesses," allowing more immediate "contact" between language and the world.[77] Whereas for Keats avoiding statement and abstraction requires "becom[ing] a sod," Williams dramatizes the limits of an expressive mode by turning to a disjunctive one that demotes the subject—performing a turn to new conventions of language intended to achieve an unhanding of its objects. Indeed, the disjunctive and antiabsorptive enter with closing lines whose sharp enjambment and use of transferred epithet notably foreground the refusal of subjective priority: now "vistas" belong to a "delight" not quite human and able to "wake" on their own: "Vistas / of delight waking suddenly / before a cheated world" (*CP1*, 405). Notably, there is no way to "say" what has been said here, for syntactic disruption and resulting ambiguity forbid it. Does "before" recommend the existence of these vistas (and their delight) in temporal priority or spatial relation to human concern? Or do these vistas get animated (awakened) only at the risk of their being cheated? Williams's refusal takes *form:* we are refused, by dint of disjunctive technique, the poet's guidance for how to interpret the lines.

For many avant-garde readers of Williams, this move has been paramount: the answer to the question "What can I say?" has been to insist that poetry should not "say" anything (contra Williams's own speech-based poetic), for in too-legible modes of "saying," the poet engages a falsely coherent traditional subjectivity and projects a falsifying logic onto senseless and contingent "reality."[78] Bishop admired and felt called to account by the ethical grounds for such refusals and explored their critical potential, but her work did not take up the disjunctive methods most often taken to be their sign. Yet she does take a cue from Williams's self-reflexive, self-dramatizing play, evident in her own tendency to highlight the amusing failures (and their mechanics of shame) that an antisubjective agenda (later identified with the refusal of "lyric") produces. Called by early modernist ethical poetics to epistemic maturity, and all the while doubting its premises, Bishop turns to dramatize the problem of trying, and failing, to shirk the shame of forms of poetic meaning making, a shame that Williams himself performed in poems from *The Desert Music* (1954) that explore the mimesis of nature as "a shameful thing" and in which the "I" asserts itself with shame: "I *am* a poet! I / am. I am. I am a poet, I reaffirmed, ashamed" (*CP2*, 276, 284). Bishop similarly explores dynamics of poetic attention and acts of interpretation in poems that use narrative to dramatize lyric subjects encountering the force of tradition, the social, history, and discourse as these enter, unbidden, into acts of interpretation, not so easily "escaped."[79]

Many of Bishop's poems of the era after her engagement with Williams, beginning with "Florida" (and the contemporaneous "Seascape"), can be read as explorations of the making and consuming of art as these processes entangle subjects in forms of self-projection. They show a continuity between Williams and Bishop that has been obscured by a divisive boundary resulting from a hegemony of midcentury lyric reading and later resistances to that hegemony. Understanding that Bishop chose to explore what Williams recommended escaping may make her more a follower of W. H. Auden than of Pound: in Bishop's later project, she critiques lyric subjectivity by focusing on discourse as it shapes supposedly "personal" expressive moments. If it seems I here credit the shaming of lyric expressiveness in so claiming, it is not so: the ethical fantasies constructed in Williams's name at their worst reduce his work to an antiexpressiveness it surely does not live up to. Those fantasies have been important to North American poetry's ongoing sense of its vitality for contemporary concerns, an investment in poetry as capable of effecting positive deformations of the subjective logic supporting both state-sponsored violence and global high capitalism. And yet we will find, in the next section, that Bishop herself thought of discursive experiment as a form of "revolt."

"CLICK. CLICK," "BAAA, BAAA": VOICING ELIZABETH BISHOP

Bishop's concerns about lyric subjectivity and a "tradition of likenesses" intensify in the poems written after World War II and published in *A Cold Spring* (1955). In "The Bight" (first published in 1949), when the figure of a speaker fully emerges, it is in an almost exasperated way—an "I" that stagily outs itself as the source of the poem's implicit metaphors and its similes:

> The birds are outsize. Pelicans crash
> into this peculiar gas unnecessarily hard,
> *it seems to me,* like pickaxes,
> rarely coming up with anything to show for it,
> and going off with humorous elbowings. (*PPL,* 46, my emphasis)

True to Bishop's review of Williams, the poem takes up a tradition of likenesses self-consciously: the tendency to interpret things as "like" other things is an activity the poem can now associate, in the figure of a dredging machine, with the mindless, ongoing "activity" of machinery; such traditions are a cultural habit more than an individual choice. If there is something "untidy," as in "disorderly," about the bight's "activity," there is something untimely about watching a harbor dredging in a cold-war military stronghold in 1948 and expecting either to be transported in the "old" Romantic or religious sense or (even) to achieve the objectivity of a Parnassian Williams poem. We are in the realm of allegory, then, not symbolism, for "The Bight" proposes that, even given this untimeliness, things can seem endlessly, if not indiscriminately, like other things (tails like wishbones like shark tails like plowshares, boats like torn-open, unanswered letters). By the end, the poem implies that it is our peculiar lot to go on performing (or being performed by) this "untidy activity."

The pervasive images and figure of trade in the poem may also warrant our reading it as reflecting on contemporary norms of the poetic trade, whose New Critical stock-in-trade was lyric speech as interpretable material (material to dredge). Composed sometime in the late winter or spring of 1948, "The Bight" was one of the first poems Bishop had written since the 1947 publication of her first collection. Bishop was quickly becoming an established poet, one who was reluctantly (and, in part, tutored by her famous new friend and correspondent, Robert Lowell) taking on the role of trade poet. Bishop had difficulty with most of what defined the poetry business in the late 1940s: she found the culture of public poetry readings by the author unbearable, avoiding them for most of her career; she did not want to teach (increasingly the norm); and she mostly suffered the few times she tried out residencies at writers' colonies.[80] These facts make the emphasis on "trade," in combination with the unprecedented willingness to attach her own authorial identity to the poem (with the epigraph, "On my Birthday"), read as a self-conscious admission that "Bishop the author" mediates this view and invites our viewing it as, at some level, "about" the poetry business and the attachment of a name to a style. The poem imagines how the low tide would look "if one were Baudelaire"; but "one" is not "one"—"one" is the literary figure Elizabeth Bishop.

This emphasis on the personal is all the more complicated given that the poem foregrounds the "voice" of the figured dredging machine (to which the poet implicitly and now famously compares the "untidy activity" of poetry making) as—quite specifically—a textual effect. The poem foregrounds the sound the dredge makes to be both spoken and not spoken:

> Click. Click. Goes the dredge,
> and brings up a dripping jawful of marl.
> All the untidy activity continues,
> awful but cheerful. (*PPL*, 47)

"Click. Click. Goes the dredge"; why punctuate it this way? By making it three sentences, as opposed to one, the line stumbles just short of achieving sonic realism: because of the choppy quality that choppy syntax produces, it is very difficult to read the line "naturally" in a vocal performance of the poem—difficult, that is, to read it as a voice or, to put it another way, easy to see textuality coming to the fore at the very moment the dredge is anthropomorphized as having a mouth ("jawful") and, by association, as speaking.

This emphasis on textuality at the moment we are supposed to hear a voice is not uncommon in Bishop's work; we could call it a signature gesture in her work beginning around this point in time, and one that sees her work in tension with the lyric-reading norms of the moment in which she was writing. Though in a 1975 letter of reply to a student's query about how to figure the subject in a poem, Bishop asserts that in poems "someone *is* talking, after all," her work can be read not to *exemplify* but rather as symptomatic of a broad turn to pedagogical methods meant to render that "someone" a dramatized "speaker"—a figured *person* in whom the poem's language could cohere as expressive "voice."[81] Bishop's poems more seem to problematize that broad turn, first in work of the 1940s and 1950s, when New Critical pedagogy was becoming the American pedagogical mainstream.[82] Bishop's ironizations, testings, and exaggerations of the assumption that "voice" inheres in a speaker give the lie to the New Critical nostalgia for (and here I borrow the "voice" of Jed Rasula's text) the "'power' and 'authority' of the voice . . . [to be] traced to a plausible speaker."[83]

The textuality of Bishop's talk destabilizes poems otherwise agile in figuring the sound of peripatetic talk. This is especially true in "The Bight," given the poem's evident concern about what variety of "activity" the post-Romantic and postmodern poet performs. But a similar foregrounding of the textual production of "voice" occurs in "Cape Breton" (started 1947, published 1949) when, "Out on the high 'bird islands,' Ciboux and

Hertford / . . . / . . . the few sheep pastured there go 'Baaa, baaa.' / (Some-times, frightened by aeroplanes, they stampede / and fall over into the sea or onto the rocks.)" (*PPL*, 48–49). The quoted sheep sound emphasizes the paradoxical conventionality required to sound "real"; we all know that the way to show what sheep "say" in English is to write "baaa" (whereas, in French, sheep "say" "bêê bêê"), so it feels pointed and bizarre to "spell it out" for us here. That the "voice" of nature is culturally relative jolts us out of what, in that poem, feels like the lull of the "inner voice" of Eliotic meditation (the poet talking to himself or to no one, as Eliot had said), as is true in several places in Bishop's work of this era, in which inhuman voices, authoritarian voices, and (or) the voice foregrounded as writing wake us from out of the comfortable lull produced by the figure of talk. Bishop's parentheses around the phrase beginning "Sometimes" does a similar thing: reminds us, with the dependence on punctuation to mark the aside, that we are not hearing but reading "talk."

A different kind of explosion of the illusion of language as personal expressive "voice" or talk appears in "Over 2,000 Illustrations and a Com-plete Concordance," begun in 1945, published in 1948. At the poem's otherwise quite moving end comes the weirdly citational phrase "Open the book" (not placed in quotation marks but feeling as if it should have been), which reminds us of the fact that we have thought we had been listening to the poet's voice. The lines in several ways foreground written-ness and, again, are difficult to voice:

> Everything only connected by "and" and "and."
> Open the book. (The gilt rubs off the edges
> of the pages and pollinates the fingertips.)
> Open the heavy book. (*PPL*, 46)

Parentheses and strange vatic speech, the quoted *ands* in " 'and' and 'and,' " make a surplus of material to interpret; such strategies point the way to-ward John Ashbery's later practice, aspects of Frank O'Hara's and of James Tate's (and Dean Young's and Tony Hoagland's, as well). The "gilt" of the old "concordance"—is it like the "guilt" of old correspondences (or the belief that such correspondences "all resolve themselves" if dwelt on?): what will this pollinate? Our answer is only to "open the heavy book." The poem's irony (throughout) renders it almost unreadable: who is this speaker? Not clearly a character, not clearly the author, this "voice" (however subtly) has rendered itself neither light and casual nor "serious and engravable": as

the poem opens, who reads the pictures in the book as "foreign," for
instance—what are we to make of it?

> Thus should have been our travels:
> serious, engravable.
> The Seven Wonders of the World are tired
> and a touch familiar, but the other scenes,
> innumerable, though equally sad and still,
> are foreign. Often the squatting Arab,
> or group of Arabs, plotting, probably,
> against our Christian Empire,
> while one apart, with outstretched arm and hand
> points to the Tomb, the Pit, the Sepulcher. (*PPL*, 44)

Even read carefully, the lines are difficult to interpret as voice—to dramatize as "the reaction of a person to a situation, a scene, or an idea," remembering Brooks-Warren, because of the complex way in which discursive,
social knowledge informs and complicates the private scene of reading in
the poem. The chief difficulty is in the word "probably," which may "belong" to the ostensible speaker's personal response to the pictures before
her (she may be racist) and, at the same time, register an impersonal awareness of how often such scenes would depict Arabs as plotters. The word
could also register an older reception of the images—the "probably" could
belong sincerely to the nineteenth-century worldview in which the illustrations were made. This is related to but not exactly the same as the possibility that the poem has slipped into the credulous perspective of a child
once instructed by its problematic images.

   In any case, if the scenes are "foreign" (that is, the opposite of the more
"familiar" wonders), they should not seem so familiarly "Arab" and easy
to stereotype. That each general item that the "one [Arab] apart" may be
pointing to is capitalized ("the Tomb, the Pit, the Sepulcher") reiterates
the discourse-making power of asserting the importance of the site by
situating it in terms of the Arab and his supposed plot. Both the Arab and
the site are generic types in a binary system (us versus them) that the poem
seems—especially in its general address—to invoke ironically. Indeed, the
fact of the list suggests ever so slightly the language of a multiple-choice
test given in school, just as sections of Bishop's epigraph to her last book,
quoted from James Monteith's 1884 "First Lessons in Geography," do: "In
what direction is the Volcano? The Cape? The Bay? The Lake? The Strait?"

(*PPL*, 148). Subtle uses of cliché (the "faithful horse," for instance) and hyperbolic adjectives further bring discourse to the fore, suggesting that the poem's knowledge derives from a source less personal than the speaker or her supposed "voice" or individual feeling. In whose perspective or person do "foreign," "familiar," and "probably" originate? The lines show Bishop's understanding of the power of discourse, a power that greatly complicates and exceeds our pedagogic paradigms for "tone" and "speaker." Indeed, the attitude of "Over 2000 Illustrations" toward the biblical images to which (at one level) "our travels" have been contrasted and found wanting cannot quite be voiced. Bishop's poem thwarts and invites our identification with its "talk," just as the subject only shakily created there seems to be drawn to identify with the pictures before her.

Rather than read the lines lyrically, then, we might think of them as, in Peter Middleton's words, "incorporating distance." For Middleton, "distance [in a text] is also a sign of a text's intersubjective embeddedness in mutually negotiated histories of cultural and social exchange."[84] And indeed the poem points to mutually negotiated forms of exchange by dislocating the intelligence about "the book" for its supposed reader. In later lines, and in a manner a bit easier to read than the dreamy, gorgeous nonsense describing the "grim lunette" of the book in the first half, the poem turns to a more "personal" memory of a travel in the Holy Land. Nevertheless, it complexly returns us, in showing the contingency of the speaker's supposed existential crisis while traveling, to the figure of the plotting Arab. "I" drifts into lyric angst upon seeing an empty grave somewhere near Marrakech:

> It was somewhere near there
> I saw what frightened me most of all:
> A holy grave, not looking particularly holy,
> one of a group under a keyhole-arched stone baldaquin
> open to every wind from the pink desert.
> An open, gritty, marble trough, carved solid
> with exhortation, yellowed
> as scattered cattle-teeth;
> half-filled with dust, not even the dust
> of the poor prophet paynim who once lay there. (*PPL*, 45–46)

The next line swiftly undercuts the speaker's lyric swoon: "In a smart burnoose Khadour looked on amused" (46). Observed by the (ostensibly) local guide to whose country tourists go in order to feel a sense of the sublime (indeed whose poems about the moment draw on Percy Bysshe Shelley's "Ozymandias" and a whole discourse of feeling about the sublime), the lyrical expression of it suddenly looks not natural and full of feeling but conventional and even amusing: Khadour has seen this moment of existential dread and sublimity played out, almost as the Western traveler's duty, before. In this (along with a "fat, old guide" at Volubulis who "made eyes," a sexual plot), he reprises the Arab figure of the opening lines with a difference—glibly servicing post-Romantic poetic transport for a fee. The poem asserts a superfluity of possible connections between its three plotting figures and the subjectivity that connects them, further resisting our reduction of its "knowledge" to the merely personal or expressive. I am not alone in feeling this: John Ashbery has identified Bishop's poem as his inspiration for the writing of "Soonest Mended," another poem whose use of cliché and the figure of intimate talk complicates and critiques the expressive and Confessional expectations they elicit.[85]

Indeed, many of Bishop's departures from the contemporary poetics of "speaker" and "drama" were politically inflected, animated by her great distaste for the cultural scene that had conditioned that poetic's success in the 1950s and after. This distaste aligns with her move to Brazil in 1951 and the critical distance it afforded her on life and culture in the United States; Bishop found herself consistently disgusted by the excessive wealth that defined the quality and tone of American life and, in an ongoing, regular correspondence with Robert Lowell over the 1950s and 1960s, often expresses intense queasiness over the excess and reach of high capitalism and the new predominance of marketing pervading the look and feel of everything.

Her critique, importantly, goes beyond a rejection of mass culture or "new money" alone. Those who would shame Bishop as a member of the "School of Quietude" might be surprised to know that, reading American literary journals, she tracks a mainstream cultural torpor that she implicitly relates to the bloating of the American pocketbook. She complains about there being "too much of everything," occasioned by her response to reading contemporary poetry in literary journals mailed from the United States: "I get so depressed with every number of POETRY, *The New Yorker* etc. (this one I am swearing off of, except for prose, forever, I hope) so much adequate poetry all sounding just alike and *so* boring."[86]

Indeed, in a March 5, 1963, letter, Bishop flags a "great American slickness"—a new cultural tone—so pervasive that outright "filth" was one of few ways to counteract it (*WIA*, 448). She found no refuge in the mainstream poetic scene and the roles it assigned poets. On June 25, 1961, not long after he had reported taking a teaching job at Harvard, she complained to Lowell that the role of "teacher-poet" produced intellectual and artistic staleness and sterility, singling out Richard Wilbur and W. S. Merwin for an overproduction of "proficient" but "glazed poems" (*WIA*, 365), and in a 1958 blurb written for May Swenson's *Cage of Spines*, charged academic poetry of the time with "formulated despair and / or careful stylishness" (*WIA*, 267). She had disparaged Wilbur's work in a May 5, 1959, letter to Lowell for "getting more and more 'nice,' careful, dry, and 'lovely'—dry isn't the word, but that kind of clever thinking-out process that leaves me cold" (*WIA*, 302). Writing on June 17, 1963, she accused Wilbur's critical work of being "class-room-ish," indicating her awareness of a New Critical lyric-reading culture's investment in "explanations, explanations" and its effects on poetic production (*WIA*, 465).[87]

Without stating it explicitly, Bishop's late 1950s and 1960s letters to Lowell suggest that she perceived no area of culture immune to an "American slickness" manifested in an unprecedented emphasis on the expressive poet-persona and a dominance of style. She found that the situation had evacuated possible avenues for poetry as a form of political revolt, once believed possible for modernists. This fact seems important to register here, given Bishop's reputation for apoliticism, "quietude," and a poetics of "voice." Taking issue with Lowell for indulging a sense of complacency about the revolutionary possibilities of early modernism in a *Paris Review* interview in 1961, she writes on the morning of June 25, 1961, "What you [Lowell] say about Marianne [Moore] is fine: 'terrible, private, and strange revolutionary poetry. There isn't the motive to do that now'" (*WIA*, 364).[88] While it may be "fine," Bishop makes a point to redress what she takes as Lowell's sense of defeat and nostalgia, in the process revealing her dismay over the totalizing effects of high capitalism: "But I wonder—isn't there [the motive]? Isn't there even more—only it's terribly hard to find the exact and right and surprising enough, or un-surprising enough, point at which to revolt now? The Beats have just fallen back on an old corpse-strewn or monument-strewn battle-field—the real protest I suspect is something quite different. (If only I could find it. Klee's picture called FEAR seems close to it, I think . . .)" (ibid., 364).[89]

In a letter from the year before, dated July 27, 1960, Bishop described the moment as an economic and literary "late" and "decadent stage" (evoking Marxist theory), and here she similarly articulates a cultural situation in which, contrary to Lowell's claims, the need to stage a poetic revolt against dominant cultural modes is just as strong as (or even stronger than) it was for early modernist predecessors, even as (indeed perhaps *because*) a viable mode of protest was out of imaginative reach (*WIA*, 335).[90] In effect, Bishop identifies a shift in the situation of language to effect, or even to aspire to, cultural change, hinting here that language and "the private" no longer function as effective grounds for the "strange" to disrupt norms of visibility—the difficulty of finding "a surprising enough, *or un-surprising enough*" form of revolt. Today, the conundrum Bishop describes might be called postmodernity, a situation in which most forms of discourse—even the extreme, private, or "raw"—feel (paradoxically) already commodified, either quickly co-opted by the cultural mainstream or always already articulated in its terms.

Bishop's response to this situation was to aim to make interpretive space in her work, a goal she associated with "modesty." On October 30, 1958, several months after writing to Lowell about modesty, Bishop congratulates Lowell's *Life Studies* for its "strangely modest tone," which, she admits, she finds surprising, "because [the poems] are all about yourself and yet do not sound conceited!" (*WIA*, 273). She recasts this paradox two years later (in a letter from May 19, 1960), when she praises Lowell's work (especially in comparison to his "better imitators," W. D. Snodgrass and Anne Sexton) for its "egocentricity," which, in his work, is "the reverse of *sub*limated" (*WIA*, 327). In light of the "modest tone" and unconceited "sound" that she earlier praised, "the reverse of sublimity" suggests the refusal to refine material to sound socially acceptable or "likeable," just what Bishop felt indicated the worst weakness of women's writing.[91] For Bishop, that is, Lowell's work is "modest," and "modest" work an appropriately unsurprising "revolt," for the apparent willingness *not* to encourage such identification and to forgo control over readers' intellectual, emotional, or readerly responses to one's work. Sublimated work, by contrast, employs "darling" gestures or efforts to be "nice" or "lovely" (as Bishop accused Sexton, Snodgrass, and Merwin of doing) in the interest of conveying personality—gestures akin to the language of advertising and its abhorrent, slick "self-consciousness," a context wherein modesty and "space" might seem, by contrast, revolutionary.

Allowing such space enables Bishop in much of her midcentury work a marked refusal of tonal specificity and thus the space to explore the discursive, public language that shapes so-called private experience and "voice" in the first place. Indeed, the "drive toward meaningful statement" that Perloff accused Bishop (and Wilbur) of, a charge that implies an effort to unify meaning in a coherent speaker, is just what Bishop greatly disliked about much midcentury work—thus my emphasis in reading "Over 2,000 Illustrations and a Complete Concordance" on the poem's undoing of its expressive logic *at just the moment* that a correspondence making (of the kind Bishop had learned to suspect in reading Williams) occurs.[92]

A similar kind of undoing occurs in many of Bishop's late-midcentury poems: In "Filling Station," for instance, after opening lines that offer a mimetic description of the "over-all" oiliness of the eponymous station, the poem alerts us to "Be careful with that match!" exaggerating the mimetic "likeness" of description with real place. As with the line's exclamation point, the poem has exaggerated voice ("Oh, but it is dirty!" for instance), and thus the line also warns us against a too-easy identification of the "I" with Bishop herself or of the reduction of the poem's figuration of speech with one psychologically distinct person (*PPL,* 123). For while the figure of voice in the opening stanza tempts us to believe that a drama of confrontation and dismissal unfolds before us—"Oh, but it is dirty!"—the line "Be careful with that match!" addresses us as suddenly also at risk of something incendiary and hysterical in immersing ourselves in this perspective, which is subtly racialized and uneasily classed (by "monkey suit," among other things). As Mutlu Konuk Blasing has argued, such lines give us "room" to be wary of the poem's own strategies, urging us to a skepticism not belonging to its speaker.[93] The poem's "I" has launched a judgmental "overall" account of the filling station and turns to a dehumanizing description of the filling station's owner and his sons:

Father wears a dirty,
oil-soaked monkey suit
that cuts him under the arms,
and several quick and saucy
and greasy sons assist him
(it's a family filling station),
all quite thoroughly dirty. (*PPL,* 123)

Lineation emphasizes "dirty" and "monkey suit" and also, more powerfully, delays passage from "saucy" to "greasy" (emphasized by rhyme), highlighting, it might seem, this speaker's association of the men with what they might have eaten or even figuring them as food-like. One could argue that in this way of making a speaker's personality unfold, however, the emphasis on line (as opposed to sentence) finally denatures voice. The poem ends up emphasizing the available discourses on which the describer draws. The parenthetical "it's a family filling station," like advertising sloganry, is undercut by that cutting "monkey suit," a term that is part of a discursive net conditioning Bishop's response to the scene. Though it is a dead metaphor, it is a "match" (between low-class labor and animality) that makes this representation problematic and incendiary (be careful with it!). What the poem does, in effect, is to "foreground[] the abstract features of the speech act rather than the authenticity of its expressive moment," as Michael Davidson describes the politics of Language technique, thus acknowledging "the contingency of utterances in social interchange."[94]

Language becomes further abstracted for the speaker (and foregrounded) as the poem drifts along the currents of anaphora across several lines, finally stumbling into the Christian slogan "Somebody loves us all": "Somebody embroidered the doily . . . / Somebody waters the plant . . . / . . . // . . . / Somebody loves us all (*PPL*,124). One of the key, repeated slogans of evangelical Christianity, this is just the sort of phrase that Bishop might dwell on in notebooks or letters, and critics have struggled to read this line.[95] Some are confident that it is spoken as part of a dramatic monologue—a sign of the speaker's disdain for the Christian idea that even the "saucy / and greasy sons" are loved by Christ (or that we all have to be loved by someone). Others locate its meaning in the speaker's psychodrama, on her coming around to a more sympathetic understanding of the filling-station owners' worth.[96] However, in league with avant-garde principles such as Davidson's, it can be read as an irresolvable remainder in the poem—one that highlights the power of language to lead subjects down chains of thought and action as if against their will, in the way an advertisement will affect one unconsciously for years afterward. What constitutes genuine experience if the language with which one experiences or describes it is inherited and often already commodified for us?

That this is one of the political questions the poem asks may be confirmed by its taking pains to confuse what is inside the frame of the poem and what is outside it. Are we the ones who are making these connections? Who has arranged things this way? Are we the ones holding the "match" that could set this encounter between white and "black," between classes, aflame? Or have we misread "monkey-suit" to mean a mechanic's coverall, when it could also mean a formal dress suit?[97] Of course, Costello would rightly correct my effort to make such a moment a willed achievement of Bishop the person (rather than a residue in language) by arguing that such is a moment when "the lyric . . . draw[s] on the 'collective substratum' [quoting Adorno] in language where 'society's inner contradictory relationships' reside."[98] And yet my ashamed desire to locate an awareness of poetry as a discursive theater within Bishop, so that she and I might identify and rescue each other from lyric shame, is one example of a process of identification that much of her late poetry was "about."

For metadiscursive and metaexpressive moments abound in Bishop's late work, foregrounding the figure of talk as neither entirely personal, nor natural, very often in poems that stage dramas of embarrassing likeness making. In "Poem" (1972), a speaker consults a tiny painting and, after noticing a near comic "likeness" between life and art, bursts (as if on cue) into a moment of recognition whose textual exuberance is overdetermined:

A specklike bird is flying to the left.
Or is it a flyspeck looking like a bird?

Heavens, I recognize the place, I know it!
It's behind—I can almost remember the farmer's name.
His barn backed on that meadow. There it is,
titanium white, one dab. The hint of steeple,
filaments of brush-hairs, barely there,
must be the Presbyterian church.
Would that be Miss Gillespie's house?
Those particular geese and cows
are naturally before my time. (*PPL,* 165, ll. 26–33)

The title of "Poem" asserts the fall into likeness making and self-projection—as in the speaker's launch to assume correspondence between the generic scene and what she already knows—to be generic, what happens in poems. The poem depends heavily on figures of voice and dramatic setting in order to foreground its unwieldy subjective power: we need the illusion of voice to see this projection of personal memory and a history take place.

The speaking subject supposes a great deal—that the painting is a "sketch for a larger one," for instance—and deduces from the quality of clouds in the painting that "they were the artist's specialty." She decides what kind of day it is in the painting ("the air is fresh and cold") and asserts that "it must be Nova Scotia; only there / does one see gabled wooden houses / painted that awful shade of brown" (165, ll. 10–12). The "must be" of lines 10 and 33 stand out as too insistent, foregrounding the speaker's projective eagerness.

Thus, while the poem creates the feeling that we are listening to someone talk here, the exaggeration of talk in the speaker's moments of identification with the work of art—that odd "Heavens!" for instance—foregrounds voice as one device on which such forms of identification depend. "There it is" does, at one level, create the illusion of a speaker addressing the reader in a comforting and familiar way (remembering Armantrout's dismissal of Ostriker's praise for Bishop's voice). However, its overinsistence on deixis also reminds us that we are *not* there (just as the speaker is not in the life of the picture described, despite her insistence that she is). In a manner having nothing to do with voice or the speaker's implied personality or the poet's person, the moment alerts readers to their own susceptibility to identify this "voice" with an actual person here with them now. Bishop's amplification of "voice"—"Heavens, I recognize the place, I know it!"—thus functions as a metaexpressive moment, even antiexpressive.[99] It is not unlike moments in Ashbery that induce the vertiginous sense that we are both inside and outside the world of the poem (just as here, our subject is both inside and outside the painting).[100] For me, this sense of vertigo more or less explodes the poem's seeming claim that a lyric subject's isolated personal experience is what we are experiencing.

Such moments in Bishop are late flowers of her early engagement with Williams's antisubjective realism in the late 1930s and 1940s and read as her answer to the question she poses to Lowell in 1961: how to find a mode of poetic revolt at a moment when poems no longer had power to effect change, either through modernist experimental technique (the "terrible, private revolution" of a poet such as Moore), or through a once-revolutionary turn to personal expression that now seemed wholly in keeping with the glib high-capitalist tone against which one wanted to rebel—how, under the conditions of postmodernity, to revive the language. These questions are not only in the main consistent with the antisubjective concerns Bishop had entertained in thinking about Williams so long ago, but they are also not far from concerns of Language poets in the 1970s and 1980s.

Indeed, it becomes possible to imagine the depth of Bishop's interest in nonexpressive speech and to regard her 1965 collection *Questions of Travel* and its foregrounding of voice and discourse as exactly *not* in keeping with an "expressive paradigm of the 60s" to which Perloff and others dismissively assign her work. Written in the period when Bishop was searching for a mode of "revolt," *Questions of Travel* echoes her discontent with the tone and excesses of American life, but Bishop's politics reside elsewhere than in what the collection explicitly says or even thematizes. Bishop explores how discursive understandings shape personal expression, how the personal is imbricated in a larger cultural logic that both implicates and forms it.

That critics have tended to read these poems as unironically expressive lyrics is not terribly surprising: most of them draw on the figure of voice, lending themselves to lyric-reading norms, even drawing on them, tempting us to imagine them as lyric monologues expressive of a speaking subject-poet's point of view. Bishop's autobiographical prose piece "In the Village" lies at the center of her first edition of the collection (much as Lowell's prose memoir "91 Revere Street" lies in the interior of his 1957 *Life Studies,* so influential at the time, especially to Bishop). And yet the poems also take pains to highlight voice as a technique.

In the opening poem, "Arrival at Santos" (1965), which dramatizes a tourist's experience of approach, by boat, to a foreign country, Bishop opens interpretive space for readers in part by disturbing our ability to identify with the poem's ostensible speaking subject. It invites and yet frustrates our reading it as a script for the "voice" of the tourist, in spite of its colloquial diction and fictional detail (detail we even can locate in Bishop's "real" life). Odd shifts in both discursive modes and subject positions distance rather than create an impression of closeness between author and speaker, or speaker and reader.

As with Bishop's most interesting poems in this vein, this distance is achieved in the tension between the figure of voice, on the one hand, and the poem's emphasis on convention and artifice, on the other. The opening four-beat line, evocative of nursery rhyme—"Here is a coast; here is a harbor"—foregrounds conventional, impersonal language rather than the prosy speech style that was then the sign of "voice," especially for admirers

of such free-verse experiments as Lowell's *Life Studies*. And when the
poem gestures overemphatically to being a "natural," real-time, spoken
account of "arrival" (insisting that this or that is happening "now," for
instance), the effort is undermined by an almost comic insistence on
maintaining its conventional rhyme scheme (abxb or abab); syntax spills
over line lengths in a remarkably awkward effort to keep to the scheme,
most baldly in Bishop's choice to move a final "s" in the place name "Glens
Falls" to the beginning of a new line and stanza to force an exact rhyme
between "Fall" and "tall" (*PPL,* 71):

> skirt! There! Miss Breen is about seventy,
> a retired police lieutenant, six feet tall,
> with beautiful bright blue eyes and a kind expression.
> Her home, when she is at home, is in Glens Fall
>
> s, New York. There. We are settled. (71–72)

The "realness" of almost comically emphatic deictic gestures and punctuated "feeling" in such lines as "Please, boy, do be more careful with that
boat hook! / Watch out! Oh! It has caught Miss Breen's / skirt! There!" are
undercut by steep enjambments that maintain rhyme: we cannot forget
that the poem is a construct and are reminded of convention at just the
moments when we are credulous that we are hearing a present-tense "experience" (71).

The odd interruption of "who knows?" in the middle of line 3 (and
"Oh, tourist" in line 7) is one of several instances of discourse shift—the
introduction of an awkward second "voice" not quite the voice of self-
address—that both elicits and undermines our taking voice as person,
establishing a colloquial tone whose very intimacy suddenly seems strange:

> Here is a coast; here is a harbor.
> here, after a meager diet of horizon, is some scenery:
> impractically shaped and—who knows?—self-pitying
>   mountains (71)

The fact that it is only in the fourth quatrain that a first-person pronoun
emerges similarly goads us into testing the assumption that we know who
or what, if not "I," had been "speaking" all along (71). The effect overall is a
deconstruction of "voice" that makes it very difficult to decide, in performing the poem, how to "speak" it: form recommends one set of possibilities;

discourse shifts another—rendering the realization of a "fixed tone" an impossible interpretive goal. Or, in Bishop's words, we lack either a strong rhetorical stance or a "clever thinking-out process" that would interpret the scene's drama, feeling, or tone for us, as the pedagogy of Brooks and Warren (realized by the "teacher-poets" whom Bishop disliked) then dictated. We are left with significant interpretive space with which to weigh the value and politics (this tourist is immodest and self-important) of the "interior" that is (ironically) offered—"we are driving to the interior"—as a symbol of authentic experience at the end of the poem (*PPL*, 72).

In the context of Bishop's views on the cultural situation informing the most prevalent poetic tendencies of her day, the poem's leaving of such space is an aesthetic-political gesture, a sharp contrast not to the revelation of intimate or shocking personal material (other forms of immodesty) but to the authority that such gestures granted author-speakers over potential meanings and the ground of pathos in their poems.[101] Bishop's critique was that to write with that kind of investment in the authority of voice was to grant aesthetic primacy to expressive personality and the illusion of spontaneity, tropes of authenticity that she seems to have taken as forms of false consciousness. In a letter from July 27, 1960, following up on her claim that Sexton was guilty of wanting poems to attest chiefly to their author's personality, Bishop subtly suggests that she takes this egocentricity as sign of a "self-conscious" quality typical in the contemporary arts, and one that served, rather than contested, the American cultural trend toward excess (*WIA*, 333, 359). In a July 12, 1960, letter to which she was responding, Lowell, in the process of qualifying his agreements with her earlier critique of Sexton's work, had dismissed meter, aligning himself with the supposed authenticity of free verse's expressive possibilities: "Meter is a puzzle to me now. . . . Something quite pleasant both to write and to read is added by meter, but it's something free verse doesn't want at all, and which seems to have little to do with experience or intuition" (*WIA*, 331). Bishop counters in her July 27, 1960, reply, "What you say about meter:. . . I have a theory that all the arts are growing more and more 'literary'; that it is a late stage, perhaps a decadent stage, and that un-metrical verse is more 'literary' and necessarily self-conscious than metrical" (*WIA*, 335).

Animating the exchange is a muted but significant disagreement about the midcentury promotion of "experience" and intuitive, personal voice as

art's best sources and payoffs. Lowell's comment makes binary opposites
of experience and convention (attributed to meter); he understands an art
of experience as expressive and thus, he implies, "free." Bishop's July 27
reply suggests that this oversimplifies a complex relationship between
subjectivity and its possible forms: notice that, in her reply, she refers to
it as "un-metrical," not "free," verse, emphasizing the conventionality of
all writing. Furthermore, she quietly corrals Lowell's "intuition and experience" with decadence and the " 'literary,' " the latter a word she elsewhere uses ironically, sometimes even associating it with provincialism
and the narrowness of coterie (in contrast with matters of broader social
import).[102]

Bishop's paradoxical sense that revolt lies in emphasizing, rather than
turning away from, convention and discourse shows even at the broadest
structural level of *Questions of Travel,* which is divided into two sections,
"Brazil" (a set of poems about Brazil and travel) and "Elsewhere" (more
autobiographical-seeming poems). Despite the opening poem's promise
that we will leave behind the conventional, if necessary, exterior world
and go "driving to [an] interior" (suggestive of the personal, emotional, and
geographic), the collection's design firmly deemphasizes personality and
interiority, reminding us instead of the superficial, social qualities of all
written material (particularly convention-bound forms). If "Arrival at
Santos" is our personal "port" to the rest of the "Brazil" section, then the
physical "interior" toward which the section drives (its innermost part) is,
at least in most editions, "The Burglar of Babylon," a ballad—significantly
one of the most conventional and least "personal" poetic forms used in the
collection and available at the time (*PPL,* 90–96). Though "In the Village"
(an autobiographical prose memoir) lies at the center of the first edition,
the story ends, we should note, by dismissing the idiosyncratic historical
detail and personal suffering that inform it—"clothes, crumbling postcards, broken china; things damaged and lost"—in favor of an image of
"the elements speaking: earth, air, fire, water" (*PPL,* 118). And though the
structure of the "Elsewhere" section moves us from the foreign to the domestic though autobiographical scenes of childhood, the final poem of
that section (and the collection) is "Visits to St. Elizabeth's," a markedly
impersonal poem only vaguely "about" Bishop's visits to Ezra Pound at
St. Elizabeth's Hospital. That it imitates the nursery rhyme "This is the
house Jack built," a form that cycles through a welter of perspectives (the
sailor, the Jew, and so on), downplays the personal (*PPL,* 127–129).

In the content of the "Elsewhere" poems, too, Bishop counters Lowell's explicit privileging of individual experience in *Life Studies,* along with his implicit privileging of an "intuiti[ve]" stylistics of voice. Several of her "Elsewhere" poems emphasize and make strange the potent, ineluctable, everyday discursive language defining our experience of experience, exploring the dialectical relationships of inner feelings and outer "conventions," discursive practice and individual experience, or, to try it another way, (personal) experience and the (social) language that describes it. This is a central concern of "Manners," which immediately follows "In the Village" in the collection (the interior, one would assume, to which we arrive). The poem presents two characters, a grandfather hoping to share his conventional wisdom about the importance of manners and a child (historicized as a "child of 1918" in the poem's epigraph) being educated to his worldview. The child dutifully repeats what the grandfather advises, a point the poem rather woodenly emphasizes for us. Here are the first four stanzas:

> My grandfather said to me
> as we sat on the wagon seat,
> "Be sure to remember to always
> speak to everyone you meet."
>
> We met a stranger on foot.
> My grandfather's whip tapped his hat.
> "Good day, sir. Good day. A fine day."
> And I said it and bowed where I sat.
>
> Then we overtook a boy we knew
> with a big pet crow on his shoulder.
> "Always offer everyone a ride;
> don't forget that when you get older,"
>
> my grandfather said. So Willy
> climbed up with us, but the crow
> gave a "Caw!" and flew off. I was worried.
> How would he know where to go? (*PPL,* 119)

The poem only very subtly shows the comic absurdity of the grandfather's supposed manners: he does not offer the "stranger" a ride, only the "boy we knew" (emphasized by the line's stress on the end word "knew"), though he also insists that the child "Always offer everyone a ride," manners he *has* forgotten, it seems, since getting "older" (119). Thus, the poem is less a "nostalgic eulogy for a passing life," as Margaret Dickie has held it to be, than a complex, ironic look at the tension between the social worldview inherited by Bishop's generation (children of 1918) and that view's lingering appeal, limitation, and increasing obsolescence in the mid-twentieth century.[103]

It is important that it is by adhering to convention, rather than by abandoning it, that Bishop's poem conveys irony and ambivalence that cannot be said to be produced by "voice" at all and thus should not quite be read as tone. The poem's pounding, mostly three-beat line often creates a tension for the reader over what to stress, as with the line, "And I said it and bowed where I sat" (*PPL*, 119). Does "I" or "said" get stress here? If we wished to emphasize the child's dutiful repetition, we would stress "I," but the accentual beat of earlier lines conditions us to stress "said." Stressing "said" rather emphasizes discourse or, to put it in Stuart Hall's terms, the force of convention to make us speak a certain way. This prosodic ambiguity is reasserted by the difficulty of knowing exactly what the child *has* repeated of the three different things grandfather says, in the second stanza, to the stranger. If the line is clumsy, it aids the poem in underscoring the only-ever-mixed value of such lessons. This happens, too, at the poem's close, with a gesture to the historical conditions (chiefly the automobile age) that render the lesson comically obsolete:

When the automobiles went by,
the dust hid the people's faces,
but we shouted "Good day! Good day!
Fine day!" at the top of our voices. (119)

Just as the grandfather is laughably emphatic about the importance of good manners when, in the fourth stanza, he anthropomorphizes Willy's crow, in this stanza, the grandfather and children overinsist on a code of manners despite the fact that the gesture of mutual respect that such behavior is meant to perform is surely lost on the passing motorists. Given Bishop's overwhelmingly negative attitude toward automobile culture at the time she was writing (something she often expressed to Lowell in the period), such moments allow her to explore—yet not through the expression of indignation—the complexity of her dismay over the current pace and tone of contemporary culture. That Bishop's poem cannot be taken as only nostalgic, *not* naively celebratory of "a social code that does not change," as Dickie claims,[104] shows it to be deeply in tune with Bishop's concern to open interpretive space as a form of "revolt," a concern that counters the lyricizing, and shaming, readings that her work has been asked to stand for.

In the "space" between the poem's adherence to convention (thematically and prosodically) and its skepticism about it (in exposing the grandfather's hypocritical manners), that is, we gain purchase on the process by which discourse asserts itself. For instance, in the last stanza, the poem seems to know that the children get out of the wagon because the grandfather has told them to, not quite for the sake of "good manners" alone; it quietly emphasizes the grandfather's power to command:

> When we came to Hustler Hill,
> he said that the mare was tired,
> so we all got down and walked,
> as our good manners required. (*PPL*, 122)

The fact of the children's willingness to repeat the lesson (without questioning its illogic) suggests that what conditions their worldview is enabled discursively, which is emphasized in the poem's many foregroundings of what gets "said." This sheds ironic light on both the poem's air of respect and also its adherence to metrical forms. As a result, what gets emphasized is *not* a set of feelings that belong to a speaker or, implicitly, to a poet. Rather, the poem draws our attention to the scene of discursive education. While Bishop no doubt found "manners" useful, she was also savvy to the way such phrases as "good manners" might get invoked to advance any number of (less homey) agendas.

Such scenes of discursive education feature in other poems in the collection: "Sestina," with its vatic line "It's time for tea now," and the nursery rhyme structuring the portrait of Pound's hospitalization in "Visits." In "First Death in Nova Scotia," which, at one level, seems to be an autobiographical narration of a child's first experience of death (of a young cousin), technical choices emphasizing discourse trouble an expressive reading of it, resulting in myriad moments that resist univocal interpretation. In setting and diction, it tempts us to take many of its descriptive lines as very nearly spoken in the voice of a child who has attempted, while looking at the body of his or her dead cousin, to embody or mobilize the culture's euphemisms for death in order to "make sense" of the body. Tense of course complicates the claim to expressive voice—this is a child's first-person experience narrated from a later vantage point. But it is the intrusion of national culture that most complicates the reading:

> Arthur was very small.
> He was all white, like a doll
> that hadn't been painted yet.
> Jack Frost had started to paint him
> the way he always painted
> the Maple Leaf (Forever). (*PPL,* 121–122)

As with Bishop's 1930s poems written in response to Williams, this scene of likeness making emphasizes discourse as it informs the attempt to figure death, especially for the very young. The parenthetical addition of "Forever" subtly but powerfully complicates our ability to "hear" a speaker's voice here. Who speaks or spoke the "forever" parenthetically added to what has so far seemed the child's imaginative description? Even if we try to take it as occurring within the real-time or dramatized unfolding of the child-adult poet's thoughts, why has Bishop bothered to show us an automatic mental association occurring in this context (Jack Frost's "always" frosting somehow makes what should be "maple leaf" "Maple Leaf," and thus we arrive at the old Canadian national anthem that one always sings)?

That the word that comes to mind is "forever"—evocative of heaven—of course fits a poem about witnessing a first "death," yet the figure of nationality that it introduces (echoed by the images of British royalty on the family's walls) suggests more at stake in these lines than a picture of personal psychology. The poem subtly suggests that the fantastic and symbolic images to which the child resorts are to be read not only as imaginative deflections of the difficulty of the first death but also as indices of how children inherit culture, including sentimental and nationalist discourses. For instance, in light of the drift into the old nationalist slogan, the claim that the deceased cousin was "all white, like a doll / that hadn't been painted yet" moves us quickly from the details that an anxious parent might ask the child to learn in order to manage the hard facts of death and burial, to the picture of nation's power to produce loyal subjects. This is how one is disciplined to one's symbolic cultural norms. Confronted not only with pictures of ancestors, celebrities, or, as in this case, one's ruling royal class but also with narratives that justify their presence, a child takes them as truth: from the child's perspective, the story that "the gracious royal couples" have invited one's dead cousin to be "the smallest page at court" is no less or more bizarre than the representation of the couples on the wall in the first place (122).

The poem hints at the gap between the child's psyche and the impersonal language that gives it shape in the closing lines, the tone of which is almost impossible to decide: "But how could Arthur go, / clutching his tiny lily, / with his eyes shut up so tight / and the roads deep in snow?" (122). Who speaks these lines? In some sense, the child does, though the words index the rebellious subject who (later) questions the fairy tale she has been offered in order to talk about death. The lines' sentimentalism is "over the top" if we expect them to fit with that adult perspective, and thus they are quite awkward to read aloud; for to try to embody them in one subjectivity oversimplifies their function in the poem. It seems that my only recourse in a vocal reading is to flatten them, so they will mark only the pattern of three stresses per line—I feel I must literally discipline the personal out—emphasizing the conventions of rhythm. In this sense, the lines thwart the identification of their rhetoric with a person (it is neither a rhetorical nor a literal question) and thus undermine the expressive gestures that Bishop has made (here and elsewhere) to "voice."

Finally, it is in the destabilization of the poem as a common ground of sympathetic identification (that is, ground that, if stable, would enable a reader's identification of text with speaker and reader with that speaking voice) that leaves us interpretive space to recognize discourse. This, I wish to identify (with) as Bishop's "revolt"—her unwillingness to arrange our understanding of the poem's implications, her attempt to show the personal and autobiographical as never not touched by social forces, including the worst of consumer capitalism. We not only cannot identify with speakers, but neither can we comprehend them as personae (characters) either. Bishop's poems treat familiar language as an object of social analysis, rather than striving to make it a conduit of voice or expression of personality.

That I believe this treatment of language brings Bishop's poems into the same universe (somewhat surprisingly, given their use of the figure of voice) with experiments from such quarters as the Language writers of the 1970s and 1980s must be a sign that the shaming of the expressive has affected me and, arguably, a body of other readers. Indeed, to see this affinity is not the only payoff here. To recast Bishop's "expressive" poetic as discursive experiment allows us to put her work in conversation with a variety of rhymed, conventional poetry of the twentieth century in the United States that nevertheless cannot be grouped with the "classroomish" examples that Bishop disliked. Just to glimpse at the possibilities, we might consider poems of two African American writers who explored the experience of being interpellated into discourses of race and who turned to rhymed, metered forms to do so. Countee Cullen's use of common meter in "Incident" (1925) makes a rich example. On a literal level, Cullen's poem is a retrospective narrative of an African American boy who, at eight years old, was called a racial slur on a Baltimore train by a white, eight-year-old boy. The poem's common meter renders it disturbingly like a nursery rhyme, marking the mindless discursive education that both boys have been subject to:

> Now I was eight and very small
> And he was no whit bigger,
> And so I smiled, but he poked out
> His tongue, and called me "Nigger."[105]

The incident, at once small, nevertheless "colors" "all" (the variety) of what happens on the boy's several-months-long visit to Baltimore in its totalizing light. "Once" innocent of race relations—"Heart-filled, head-filled with glee"—the boy is now cast into a negative identification by a totalizing discourse (a different "all"), a reading that, for me, cannot be realized without attending to how narrative, expressive, and traditional features of Cullen's poem function. Rhyme does not mark an (antimodernist) hewing to poetic tradition here but allows us to register the rote manner in which the white boy launches the slur, as well as its disciplinary force on the African American boy's experience of his own experience (he cannot remember anything else happening over the course of his stay). So, too, the simple expressive narrative (obviously) cannot be read as merely simple. As Rachel Blau Du Plessis has argued, the poem's minorness, its being an "incident," underscores one "small or minor occurrence which implicates or precipitates a public crisis."[106]

The force of Cullen's poem cannot be realized in an expressive reading of the poem, nor can that of another poem we might compare to Bishop's work of the period—Gwendolyn Brooks's "a song in the front yard" (1945), whose metrical experiments similarly complicate an expressive reading of it. Like Bishop's "First Death" and "Manners" and like Cullen's "Incident," Brooks's poem condenses a child's/adult's perspectives to explore the child's interpellation into a hegemonically white and economically determining order. Like Cullen's, Brooks's poem signals the subject's unconsciousness of the discursive education she is receiving, in this case, through her mother:

> My mother, she tells me that Johnnie Mae
> Will grow up to be a bad woman.
> That George'll be taken to Jail soon or late
> (On account of last winter he sold our back gate).[107]

We could not realize the lesson in a vocal interpretation of the poem, flagged for us by the ironic use of "song" for the title: the capital "J" in the word "Jail" indicates the grave truths subtending this seemingly simple song about desiring to step out of (economic and moral) line. The mother warns that, "on account of" the theft of their back gate, Johnnie, a neighbor "charity" boy, "will go to Jail soon or late." For the child, the prediction and the logic attending it (one childish prank predicts a criminal future) seems object of rebellion to the child; her mother's account of the "real world" is too conservative and restricting. But ballad rhythms (suggestive of the juncture of public and personal tragedy) and the capitalization of the "J" in "Jail" tell a countervailing story about how children internalize hegemonic discourse. It is not logical that Johnnie *will* go to jail (why should one prank result in future jail time?) unless jail has become, in one's imaginary and real world—by dint of racial and economic structures of injustice—a proper noun, an institutional destiny and force. The illogical situation becomes a defining imaginative limit, the poem shows us, a "truth" that determines how even the front-yard child self-expresses. Thus, Brooks's relatively straightforward poem, on one level expressive of a young girl's experience and feeling, operates at levels that exceed "our" assumptions about the self-evidence of (white, privileged) lyric subjectivity. This difference of this Jail is marked visually, in keeping with the systems that determine its particular force and difference for this child.

Expressive readings tend to attach most easily to straightforwardly "narrative" poems such as Bishop's, Cullen's, or Brooks's. And it is not that we do not (or should not) see a person here; yet expressive readings can limit what we imagine that person to look like and what we imagine the work capable of exploring and revealing. My broader point here is to maintain that writers such as Bishop or Brooks or Cullen engage a poetic politics, as did Language writers. But we could not expect it to be shown through syntactic disruption or modernist technique. Bishop even shared with Language writers the belief that the most useful way to resist high-capitalist modes as they had shaped culture was to reveal and disrupt habits of language to produce interpretive space and to foster critical self-awareness. However, Bishop researches that situation by experimenting with rhetoric and discourse, not radical syntax. So quiet is Bishop's talky, "unsurprising . . . revolt," however, that it not only has slipped notice but has been mischaracterized as "the school of Quietude" (Silliman). Critics more inclined to champion Bishop's descriptive skills or to tease out personal confessions from her understated and often oblique poems or to dismiss them as mainstream "lyric" miss their more radical nature.

The result is a Bishop canon held to exemplify post-Romantic lyric understood both as an imaginative net over "reality" and also (at the same time) as achieved personal expression—views she pointedly rejected. While Bishop used the term "lyric" (indeed to describe Brooks's *Annie Allen*), she, like many other poets, wrote poems that resist modes of lyric reading that came to overwhelm the term. Indeed, Bishop identified in that 1949 work "a strain of lyric emotion" while still insisting that Brooks's language experiments "make the tone of her work as variegated as possible," which makes the "story of Annie Allen . . . a . . . kaleidoscopic dream."[108] Such variegations—in fact resistant to readings for tone—characterize those of Bishop's experiments derived from strains of early modernism, particularly from Williams, whose texts are central to an American avant-garde canon. The avant-garde antilyric agenda, as Virginia Jackson argues in her entry on "lyric" in *The Princeton Encyclopedia of Poetry and Poetics,* grew in "reaction formation" to hegemonic forms of lyric reading.[109] What we have missed in lyricizing Bishop is the possibility of another strain of response to that shared concern about the subjective-expressive mode in American lyric reading and writing, one shared by Ashbery and O'Hara, too. The next chapter, on Anne Sexton's poetry, turns to a poet who, in her associations with the anti-idealized epitome of lyric—the Confessional poem—has been asked to serve as the abjected repository of "our" lyric shame. By reading her work both to grotesque and problematize the standards to which she has been held, I will experiment further with the limits of lyric-reading practices.

CHAPTER TWO

Something for Someone

*Anne Sexton, Interpretation, and
the Shame of the Confessional*

> If language is conceived as a medium, . . . it is a medium in
> the sense of a membrane, as capable of blocking the real as
> of letting it in.
>
> —*Ron Silliman,* The New Sentence

THE TRICK OF WORDS WRITING THEMSELVES

I was acutely aware that I should dislike Anne Sexton's poetry long before
I had ever read a single Sexton poem. While lyric readings of Bishop's
work have secured for it a problematic reputation for aesthetic-interpretive
mastery and controlled "voice," lyric readings of Sexton's work dictate
that we see it as sloppy, and thus failed, traditional lyric, with Sexton
drifting perilously from serving the lyric-reading assumption that good
poems process experience into finished forms. On these terms, Sexton
stands as an object of shame for the mainstream critical culture that at
first endorsed her. At the same time, those who are affiliated with avant-
garde and antilyric discourse also identify Sexton's failure with laxity and
expressive overindulgence.[1] This suggests that the abject status of expres-
sionist Confessional work is agreed on by two otherwise deeply opposed
"camps"—the lyric and the antilyric. One might say that if Bishop is for
some people the "most beloved" lyric poet, Sexton is *everybody's* least beloved lyric poet.[2] Indeed, if the anxiety for me of identifying with Bishop
is that I might be thought to have conservative and naïvely expressivist

tastes (and thus be caught serving dominant modes of culture), the risk of identifying with Sexton is that I might be accused of having no taste.

The terms of disapprobation for Sexton tell us a great deal about the challenge that much mid- to late-twentieth-century poetry presented to Mill-derived norms of lyric reading codified in the twentieth century. In Robert Lowell's remembrance of Sexton written after her death, he says of his former student's work, "Many of her most embarrassing poems would have been fascinating if someone had put them in quotes, as the presentation of some character, not the author."[3] Lowell assumes an identity between Sexton's poems and her self that, by the mid-to-late 1970s, was becoming ever more embarrassing, though it is an assumption once central to the success of both Sexton's and Lowell's midcentury "Confessional" poems.[4] Lowell's return to impersonal tastes and norms that he had once been thought to "break through" may in fact have been informed by some shaming responses to the closeness between life and art that he had courted. In *The Dolphin* (1973), Lowell infamously printed the letters of his still-living ex-wife, receiving scathing reviews for it, even from his fans, including the following, from a very Eliotic-sounding Marjorie Perloff in 1973: "Lowell no longer quite succeeds in transforming his life into art, and his reservation, sometimes embarrassingly personal, sometimes boring, should indeed have remained 'sealed like private letters.' Here, if anywhere, the famed Confessional mode, inaugurated by Lowell's beautiful *Life Studies* of 1959, reaches its point of no return."[5] Lowell's midcentury work, along with that of Sexton, Sylvia Plath, and W. D. Snodgrass, had once seemed radical—a liberating correction to the impersonal poetics of T. S. Eliot and some New Critics, particularly to the idea that the successful poem must achieve an ideal transformation of the merely personal. By the mid-1970s, clearly, much had changed.

Lowell's suggestion about Sexton's work is a quintessential New Critical move: the right *interpretive* move (those quotation marks) could transform the embarrassments of the Confessional lyric into the "fascination[s]" of the impersonal dramatic lyric or dramatic monologue. At the risk of repeating commonplaces about the New Criticism, at stake in the ideal of distance between authors and their poems is Eliot's famous belief that good poems "digest and transmute" the merely personal, historically particular feelings of their authors into *"significant* emotion," which allows access to a "main current" of "tradition."[6] Eliot's faith was in a somewhat mystical, writerly process whereby study in combination with passive receptivity produces a new work that perpetuates and draws from a body of texts whose greatness transcends particulars of time and place.[7]

While Eliot imagined this digestion of emotion and processing of the personal as the writer's responsibility, Lowell's suggested quotation marks imagine that process of dramatization managed by the critical interpreter. In this, he also follows Brooks and Warren and Wimsatt's lead: remember Brooks and Wimsatt's 1957 assertion in *Literary Criticism,* absolutely definitive of the pedagogical norms for poetry reading in place for Anglophone readers and writers since the 1930s, "Once we have dissociated the speaker of the lyric from the personality of the poet, even the tiniest lyric reveals itself as drama."[8]

This shift to *interpretative* processes that realize a poem's dramatic qualities was central for a pedagogical program concerned to shore up conventional notions about art's social function and value that had been eroded across several decades, beginning with various modernisms. How could artworks be understood as useful or to speak to universals? Lowell's late 1970s comment about Sexton is thus a very late version of that New Critical orthodoxy (and we might notice that Lowell seems almost to parody the critic's power over the artwork). It admits, more openly than the New Critics did, the oddly protean, and even phantasmal, ontology of the artwork in such a critic-centric situation. If the work fails to speak to broadly held moral standards, Lowell seems to suggest, then just transform it to a dramatic monologue and make it a lesson in character failure.

In this, Lowell's comment also raises the complex, contradictory knot of attitudes that describes the status of New Critical imperatives for poets of Lowell's and, more so, Sexton's postmodern generation. However expressive a poem was expected to be—always to be read, that is, as the response of a speaker to a situation—it also had to announce its distance from its author, either through its surface difficulty or in its dramatization of the personal, so that it would warrant and support close critical scrutiny and not, one could argue, embarrass the critic for his or her sheer redundancy. Indeed, the midcentury American canon's near dismissal of Walt Whitman, whose work's "naïve affirmations" and directness did not seem to support the professional critic's centrality to poetic reading, points to just such a fear of redundancy, as Alan Golding suggests in his discussion of New Critical canons of taste.[9] Another set of then-current reading imperatives (somewhat at odds with the imperative to preserve and sustain the critical endeavor) dictated that, however difficult the good poem was to be, it should not be so difficult as to be uninterpretable, because that would render it not useful. In all ways, the poem was not to be for the author alone but to serve as part of a verse culture still attached to an Arnoldian notion of art's edifying and instructive function.

In fact, haunting Lowell's assertion of Sexton's affront to expectations for poetry to dramatize the self is the dismay that Allen Tate, Lowell's own New Critical mentor, expressed over the autobiographical poems of *Life Studies* in 1957, before Lowell published them: "All the poems about your family . . . are definitely *bad*," he wrote to Lowell. "I do not think you ought to publish them. . . . The poems are composed of unassimilated details, terribly intimate, and coldly noted [and] . . . of interest only to you. . . . They have no public or literary interest."[10] Sexton's own mentor, John Holmes, had similarly protested her publication of poems, in *To Bedlam and Part Way Back* (1960), that he knew referenced her stay in a mental institution. He found the poems "very selfish—all a forcing others to listen to you, and nothing given the listeners, nothing that teaches them or helps them": "It bothers me that you use poetry this way. It's all a release for you, but what is it for anybody else except a spectacle of someone experiencing release?"[11] These sets of advice about the need to objectify the personal content of the poems occur just around the time that Wimsatt and Brooks were advising students to put quotation marks around all lyrics in order to read them as dramas (not personal expressions).[12]

At stake in such imperatives—still quite strong—were broadly humanist assumptions and tastes: poetry should speak to and for general human experience. Thus, the early promise and excitement of the "personal" for those poets who got identified as "Confessional" was in imagining that poetry could attest to aspects of experience theretofore counted *out* by such universalizing assumptions. Though the impersonal poetics of Eliot and the New Critics figured the successful lyric poem as a work seemingly undertaken as if with no concern for audience, drawing on Mill's mid-nineteenth-century idea that poetry at its lyric best was "feeling confessing itself to itself" in "utter unconsciousness of a listener," Confessionals turned *their* back on listeners by ignoring standards of decorum.[13]

Indeed, the presumption implicit in Mill—that this intensely lyric, inward poetry would nevertheless be perfectly legible to anyone who happened upon it—is to assume that nothing in the poem would prove so particular to the poet's experience or so countercultural or so peculiarly put as to thwart the reader's identification with the poem and the subject in it. For Mill, poetry is "the delineation of the deeper and more secret workings of human emotion" and thus "interesting only to those to whom it recalls what they have felt, or whose imagination it stirs up to conceive what they could feel, or what they might have been able to feel, had their outward circumstances been different."[14] The underlying assumption of this hugely influential idea is that, however distinct one's actual historical experience, all "truly" poetic experiences will allow their readers to identify with the generalized "human heart" they realize.[15]

To say that Sexton flouted this injunction sounds obvious at first. One need only cite the title "In Praise of My Uterus," for instance. Furthermore, many postwar, mid-twentieth-century American poetic projects sought to test the limits of what subjects were thought to befit the imaginative stirrings that such a lyric theory accorded to poetry: Allen Ginsberg's "Howl" brought the pains and pleasures of a homosexual life, Communism, and countercultural choices to bear on the assumptions of lyric humanism; the Confessionals, especially Robert Lowell, made it difficult to think of their "I" as anyone but the author; and female writers, including Sexton and Sylvia Plath, wrote poems emphasizing experiences necessarily belonging to female bodies, thus testing the implicit assumptions for the lyric speaker to be male. As Adrienne Rich put it, thinking about the turn to the autobiographical and personal in post–World War II poetry, "We were trying to live a personal life," the "only one we could attest to."[16]

Rich's line comes from the poem "In Those Years" (1991), which actually critiques the midcentury turn to the personal from forty years later, regretting its consequences: "We found ourselves / reduced to I," Rich writes—that is, cut off from the potential power of the communal, the human, the "we."[17] Rich is writing in the early 1990s, when the Confessional, along with Deep Image, the so-called epiphanic lyric, and other such "testamentary" American poetic styles (as Michael Davidson has named them), had fallen into disrepute, not only among poets longing for a more explicitly social and political grounding for poetry (as was Rich) but quite keenly among Language poets and others who, in the wake of 1970s poststructural ideas, made it a mission to deconstruct the poetics of "voice" that they saw dominating the MFA-influenced mainstream canon of contemporary poetics.[18] That poetics of voice, implicitly invested in a coherent subject, seemed continuous with a mystifying late-capitalist social imaginary, in which the ideal of a poem as a "lyric . . . message in bottle" that "speaks out of a solitude to a solitude," in Edward Hirsch's words, seemed to Language poets to maintain "a marginal, isolated individualism . . . as an heroic and transcendent project," as Silliman, Carla Harryman, and others posited their resistance to the lyric ideal of the 1980s.[19]

Where should we place Sexton in this binary of personal expressive lyric and antilyric? Long after critics committed to an Eliotic sense of poetry's achievement had come around to valuing the ability of Lowell's work's to analyze the self in history, Sexton's poems still seemed only to have been written all for herself, as Holmes's critique suggests. Why so? Here I would like to propose that what made Sexton so radical as to require abjection, was not, as is usually assumed, her standing for the "reduc[tion] to I" that Rich and Language writers shared as a concern but rather her unwillingness to stick to the imperative for poetry to function as achieved craft.

As I will suggest in more detail through the body of this chapter, Sexton's work often resists the kinds of analysis that were paramount for any number of critics encountering her work in her lifetime. But what strikes me as odd is how, when Sexton's work is turned ever so slightly away from lyric readings of it, it can feel continuous in some of its effects and goals with late 1970s avant-garde projects that refused to value emblems of heroic and transcendent isolation. Sexton's poems—so often epistolary or dramatic monologue or addressed to a responsive "you" or interested in intersubjectivity—refuse that image of isolation and in fact expose and foreground the audience function that Mill shakily and incompletely suppressed. Why have we not read Sexton's experiments with subjectivity and lyric isolation as avant-garde?

In Hirsch's figure for the lyric poem that "speaks" across time, disembodied and ahistorical, as in Mill's figure of a poem unconcerned to meet the specific, conventional needs of specific audiences, there is a presumption that good poems inspire effortless moments of identification between themselves (as persons) and their readers. In a way, the process of depersonalization valued by (some) New Critics and, later, widely fostered in pedagogical readings for a dramatized speaker was animated by a similar presumption: as David Orr has suggested about the risk of engaging "the personal" in a poem, in order for "the personal" to work, it has nevertheless to seem crafted.[20]

Here it seems important to reiterate my wariness about identifying with Sexton-the-writer and my desire to do so in such a way that does not reduce her to her alcoholism, marital instabilities, and suicide—to unashame her work so my taking it on will not shame me. Even if one chooses not to identify with a heroic image of the poet's person or the poem's protagonist, there is nevertheless a pull to identify with the poet's achievement (or perhaps the poem's achievedness). Indeed, that pull may be usefully described as a reading horizon, a basic, if tacit, aspect to lyric-reading strategies that many people have inherited. Recognizing, then, that to do so must mark my own concern to justify taking Sexton's work seriously, I will argue that her work foregrounds and complicates the fictions of "voicing" and "overhearing" that were so important to the New Critical fantasy of lyric identification and control, and it invites us to think twice about processes of identification that enter into lyric readings, as well as the culture of professional criticism that fosters them.

As Sexton's biographer Diane Middlebrook and others have helped to show, Sexton was sharply aware that the published poem produced an identity that was illusory and yet a powerful ground of identification for her readers and even for herself. She wrote to her psychiatrist, Martin T. Orne, "I made up a whole person, a poet, Anne Sexton, who would be worth something to you. . . . All those people who write to me and believe in me. God! I don't even exist."[21] She was also aware of herself as part of a poetic culture that would require her to think cannily about her public persona and the appeal of her "self" as a public fascination: she called herself "a person selling poetry" and "an actress in my own autobiographical play."[22] At the same time, Sexton was thinking about the power of language to construct, in effect, its "own" agenda and to produce an authorial identity separate from herself. In a letter to Orne from the same year that she wrote "Said the Poet to the Analyst," Sexton describes language as a "counting" game, perhaps the poem's *donné:*

> Of course I KNOW that words are just a counting, I know this until the words start to arrange themselves and write something better than *I* would ever know. . . . I don't really believe the poem, but the name is surely mine so I must belong to the poem. So I must be real. . . . When you say "words mean nothing" then it means that the real me is nothing. All I am is the trick of words writing themselves.[23]

Given Sexton's reputation for uncritical, naïve expressiveness, her insights about language as it shapes a writing subject distinct from (but influential on) the self, and about the market's ability to create an author-function, might seem surprising. One might more readily expect them from a much more contemporary writer, perhaps affiliated with avant-garde poetics. While Sexton's most sympathetic critics of late have been able to recognize her savvy about subjectivity and language, more so than her Confessional reputation has allowed, most critics have missed the often quite remarkable ways in which Sexton's work exposes and exaggerates the very premises of midcentury lyric reading that produced that reputation in the first place. Sexton's work resists, at several levels, our identification with it; and it is difficult to read in ways that test the centrality of *criticism* to poetic value that was in place when she was writing.

SEXTON'S POETIC CULTURE

One of Sexton's first published poems, "The Reading" (1958)—not included in her *Collected Poems*—indicates that at the start of her quite self-conscious study of how to write publishable poetry, Sexton's sense of what constituted poetry involved a keen and uneasy awareness of an academic proving ground teeming with professor-critics.[24] Furthermore, it shows that Sexton understood that, in the poetic culture she would have to master, poems were to be performed before audiences of judgmental, professional academics eager to authenticate the poem as "spoken," achieved, and personal. Throughout, the poem courts a confusion of writing with speaking and of interpretation with speech that illustrates this understanding:

The Reading

This poet could speak,
There was no doubt about it.
The top professor nodded
To the next professor and he
Agreed with the other teacher,
Who wasn't exactly a professor at all.
There were plenty of poets,
Delaying their briefcase
To touch these honored words.
They envied his reading

And the ones with books
Approved and smiled
At the lesser poets who
Moved unsurely, but knew,
Of course, what they heard
Was a notable thing.[25]

Though the poem on its surface flatly describes the academic poetry
reading as a proving ground, its stilted, choppy lines and antipoetic
and unlike-natural speech highlight that poetic culture's attachment to a
mode of poetic reception that assumed the identity of writing and speaking. The observed poet "speaks" his words, but the professor-poets in the
audience linger to "touch" them (l. 9); and though what they have "heard"
is a poet reading aloud, they have heard not speech but "a notable thing"
(l. 16). The confusion of vocal performance with something static and
thingly (such as text) continues in the second verse paragraph, further
emphasizing the fact that the listeners experience not a poem (not even its
audible elements) but the poet (metonymized by his "famous name"):

After the clapping they bundled out,
Not testing their fingers
On his climate of rhymes.
Not thinking how sound crumbles,
That even honor can happen too long.
A poet of note had read,
Had read them his smiles
And spilled what was left
On the stage.
All of them nodded,
Tasting this fame
And forgot how the poems said nothing,
Remembering just—
We heard him,
That famous name. (30, ll. 18–32)

Sexton emphasizes the author's fame and his person as these dwarf the
experience of his poem—the audience hears "him, / That famous name,"
and he reads them "his smiles," rather than his poem. This suggests how
little the poem within the poem (which is untested and unthought of in

lines 19–21) matters; it is overshadowed by the academic "reading" culture of the day. The text sees Sexton sizing up the 1950s poetry business
and the academic social scene that conditioned norms for consuming poems and for generating "readings" of them and establishing their cultural
capital. Flat, unpoetical description and what seem arbitrary line breaks
over the first thirteen lines suggest the possible badness of the famous
name's poem, highlighting the social nature of the culture in question. In
all, this reads as a sardonic comment on the academic culture that would
determine the results of Sexton's own first forays into print: Sexton was
savvy about the cultural forms that determined and indicated a poet's
success. Why else would she emphasize so awkwardly the fine distinctions of hierarchy dictating the differences among "top professor," "next,"
and "other teacher," who "wasn't exactly a professor at all"?

Given this canniness about the dominant, New Critical–influenced
poetic culture, the poem's emphasis on sound and speaking takes on a
remarkably specific character, seeming to reference the pedagogical expectation, assumed broadly, for poems to be read as having speakers. What
the audience has forgotten, in fact, perhaps in the rush to fame and to
please "top professors," is "how the poem said nothing." Sexton emphasizes writing in a poem about public speaking, speech you can touch, as if
to suggest that the slippage between the two is a critical value that originates
in a poetic social culture, rather than as a description of what poetic texts
do or how poets write. This emphasis may well indicate self-consciousness
and often flagrant attention (if not quite resistance) to critical emphasis
on voice as that dovetailed with the U.S. poetry scene's and broader
culture's emphasis on personality—star power.[26]

In the same year that this poem was published, Sexton expressed concern in several letters to professional readers of her earliest work about the
frequently heard admonition that she needed still to "find her voice." To
Nolan Miller (editor at *Antioch Review*) she wrote in November 1958,
"People keep telling me that I haven't found my 'voice' yet and I have
spent considerable time fishing around in my desk drawers and under old
ms. and have found no new notable sound. Therefore I wrote this long
poem ["The Double Image"] on my best bond paper as if it deserved it
from the beginning. Etc. Etc." (*Letters*, 44–45). Here, as in "The Reading," Sexton figures poetic "voice" as a thing she will find not in her self
but in her desk. While this might be read in light of the rise of the personal "voice" as a sign of political liberation, it more likely emphasizes the

fact that, in the day's poetry market, the figure of "voice" was becoming a metonym for print worthiness and success.[27] Reversing the logic wherein finding one's voice leads to the best "bond paper," Sexton will use the bond paper anyway, as if to fool others into hearing her "voice." In "The Reading," emphasis on the social, academic settings in which the value of poems was to be determined similarly suggests the artwork's contingency to its culture of consumption; for "top professors" of the day (and the "teacher" and student minions hoping to please them), the idea that every poem has a solitary speaker and should be read (interpreted, that is) to identify the speaker was a norm of lyric reading—indeed, what Virginia Jackson calls "*the* lyric metaphor."[28] Indeed "voice" (and speaker and tone) had been important interpretive and critical concerns for twenty years' worth of academic poetry readings, reinforced in the pedagogical writings of Ruben Brower, Rene Wellek, and Warren Austin and, in the later 1950s, by Wimsatt and Brooks, among many others, and still used today. Among other things, "speaker" and "situation," as Vernon Shetley has argued, were reading methods that made difficult texts teachable, absorbing gaps and lacunae into the psychology of a speaker, which points to a major weakness of the model: its tendency to privilege poetic techniques that *can* be read as indices of voice or personality and to deemphasize those that cannot.[29] It is important to add, however, that the speaker model is problematic even for poems that, at first, might seem tailored to it. For it is not true that all poems that make it possible to identify a potential speaker and setting or whose narrative is legible enough to allow (or even encourage) a dramatic reading are best served, or most fully served, by a reading that emphasizes voice, character, situation, and unified psychology.

Indeed, as Sexton's awareness of "voice" as a trope of authenticity prepares us to see, her poems often foreground the presence of their speaker as if to exaggerate, explore, and sometimes explode the tacit premises of the lyric-reading models then being established and still potent today: chiefly, that poems were produced to be analyzed into legible moral content, as speech, by academic critics.[30] This claim brings my argument in line with a small but growing body of Sexton criticism that aims to save her work from narrow biographical and expressive readings.[31] Most notable of these is the work of Jo Gill, which asks us to see Sexton exploring "the liminal space between I and you, speaker and reader, . . . self and object world," so that we might understand her to "foreshadow . . . the markedly self-reflexive tendencies of more recent American poetry."[32] As welcome as Gill's work is, it nevertheless mounts its recovery effort—a project, like mine, to save Sexton from the worst shame of "lyric" (read as narcissism and naïve self-expression)—by depending on the very lyric-reading norms that help produce that shame in the first place. Gill qualifies that to argue for Sexton's self-reflexivity is not "to assert that [Sexton's work] represents a proto-postmodern rejection of authenticity, referentiality, or expression but rather to suggest that it is skeptical, knowing, and inquisitive about the status of these and about the processes by which they are established and understood."[33] I will amend this useful claim by specifying that the processes about which Sexton is most "knowing" and "skeptical" seem to be the lyric-reading processes that Gill turns to in evidencing her claim. This is a slight but important specification of Gill's argument that asks us to flesh out what is at stake for Gill in marking a difference between "rejecting" expression, authenticity, and referentiality, on the one hand, and being "inquisitive" or "knowing" about these and how they are established or understood, on the other.

In other words, conventions of lyric reading and interpretation that made it difficult for critics before Gill to even consider the possibility that Sexton was not operating in an unselfconsciously expressive mode *also* conditioned the perceived need for a wholesale rejection of such a mode (as was true in self-identified antilyric movements such as Language and the New York School). Both Gill and the Language writers mistake as a poetic writing mode what may in fact have been a way of reading. Admittedly, most of us slip into these conventions rather easily, sometimes in counterintuitive moments. We may be so habituated to them that we find it difficult, for example, to imagine that Sexton herself confronted the speaker model as a rather bizarre critical invention and a limiting fiction for a "business" (as she puts it in one poem) made of written words. For the young Sexton, what appealed about such a "business" was that words could so quickly drift from an author's intended meaning, even becoming loosed from referential meaning or oddly separated from their expected uses in the writing process. Such drift is ill suited to the metaphor of speech and hearing, which presumes a tonal immediacy.

Indeed, what surprised me when I finally picked up Sexton's poetry (feeling obliged to consider it in the context of my field studies) was how ill fitting her poems seem to the shamefully "lyric" role they have been asked to play: that is, as self-referential, narrative poems cohering around and through the figure of a speaker. I was surprised to find that Sexton's poems often seem not only not expressive but not even dramatic; rather, they tend to foreground writing and to destabilize their metaphoric frame to an extent that makes it difficult to read them as even coherent. They are fascinating not because dramatic strategies allow us to analyze her words as spoken by "some character" (now relieved, as with Lowell, of our and her embarrassment) but rather because they draw on, foreground, and complicate the very fiction of "voicing" and "overhearing" that was so important to the conventional constructions of lyric that were paramount as Sexton began writing poems. Consider "Said the Poet to the Analyst" in full:

> My business is words. Words are like labels,
> or coins, or better, like swarming bees.
> I confess I am only broken by the sources of things;
> as if words were counted like dead bees in the attic,
> unbuckled from their yellow eyes and their dry wings.
> I must always forget how one word is able to pick
> out another, to manner another, until I have got
> something I might have said . . .
> but did not.
>
> Your business is watching my words. But I
> admit nothing. I work with my best, for instance,
> when I can write my praise for a nickel machine,
> that one night in Nevada: telling how the magic jackpot
> came clacking three bells out, over the lucky screen.
> But if you should say this is something it is not,
> then I grow weak, remembering how my hands felt funny
> and ridiculous and crowded with all
> the believing money.[34]

Sexton's title implies the quotation marks for which Lowell called. However, the poem troubles the paradigm of a speaker-character whose unity we can "overhear" as speech. The lyric endeavor is framed as a "business" (*CP*, l. 1), hardly spontaneous and feeling speech; words are calculated for profit as much as effect. Second, the chain of similes running from lines 1 to 3 figures a progressive veering of language from reference:

words go from being like labels, mimetic signifiers, to being like coins—
tokens of the hovering abstractions on which value systems such as language or capital depend—and then to being like "swarming bees," loosed
and unmanageable. At the formal level, the poem's sonic hum of rhyme
(ending in the funny rhyme "funny/money") reiterates the idea that poems "say" things at subrational levels having nothing to do with semantics
or expressive subjectivity.

Furthermore, the poem highlights the presence of a "you" who ana-
lyzes and the problem that social fact presents to the model of lyric address and expression: All "saying" in the poem is provisional and happens
in imaginary addresses that are, nevertheless, not exactly private. Indeed,
by the second stanza, the imagined "you's" response (which can be read as
belonging either to "I" or "you") has the power to recalibrate the narrative
of the magic jackpot and the lucky screen: "But if you should say this is
something it is not / then 'I'" (ll. 15–16), in effect, must recalibrate the
ideation that has just happened.

As with the "top professor" who adjudicates the reading and writing of
poems, the poem highlights an interpreting audience on whom the very
idea of an internal, private lyric moment depends; whatever private
thoughts might here be shared are already informed by a social imaginary.
This is not quite the same thing as to say that Sexton is interested in the
"hermeneutics" of the space between "I" and you, though it is very close.
Sexton, in effect, explodes a fiction of productive isolation that midcentury lyric readers drew from Mill, that lyric is "the lament of a prisoner in
a solitary cell, ourselves listening, unseen, in the next."[35] Sexton's exposure
of audience underlies what made her work most embarrassing; by figuring
the lyric audience and foregrounding the lyric addressee, it reminds us
that lyric is an exchange subject to a poetic culture. This represents an
intensification of the metadiscursive play that Bishop aimed for in her work:
for Sexton, the personal poem is ever aware, in turning its back on its listener,
that it is a spectacle.

This awareness does not produce clarity in the poem; indeed, what the
poem "confesses" to its analyst is remarkably obscure. Rather than inviting identification with a speaker, it revolves around that expectation, refusing to be useful and legible for all. There is a good deal of ambiguity as
to how to voice it; one question is whether to voice it at all. For instance,
the ambiguity of the line "I confess I am only broken by the sources of
things" (l. 3) would be hard to unify in interpretation: is it that "I" is not

broken by anything else? Is it that *only* "I" am broken by the sources of things? Or is it that the sources of things, despite what one might assume, only serve to "break" I (as opposed, say, to shoring "I" up)? Similarly, the grammar of line 6 is such that one struggles to voice it with any confidence: "I must always forget" might mean "it must be that I always forget," or it might function more like a command, as in "I must, truly I must always forget." What must be forgotten (or must have been forgotten) seems to have everything to do with the ways in which language can have a mind of its own—how, against the logic of self-expression and hermeneutic analysis, systems of signification can produce waywardness: "how one word is able to pick / out another, to manner another, until I have got / something I might have said . . . / but did not" (ll. 6–9).

Also in tension with the figure of "voice" is the frequently occurring figure of ellipses in Sexton's work (and in Lowell's, too, we might note). As seemingly negligible as they are, ellipses complicate a Confessional, lyric reading of "Said the Poet," among other poems in Sexton's canon.[36] Ellipses can be read to suggest many things—a lapse of time between one statement and another, a drifting of internal thought for a character, something a character or writer has specifically left out. A habit of lyric reading would ask us to skip over an ellipsis, because it is a sign that only awkwardly asks to be voiced as speech. In its material presence and in its very ambiguity as a referent—the very fact that one has to decide which role the ellipsis is meant to play (how to read it)—the ellipsis introduces a situation that can exceed lyric- and even dramatic lyric-reading strategies. As Jenny Chamarette puts it, ellipses announce a "rupture. . . . The 'break' serves to heighten the reader's perceptual awareness of the sign itself as material imprint[—]equally formative of a drawing toward, or departure from, meaning."[37] In other words, ellipses assert, rather than repress, the fact of a text's material conditions.

In Sexton's poem, a lyric-reading paradigm would dictate we read the ellipsis to indicate that the speaker (or poet as speaker) has left something out that either was said or might have been said. It could be taken to signify a speaker's thoughts trailing off as she lets her mind dwell for a moment on "something [she] might have said . . . / but did not." But notice that Sexton's poem foregrounds the oddity of the lyric reader's expectation for poems to "speak," by, in effect, rhyming an unlikely vocal performance of the graphic symbol ". . . "—a symbol of what is *not* to be said— with the end phrases, "until I have got" and "but did not." That is, if in reading the poem, we literally *voice* the ellipsis as a graphic mark ("dot dot dot"), its rhyme becomes a gross literalization of something "I" or a poem's speaker "might have said" but (in a conventional public performance of a poem) probably would not "say." In so foregrounding the problem of what does and does not get "said" in a poem, Sexton's poem brings into surprisingly sharp comic relief the fact that "the speaker" paradigm clashes with the poem's material existence.[38]

By serving as a rupture that highlights the materiality of the sign (what "the speaker" typically does not say), the ellipsis brings to the fore a lyric-reading paradigm that is normally tacit, allowing us to feel, as a fresh oddity, the concept that these words do not only (or even) belong to a speaker at all but do belong to a system of signs. Thus "I," in the next stanza, "admit[s] nothing"; what is admitted or not in this poem is revealed to be a function of the *analysis* that comes to bear on mere words, an "I" who is the result of "the trick of words writing themselves" and a "you" who also writes them. That the poem's stanza structure mirrors the presence of both "you" *and* "I," poet and analyst, brings the supposedly covert hearer/analyst into the body of the poem, reminding us that conventions of print and lyric reading condition our experience of the poet's voice, or not.

Twenty years later, Sexton, by now a "famous name" herself, writes a fable called "The Letting Down of the Hair," published in 1972 in *Atlantic Monthly,* that is even more self-conscious in exploring the expectation that lyric behave as a sign not only of a speaker's but also of an author's "famous" speech.[39] The fable imagines a woman who has become famous for her Rapunzel-length hair, which she must let down out of her window once a day to dry. The fable is comically clear that this daily occurrence, which has attracted fans and taken on the quality of a performance, is an allegory for "the life of a poet."[40] Against her intentions, the woman explains, she is "becoming a tourist attraction": "The Gray Line bus arrives daily with a taped recording of facts—usually false—about what I do and who I am."[41] A Hollywood-style spectacle surrounding the letting down of the hair has caused the woman's fans to mistakenly identify her with her hair. In the course of making this point, Sexton's fable frames the notion that poems speak for their authors as a misidentification: "The people have become very devoted or very disgusted. They often write to me. I don't answer them, of course, for *my hair cannot speak* and it is the hair they write to."[42] In analogizing the production of poems to "the letting down of the hair," the fable indicates that fans might do better to write letters not to poets but to their poems. Of course, it is clear that the reputation for "uninhibitedness" in Sexton's work (as if Sexton were "letting down her [own] hair") had much to do with its revelations of a repressed order of knowledge; by writing about specifically female experiences and the female body in particular, Sexton in her Confessional stance implied the awakening of a political "voice" seen to be newly uninhibited.

But the fable laments the ways Sexton's writing was often identified with her self and as her *personal* "voice." Here we might remember the paratext that first supported Sexton's work in the public eye. In Robert Lowell's jacket blurb for Sexton's first book, for instance, he frames the poems as written with "the now enviable swift lyrical openness of a Romantic poet. Yet in her content she is a realist and describes her very personal experience with an almost Russian accuracy and abundance."[43] The assessment would work well to sum up Lowell's own *Life Studies,* published the year before Sexton's *To Bedlam and Part Way Back,* with its exhaustive novelistic attention to detail and its invitation, even insistence in several places, that we read the life studied as quite specifically Lowell's. Throughout his autobiographical prose memoir in *Life Studies,* Lowell laces the full proper names of his well-known family (that is, a family known in the historical record) and includes historically verifiable details about his own life, including, in one poem about a failed marriage, the "famous" name of a contemporary friend, Philip Rahv, well known to be the editor of *Partisan Review,* in which many of Lowell's poems appeared. Sexton's work in *Bedlam,* by contrast, very often generalizes aspects of her life and tends to employ persona. Though she uses her daughter's first name in several poems and the first names of friends, they were not publicly "known" figures. Thus, our strongest invitations to identify the poems with Sexton's real life come from Lowell's jacket blurb and the book's back-jacket copy, which sells the poet's ability to "so plainly confront[] guilt, loss, the intractability of events," thus arranging our understanding of these poems as autobiographical and confessional, as a "letting down" of Sexton's "hair."[44]

In the late-career fable, then, it is the highly mediated spectacle of celebrity that encourages a false sense of immediacy—and the illusion of intimacy—for Sexton's fans: "Fifty letters came just last week in response to a TV crew that came out on Monday to film the letting down of the hair."[45] The letters come "in response to a TV crew"; Sexton implies that the fans should be writing to the crew, pointing again to the error of identifying the hair (or poems) with intentional subjects.[46] Here, as elsewhere, Sexton's work flaunts the expectation that writing is the self's expressive extroversion, even as it implies it to be a species of misidentification. In so doing, Sexton foregrounds, even exaggerates, and in effect exposes tacit norms of lyric reading. Perhaps the culture's critical and poetic embarrassment (and even shame) over Sexton's work derives not just from the work's revelation of intimate details and taboo subjects (central to accounts of the Confessional and the source of its feminist possibilities) but also from its being overtly and self-consciously *staged*. Sexton renders the lyric scene of overhearing comically exaggerated, unveiling its technologies. James Dickey figured Sexton's first book, for instance, as coercing the reader into an uncomfortable voyeurism, arguing that because the poems "so obviously come out of deep, painful sections of the author's life . . . one's literary opinions scarcely seem to matter; one feels tempted to drop them furtively into the nearest ashcan, rather than be caught with them in the presence of so much naked suffering."[47] Dickey's assumption that Sexton's poems reflect her lived life (so often untrue) is not all that conditions his sense that these poems fail and ashame him; reading them, he feels suddenly addressed by, or in the presence of, a historically verifiable person, a feeling that disturbs conventions dictating his role in relation to the work, which is to be the unseen overhearer (the "invisible listener," as Vendler would say).[48] Dickey was not alone in this oddly paradoxical situation, one that produced embarrassment, even shame: among others, Peggy Rizza (another reviewer) complains that Sexton is "excessively personal" and that, reading her work, "we feel like voyeurs, *as though we have read something we hadn't quite intended to read,* something which is revealing or embarrassing but in no way instructive."[49] Though the claim in all cases is that the work is marked by an uncomfortable immediacy and presence (its "naked suffering," the intrusion of "personal" experience), what is asserted, paradoxically, is these readers' sudden, problematic awareness of their own mediating presence as readers. They are no longer "invisible listeners" but intimated readers "caught" in the act as unseemly voyeurs. The figure of the voyeur literalizes and grotesques the Millean scene of "overhearing" into overseeing, or peeping, with the risk of punishment.

Here we might pause to draw out (again) Mill's theatrical figure for the quasi-invisible listener, in which poetry is a "soliloquy" in "full dress and upon the stage," performed as if with no awareness of the audience: the figure informs the foregoing readings of Sexton, wherein critics found not quite acknowledgment of an audience (what for Mill would make it lesser "eloquence") but a breach of the theatrical "fourth wall," the effect being its turning the spot light meant to shine on the speaker on the audience member instead: "All poetry is of the nature of soliloquy. . . . The actor knows that there is an audience present; but if he acts as though he knew it, he acts ill. . . . But when he turns round, and addresses himself to another person; when the act of utterance is not itself the end . . . then it ceases to be poetry, and becomes eloquence."[50] The conventional "lyric" arrangement is for everyone to act as though no one is in the audience. Sexton's work, these critics imply, exposed that technology to view.

Though this particular lyric-reading ideal was emphasized by Mill, it became codified by the classroom lyric-reading culture that mushroomed in the United States after the 1930s. Reuben Brower, legendary teacher of close reading (a term he coined) at Harvard and Amherst in the 1940s and 1950s, mobilizes the Millean theatrical figure to suggest the embarrassment of being caught in the act of watching an actual person, as opposed to hearing a "speaker" speak: "The voice we hear in a lyric, however piercingly real, is not Keats's or Shakespeare's; or if it seems to be . . . we are embarrassed and thrown off as if an actor had stopped and spoken to the audience in his own person."[51] Northrop Frye famously echoed Mill by saying that the poet "turns his back on his listeners."[52] Brower also fears being caught in the act, and he takes his fantasy of embarrassment about the potential for a too-direct address from Keats beyond Mill's terms. For Mill, eloquence was not embarrassing, it was just not poetry, which, ideally, should be untouched by the marketplace and its purposes. For Brower, the marketplace (implied by the theater figure) is the source of embarrassment, and embarrassment (like shame) alerts one to one's place in a social configuration; in being embarrassed, the reader becomes aware of him- or herself as in an audience/market, with the poet a kind of performer.

Thus, Brower's claim is Eliotic, too, addressing a moment when craft slips so far out of sight that we sense its presence negatively—feel the failure of craft exposing our awareness of its want. Though only inexplicitly, what gets (awkwardly) admitted is that *writing* has gone out of control. A disinterest in craft norms gets exposed, similar to the way that, if an actor turns to address the audience, he or she breaks down the "fourth wall," exposing the suspension of disbelief and other conventions of theatergoing, exposing the audience. Recall that this is precisely the metaphor that

Charles Bernstein (referencing Ford Madox Ford's realism and, tacitly, Mill) invokes to describe the absorptive text, suggesting, "Nothing / in the text should cause self-consciousness / about the reading process: it should be as if / the writer & the reader are not present."[53]

This prescription is precisely what Sexton's work failed to serve: instead of parallel privacies (as Mill figures it, two people in adjacent solitary-confinement cells), Sexton's work insists (by negative fiat) on readers and writers participating in something together. Critic David Orr describes such poetic embarrassment in terms of an "other presence" entering the field of the page: "We have trouble keeping the poet-as-author 'sustained in harmony' with this new identity . . . in part because the writer himself seems to struggle to do so." The "friction" between supposed identities on the page "can be exciting," Orr supposes. "Or as it happens, embarrassing."[54] In Orr's poetics, a poem embarrasses when an expected level of tension between what is seemingly "personal," and thus supposedly artless in a poem, and what is "skillful," and thus artificial, is thrown out of balance: personal poems "make the distinction between words like 'artful' and 'artless' so complicated as to be almost impenetrable."[55]

Orr, much like Sexton's critics, would read "this other presence" as an authorial "identity," but we could read it as a technique of writing that flusters a process of easy identification that the lyric ideal posits as necessary. We could read, that is, the embarrassment that Brower and Orr describe as involving the intrusion of writing qua writing (instead of as taste, much as Bernstein supposes). It is as if, at the moment that writing is suddenly felt to fail as acceptable poetic "speech," it is outed as never having been "speech"; and in that moment, it threatens to expose or explode the very fiction that sustains the lyric interpretive endeavor—the idea that we are overhearing something not addressed to anyone at all, not conditioned by a specific literary context or situation of address, and yet nevertheless perfectly clear. Sexton's work often brings this suppressed social element of lyric to the fore.[56]

THE INTERCOM PAGES YOU: SEXTON'S EXPOSED ANALYST

Like much of Sexton's work in *To Bedlam,* "You, Doctor Martin" emphasizes the written page in a way that tests our ability to read it as speech. But "You, Doctor Martin" is especially interesting for exposing processes of identification that enter into lyric reading, as well as the trope of lyric expression that those processes depend on. The poem's mode of address is not at all typical of the lyric's reputation: as William Waters puts it, "lyric is famous for calling upon things that do not hear," and many critics after Mill have imagined that the addressee of most lyric poems is only second-ary. Waters explains the tendency for lyric to be understood as a mono-logic genre: "Who (or what) gets addressed, when and how, will say little about the work's artistic or human concerns if all a poem's hailings are equally void of effect and therefore essentially interchangeable."[57] The specificity of Sexton's address in this poem (and, as we shall see, in such late poems as "The Gold Key") foregrounds and problematizes this repu-tation, immediately identifying the poem's addressee as so particular and central to the poem that it cannot be taken as universally relevant.

In fact, tension between address and typography shows Dr. Martin's part in the poem to be anything but negligible. Sexton foregrounds Mar-tin's power to analyze what is pointedly *written* (and printed) mad:

> You, Doctor Martin, walk
> from breakfast to madness. Late August,
> I speed through the antiseptic tunnel
> where the moving dead still talk
> of pushing their bones against the thrust
> of cure. And I am queen of this summer hotel
> or the laughing bee on a stalk
>
> of death. . . . (*CP*, 3)

Highly enjambed lines from the start create orphaned phrases (what Mary Kinzie calls "half meanings") and break the fluidity of "voice" as expres-sive speech, denaturing line's connection to breath.[58] The poem's centered alignment is anachronistic, atypical for the collection and the day. Sex-ton's poem even seems to acknowledge the effect of radical enjamb-ments—"broken lines"—that both interrupt our expectation for singular voice and render the poem's speaking subject dizzyingly multiple.

But here we see how the shame of Sexton's lyric reputation can be fos-tered or diminished using such tools of analysis. Readers such as Kinzie and Laurence Lerner have taken radical enjambments, "half meanings," and violent imagery in Confessional poems as mimetic of feeling or of a speaker's psychology, and this (for Lerner) justifies Confessional methods "that do not always seem to be under control."[59] However, even when read through the lyric expectation that what we are overhearing is a voice attesting to, or mastering, personal experience of the madhouse (that is, where the specific address does not matter), "You, Dr. Martin" jars in its emphasis on diction and on figures related to speech. Patients are in "boxes / where we sleep or cry" (*CP*, 4, ll. 27–28).[60] Chalk whines, "knives" are "for cutting your throat" (3, ll. 14, 16). In a later image, patients are not speaking subjects but "magic talking to itself" (4, l. 37). The doctor "*calls*[*s*] at the madhouse" (4, l. 32) but is only an "oracular / eye in our nest" (4, ll. 32–33). In one image, voice, text, and identity merge when the "intercom *pages* you" (4, l. 34, my emphasis). Enjambment emphasizes these phrases, as well as denaturalizes them as speech:

> of smiles. We chew in rows, our plates
> scratch and whine like chalk
>
> in school. There are no knives
> for cutting your throat. I make
> moccasins all morning. At first my hands
> kept empty, unraveled for the lives
> they used to work. Now I learn to take
> them back, each angry finger that demands
> I mend what another will break
>
> tomorrow. Of course, I love you; (3, ll. 15–22)

As the first poem in a collection sold for its poet's ability to "so plainly confront[] guilt, loss, the intractability of events" and for its narrative legibility ("This book of poems has the cumulative impact of a good novel"), it is surprising how often the poem deflects, rather than encourages, our identifying a clear speaking subject or a narrative thread.[61] Surface difficulties—excessive pronominal shifts and enjambments that serve rhyme but break syntax—expose our desire to identify, more easily than at first we can, a person in its broken lines.[62]

Furthermore, the poem explores the lyric-reading process (through the figure of analysis) that turns text into people. The analyst's "business is people"; as the voyeuristic overhearer of his patients' semipublic madness, Martin literally hangs over each subject in Sexton's poem-box— "light[ing] . . . up" each, transforming a din of inhuman "magic talking to itself / noisy and alone" into "people." Martin's figure brings to view both the theatrics and the "business" of the analyst not only whose job is to witness, cure, and contain madness but also whose very presence determines madness in the first place. This might be analogized to the lyric reader whose presence dictates the terms by which a poem gets read as spoken expression. "Of course I love you; / you lean above the plastic sky" (*CP*, 3, ll. 22–23) suggests, for instance, the problematic (compulsory?) "loving" of someone who posits himself professionally "above" the subject, the subject's Godlike adjudicator. Could the figure also refer us to the process of poetic "overhearing" that turns on the analysis identification of a rational speaking subject in a kind of box?

My point here is that though the poem clearly serves as testament to (and gets read as) a patient's frustrated experience of confinement in an asylum, it importantly does *not* "sp[eak] frankly and eloquently of mental illness," as the common reception of Sexton would dictate.[63] Indeed, critics who reduce the poem to frank expression in effect repeat the Dr. Martin role. In the poem's almost obsessive focus on "you," it boldly draws the curtain from the Millean scene of lyric utterance—the seeming "utter unconsciousness of a listener," in Mill's words—revealing the important context-specific social theatrics that (paradoxically) produce the privacy of lyric: even "magic talking to itself" depends on the analytic audience that will frame it as such, a figure linking lyric analysis to other forms of discursivity.[64] Again, Mill's own figure for how that privacy works only messily suppressed the social. Susan Rosenbaum suggests that "the expansion of commercial culture in the eighteenth century engendered deep-seated moral anxieties about the marketing, sale, and circulation of 'private' expression."[65] As Virginia Jackson points out, we see Mill's "double bind" in making lyric address "the defining feature of the poetic," evident in his extension of the soliloquy metaphor, which troubles the figure of voice with which, by now, the twentieth-century lyric is almost completely identified: poetry, Mill writes, is "on paper" and in a "shop" but also "on stage": "the actor knows that there is an audience present; but if he act as though he knew it, he acts ill."[66]

While it might overstate things to claim that Sexton's poem and indeed many of her poems are *about* twentieth-century uses of Mill's figure for lyric, "You, Dr. Martin" surely does illustrate Jane Hedley's broad claim, in her study of gender and lyric address in contemporary American poetry, that Sexton, like other female poets writing in the mid-twentieth century, needed to come "to grips" with problems of subject position and address, with "the problem of the 'I' [and] . . . the problem of the 'you.'"

But we can go further; for while Hedley must be correct in part that solving these problems had to do with Sexton's specifically expressive lyric ambitions—"of how to write from the perspective of a woman's experience and yet be taken seriously as a poet"—Sexton's work also challenges the premises that underwrite such a goal.[67]

"THE GOLD KEY": DISCURSIVE SHIFTS

Another of Sexton's chief challenges to the premises of the expressive as a poetic goal is evident in her work's resistance to a hermeneutic in which tone—a key "element" of interpretation in the lyric speaker model—rules. Tone was a key term assumed by several generations of academic readers (including my own), one by now so fully ingrained that it may help to remember the recent rise of this interpretive tool. In *The Fields of Light*, Brower argues, "Our whole aim in analysis of tone is to delineate the exact speaking voice in every poem we read . . . by attending to the special, often minute language signs by which the poet fixes the tone for us."[68] Tone, for Brower (as for I. A. Richards and others) is "1/ the implied social relationship of the speaker to his auditor and 2/ the manner he adopts in addressing his auditor" (22). He goes on to argue, "In every line and phrase the poet is conveying some sense of experience, and we are registering it" (31–32). Brower's sense that tone is "fixed" for us by the poet and analyzable by the professional interpreter is undergirded by a faith in right interpretations of poems, in expressive aesthetics, and in the professional expertise needed to arrive at the interpretive mastery involved in both reading and writing poetry. Brower held that poems turn readers into specific kinds of auditors; a dramatic situation makes us into "brother, lover," eavesdropper, or friend, for instance, and tone suggests the manner in which, as the poem's ideal auditor, we are being addressed (23). This would suggest that it is when we are exposed as a specific reader reading a specific poet's work (Keats's or Sexton's), rather than imagining ourselves as ideal auditors of a speaker's voice, that embarrassment arises.

I have argued that Sexton's exaggerated performances as the lyric speaker expose us as her readers; it is the breakdown of the tone contract wherein our power as interpreters is challenged. Consider, for instance, the late poem "The Gold Key," the first poem in *Transformations* (1971), which resists tonal reading and the paradigm of interpretability by stagily exposing the requisite dramatized speaker that was so central to lyric-reading pedagogy of the day. That Sexton's major critics give little mention to the poem is surprising, given its pointed effort to frame its parent collection (which retells tales of the Brothers Grimm) by questioning the tales' interpretability, the value of a hermeneutic approach to poems, and even her own collection's artistic value. The poem is based on the Grimms' tale "The Golden Key," here translated by D. L. Ashliman:

> Once in the wintertime when the snow was very deep, a poor boy had to go out and fetch wood on a sled. After he had gathered it together and loaded it, he did not want to go straight home, because he was so frozen, but instead to make a fire and warm himself a little first. So he scraped the snow away, and while he was thus clearing the ground he found a small golden key. Now he believed that where there was a key, there must also be a lock, so he dug in the ground and found a little iron chest. "If only the key fits!" he thought. "Certainly there are valuable things in the chest." He looked, but there was no keyhole. Finally he found one, but so small that it could scarcely be seen. He tried the key, and fortunately it fitted. Then he turned it once, and now we must wait until he has finished unlocking it and has opened the lid. Then we shall find out what kind of wonderful things there were in the little chest.[69]

As Ashliman indicates in a note, from the Grimms' second edition of the tales (in 1819) onward, they always printed "The Golden Key" as the last in the collection. As a last word, it keeps us (literally) in suspense, inviting and fending off its readers' hunger for the satisfaction of "an answer" to the box's contents. As an allegory of reading tales, it supposes that the meanings or values of the tales are not necessarily "in" them (the way a treasure might be inside a box); taken one way, the ending emphasizes the pleasure of reading (a process close to adventure) rather than the interpretive moral or payoff it will produce (its product); and, taken another way, it refers us to the potential identificatory projections that readerly desires can produce.

Sexton begins her retellings by proposing that her own collection is what the boy finds at the bottom of his box. At the end of "The Gold Key," she retells "The Golden Key" as follows:

> He turns the key.
> Presto!
> It opens this book of odd tales
> which transform the Brothers Grimm. (*CP*, 224, ll. 43–46)

That the original tale is now imagined to beget more tales (or Sexton's "transformations" of other tales) reiterates the ironic expletive gusto of Sexton's "Presto"; if there is a wonderful "thing" to discover at the bottom of the box, it utterly lacks the facticity of a "thing." In keeping with the original tale's turn from the discovery of a message or meaning at the bottom of the box (in effect we find instead another box), Sexton's poem proceeds to defeat the reading in search of "attitude" and "tone." Discursive shifts, which make "tone" in Brower's terms—fixing a relationship between speaker and audience—impossible to glean, recall the original tale's insistence on *not* telling us what the golden key opens (a metaphor, perhaps more clearly in Sexton than in Grimm, for what interpretation "should" yield). Indeed, the impossibility of determining a fixed tone in Sexton's poem renders the fact that it begins by unmasking its "speaker—a hyper-"lyric" gesture—all the more interesting. Sexton appears to be performing an exaggeration of the fiction that poems are spoken:

> The speaker in this case
> is a middle-aged witch, me—
> tangled on my two great arms,
> my face in a book
> and my mouth wide,
> ready to tell you a story or two. (223, ll. 1–6)

Sexton pokes fun at the New Critical schoolroom question often asked of lyric—"who is the speaker?"—by identifying "the speaker" from the outset, yet only to insist on identity between "the speaker" and "me." Still, the gesture does not assure us that this is a "confessional" speaker-author in the expected sense. After the overdetermined identification, the description of the "me" speaker that follows presents an image remarkably *in*human: what *part* of this "me" is tangled "on [her] two great arms" (l. 3)? (It seems anatomically impossible.) The grotesque "mouth wide" and "face in a book" (ll. 4–5) are hyperliteralizations of the speaker figure, which renders the image, ostensibly produced to unmask "the speaker" as "me," rather more like an exaggerated mask, depersonified.

The poem then names a variety of possible "yous" it might address, lending an almost comic specificity to the apostrophic situation, exaggerating the problem of address suppressed by an interpretation for tone:

> I have come to remind you,
> all of you:

> Alice, Samuel, Kurt, Eleanor,
> Jane, Brian, Maryel,
> all of you draw near. (223, ll. 7–11)

Here, two lyric norms clash: on one hand, the norm is for the "you" addressed to be always so universal as to be "all of you," "ourselves unseen listening," as Mill puts it; and on the other, the norm is to identify "where in the social hierarchy the fictional speaker and auditor stand, . . . lover and beloved, brother and sister, man and wife, servant and master" (Brower, *Fields,* 22–23). Sexton exposes these conflicting expectations, for what seems at first to be a general address is then comically specified by the list of quite particular names. The poem seeds the expectation that its addressees are children with the beckoning "all of you draw near" but then contradicts that expectation, aging the child, turning a light on her specificity in a discomforting way: "Alice, / at fifty-six do you remember?" A discourse shift toward the surreal and confrontational then goes on: "Are you comatose? / Are you undersea?" (*CP,* 223, ll. 21–22). In all, the poem's unsettling mode of address defeats the conditions necessary for determining a writer's tone—the "implied social relationship of the speaker to his auditor" that would fix attitude and the range of interpretive possibilities (Brower, *Fields,* 22).

Sexton's poem then moves to its version of the tale, in this case, about a boy who also figures for "the reader":

> He is sixteen and he wants some answers.
> He is each of us.
> I mean you.
> I mean me. (*CP,* 223, ll. 26–29).

At first, in framing the reader/subject as "each of us," Sexton seems to gesture to a universalism we might associate with Mill's figure. But as the poem continues, the generality of "you" has to meet the odd idiosyncrasy of her appeal to it—"It is not enough to read Hesse / and drink clam chowder" (ll. 30–31)—which makes it difficult to think of this boy (who is also "you" and "me") as "each of us" or "all of you." The reference is too intimate, too specific. Indeed, Sexton's dedicatory note to the book *Transformations* (which directly precedes the poem) reveals "Linda" (Sexton's daughter) as she who "reads Hesse and drinks clam chowder" (*CP,* 221).

What is produced by the flaunting of general appeal is a nearly surreal discursive instability that marks the poem throughout, ending with two sharp rhetorical shifts in its last few lines. The lines reveal the box's "contents"—"this book of odd tales / which transform the Brothers Grimm" (*CP*, 224, ll. 46–47). But Sexton's poem now turns on itself in a nearly unparsable way:

> Transform?
> As if an enlarged paper clip
> could be a piece of sculpture.
> (And it could). (ll. 48–51)

These shifts destabilize the figure of a unified speaker's voice, leaving us with a "discovery" at the bottom of the poem/box that paradoxically refuses to function as an answer. For one, it is entirely unclear who (what subject position or, more pointedly, what "speaker") doubts that these tales "transform." Is it the author? A "speaker"? A different speaker? The poem? And what is the value that the "transformation" figured (paper clip as art object)? This is an important question, given that *Transformations* is the title under whose sign these tales unfold.

One strong possibility is that an enlarged paper clip presented as sculpture stands as antiart. The everyday object becoming art recalls Marcel Duchamp's "readymades" and other such early-twentieth-century artistic challenges to the idea of "high art" as specifically skilled and retinal. The poem's mixed assertion that the poem/object both is and is not art (especially in the last, parenthetical line) resembles Robert Rauschenberg's famous 1961 conceptual "portrait" of Iris Clert—a telegram reading, "THIS IS A PORTRAIT OF IRIS CLERT IF I SAY SO. ROBERT RAUSCHEN-BERG." Rauschenberg's performance of his own power to interpret his work takes a stance against mimetic expectations for portraiture.

It seems fair to say that Sexton's poem similarly turns against conventional expectations of lyric. Along with flouting the problem of address that defines lyric readings and exaggerating the speaker model, *Transformations* is representative in its resistance to the interpretability or universal appeal expected of lyric at midcentury, opposing a culture inclined to use the fairy tale and romance to promote consumer conformism, which explains the mix of mostly legible feminist allegories about marriage and modern psychology with tales emphasizing moral complexity and even surreality.[70] These latter often invoke and test an addressee for whom fairy tales would offer up a useful "answer," such as a moral (or antimoral) with universalist appeal.[71]

In resisting paradigms of transformation (and transport), as well as the speaker model, Sexton's "The Gold Key" resists what that model demands—interpretability. Sexton defies mainstream, Eliotic critical standards, which, as late as the 1960s and 1970s, dictated that good poetry transmute (transform?) its raw materials into something coherent enough to, if not delight, then in some sense instruct others. For instance, Joyce Carol Oates complains that Sexton, after her second book, stopped working to render the work's universal appeal, failing to "translat[e] emotion into a coherent poetic 'image.' . . . The almost unnamable lust of [Sexton's later work] becomes, finally, a lust to destroy poetry itself," a failure Oates finds in Sexton's failure to work hard enough to "imagine a structure that would contain her own small despairing voice amid many other voices; she did not commit herself to the *labor* of such a creation."[72] Patricia Meyer Spacks found Sexton's later work "grotesquely uncontrolled," lacking the containing "structure" Oates called for, views that bespeak the common understanding of lyric as a genre expected to master psychological and phenomenological muddle in controlled language.[73] As Helen Vendler has articulated in a similar line about successful Confessional lyric, "without analysis, there is no poem."[74]

It is important to pressure such assumptions about "poetry," including the one dictating that Sexton's unwillingness to *"labor"* to "contain" (perhaps with a paper clip?) her only "small despairing voice" might nevertheless "destroy" it (poetry). The implication that the merging of the singular into the collective is the form of intellectual and analytic containment that renders poetry Poetry may help us to imagine what might have compelled Sexton to refuse the aesthetic control that for Oates signified "poetry" (not to mention the collective) as such. The figure reiterates the problematic public-private space of Mill that Brower, as well as Sexton and other critics, confronted as even more problematic. Oates presumes the successful, well-behaved lyric as a space in which a reader eavesdrops on voiced intimacy that, paradoxically, nevertheless accords (or should accord, through labor) with norms of socially sanctioned, if not exactly "public," behavior. Thinking in similar terms, James Dickey's literary opinions do not "matter" when he reads Sexton because what Sexton writes is ("obviously") too particular to her own life (he assumes) to speak to and, moreover, *for* him: in lyric-reading terms, Sexton fails to promote the illusion of an *identity* between reader and writer, one that depends on these figures' twinned isolation. Even in 1977 (the date of Oates's writing), the refusal to write poems of an impersonal but "universal" character is construed as a failure of spirit and an offensive missing of the lyric literary mark.

But "melodrama" of Sexton's work (the word Charles Gullans uses to express his irritation and embarrassment about the poems in *Live or Die*) helps us to bring to light some of the complexity of the lyric-reading situation in the early 1970s, a complexity that dogs us still. The value of the personal, on the one hand, once seemed to be its ability to challenge the mystifications of supposed universalism; on the other, feminist poetry was still held to an Eliotic standard of the universally cathartic "significant" poem.[75] For instance, Alicia Ostriker disparages Sexton's long sequence *The Jesus Papers* (1972) in terms much like Oates's; the work's feminist agenda fails because it is subversive but not cathartic. Ostriker's evidence is the sequence's surrealism, taken, among others, as sign of its anti-"lyric" qualities. She writes,

> Reading . . . *The Jesus Papers* is like walking barefoot on broken glass. But the surrealist mode subverts one's ability to accept suffering as ultimately necessary or ennobling. In contrast to tragic and lyric modes, which persuade us that their visionary worlds are deeply true, and must be accepted, surrealism persuades us that its world is arbitrary and questionable. The confusion between "truth" and "lies" insisted on in [this] sequence[] reinforces this subversive effect, as do key formal devices designed to disorient the reader:. . . progressive (but potholed) sequence followed by regression, . . . the collapse of past and present, the flaunted anachronisms.[76]

Ostriker finds that, in questioning the value of patriarchal "pattern" without transcending to some more universal pattern (that is nevertheless not patriarchal—a conundrum for sure), Sexton's work fails to adhere to standards that Ostriker identifies with "lyric"; for Ostriker, the job of "lyric" is to transform suffering into something ennobling and "true."

Though Sexton's departures from "traditional" lyric virtues proved damning for her reputation among establishment critics, we might ask why

their raising concerns about her antilyricism did not result in its constellation among poetic experiments of the time, including Language writing,
that challenged critical norms regarding lyric "speakers," interpretability,
and address. Is it only my own shame about Sexton informing my desire
to read her 1970s work in light of the avant-garde aesthetics? Both Sexton and Language writers (publishing at the time "The Gold Key" and
The Jesus Papers appeared) received negative reviews concerning the works'
transgressions of the norm for poetry to "speak" clearly to and for human
concerns. These were often articulated in what Ron Silliman has called
"the threatened rhetoric of fury" and with a similar paranoia about the
mode's potential power to destroy "poetry." Seen from the vantage of
mainstream lyric expectations, Sexton's work and many Language experiments seemed gross signs of a "lack [of] discipline," and their experiments
with address and subjectivity get read (or misread) by more "mainstream"
critics as indicating an unbearable want of aesthetic control—and even,
again, as reflecting a desire to "destroy poetry."[77]

This is not to say that a poem such as "Live" from Sexton's *Live or Die*
(1966) is transgressive in just the way of an avant-garde poem from
roughly the same time. Indeed, though Gullans and others attacked *Live
or Die* in the press, it won the Pulitzer, and most of its poems follow contemporary conventions of autobiographical monologues, retaining most
establishment conventions for expressive poetry. Looked at as a whole
structure, the talky, loose unfolding of its plot is more or less familiar,
moving over 106 lines and six verse paragraphs from the (albeit bizarrely)
colloquial "Well, death's been here" (*CP,* 167, l. 1) to "Even so, / I kept
right on going on" (l. 19), to the hackneyed "Is life something you play? /
And all the time wanting to get rid of it?" (168, l. 34), to a meditation on
family life at line 45, to an address to (perhaps) family at line 85, and closing with a vow to live at line 107. Focused on one subject's internal state,
"Live" could not be farther from Language-centered avant-garde concerns
of the time, whose tendencies were, even in evidently autobiographical
modes, to decenter the "I's" priority and to emphasize "the self as a relationship rather than an essence."[78]

And yet "Live" is an interesting point of comparison; throughout, a
mixture of lazy and extravagant expression, in concert with morbid imagery, exaggerates the metaphoric orbit of the personal emblem, courting
melodrama and exposing how deeply rooted was the interpretive decorum of epiphanic, meditative poetry at the time. In the opening verse

paragraph, the subjectivity on display is lost in lines and images that move too quickly and resist cohering as a net of interinterpretable metaphors:

> Well, death's been here
> for a long time—
> it has a hell of a lot
> to do with hell
> and suspicion of the eye
> and the religious objects
> and how I mourned them
> when they were made obscene
> by my dwarf-heart's doodle.
> The chief ingredient
> is mutilation. (*CP*, 167, ll. 1–12)

Mutilating conventions of the well-wrought confession, what is on offer is a little too obscure to function as an allegory of the self. Melodramatic images from tabloid horrors are surreally natural, out of sync with the casual, talky, daily quality of the piece:

> And mud, day after day,
> mud like a ritual,
> and the baby on the platter,
> cooked but still human,
> cooked also with little maggots,
> sewn onto it maybe by somebody's mother,
> the damn bitch!
>
> Even so,
> I kept right on going on
> a sort of human statement,
> lugging myself as if
> I were a sawed-off body
> in the trunk, the steamer trunk. (167, ll. 12–24)

As Abigail Child has written of melodrama, it "throws a wrench into rational analysis that seeks to authorize its status outside the context of desire and distortion. . . . [It] equals the theatricalizing gesture itself, framing a world of unspoken relations, exhibitor of the repressed."[79] Sexton's "Live" seems similarly disruptive, the kind of "mad poem" of Sexton's that

Bishop said she admired. It is not a poem we can straighten out by reading it expressively as "about" or as a mimesis of madness, however; it is "mad" or errant in that surplus of jarring imagery and sudden affect, which sees it stray from conventional views of what belonged on the lyric stage. Sexton's challenge, that is, is to the expected balance of artlessness and control—the twentieth century's version of poetic decorum.[80]

Though this choice gets read expressively and as sign of personal dissolution (what made Lowell wonder if quotation marks would have rendered these poems fascinating), we can think historically about Sexton's choice to diminish the certainty of the text's interpretive destiny. The late 1960s see a number of poetic movements inclining away from New Critical standards. Indeed, the possibility that Lowell himself imagines New Critical processes working in so flippant a manner on Sexton's failed poems seems a sign of the culture's drift away from the premises subtending New Critical hermeneutics. Much of Frank O'Hara's work makes a fine example of this shift, and his 1959 poetics essay "Personism" figures the moribund Eliotic poem as an anxious mother trying to force-feed her children meaning, a note to a critic who reduces his poem's "confusion" to O'Hara's confusion while writing.[81] Sexton's "The Silence" (1972) alludes to a similar refusal of controlled craft geared toward the production of useful poems, figuring a writer-subject "filling the room / with the words from [her] pen. / Words leak out of it like a miscarriage" (*CP*, 318–319). In the eyes of Sexton's critics, miscarried writing was an aberration or malfunction of a process thought to be both exemplary and "natural" and confirmed at last by the expert critic's reception (delivery) of the poem. Yet even Sexton's earliest, most controlled writing sought release from that interpretive logic.

ALL GOD'S CHILDREN NEED RADIOS

As the early poem "The Reading" and the late prose fable "The Letting Down of the Hair" suggest, over the whole of Sexton's career, she produced work that demystifies the identification of writing with speech and person (and textual conditions with the author's psychology), an association she both courted and resisted, ever aware of celebrity culture. This might read as a bit of a contradiction: Sexton courted the public eye in performances that drew very much on the "reality trope" common to midcentury work, especially that identified as Confessional. That is, Sexton's actual performances tended to suggest her desire to erode the distance between written work and lived life. As David Haven Blake puts it in his study of the Confessional's complicity with twentieth-century celebrity and consumer culture, though it "occurred on an overtly public stage, the confessional style helped foster an illusion of intimacy among the reading public." Blake's point is to show us how the Confessional is in fact "immersed in the commercial world it purported to resist" and to view confession "as a staple of the celebrity industry, a speech act employed to foster the illusion that fans have glimpsed the paradox of a publicly legitimate but authentically private self."[82]

But as this chapter has tried to show, and as Susan Rosenbaum argues, this paradox—of what Blake calls a "publicly legitimate but authentically private self," a "fusion of intimacy and publicity"—is not just symptomatic of twentieth-century culture and the "modern era of advertising," as he supposes.[83] These also describe the paradox that Mill's work presented to mid-nineteenth-century audiences: with the image of lyric as ideally private utterances nevertheless printed on hot-pressed paper and sold at bookshops. This is a longstanding paradox concerning poetry's status and place in a verse market and culture. We can read Sexton's bold performance of that paradox both as symptomatic of the modern era of advertising and yet also as an explosion of the mid-twentieth-century critical demotion of it. Then it might seem less surprising that, at one and the same time, Sexton was imagining writing in terms that seem very nearly Barthesian, even as she maintained conventions of autobiographical lyric common to her moment.

Sexton's 1973 prose writing *All God's Children Need Radios,* first published in *Ms.* magazine under the title "A Small Journal," highlights this mixed quality of her work.[84] Consisting of fifteen short prose blocks, all individually titled and dated—from November 6, 1971, to January 1, 1972—it reads, on the one hand, as realistic and narrative. Read as a journal, as *Ms.* magazine would have had us do, several entries begin by locating us in a real place ("'O Lord,' they said last night on TV") or in a realistic narrative locale (the entry for November 25 refers us to "the turkey" and Thanksgiving), gesturing to "setting" (another interpretive field emphasized in college explication). Furthermore, entries cross-reference in small details (roses received as a gift in the first entry are referenced in the fourth), and named characters reappear throughout the work ("Sweeney" and "Mother," most forcefully). In this, the piece accords with its supposed "journal"-like quality.

On the other hand, thwarting the coherent speaker model, entries function more like snippets of language that one might channel through a radio, because they are not particularly "lyric" and are more everyday. The effect is of a mixed genre piece: though in reprints the piece tends to be framed as a fiction, its resistance to generic categorization is important, which Sexton highlighted by referring to the entries this way: "prose poems that I call stories."[85] In the early 1970s, Sexton would have been acutely aware that her readers were hungry for a "real" picture of her "real life" in journal form ("The Letting Down of the Hair" is also from this period), so the piece's working with and against the modern reader's desire to peer through lyric or memoir into intimate details of its celebrity author's life is key. In fact, by emphasizing mediation of voice with the figure of the radio, even the title seems to address the problem of anthropomorphism and the lyric.

The poem resists organizing (true of much of Sexton's work) around an expressive voice or a coherent lyric "now" that would encourage our identification with a speaker, even though, at its start, it draws on a comically expected notion of a lyric situation, addressed to an unspecified "you" who has sent roses. The poem quickly makes us feel privy to a drama in which we are not included: "Thank you for the red roses. They were lovely. Listen, Skeezix, I know you didn't give them to me, but I like to pretend you did because, as you know, when you give me something my heart faints on the pillow" (NE, 23). The "journal" is already swerving out of its proper generic category: we are voyeurs/hearers not of a private soliloquy but of an exchange that hovers between "overheard" address ("Listen" seems almost an ironic command here) and epistle (perhaps a thank-you note). Antilyric and antipoetic, the entry also challenges our sense of where to locate ourselves in relation to the piece: who are we in this economy of speaker and addressee; what is "real" in this journal, and what is not?

Furthermore, like other serial poems of this period (notably, those in Words for Dr. Y [1978]), All God's Children foregrounds what Barthes called—in his famous "Death of the Author" essay from 1967, published in English just a few years before All God's Children was written—the social "tissue of quotations" from which writing comes and that mediates any act of self-projection or lyric identification.[86] The section titled "Some Things around My Desk," which would seem to promise just the kind of autobiographical information that a fan eager to know the "real" Anne Sexton might want from a poet's "journal," highlights the mediations of her work by other texts, not the kind of details that would particularize her as an author. The entry pokes fun at the idea that writing bespeaks its author's presence or "voice": "If you put your ear close to a book, you can hear it talking. A tin voice, very small, somewhat like a puppet, asexual. Yet all at once? Over my head JOHN BROWN'S BODY is dictating to EROTIC POETRY. And so forth" (*NE*, 24). If writing speaks, what will shut it up? Sexton humorously literalizes the confusion of writing with person in such exaggerated anthropomorphisms, enumerating various quotations—pointedly "anonymous"—that have been "Scotch-taped up" over the desk (24). These quotations are italicized (that is, notably, not in quotation marks), and most figure writing as distinct, even radically separate, from the author's self or body. The first quotation, *"Poets and pigs are not appreciated until they are dead"* (24), grossly confuses the increased value of the pig's body (as food) after death with the appreciation (and increased value) of the author's corpus after death. In the second quotation—*"The more I write, the more the silence seems to be eating away at me"* (24; a quotation Sexton elsewhere credits to C. K. Williams)—writing is not only not identical to author's voice or author's person, but it in fact effects self-erasure and silencing. The selection continues, "And here is Pushkin, not quite anonymous: *And reading my own life with loathing, I tremble and curse*" (24); this quote is from Pushkin's "Remembrance" (1828), a figure that emphasizes the alien quality of text for the self who wrote it.[87] Sexton's passage goes on, "And: *Unhappiness is more beautiful when seen through a window than from within*. And so forth" (24). That Sexton leaves it ambiguous as to whether the second quotation is also Pushkin's (it is in fact from the Japanese novelist Yukio Mishima) seems in keeping with the deemphasis in the section on authorship as such.[88]

I wish to emphasize that what is "around" Sexton's desk is, finally, treated as text—comically garrulous but pointedly "anonymous"—a figure that emphasizes "voice" to be publicly constructed, and personal writing, derivative, not original. If garrulous here, writing and authorship are not heroic. It is worth quoting the rest of the entry in full, for its subtle play, often through the figure of address, with the problem of what writing has to do with the person:

Sweeney's telegram is also up there. *You are lucky,* he cables. Are you jealous? No, you are reading the Town Report, frequently you read something aloud and it almost mixes up my meditations. Now you're looking at the trout. Doomed. My mother's picture is on the right up above the desk. When that picture was taken, she too was doomed. You read aloud: *Forty-five dog bites in town.* Not us. Our dog bites frogs only. *Five runaways and five stubborn children.* Children stubborn but not reported. The phone, at my back and a little to the right, sits like a General (German) (SS). It holds the voices that I love as well as strangers, a platoon of beggars asking me to dress their wounds. The trout are getting peppier. My mother seems to be looking at them. Speaking of the phone, yesterday Sweeney called from Australia to wish me a happy birthday. (Wrong day. I'm November ninth.) I put my books on the line and they said, "Move along, Buster." And why not? All things made lovely are doomed. *Two cases of chancres,* you read. (24–25)

The shift from Sweeney's telegram address *("You are lucky")* to the ambiguously addressed and typographically different "Are you jealous?" confuses "you" with "you," along with our sense of whom the poem addresses. We are further confused by the fact that, as the passage continues, the second "you" is described as in the process of reading. After all, *we* are, I am, you are reading; before the sentence continues to identify what is being read (the "Town Report"), we—I—am put into passing identity with that lucky "you" and then that jealous "you." The passage acknowledges the pronominal confusion it courts when it continues, in a run-on sentence that renders agency confusing, "frequently you read something aloud" and admits, "it almost mixes up my meditations" (25).

Whose meditations are whose here? Sexton's figure performs a humorous complication of Eliot's third, "meditative" voice in *The Three Voices of Poetry*—"the poet talking to himself—or to nobody."[89] It suggests that, even if taken in a "lyric" spirit (that is, as though produced without thought of a particular audience), a poet's meditations nevertheless cannot be isolated; they will involve what is "around [her] desk" and also the interpretive lenses of readings and interpretations of them. If the "you" reading aloud reads Sexton's text (as I am reading it now), "her" meditations are quite literally "mixe[d] up." Indeed, this mixing up (a gesture to intersubjectivity and the interplay of possible readings) might almost be taken as an *ars poetica* for the whole text, with its insistent confusion of text with author and its comic exaggeration of the idea that texts perform disembodied "talking," as well as its tendency to confuse me (the text's reader) with the underspecified figure of an implied listener ("you") in its moments of underspecified address.

The claim that it is by reading aloud that "you" mix up "my" meditations cites and foregrounds the species of subjective identification emphasized by normative conventions of meditative lyric reading, particularly the Vendlerian idea that lyric is private speech rendered as a script for the reader's voice. In all, this section reminds of what many twentieth-century readings of Mill repress—the scene of the writer's desk and poetic culture, whose public awareness exceeds the scene of seclusion that Mill could (albeit shakily) entertain as a possibility. The piece as a whole thus directs itself away from a voice-centered model of poetic originality or personal expressive "lyric" confessionalism and toward a scene of intertextual writing.

One might here counterargue with reference to the fact that the section titled "Mother's Radio" emphasizes a potential psychology driving the whole piece, for here, the dying "mother" is figured in such a way as to resonate symbolically with the aforementioned trout as a fish "under water, her gills pumping, her brain numb" (26). This symbolic matrix is what Helen Vendler's "Freudian lyric" reading would ask us to find ("Freudian lyric" serving as Vendler's alternative term to "Confessional")—a text that seeds psychological details that would allow a reader's "analysis" to resolve the poem into a symbolic study of a speaker's psychology, an operation (analysis by the poet for the reader) without which (for Vendler) there is "no poem."[90] However, at the same time, the section emphasizes proxies that mediate for real people: "Mother's radio" is a figure for the mother and also, somewhat confusingly, the name given to two different radios, as well as the section as a whole. Both radios and the title of the section are always in italics; the effect is a confusion of "mother," "radio," and writing.

This confusion reiterates the piece's tendency to rescind its offer of the "real" Sexton, reading neither as realistic details representing madness nor as indices of an expressive aesthetic. A section titled "Dog" similarly recalls Gertrude Stein's "The question of identity: a Play" (1936), and anticipates aspects of Lyn Hejinian's impersonal personal autobiography, *My Life* (1980), by foregrounding overhearing as a production of meaning (rather than its revelation):

"O Lord," they said last night on TV, "the sea is so mighty and my dog is so small." I *heard* dog. You say, they said *boat* and not *dog* and further *dog* would have no meaning. But it does mean. . . . Dog stands for me and the new puppy, Daisy. I wouldn't have kept her if we hadn't named her Daisy. (You brought me daisies yesterday, not roses, daisies. A proper flower. It outlives any other in its little vessel of water. You must have given them to me! If you didn't give them to me, who did?) (29)

"But it does mean" may be said by "you" or "I," producing muddled ground between us, thus highlighting the identificatory urge to make the text "stand for" Sexton. Indeed, the section's later move to construct a highly idiosyncratic reading of the sentence "O Lord, the sea is so mighty and my dog is so small" recalls what Paul De Man, in "Anthropomorphism and Trope in the Lyric," calls a "hermeneutical, fallacious lyrical reading of the unintelligible":[91]

"My dog is so small" means that even the two of us will be stamped under. . . . The sea is a mother, larger than Asia, both lowering their large breasts onto the coastline. Thus we ride on her praying for good moods. . . . She is mighty, oh Lord, but I wish my little puppy, Daisy, remain a child.

Too complicated, eh?

Just a thought in passing, just something about a lady and her dog, setting forth as they do, on a new life. (29)

At just the moment that the explanation of what the sentence might "mean" becomes overtly psychologized and theologized, linked to the demise of "Mother" in the piece, the discourse shifts, by virtue of an exaggerated address, it seems, to a reader—"Too complicated, eh?"—refusing depth-psychology and complicating our sense of whether the personal grounds this project.

In this refusal, "Dog" flags the expectation for writing to provide the semantic means to its own interpretive closure by failing to satisfy it. Asking the authoritative "you" to believe what the nonsense phrase "does mean," it nevertheless offers a meaning that is comically idiosyncratic, even nonsensical, and indicative of defensive projection. The section's last sentence performs this unhanding of interpretation by re-presenting the reading of the television phrase as "just something about a lady and her dog"—not a portrait of a speaker longing to interpret the world as about her but a thought and text that plays and "passes" (29). The "I" initially so attached to her reading of the sentence "The sea is so mighty and my dog is so small" now becomes "a lady" and "Daisy," "her dog." All that went before now reads as cited material, and Sexton exposes the citational, performed quality of the supposed "voice" of the diarylike journal entry.

Such gestures free the section (and perhaps the whole poem) from the Freudian interpretive logic that Vendler takes as definitive of postwar lyric and always implicitly the province of "lyric." For Vendler, "the experience of Freudian therapy generated new formal subgenres of lyric" and "new formal procedures for shaping it," an argument that puts a new historical-psychological twist on New Critical modes of lyric reading but in effect asserts that poems should be read (true to New Critical pedagogy) as dramas revelatory of their subjects' (if not their authors') depth-psychologies.[92] Vendler encourages us to read aspects of a poem as a sign "of something repressed, not consciously available," and as the author's "aesthetic means to enact its analysis."[93]

ANTILYRIC READING

I would like to linger on "the lyric" understood as a genre defined, since the mid-twentieth century, by its supposed openness to interpretive analysis. Interpretability is what many *critiques* of "lyric," made especially by those who align themselves with American avant-gardes and Language writing, identify as lyric's most shameful aspect, one often tacitly or explicitly identified with the Confessional. Craig Dworkin describes the 1970s avant-garde as "explicitly positioning itself against the increasingly canonical poetics of those 'confessional' writers who had come to prominence in the previous decade," and one primary feature of the Confessional's bad legacy, at least according to that generation of avant-gardes, is the processing of experience into closural poems.[94] Here we should remember that the aforementioned group manifesto by Language writers identifies the canonical voice poem as one in which experience is "worked-over" and "specifics of experience dissolve into the pseudo-intimacy of an overarching authorial 'voice,'" an aesthetic tendency they relate, "genetically" to the "confessional voice poem."[95] One of Lyn Hejinian's most famous poetics essays, "The Rejection of Closure" (1983), argues against the "closed text," which it defines as "one in which all the elements of the work are directed toward a single reading of it. Each element confirms that reading and delivers the text from any lurking ambiguity."[96] In a preface written for the essay's reprinting in *The Language of Inquiry* (2000), Hejinian offers as her example of a "negative model" of the "closed text" something that sounds very much like what many people associate with Confessionalism: "the coercive, epiphanic mode in some contemporary lyric poetry, . . . with its smug pretension to universality and its tendency to cast the poet as guardian to Truth."[97] Telling, too, is her depiction of "confession" in the essay "Language and 'Paradise'" (1984), as "a strange form of aestheticization" motivated "by the desire to know but also a desire to make known," a desire that attempts to be fulfilled by the confessional subject's "reach[ing] across events to another person and attempt[ing] to introduce a witness" who will become "a first and original as well as complete knower of the narrative" desired.[98]

We do not have to look very far to find critical corroboration of the association of contemporary lyric with smug and carefully crafted or "coercive" epiphany and with a "closed," as in too readily interpretable, quality.[99] And Sexton's work, which has been received as quintessentially "personal," expressive, and Confessional lyric, is not usually credited with waging critique against or resistance to that mode. To the contrary, the chief features supposed to define her Confessional lyrics—authentic voice and expression—tend to be those against which antilyric statements are made. Charles Bernstein, perhaps (along with Hejinian) one of the most noted of poets and theorists associated with Language writing, presents the link between speaker, "voice," and the degrading interpretability that Hejinian calls "closure" as quite clearly an issue of interpretation when he offers, in his poetic essay "Stray Straws and Straw Men," that

> there is the assumption that poetry matures in the location of "one's own voice," which as often as not is no more than a consistency of style & presentation. "The voice of the poet" is an easy way of contextualizing poetry so that it can be more readily understood (indiscriminately plugged into) as listening to someone talk in their distinctive manner (i.e., listen for the person beyond or underneath the poem); but this theatricalization does not necessarily do the individual poem any service & has the tendency to reduce the body of a poet's work to little more than personality.[100]

"Readily understood" and "indiscriminately plugged into" as "talk" suggest the interpretability often ascribed to "lyric" (by antilyric opinion), a reduction (or grotesquing) of Brower's methodological conditions for reading lyric. That is, though expert interpretation and a "fixed" tone were chief critical ideals for Brower, his work insisted that poetic analysis for tone and attitude could be achieved only with great labor. It would be a gross reduction (and in some cases a simple error) to assume that all those critics who were associated with New Criticism advocated poems that produced a mindless receptivity in their reader, without any linguistic or conceptual interference expected. Yet ease of interpretability has become one the most frequently sounded contemporary charges made against "lyric" (indeed a way of defining "bad"—New Critical, mainstream, Confessional, Romantic—lyric), or against expectations about lyric interpretation, making these charges surely a "reaction formation," as Jackson argues, to the dominance of (a reduced version) of New Criticism and a "lyric" ideal "that could exist only in theory."[101]

In a move related to this confusion of poems with interpretive norms, "lyric" gets associated with "clarity," as in Rae Armantrout's identification of antilyric's liberatory potential with the refusal of clarity as a compositional goal. That Armantrout takes to task "feminist critics . . . [who nevertheless] continue to valorize the poem dominated by a single image or trope and a trustworthy (authoritative) narrational voice," singling out Ostriker's admiration for Bishop's "usual tone of trustworthy casualness," again suggests to me that neither critic has fully imagined the extent of Bishop's experiments with rhetoric or her suspicion of a "tradition of likenesses." In Armantrout's reading of a Sharon Olds poem, "The Only Girl at the Boys' Party," she critiques its "readability," which she identifies with an "imperialism" of "voice," a view that resembles Hejinian's sense of the "coercive[ness]" of the epiphanic contemporary lyric. Armantrout argues, "When Olds claims to know what is in her daughter's mind [a surprisingly literal reading of the poem] . . . I am repelled as by a presumptuous intrusion." Forgoing the possibility that the poem is not a record of Olds's voice and that projection and fantasy are the poem's subject (though I am not necessarily claiming that they are), Armantrout sums up her argument against the supposed clarity of Olds's poem by arguing, "Only information tailored to the controlling code is admissible; no second thoughts or outside voices are allowed. Whether such a poem is clear depends upon what one means by clarity. Certainly it is quite readable." Language writing, by contrast, works like "contrapuntal systems in which conflicting forces and voices (inner and outer) are allowed to work."[102]

We can detect just a bit of the shaming charge of almost neurotic attachment to control attributed to the Confessional and to the "lyric"
here—"allowed," for instance, implies that the Olds poem has, in discipli-
narian mode, repressed conflict and dissent and controlled the reader's
response. Armantrout closes with several suggestive questions that inform
much Language-oriented writing: "What is the relation of readability to
convention? How might conventions of legibility enforce social codes?"[103]
Armantrout's interrogative mode indicates her desire to stay open, but
she also already has an answer: conventions of readability reiterate and
affirm conservative politics. For this clarity of legibility, of being "closed"
in Hejinian's terms, is what most avant-garde-inclined critics of voice
"lyric" (understood as Romantic, or confessional) would identify as its
shameful complicity with authoritarian forms of power and lack of critical potential—the chief charge against it and the reason lyric is targeted
for critique, or is outright rejected, and cast as antitype.

Though most of these arguments originate in conversations that we can
date to the late 1970s and early 1980s, one earlier key moment in the mis-
trust of confessional lyric as "coercive" in its "epiphanic," "legible" mode
occurs in the mid-1960s, when the New Critical agenda had taken firm
hold in the university but before Language had formed as a distinct literary movement. In 1965, Frank O'Hara expresses his fatigue with and mis-
trust of the wildly influential "Skunk Hour" of Robert Lowell: "I don't
think that anyone has to get themselves to go and watch lovers in a park-
ing lot necking in order to write a poem, and I don't see why it's admirable
if they feel guilty about it. They should feel guilty. Why are they snoop-
ing? What's so wonderful about a Peeping Tom?"[104] As Anne Hartman
glosses it, what O'Hara critiques in Lowell's "confessional mode" is its
"spurious claims to sincerity and cathartic release from a guilt that is in
fact its precondition."[105] This "mode" that O'Hara helps Hartman identify,
in which interpretable material is (ostensibly) seeded in a text in such a
way as to seem spontaneous and unwitting, very much resembles the
terms (if not the spirit) of Vendler's redescription of Confessional work as
"Freudian lyric." Again, for Vendler such lyric structures itself to promote
its own analysis: "It . . . traces guilt or madness to its origin in family history, or to its origins in a pathological scrupulosity, or to a repression of
one side of the self; it then finds aesthetic means to enact its analysis, and
can go no further." Freudian lyrics succeed by rescuing the "demons of
the given" (real facts of personal breakdown) with the "seraphs of the

made," by which I think she means artful arrangement leading to the interpretive "analysis" without which, for Vendler, "there is no poem."[106] With
the poet's preseeding of the terms by which a reader (a critic? an analyst?)
can analyze a subject's psychology, the Vendlerian Freudian lyric entails
just that kind of epiphanic solution that Armantrout calls "clarity," that
Bernstein finds "reduc[tive]," that Hejinian calls "smug," and that O'Hara
(first) dismissed as a contrivance.[107]

If discursive trends in literary history have led us to too easily group
Sexton's work with the Freudian lyric that Vendler admires and the American poetic avant-garde reviles, it does a disservice to quite a lot of Sexton's
work, as well as to our sense of American literary history. Though Sexton's
poems are, without doubt, far more narrative and, at least on their surface, more "speaker"-driven than Language-centered writing, I do not believe her work fits the bill of the preseeded, clear text that its Confessional
reputation foists on it. Indeed, I have supposed, to the contrary, that what
disturbed reviewers about her work throughout her career involved its resistance to the lyric-reading premise that writing is "something that is to
be interpreted," as Jerome McGann puts it.[108]

Could we consider the antilyric strategies of some Language-centered
practices and Sexton's exaggerated performances of lyric norms as being
more continuous than conventions of lyric reading have allowed us to see?
Are readability and clarity in fact the same thing? Like Armantrout, I
know my answers: both avant-garde rejections of "Confessional" and the
mainstream rejections of Sexton have failed to note their investment in an
interpretive mode of reading (lyric reading) that renders syntactically cohesive works more *clear*—or less strange—than they perhaps need, or
ought, be made. Once again, our status and function as critics is very much
at issue in supposing this, as John Ashbery understood in 1968 when he
noted, in a review of Ted Berrigan's *Sonnets* (which the *New York Times*
chose not to publish) that the "polyphonic style" of Berrigan's poems and
of the New York School is "one of [their] real achievements" and one that
"renders criticism obsolete."[109]

I am tempted to think that Ashbery knew how incendiary and challenging such a claim (and such poems) could be: what is there to do with
a short poem that can exist (and even be admired as "achieved") in spite
of its failure to invite the "analysis" that Vendler and others take to be
fundamental to the lyric? The avant-garde has been eager to part with interpretable texts in the writing of "open" texts, but it has been slower to

part with the reading strategies that lyricize and in effect "close" other kinds of poems.[110] Common critical wisdom assumes that choices made in poems such as Berrigan's, such as encouraging "polyphony" by "breaking up the traditional structure of poems," as Ashbery puts it, and deauthorizing a speaking subject, produce the polyphony and the obviation of analysis that Ashbery flags.[111] However, even many of Sexton's poems that do not employ those techniques can raise questions about where, in fact, "analysis" resides: Does a writer produce it? Does the critic produce it? "For John, Who Begs Me Not to Enquire Further," for instance, invites our dwelling on a queasy boundary between the legible and illegible, clarity and obscurity, without relying on radical syntactic disruption or an undoing of the "I" to do it (CP, 34). This has been downplayed by readings—paradoxically, even those made in service of less biographically focused readings of Sexton—that focus on the biographical backgrounds of the poem (particularly, those in the letter from Sexton's mentor about her work). It is not that the biographical background is not there: it is verifiably "true" that Sexton's poem addresses Holmes and reprises exact phrases from Holmes's letter.[112] But what of the poem read outside the context of the Holmes letter, either by first-time or nonscholarly readers?

This question is well worth asking, for even if "For John" is clearer or more "legible" than a Berrigan sonnet, it resists the ready interpretability charged to lyric. Even with biography in hand, and even as the poem unfolds, underspecified referents obscure what the poem is "about," as though (in a way that reminds me of what Perloff argues of O'Hara's poems and "Personism") we are overhearing one half of an intimate telephone conversation for which we lack sufficient context[113] The poem's complex opening sentence unfolds over nine lines, beginning,

> Not that it was beautiful,
> but that, in the end, there was
> a certain sense of order there;
> something worth learning
> in that narrow diary of my mind,
> in the commonplaces of the asylum. (CP, 34)

We are left quite unsure, through the sentence and the poem, what "it" is. Does "there" refer to "the narrow diary of my mind" or "the commonplaces of the asylum" (both grammatically plausible)?[114] Given "John's" urgent refusal of enquiry, questions, and their perhaps unwanted intrusive nature, are foregrounded.

As with many O'Hara poems, the would-be interpreter's disrupted access to this material results from the poem's structure of address, not the thwarting of syntax or marked elliptical tendencies (as we might find in much Language-centered writing): we are made privy to a discussion whose backstory Sexton could not have expected others to know. Though the poem elicits our interest in its context (literally, it is a private address made in public, as we expect of lyric), the address is not made "for" a universalized "ourselves," as Mill's nineteenth-century view of lyric would dictate. This, in fact, was Holmes's concern about Sexton's poems, as expressed in his letter (and here I go slipping into biographical reading, too): "but what is [your poetry] for somebody else?" As Sexton knew, her refusal to speak "for" others had made her poems seem shameful to Holmes, to whom she wrote in a letter of response on January 30, 1961, "In the long pull, John, where you might be proud of me, you are ashamed of me" (*Letters,* 119). But Holmes errs in assuming that his own identification with the piece will match everyone's; in fact, the poem performs a veering away from such an identificatory model of lyric reading by foregrounding the sound of imploring speech, only to insistently withhold the context that would render it meaningful. We have almost no access to the confession and argument that plays out on the page.

The longer conceit (fifteen lines) that extends the address we overhear in fact deflects both an anthropomorphic reading and a closural interpretation. It begins and ends with a slightly surreal image of the poet's head as a sort of fishbowl:

> I tapped my own head;
> it was a glass, an inverted bowl.
> It is a small thing
> to rage in your own bowl.
> At first it was private.
> Then it was more than myself;
> it was you, or your house
> or your kitchen.
> And if you turn away
> because there is no lesson here
> I will hold my awkward bowl,

with all its cracked stars shining
like a complicated lie,
and fasten a new skin around it
as if I were dressing an orange
or a strange sun. (*CP*, 34, ll. 17–32)

Resisting the contract for poems to clarify a subject to a reader, the poem proceeds by way of a remarkably difficult series of pronoun shifts and images that are vague and strange in part because they keep turning people (or is it emotions?) into spaces and things: "myself" becomes "you" becomes "your house / or your kitchen"; "I" becomes "you," who turns away, readmitting an "I" described by its thinglike ability to "hold" "my" (once) head, now an "awkward bowl." Such identity shifts and depersonifications contribute to the lines' resistance to any single reading and unsettle the image of the "speaker" it presents.

The refusal of clarity and mimesis is produced by something that closely (perhaps uncomfortably) resembles "bad," as in imprecise, writing. Ambiguities border on downright vagueness: Is it the way that stars shine that makes them a "complicated lie"? Is it that they are cracked *and* shining? And what, most importantly, does this gesture hope to achieve "for John"? To keep his attention? To repel him, creating more distance between them? It is not at all clear. Orange, skin, sunlight, and glass (three images we are offered for the "it" that will be refashioned for John in consequence of his "turn away") do not fall into the clear dictional or metaphorical pattern that Armantrout disparages in mainstream writing. And then "dressing" an orange is hard to imagine: is the skin of the orange already off? Is this clothing—or salad dressing?—applied to fruit (what is inside the orange peel) or to skin (the orange peel itself)? Given that bowl, skin, oranges, and sun might metonymically link to "face" (what a model of lyric reading would have us expect to see as the "fruit" (person?) of the labor of interpretation, the thing reflected or seen through a glass darkly), the effect is rather a sense of endless masking and obfuscation. The vagueness of the following lines is difficult not to notice: "There ought to be something special / for someone / in this kind of hope" (35). The near repetition of unspecified "something" and "someone" makes it clear that the poem refuses the clarity of anthropomorphic identification and instead holds out its something only *in potentia* and in the least predictive and universalizing terms. Language seems ever to be getting in the way:

What kind of "hope" is this? How is dressing an orange or a "strange sun" a "kind of hope"? And so on.

The obscure poem and its paratext of biographical readings thus raise important questions about how, on what terms, readers identify (with) poems, their speaking subjects, and their authors. Though the early Language critique of the "voice" poem implicitly charges "I"-centered, "confessional," and "workshop" poems (different ways of identifying what was widely understood to be the paragon of "lyric" of "official verse culture" of the 1970s and 1980s) with producing such acts of identification—with assuming and endorsing an overly simplistic model of communication coincident with the worst of consumer capitalism—"For John" asks us to think again: it in fact resists Holmes and satisfies Armantrout's desire for a subtler, less consumable, more multivocal poem by testing our desire to identify (with) it.[115]

That it does so raises the issue of what gets valued, in contemporary poetics cultures, as "poetic" difficulty, which Andrew Osborn, in his entry on "difficulty" in *The Princeton Encyclopedia of Poetry and Poetics,* defines as "resistance to swift and confident interpretation." Osborn is shrewd to note that, though "difficulty" is "conventionally attributed to poems themselves," in fact, it more "accurately denotes an interpretive experience in affective terms," a point that highlights the ineluctable anthropomorphics that attend lyric readings.[116] The kinds of "tactical" and "ontological" difficulties (breaches of the contract for a writer to communicate with readers) that many lyric readers of the midcentury valued in radical modernist works—especially forms of parataxis and ellipsis—were those that could be brought, nevertheless, into legible order by the exacting critic, which suggests the part that analysis plays in defining, and resolving, the terms of what is difficult. It is the opening to resolve its difficulties that Sexton's work could be said to resist; Sexton's project might be thought to align in this sense with what Vernon Shetley has argued about John Ashbery's particular form of "difficulty"—a forgoing of the "conventions . . . generated by the academic appropriation of modernism" and the decision "not to produce within the [interpretive] paradigms offered by the New Criticism."[117]

This is to say that the final figure in "For John" emphasizes "the presence and character of reading codes," as McGann has written of Charles Bernstein's work, but in ways that we are not used to looking for in Confessional work.[118] The poem's closing sounds like a revelation or an epiphany but shows us little more than our expectation for one meaning to emerge (like a face we long to see emerge from behind a veil) and a universal interpretive key by which to read the rest:

> although your fear is anyone's fear,
> like an invisible veil between us all . . .
> and sometimes in private,
> my kitchen, your kitchen,
> my face, your face. (*CP*, 35, ll. 40–44)

Though many critics have read these lines and the poem in general as a defense of the Confessional and its potential uses to others or, as Gill does, a representation of how confession works ("a moment of crisis in the subject's sense of self . . . laid bare for contemplation by both speaker and reader"), I wish to emphasize again the poem's utter resistance to specifying its contents.[119] Indeed, we reach a far point of unspecificity in these closing lines. The figure of a "veil" that is somehow "between us all" emphasizes the poem's dismanagement of a reading code in which surface gives way to depth, for something "invisible" and "between us all" is quite *unlike* a veil. Veils typically separate one thing from another (they establish the binaries of inside and outside, private face and public world) and thus usually involve things understood in binary relation of surface and depth. That this veil is positioned "between us all" makes it more like air—something omnipresent but invisible, whose presence (and power) we take for granted or have neglected to notice. Because we do not know what "it" or "something" are, the "fear" they provoke, belonging not to "everyone" (the universal) but to "anyone" (the anonymous, each in his or her own person) is difficult to imagine:

> This is something [what is?] I would never find
> in a lovelier place, my dear,
> although your fear is anyone's fear,
> like an invisible veil between us all . . . (ll. 38–41)

Here I can, at last, call on this chapter's epigraph from Silliman, "if language is conceived as a medium . . . it is a medium in the sense of a membrane, as capable of blocking the real as of letting it in."[120] Language functions like a veil if we render it more visible, and Sexton both does and does not do that here. The poem seems at first like "absorptive" text, but "For John" drifts off into an ellipsis at this point, gesturing to the materiality of language, a reminder that what is "between us all" most of the time is language. Language is not abstract but social; and the uses of poems are context specific, given that poems are between people. Sometimes, context enables a piece of writing to feel like "anyone's," open to projective identification. And it is that context specificity that can make a poem that is quite ambiguous, abstract, and impersonal for most readers nevertheless read to one's writing teacher as scandalous and "too private" for all. Rather than defending a particular kind of poem or poetics for all, Sexton's poem offers a performance that sounds like self-revelatory talk and imploring speech, all the while insisting on how little has been said.[121]

What the poem foregrounds is the fact that, even when forged in private, thoughts about myself are not only about myself: not simply about "you" or "me," they participate in larger discursive problems and are thus "something" for "someone." If that "something" is not originated or fixed by the poet, neither will every recipient experience "it" the same way: "And if I tried / to give you something else," the poem warns, "you would not know." Though the sentence does not end there, the half meaning—which raises the specter of a message that will fail to reach its intended interpretive fulfillment—has special significance, for Sexton often complained about her critics' tendency to insist on identifying her poems with her self.[122]

THE BLEATING RADIO AND THE CONFESSIONAL SUBJECT

My aim in this chapter has been to prize Sexton's work from the grip that the term "Confessional" has on it. Avant-garde poetics have influenced my sense of how to read contemporary poems, yet I can see that one lasting, unfortunate legacy of antilyric discourse has been the preservation of the very terms—Confessional, lyric, voice—that new reading and writing practices sought to reform, problematize, and critique. Though the anti-ideals of "the voice poem," "the workshop poem," and "the Confessional" are vivid and oppressive, one wonders if they ever are—or were—actually written. Discovering how little of Sexton fits the "Confessionalism" with which she has become identified has led me to wonder whether such a quintessential Confessional poem has ever existed. The critical tendency has been to displace the shame of the Confessional "lyric" onto some lesser, inferior, or "bad" Confessional. But who, what poem, is the quintessential Confessional? Now that some writers affiliated with Language have taken in Sylvia Plath, to whom should we turn as the "real" Confessional?[123] Perhaps Snodgrass, since he is read even less than Sexton?

As discussed earlier, O'Hara and later Vendler have made it easy to take Lowell's "Skunk Hour" as definitive of the Freudian analytic mode. I find the claim convincing, especially given the care with which *Life Studies* lays the interpretive path by which to read this last poem as culminating the book-long "study" of the origins and outcomes of "Lowell's" mental breakdown. But even "Skunk Hour" can be read as problematizing the figure of voice and the fulfillments of voice as personality on which Lowell and his critics so clearly relied.

The poem (you may know) carefully stages an abrupt shift after four stanzas of rather unselfconscious present-tense narrative description to a narrative past that, true to O'Hara's reading, feels like a rather self-conscious setup for a lyric, confessional moment to occur:

> One dark night,
> my Tudor Ford climbed the hill's skull;
> I watched for love-cars. Lights turned down,
> they lay together, hull to hull,
> where the graveyard shelves on the town. . . .
> My mind's not right.[124]

Why does the poem bother to use an ellipsis in this way? Read lyrically and because it precedes the poem's shift from past-tense narration into a self-realizing, expressive claim, it indicates an elapse of time between the dark description and the recognition (psycho- or literary analysis style) that the mind generating it is not quite "right." It is as a dramatic cue—a note in a script suggesting the "beats" or timing of how this act of mind, checked by the light of self-scrutiny, should be performed. But in the very next stanza, an ellipsis now occurs within quotation marks, a visual repetition with a difference that draws Lowell's personal cri de coeur ("my mind's not right") into analogy with to the "voice" of a car radio, sheeplike in its mechanical bleating out of the popular blues and folk song "Careless Love":

> > they lay together, hull to hull,
> > where the graveyard shelves on the town. . . .
> > My mind's not right.
> > A car radio bleats,

"Love, O careless Love. . . ." I hear
my ill-spirit sob in each blood cell,
as if my hand were at its throat. . . .
I myself am hell;
nobody's here— (95)

What is the ellipsis within the quoted song title telling us, and is it the same thing as those that precede and follow it (which are not in quotation marks), ostensibly "spoken" lines? That Lowell turns us to an overheard radio, and one that mediates a lyric *cri de coeur* that is mechanically reproduced, troubles the figure of lyric as personal and expressive. Further, because "Careless Love" is a standard folk form that has proliferated myriad interpretations since its first recording in the 1920s, the song here asserts the conventionality of this private anguish at just the moment when the poem seems poised to assert its individuality ("my mind's not right"). As Lowell was writing the poems in *Life Studies,* he might have heard Fats Domino's 1951 recording of the song or perhaps Ottilie Patterson's 1955 version or Pete Seeger's 1958 version on the radio, just to name a few. Each recording changed the traditional content of the folk song, thus modifying W. C. Handy's 1920s modernization of the "original." Of course, "original" has to go in scare quotes here because, as a folk form, the transcription of the song at any given moment necessarily could not make a claim to be the song's original form. Taken in this context, the three visually aligned ellipses make strange the illusion that what we are overhearing is the real suicidal angst of a real speaker (indeed, of Lowell). This is true not just because the speaker also "hears" here—first the radio, then his "ill-spirit sob"—but also because the personal confession that follows the radio bleat is brought into implicit typographical and orthographic comparison (by dint of the ellipses) with the radio bleat itself. We are left feeling that what we are meant to feel we have just overheard might be rather generic, just another version of something quite conventional.

So is it the poem that does this? Is it Lowell? Is it a style of reading that allows for it? For Lowell's contemporary readers, the confession "my mind's not right" might have produced the feeling of being privy to speech overheard by a poet operating without consciousness of a listener. But the poem suggests a different kind of overhearing—we have heard it (or something like it) too many times; the poem's individuating gesture is, like the recorded version of "Careless Love," in fact more of the same. What these overdeterminations of "voice" in the poem complicate is the very "clarity" and unashamed mastery over both the self and the world that the lyric performance claims to stand above.

Sexton picks up several of Lowell's "Skunk Hour" images in one of her poems from the late sequence "Letters to Dr. Y," published posthumously in *Words for Dr. Y* (1978). Overall, the sequence foregrounds lyric as an intersubjective space; many poems are dialogic, with Sexton's characteristic tendency to turn from "me" to "you." The second poem in the section, dated from 1960, imagines an analyst "you" who, seemingly personifying the aims of lyric reading, asks of the poet after she presents her words, *"And where is the order?"* As is true in "You, Dr. Martin," Sexton explicitly associates the analytic therapist's order with that of the lyric reader, refusing lyric-reading paradigms by insisting on a "disorderly display of words" that "know[] their rights" and aim for a messy, dialogic space (*CP*, 562–563). In another poem, the interlocutor doctor's last words identify the space of confession as "A strange theater," reminding us of the audience that conditions the lyric soliloquy, figured only awkwardly by Mill but suppressed by Mill's later readers (577). In the most interesting poem of the series, dated from 1967, Sexton takes up Lowell's images quite specifically: "It's music you've never heard / that I've heard / that makes me think of you." The "music" in question is

> but pop songs on my kitchen radio
> bleating like a goat.
> *I know a little bit*
> *about a lot of things*
> *but I don't know enough about you . . .*
> Songs like cherries in a bowl,
> sweet and sour and small.
> *Suddenly I'm not half the girl*
> *I used to be.*
> *There's a shadow hanging over me . . .*
> From me to you out of my electric devil
> but easy like the long skirts
> in a Renoir picnic with clouds and parasols. (572)

Sexton is amusing in figuring the progress "from me to you" (the process of poetic reception that she often explores) as intertextually mediated.

With the radio serving as concrete reminder of technologies of reception and dissemination, we move from the Peggy Lee lyrics' humorous reminder of the impersonality with which the Freudian analyst is supposed to conduct himself, to the Beatles, to an entirely different discursive realm (Renoir and painting) to define the force of the music. Everything is read through by something else here: as the songs help "I" to understand "you," Renoir helps us read Peggy Lee and therapy, itself a reading of the self. Alluding to the paradigm of Confessional shame—the "love cars" scene in Lowell's "Skunk Hour"—the "I" then imagines (or sees) "Fourteen boys in cars . . . parked,"

> with fourteen girls in cars and they
> are listening to our song with one blood.
> No one is ruined. Everyone is in
> a delight at this ardor.
>
> I am in a delight with you, Music Man.
> Your name is Dr. Y. My name is Anne. (573)

In Lowell's poem, the presence of others recalls the solitude and loneliness that constitutes a paradigmatic lyric isolation (even as the radio song reminds us of the conventional and thereby social nature of the trope). In Sexton's poem, the intertext of pop music (perhaps even "Careless Love") makes "one blood" of patient, therapist, and a diverse group of lovers in the park and, by way of allusion, of Lowell. The music, "our song" but belonging to many, charts a course "from me to you" and results not in shame but in "delight," in an ardor by which "No one is ruined." In other words, Sexton's address does not refer us to or even quite "resist the essential isolation of lyric" as Ann Keniston argues about contemporary lyric address.[125] Instead, it reminds us that lyric circulation constitutes a social arena and a form of community, that the personal, private, and intimate are intermediated by public concerns and language in any case. It also indicates an unwillingness to perform the epiphanic, contrived unburdening of guilt that O'Hara felt defined Lowell's Confessional mode. This is all the more interesting, perhaps, if we consider the fact that one very plausible biographical background to Sexton's poem is the (truly scandalous) affair that she was then engaged in with her therapist.[126] All the more counter-Confessional is the fact that the next poem in Sexton's sequence begins "I am no longer at war with sin" (*CP*, 573). At the same time, we should remember, before we project the Confessional onto Lowell in the process of rescuing Sexton, that Sexton takes her cue and images from Lowell, turning his images to use in her own poem, which helps to show Lowell's poem's own foregrounding of its social embeddedness.

If my aim here has been to find in Sexton's work more openness than has been attributed to it (more polyphony and self-awareness), I have risked reanimating the shame of the Confessional; in refusing the lyric reading that produces midcentury lyric Confessionalism, I have nevertheless drawn on modes of antilyric reading and thinking, whose aim is to produce avant-garde lyric. In the next chapter, I consider the work of Bernadette Mayer, whose turn away from the avant-garde community and aesthetic norms that fostered her early career sees her adopt, quite self-consciously, the ashamed "Confessional," taking on the expressive charge from which I have tried to rescue Sexton. Like Sexton, but a generation wiser, Mayer flaunts the "speaker" paradigm that structures lyric-reading practices. But the effect and the concerns are different, for Mayer takes on what we are sure she already knows has been repressed and rejected by her rather small and specialized poetic community. Finally, if Sexton grotesques, parodies, exaggerates, and flaunts certain lyric expectations, that fact has been underexplored—as our available logic for reading her makes it so easy to read Sexton's work either as failed conventional lyric or as naïve to poststructuralist techniques of the day. Charles Bernstein has described the work of O'Hara and Mayer as a "fronting" of the assumptions of the personal, expressive lyric.[127] Bernstein invokes Mayer (though he later critiques her personal work), O'Hara, and Jack Kerouac to problematize a distinction he himself raises between, on the one hand, "a poetry of visible borders: a poetry of shape . . . [that] emphasizes its medium as being constructed" and, on the other, a desired poetry of "primarily . . . personal communication, flowing freely from the inside with the words of a natural rhythm of life, lived daily." Bernstein's point is to denaturalize the idea of poetry as personal communication, so that he may argue that there is no "natural look" to a poem: writing belies the fantasy that it is produced by "letting it happen," a fantasy animated by an aesthetic of "honesty," "artlessness," "sincerity," and "personal expressiveness."[128] Nevertheless, he avers (without elaborating) that poets such as O'Hara and Mayer complicate the distinction. If Bernstein and others affiliated with Language tendencies have tended to assume we *cannot* make that claim for Bishop or Sexton, it is worth wondering why. It is also worth wondering what it means to perpetuate the shame of lyric by asking Sexton to become a Language poet in order to be likable. Mayer's work takes on that very double bind in order to explore the possibilities of the shame that the Confessional lyric's dismissal tries to will away.

CHAPTER THREE

"Speaking in Effect"

*Identifying (with) Bernadette Mayer's
Shamed Expressive Practice*

> Well meanwhile Elizabeth Bishop has up and died in the
> middle of our conversation. And, I heard, she died an
> hour before she was supposed to give a reading which was
> something evidently she feared doing. So I started reading
> her complete works, just like you, and I must say I found
> the works sustaining and sustained, perhaps in a cold way,
> almost too good or perfect, did you know she's gay? She
> was gay, she managed to live a pretty long life for a poet
> too. And her sestina, as you say, is great.
>
> —*Bernadette Mayer, from "Equinoctial Tears," in*
> The Desires of Mothers to Please Others in Letters

IT COMES AS a surprise on page 111 of Bernadette Mayer's book-length
poem *Midwinter Day* (1978) to find Anne Sexton named among a list of
twenty-seven female writers "and the saints," whom Mayer's "I" celebrates
for having had "the time, chance, education or notion / To write some
poetry so she could know / What she thought about things."[1] Mayer, a
second-generation poet of the New York School,[2] has avant-garde affiliations that make her naming of Sexton (among others) in 1978 a self-
conscious transgression of avant-garde codes of taste.[3] Sexton's suicide in
1974 secured her a sensational literary fame; each of the first five years
following her death, a new, posthumous Sexton book appeared in print.
Even without this kind of visibility, Mayer was doubtless aware that both

Sexton and Sylvia Plath (also named) represented the Confessional main-stream of expressive tendencies that so much avant-garde experiment op-posed. With few exceptions, Mayer names late-twentieth-century writers significantly varied in school and style:

> There's Anne Bradstreet and Tsai Wen Gi,
> Elizabeth Barrett Browning, Alice Notley and me,
> Adrienne Rich, Sylvia Plath, Anne Sexton,
> Elinor Wylie, Louise Bogan, Denise Levertov,
> There's Barbara Guest, H.D. and Harriet Beecher Stowe,
> Murasaki Shikibu, Fanny Howe and Susan Howe,
> Muriel Rukeyser, Mina Loy, Lorine Neidecker,
> Gwendolyn Brooks, Marina Tsvetayeva and Anna Akhmatova,
> There's Rebecca Wright
> And the saints
>   I read in the papers that women live longer
> Because they don't do all of this
> And as they begin to become more like men
> In all these ways they'll die equally soon
>   I forgot to mention
> George Sand,
>   As if death were not life
>   and I was dressed as a man
>   (*MD*, 111)

The lines show Mayer's typical wit: if the 1970s popular press framed women's liberation and career ambitions as potentially *deadly*, Mayer rather celebrates that we will soon see women "die equally" by "doing all of this": death as a published writer is the afterlife Mayer wants. Naming not only Sexton and Plath but also the American formalists Louise Bogan and Gwendolyn Brooks, Mayer makes a feminist canon that boldly cuts across the divide between mainstream and avant-garde that was then important to the American avant-garde's distinctiveness. Increasingly since the 1960s (after the appearance of Donald Allen's anthology *New American Poetry, 1945–1960*), the discourse of divide asserted the impor-tance of rejecting traditional formalism and expressive aesthetics; as May-er's riff on Roman tribalism in lines preceding the list shows, she knew that to propose an all-female canon that crossed the divide was to turn from the tribe.[4] It is a gesture apt for framing Mayer's work's vexed, self-conscious turn, in the late 1970s and 1980s, from the aesthetic dictates of the avant-garde community in which her work had emerged.

As is true of Bishop's work, Mayer's troubles the logic of groups and schools by which scholars describe the diversity of the late 1970s poetries. While I read her experiments with the expressive figure and the personal in her late 1970s works as constituting a conscious defection from antiexpressive avant-garde dictates, it is important to qualify the terms a bit (as well as to admit that the reading is, in part, a fantasy inspired by my own lyric shame). The conceit of *Midwinter Day* is that it was written in and about the events of one day in Mayer's life (December 22, the solstice, in 1978). The work unfolds in a mix of prose forms and verse sections, and like many New York School projects that explore dailiness, it offers an astounding, detailed recounting of the day, mundanities and all. Mayer moves from her morning's dreams to details of the day spent with her two small daughters in Lenox, Massachusetts, where she had recently moved—a run of errands, a trip to the public library, visits from a repair man and a friend, cooking dinner and putting the children to bed, to her nightly writing session and sleep.

However personal the work is, its length, along with its loose syntax and temporal structure, delivers its substantial pleasures and celebration of the personal in a form utterly unlike the canonical personal lyric of the day. As Peter Baker argues in his 1991 book on modern and postmodern long poems (with perspicacious sensitivity to the idea of "lyric" as a form of interpretation derived from a "certain view of Romantic and post-Romantic poetry"), Mayer "eschew[s a] model of textual production" produced by the dominant "interpretive model" based on "interiority."[5] Indeed, in *Midwinter Day*'s length and epic ambitions (it invokes Joyce's *Ulysses* in its opening words) and in its resistance to interpretive summary, it keeps faith with many antilyric techniques and concerns of the period. It opposes a dominant poetic culture that valued the consumable, well-wrought poem that is interpretable in a single classroom session. Though it moves in and out of meditations (many on the situation of the woman writer with children) and though its last section soars, it refuses moral take-away points. Meditative moments cut short, mimicking an "associative" logic and the interruptive rhythms that parental-care tasks produce:

> What an associative way to live this is, dreams of hearts beating like
> sudden mountain peaks I can see in my chest like other breasts then in

one vertiginous moment I can forget all but the reunion and your original face, two shirts each under overalls over tights under shoes then one sweater, outer suits with legs or leggings, mittens attached, hats and overshoes. Everybody wanting something or nothing to be done to them, then one of the shoes falls off again. (*MD*, 35)

Other sections include documentary lists—Lenox town buildings and store names, titles of books on the display table at Matthew Tannenbaum's Bookstore, styles of painting, scientific inventions, and concepts in the news ("The conditioned reflex, the cyclotron, the neon lamp / . . . / Nylon, 'heat death,' recombinant DNA techniques, the laser")—that extend to forty lines (114–115). The dinner-making section is structured around abridged versions of books that Mayer was reading to her girls (including her toddler daughter Marie), interrupted by sudden personal memories or free association or what feels like plain gossip:

Marie's painting with tempera colors. Raphael once told me he thought Diane di Prima's work was difficult and somewhat crazy until he read mine, though he's sympathetic and sees our writing as a symptom of what he thinks of as the crazy times. William Shirer surely wouldn't like my work, he says Gertrude Stein was a megalomaniac and the ugliest woman he ever saw and that her writing is just silly. I wonder what he'd have thought of Margaret Fuller Ossoli. Barry told Clark I shouldn't write about Lenox he didn't like Lenox. Someone else said I was no longer a true experimentalist. Alex once said my writing was rude and Les thought my photographs in Memory were too pretty. Marie's paintings are bright and done quickly. (64)

If in these ways the poem mobilizes techniques in keeping with avant-garde antilyricism, it also marks Mayer's geographic and aesthetic defection from her avant-garde community around questions pertinent to lyric shame. The book and the aesthetic and political concerns that animated it exposed Mayer to a sense of failure and made her an object of discomfort (even shame), I would argue, for the Language-centered avant-garde. We glimpse this in Mayer's indulgence in imagining her coterie's disapprobation (and that of the historian William Shirer, a famous resident of Lenox), all in terms peppered by misogyny. In the year she wrote *Midwinter Day*, Mayer moved to Lenox from the Lower East Side, the geographic locus of her artistic and poetic community; in the autobiographical books that followed—*Midwinter Day, The Desires of Mothers to Please Others in Letters* (a book-length epistolary prose-poem procession she started the next year), and *The Golden Book of Words* (a collection of short, stand-alone poems)—Mayer indicates that the move felt like both a defection and a form of exile.[6] In interviews she has said she moved in part to distance herself from the "blatant sexism" that was surprisingly "so acceptable among people you would respect" in the downtown art scene.[7] And she has said that a life raising children and running a small press in the country with her husband, Lewis Warsh, enabled important aesthetic shifts, as well. With distance from her community, Mayer found herself entertaining the desire to imagine and please a wider audience. She confesses that "even traditional forms" were part of the pleasures that she newly imagined giving and getting in writing.[8] Much of *Midwinter Day* rhymes (sometimes with an artificiality that predicts the self-conscious campy formalism of 1980s rap, sometimes in a more "sincere"-seeming way). Mayer began experimenting with the sonnet form at this time and has continued to do so since.

Despite Mayer's apparent interest in what distance from her community enabled, apparently, these shifts were not easy; her work of the period frequently references and performs shame and anxiety about them. The work engages the complex politics and feminist concerns that surrounded her self-conscious adoption of some of the expressive gestures (first-person narrative, autobiographical writing, relative clarity) that Language writers (in particular) had begun to associate with the "workshop" and "voice" poem—taken as late flowers of "the Romantic lyric" and against which they articulated their aesthetic critique of "lyric" subjectivity.[9] Mayer seems to anticipate the disapprobation of her audience of avant-garde readers, some of whom took her turn to expressive gestures as a kind of "fall from grace," as critic Ann Vickery has put it.[10] Yet in Mayer's attempts to imagine and address an audience outside the dictates of anti-lyric practice, her work explores processes of readerly identification and self-projection, arriving at a critique of lyric reading whose metapoetic implications resemble those that follow from Bishop's dramas of interpretation. In taking on the personal from what I read as a self-consciously ashamed position, Mayer's work challenges the identification of first-person practice with the ashamed anthropomorphics of lyric reading. Though many of the works I discuss in this chapter are prose experiment (not lyric), they indicate Mayer's research into norms of lyric reading as perpetuated by the Language assumptions that shamed her.

LANGUAGE AND "THE SPEAKING WORLD"

Though Mayer's strongest affiliations across her career have been with New York School poets (her former husband, best friends, and the poets she revered were New York School writers), in her early career, she was also strongly identified with Language poets. In particular, her earliest work advanced a critique of the expressive norms that, in part through the success of Language discourse, became synonymous with "lyric" and "mainstream." That critique was also directed against the speech-based poetic of Beat and New York School poetries, both of which experimented with the personal and quotidian. Mayer's public stances toward the literary, and much of her published work before *Midwinter Day,* epitomize the oppositional stance of the Language-centered avant-garde, evident in her advice to students in one technical "experiment" to "work your ass off to change the language & dont ever get famous."[11] And though later the New York School and Language poetry would be viewed as distinct—even rival—avant-garde camps, early iterations of the Language movement were formed in part in the poetry workshops that Mayer led: Charles Bernstein, Hannah Weiner, and Nick Piombino (all canonized as Language writers) found opportunities to "socialize[] and theorize[] with one another" in Mayer's classes.[12] Indeed, in Daniel Kane's literary history of poetic avant-gardes in downtown New York in the 1970s, which details the increasingly contentious expressions of theoretical differences between New York School and Language writers, Mayer features as a bridge figure:[13]

> Mayer proved to be an alternative to the "alternative" defined by Second-Generation New York School writers [such as Ted Berrigan], and she offered a set of new literary and evaluative standards that moved toward a more overtly theoretical poetics of multiple referentiality and syntactical rupture that was generally suspicious of the poem as an emotive or expressivist composition.[14]

Kane's descriptors—"multiple referentiality," "syntactical rupture," "suspicion" toward "emotive and expressivist composition"—identify Mayer with techniques and poetic politics that are common to the otherwise

diverse practices identified by "Language." Indeed, much of Mayer's earliest work gives support to Jerome McGann's claim for Mayer's clear influence on early Language writing.[15]

Mayer's *Ceremony Latin* (1964, published in 1975), for instance, alter-
nates slight, first-person expressive (if disjunctive) moments—"I can see
praying to the sun / or maybe the rain because they cover / everything &
come from apparently nowhere"—with writings that foil lyric-reading
strategies, by radically deemphasizing the experiencing subject's point of
view and insisting on printed language as *not* speech, thus invoking but
also significantly parting company with much New York School and Objectivist work (Frank O'Hara, George Oppen, and William Carlos Williams, for instance), gesturing toward a more Steinian poetic.[16] The collection's third (untitled) poem,

> reading a poet's life
> preconceived ends
> real life of the poet
>
> impressions accidental
>   animals' intelligence[17]

not only does not offer a central subjective perspective; it also wittily un-
packs the phrase "poet's life," critiquing the divining of a poet's "real life"
as an interpretive aim. A "life of the poet" (a biography) is a life construct
written to emphasize particular aspects in the life, thus lending it (false?)
shape. Then again, a real life does have "preconceived ends"—the necessity of the body's death. Contrasted in the closing couplet are more "acci-
dental" impressions and, even less tidy, "animals' intelligence," phrases
that reject the subjective heroics of the written life.

Stand-alone poems in *Ceremony Latin,* and the earliest-written poems
collected in *Poetry* (1976), undercut "lyric" conventions and personal tropes:

> Mary Jemison   White Woman
> of the Genesee
> simple writing w. form personal (*CL,* Eclipse 005)

In her early prose poems, too, narrative logic is undercut by surrealistic,
radically disjunctive gestures that swerve from reference. If they often offer a whiff of personal experience, it tends to be experience of a kind that
cannot be subsumed into moral, universal appeal, that lacks narrative

finish, and that is dominated by overtones of unreality and dream logic. None of the poems invite an audience's identification with a distinct speaker figure.

The deemphasis on individual authorship is paramount also in Mayer's joint publishing project of a few years later, *Unnatural Acts*—a series of collaborative print publications that emerged from the Poetry Project Workshop in 1972. The first issue does not credit its individual authors and suppresses all its editorial information.[18] An excerpt on the cover of issue 2 reads, "Our poems aren't our appearances," arguing, "When you take out the 'I's' / Everybody is matched." As Libbie Rifkin describes the piece, "In its desire to take on the 'unnatural' as its primary model for producing artworks" and in "Mayer's near-invisible self-positioning," *Unnatural Acts* and the workshops that informed it "deviate[] radically from . . . fantasies of self-legitimation and organicism."[19]

STORY, Mayer's first published book (which appeared in stapled, mimeographed form in 1968, from 0–9 Press, her project with the performance artist and poet Vito Acconci) is a thirty-five-page, extended poetic play with narrative forms; titles of its quite short sections (often in irregular, end-stopped lines) refer to genre or narrative forms: "Love Story," "Western," "Anecdote," "Saga," "Fable," "Bedtime Story," "Narrative Poem," and so on.[20] The writing is resolutely impersonal, seemingly both "about" and yet keen to denature the generic logic of the "stories" we tell, as is evident in "Scenario," consisting entirely of one line: "We all live under some of this and that" (Eclipse 004). There is often no clear relationship between the titles of sections and the generic expectations they raise. "Bedtime Story," for instance, raises expectations for a certain kind of story (something soothing, that closes, as is conventional, on sleep or an image of night) and yet proceeds as follows:

> There was a young man who went out alot at night; he
> was never at home.
> A piece of history.
> A slender thread. (Eclipse 012)

Mayer claims that the book, derivative of "myths, fairly tales, the dictionary, and some lists," is composed of "fourteen stories . . . told in interweaving sentences so that the fourteen stories are all going on simultaneously at the middle of the book."[21] It is difficult to divine the "diamond shape" that Mayer says defines the interlocking of these stories, but narrative threads do run through. Working with the unit of the sentence (coherent sentences run throughout), Mayer's technique resembles Lyn Hejinian's in *MY LIFE* (1980). However accessible in glimpses and in parts, both refuse to cohere even as they incite a desire for coherence.[22]

These and the stand-alone poems in *Poetry*—her first major collection—show the potential appeal of her early work for others pursuing experiments that privilege the materiality of language over its reference. Poems such as "Three Men" emphasize repetition and semantic parataxis and seem "about" syntax, lacking any conventional signs of a self behind the writing.[23] The beginning of "Meissen," a paragraph-long prose poem, indicates the disjunction and surrealism marking much of Mayer's early work:

> Have them come. The best is in the beginning. Armies may falter. A detour may deter. So rest in the middle. A doctor is in error. He denies defiling the child. The denial is then disavowed. The doctor's office is full. Above the wainscot, Dresden china, made in two firings, hangs in the antechamber or waiting room. China, the doctor explains, is a vitrified ceramic ware of clay, feldspar, and flint. Despite the name, Dresden china was made in Meissen. The doctor throws this in as a feeler. (10, Eclipse 014)

The relation of these sentences is just hypotactic enough to invite us to construct a narrative (perhaps of the "defiling" mentioned), yet the piece as a whole invites us to consider meaning as constructed by contingent processes rather than as immanent. Prose progresses by associative logic, and it would only be by ignoring those sentences that do not fit the dominant semantic code that we could construct a narrative line.

Thus, the poem very cleverly leaves us hanging as to how best to engage it, emphasizing (by negative fiat) the lyric-reading conventions that would have us identify (with) a speaker. On the one hand, the associative logic of the words might reflect an analysand's psychology; wordplay could be working with a psychoanalytic "plot" (an office-room consultation, the scene of defiling). On the other hand, assertions of chance connections between sounds of words cut against that logic. "Falter" is consonant in sound with "detour," and the "d-e-t" of "detour" leads to "deter" through a phonemic resemblance (producing a near homophony); "rest" dimly relates semantically to "deter" (as deterrence enforces something like rest, both are forms of cessation); "doctor" nearly rhymes with "deter" and "detour" and "error," which follows. "Firings" recalls "armies" and "defiling" and so on. The assonance of the long *i* sound of "deny" and "defi-" puts the "defy" in "defiling." "Feeler" returns us to "feldspar," the "w-a-i" of "waiting" is also in "wainscot," and on and on. Thus, a doctor in error begins to suggest studied verbal errancy (rather than a psychological plot).

As with much of Mayer's work of this period, her great skill in this poem is in eliciting readerly expectations for an interpretive whole, even while casting a skeptical eye on the drive to interpretation. Charged by the thrill of rhymes both aural and visual, the more associations a reader finds between words and letters and sounds, the more the reader grows aware of him- or herself as a contingent force of meaning making and interpretation on these words: there is no place, after all, that the visual rhyme of "w-a-i" with "w-a-i" *must* lead an interpretation. The poem's openness to interpretive play winks at its own suggestion of "a" logic of interpretation, such as is incited by the conjunction of "doctor," the "defiling," the German place name "Meissen," and (later) the phrase "bringing to light," a constellation that strongly (for me, at least) evokes a scene of Freudian psychoanalysis.

The difficulty of keeping language in line with the facts it is supposed to reference ends up suggesting our susceptibility to connotation and language's susceptibility to human history: China does not to refer to the country, after all; this is Dresden china, which is in fact porcelain produced in Meissen, all somehow secondary to the more urgent interpretive question that the passage raises—the possible "defiling" (another kind of dislocation) of a child by a doctor and its relation to the scene of analysis. Is the scene of defiling the scene of analysis? If china is not China, who knows?

If read lyrically, the passage's semantic drift can serve as a scene of Freudian (or lyric) analysis, in which the poem or analysand free-associates and provides us an analytic text. A discourse shift introduces a voice that might even be taken as the (German?) doctor's:

> Now if you are here for a visit there's no point in saying so repeatedly, therefore, the doctor says again, we will sit through more and more consultations but never, he impresses, learn when or where or why or how or how often the habit may have been broken and who began it and who first brought it to light and then how to end it.
> The door opens then closes. (10, Eclipse 014)

And yet Mayer obscures who or what, if anything, needs analysis here—the doctor or the child or the text—inviting us to take our interpretive pleasure and yet proposing analysis as a frustrated scene in which we might "never . . . learn." The scene of analysis that is represented only barely and unstably figures a psyche or a speaker ("you" might be "he"): we cannot quite resolve any of the suggestions as belonging to one subject.

Such examples from the early work show Mayer exploring techniques and politics of interpretation in modes common to a variety of Language poems, and her work over the course of her career to date never moves terribly far from the disjunctiveness and parataxis here evident. Mayer has even gone so far as to claim for herself a formative role in the genesis of Language practice: "The language thing happened because I was teaching all the things [chiefly theory texts] they wanted to know."[24] Though this is probably true in part, Mayer exaggerates, perhaps in defense of her falling out with that group, which some critics have supposed resulted from her "return to traditional forms."[25] Critic Peter Baker notes that for some poets associated with the "Language circle and experimental poetry," Mayer's use of "more traditional conventions of poetry" seemed a "betrayal of the movement." Without specifying which conventions or traditions, he implies that Mayer's adoption of "a more personal style of expression" was to blame.[26]

This explanation fits Mayer's claim that her move toward "clarity"—by which she means, chiefly, legibility—dismayed Language writers.[27] Indeed, Mayer's abjection helps to show discourses of "the personal" and the legible dovetailing in the shaming of lyric, for the only thing that strongly distinguishes Mayer's late 1970s work from earlier experiments with the personal is the later work's openness to being read as autobiographical and explicitly concerned with communicating experiences of bearing and raising children. In poems written in the late 1970s in *The Golden Book of Words* (1978; the title references the then-ubiquitous children's word book and series), in some of *Poetry* (1976), and in *Midwinter Day* (1978), as well as in the prose work *The Desires of Mothers to Please Others in Letters* (1979–1980), Mayer draws on such chronicling forms as the journal, the diary, and the letter, recounting details strongly suggesting "facts" of her daily life. In these works, too, the use of narrative techniques, proper names, and other such "reality effects" suggest that she was pursing a "personal" poetics that marked a return to both New York School attention to the self and even some confessional gestures from the 1960s and early 1970s, both abjected by Language poetry's critique of expressivity.

However, it is also worth considering several of Mayer's early, "objective" projects as quasi-scientific language experiments (even Language experiments) intended to discover methods of writing about the self in an ethically sound manner. In an interview from 1992, asked about whether the issue of "clarity" and "sincere expression" came up in the first workshops at St. Marks, Mayer's response suggests that, however carefully she engaged poststructural ideas about the subject, she believed she would find an expressive mode to engage without guilt or a sense of failure: "At that point in time, everybody was trying to avoid [clarity and sincere expression]. But I always assumed that eventually, someday, that I would learn how to do it."[28]

Memory, the 1971–1972 conceptual art project that attracted many New York–based, Language-oriented writers, began as an exhibit of photographs that Mayer took every day in July 1971, along with text and taped narration of Mayer responding to the photographs, all attempting a "scientific" study of memory's processes and its shaping power over experience.[29] In a surprising coincidence with some confessional work of the time, Mayer attached a preface written by her analyst, David Rubinfine, when she published her transcription of the taped narration in 1975.[30] Though the work seems far from what we might associate with "sincere expression," Rubinfine's framing the work as a "new kind of autobiography" seems of the moment. His diction, however, puts a scientific spin on the work: *Memory* "provides us with data from the past, recent and remote, but [Mayer] has somehow found the means to recreate archaic modes of representation of inner and outer sensory data, by reviving the quality of consciousness in which they occurred."[31] It was in the course of psychoanalysis with Rubinfine in 1972 that Mayer wrote *Studying Hunger Journals,* from which the prose work *Studying Hunger* derived. Over four hundred pages long, the journals were undertaken to aid the process of analysis. Both projects and the preface recall Anne Sexton's and Robert Lowell's breakthroughs into new forms of writing with the help of analysis, and Mayer frames *Studying Hunger* as her search for "a workable code, or shorthand, for the transcription of every event, every motion, every transition of [her] mind": to "record . . . states of consciousness, my states of consciousness, as fully as I could."[32] The text transcription of the *Memory* exhibit recording is largely prose blocks of loosely punctuated stream-of-consciousness prose, whose logic is associative and nonnarrative. Occasionally, prose forms into lines, as from one of the sixteen pages devoted to July 1, for instance:

> i spend my time looking at projections of weeks ago
> on the wall what was downstairs were they the same which are the
> lathes you have it printed on glass DBH 14 scoop & a hole in the
>   ground
> they've just taken the pipes away and chain saw
> ones are the ones on the wall the same ones is the wall moving
>   (Eclipse 008)

Along with other of Mayer's nonlyric works of the period, *Memory* may be taken, as Douglas Messerli said of her *Eruditio Ex Memoria* in 1979, as research of the "self as defined by the knowledge which makes up the self, which perceives the world in which the self lives."[33] Both texts respond to earlier Mayer texts, reflecting on what a past self had produced (and had taken in that led to its production) and, in the act of remembering, making a new text. The effect is not unlike looking into a hall of Mayer mirrors, a complex figuring of past and present that thwarts the hierarchizing of these that might occur in a Confessional text informed by depth psychology.

In *Eruditio,* Mayer responds to the text of her school notebooks, weaving tangentially related sentences that both reproduce and reflect on various of her academic subjects—Boolean algebra, modern Irish playwrights, Latin texts, modern American poets, Continental philosophers—strung together in a nonnarrative logic reminiscent of associational consciousness. Many sections join simple, first-person phrases in run-on sentences, producing exaggerated self-report. The overall effect is an account of sources of Mayer's self and knowledge that disrupts "usual" confession, though it seems "sincere" expression nevertheless: "No coy discontinuity is this, no clever disassociations," as Messerli writes (Eclipse 010).

Indeed, though neither *Memory* nor *Eruditio* resembles lyric, both address the contemporary vogue for autobiography and confession by exploring and challenging modes of lyric reading that conditioned their reception. *Eruditio*'s challenge comes in the work's ongoing tendency to confuse us as to whether and when Mayer is the writer or reader of her works and memories.[34]

I write stick letters on this page of philosophy to see how the letters of a poem may all begin to look alike, a poem about color which is sentimental and imitative of Dylan Thomas, he was popular in that Catholic school. Dun Scotus was the subtle doctor, I don't know any doctors who are subtle, yes I did know one, a woman, she always said to wait and see, something about God's simplicity and a first Cause: the moon is moving over, it makes me feel desperate, as if I must finish my thesis tonight. (*Eruditio* 35, Eclipse 037)

It is difficult to decide the locus of what is "happening" in this reading/writing event. We make out a loquacious, meditative stream of thought in process—"I don't know . . . yes I did know . . . the moon is moving over, it makes me feel desperate, as if I must finish my thesis tonight"—but the passage confuses the "present" moment of Mayer's (and a reader's) reading with the past moment of Mayer's and others' writings. When is Mayer "reading" (interpreting) her school notes? When is she commenting on what she was then feeling and when on what she is now feeling? Surely she need not "finish her thesis tonight," so those feelings produced by the moon, do they belong to the past or the present? Multilayered processes of reading become the subject here, clearer in a later passage that directly references norms of lyric reading—chiefly the idea that we are "listeners" when we read and speakers when we write, the dominant poetic interpretative rubric in place when Mayer was in school. The section begins with an address to a "you" that may be the audience but that also, dizzyingly, includes Mayer:

There is a problem in writing and in writing from my notes I am beginning to see that I make some assumptions about my age and about my language. I expect something and I think you know exactly where I am and what I am doing when that might not be so I have a memory and a backlog of knowledge and information that is not necessarily complete for you. . . . *The bourgeois audience is accustomed to listen,* at least for a while and it is a useful and understandable act, an art in itself, to be alerted to levels of meaning, to expect to understand. I do not understand the Norman influence on literature, the time of the courtly romance, I do not understand the language of the nobility, I understand better this bug on the table. This florid bug. (38, Eclipse 040, my emphasis)

Mayer is reflecting both on writing and reading the self, and thus she
reflects on what readers of *Eruditio* may be experiencing, too. The inevitable pleasure and "problem in writing" and reading appears to be the
power of identification: Mayer has not only assumed that readers know
more about her than they do, but she (somewhat comically) over- or misidentified with "I," reading-writing "from her notes" and projecting "assumptions" onto that "I" that she reads-rewrites. She frames this as a conventional lyric-reading "problem"; the "bourgeois audience" that includes
herself and other school-educated people expects "to understand" and
"listen." Mayer goes on to call herself the "speaker," emphasizing that
classroom metaphor that, as in Mill, collapses distances between writers
and readers and, through the figure of expressive feeling ("feeling confessing itself to itself"), allows the powerful identifications between reader
and writer that are Mayer's subject here. Mayer's touching metapoetic admission that she projects onto her own notes shifts imperceptibly to an
address to an audience figure ("you") and an onrush of information
detailing what "you" (reader/audience figure) cannot be expected to remember or know about "I." Mayer disrupts the "bourgeois" audience role
with frequent gestures to this "you" with whom, she admits, she has
overidentified and who might, in an almost comically literal way, overi-
dentify with her:

> I have a method of surviving and it affects you because I bestow it
> quickly as if I am hoping that you will not suddenly disappear or
> choose to leave and never return. I also have a theory of energy though
> I do not think I use symbols, and I want to be perfect, yet in the mo-
> ments that I am on the outside, forced to be without you, I cannot al-
> ways control this, I see the horrible news happening and though I ad-
> vocate change, I cannot always stand this, my language always reflects
> this. I am of a different generation from my parents and from my chil-
> dren. I have had a father and an uncle. And some men and women of
> my generation are of a different age from my own. I am of the female
> sex, I the speaker. I have a husband who is perhaps your son or brother,
> or friend. I have a blood relation in my sister and in my daughter. Per-
> haps you knew my mother or my father. My name is Bernadette Mayer.
> (37–38, Eclipse 039)

Given the underspecified nature of this "you," we cannot help but feel addressed; the passage is concerned to keep our attention, lest we "suddenly

disappear or choose to leave." Then again, this "I" is engaged in self-analysis, which could render the "you" one aspect of the "I." Several sentences are pointedly ambiguous, now readable as Mayer's report on what a past self "did" in her school notes (the record of them) and now as assessments of the character of a present self. For instance, "I have a theory of energy" might be read as, "here, on this page of (physics? philosophy?) notes, I wrote down a theory of energy," or it might on the other hand be read as an expressive assertion belonging to the present. The rhetorical thrust of "I want to be perfect" could similarly stand as an assessment of a past self "read" in writing and also as a present-day confession about the self: "I see the horrible news happening and though I advocate change, I cannot always stand this, my language always reflects this." Mayer could be reading herself as a text or expressing something through the text. Which is which?

The tension that these ambiguities produce depends on our habituation, as lyric readers, to the figure of voice, to turning writing into a speaking self that we can analyze psychologically.[35] Mayer's work foils a lyric reading by emphasizing the limits to "understand[ing]" this text by *listening* to it. The I's "survival" is at stake: what keeps the personal presence lively on the page, especially under the pressure of our effort to comprehend it? And it also asks, *is* there a personal presence here? Where? The "I" invoked through an interwoven act of memory, reading, and writing is never stably in view. Is it in slippage that survival happens? Or is slippage what we need to rescue the "I" from? In a comic solution to such questions, the passage turns to what "the bourgeois audience" might also expect from memoir: verifiable statistics. In naming herself the "speaker," Mayer relieves our anxiety about who the "I" of this work is (one version of the text's meaning), and yet, in the summoning of the "you"/audience into the bosom of her family circle, she exposes the desire for bonds of intimacy that readerly identifications seem to promise: "I have a husband who is perhaps your son or brother, or friend" (38, Eclipse 039).

The earlier, less traditionally narrative work *Moving* (1971) more aggressively invokes figures of "speaking" and "listening" but can be taken also to explore the effects of first-person enunciation and the desire to express. The work begins with the line, "fear sure voice music body time listen / being part. being trapped / being part being trapped which is it?"[36] With "voice" and "listen," Mayer proffers terms of lyric reading that her work refuses, asking us to listen but offering no voice. A short excerpt of a much-longer passage, more insistently structured around the command to "listen," seems to want to speak of a death (or to remember or address a dead person) in a "spontaneous overflow of powerful feelings." But the passage gets stuck on enunciating the I's departure from the graveside (or is it a figure for a lyric spilling out?) in a string of possible ways to put it:

> listen, whatever-your-name-is, listen i'll cover your bones with
>   rocks & feathers because you're going where it's empty listen the
>   black earth
>   will hide you, a black hut, a black box, a grave with black
>   pebbles, listen your soul's spilling out listen it's blue   & i'm leaving.
>   i'm departing. i'm taking my departure i'm going, i'm going away.
>   i'm going
>   off. i'm getting away i'm going my way. i'm getting along, i'm
>   going on.
>   i'm shoving on. i'm trotting along. i'm staggering along. i'm
>   moseying
>   along. i'm buzzing off. i'm moving off. i'm marching away. i'm
>   pulling out.
>   i'm leaving home. i'm going from home. i'm exiting. i'm breaking
>   away. i'm . . .
>   . . . i'm ceasing to be. (Eclipse 023)

The poem barrages us with first-person statement here, on the verge of producing a coherent speaking subject. Short bits of gossipy biographical prose drift into surrealisms that refuse the trope of confessional or auto-biographical speech. In one section (typically disorienting), "I" suddenly works for the CIA, is male, and has his car blown up on vacation. Rare subjective moments refuse to produce a sustained image of a continuous self and cannot be taken as expressive, yet they prefigure Mayer's later, explicitly personal work and help theorize the process of identification as problems inherent in processes of reading and writing.

As differences between *Eruditio* and the earlier *Memory* and *Moving* show, however, Mayer's later work's explicit concern with the personal and its frank admission of desire for audience mark a significant shift. "I Imagine Things," from *The Golden Book of Words*, announces that it is "time to think it's made by you, made by me," for instance.[37] *Midwinter Day*'s last pages address (her husband) Lewis as he goes "out for cigarettes," and rhetoric flies high in the face of what by then was a clearly articulated contemporary antilyricism:

> As if love is not the food
> Of those of us satisfied enough to write
> To write to lend urgency pleasure, to sing,
> To celebrate, to inspire, to reveal (*MD*, 115)

Such frankly old-fashioned poetic rhetoric—"pleasure," song, celebration, inspiration—had been unfashionable at best in the twentieth century and was part of what made some of Mayer's supporters uncomfortable.

Mayer's turn from that community comes clearest in a 1984 satire of Language writers, "Homage to Jonathan Swift: another story told / about the language of the past," which accelerated her into a break. Written as a mock travelogue, the piece is one chapter of Mayer's *Utopia,* a traditional utopia comprised of writing by Mayer and others, edited and compiled by Mayer.[38] The "Homage," by Mayer, describes a female traveler's visit to an "island . . . in the air," first as guest, later as captive, depicting the Language community as a colony of monkish, bespectacled men garbed in gray.[39] Mayer's satire emphasizes, often heavy-handedly, the male community's insensitivities to gender and their prohibitions of expressive speech and "emotion." Taken to a lecture hall to hear "confusing speeches, or whatever they were," the female traveler recalls one—"aplumb eplettes iplitty abilullty ebullient scribblier afloont effluvivial iffling asslong (at which word everyone tittered so they must have the same devotions as humans)" (42)—mocking the men's fussy immaturity. She compares Language aesthetics to Catholic-school Latin lessons of her (oppressed) youth, reporting her disappointment: "just as I'd get interested they would leave off and continue with something like: vivo I live voco I call volo I will" (42).

The piece further suggests that Language politics/aesthetics realize a perverse self-isolation motivated by deep distrust of any audience that would embrace it. Mayer frames this distrust as symptomatic of widespread alienation of poetry from social life in the late-twentieth-century United States. Throughout, she emphasizes the noncommunicative drive of the community as peculiar and willful. "Though we spoke the same language they had no desire to communicate with me as yet," the traveler reports, marveling at the men's isolation from "the speaking world" (41–42).[40]

One imagines that the depiction did not go over well with the audience for *Utopia,* many of whom were or were affiliated with Language writers and who would have felt singled out by its heavy-handed, even insulting depictions. Mayer invited Charles Bernstein (original editor of *L=A=N=G=U=A=G=E* and frequently, throughout the 1970s, Mayer's advocate in print) to respond to the work. Not surprisingly, his response, titled "The Only Utopia Is in a Now" (included in Mayer's book and later reprinted by Bernstein) seeks to refine her depiction of Language's stance toward norms of poetic communication. Continuing in Mayer's eighteenth-century mock travelogue mode, Bernstein's traveler also visits "Utopia," where writer inhabitants are forbidden to *think* and are convention bound: "You're only supposed to write and say what everyone else knows, and to write and say it in the way everyone else has already heard it. In fact, they issue a manual, Acceptable Words and Word Combinations. . . . It's no use arguing, since anyone who disagrees is called anti-emotional and, regardless of their gender, is also called 'male.' "[41] Bernstein here critiques the legibility (what Mayer called "clarity") that Mayer newly valued as a writing goal; he complains that it results in tired cultural repetitions marked by political restraint and the false consciousness of (irrational) feminists. One assumes that aspects of Bernstein's retort contributed to Mayer's feeling shamefully identified as a "failed experimentalist," a charge made by one (unnamed) avant-garde poet that she often recounts in interviews.[42]

Though the exchange marked a breach between the two poets, even Bernstein's early interest in Mayer's work bordered on critique: responding to Mayer's very early *Memory,* he finds her work "rooted" in the "assumptions" of "the naturalness" of poetic language: its supposed "honesty, its directness, its authenticity, its artlessness, its sincerity, its spontaneity, its personal expressiveness." Her achievement, he felt, was in how she "fronted these assumptions," suggesting both a false front and a confrontation of them.[43] Bernstein's point was to question and dislodge the supposed "naturalness" of the personal and expressive tendencies in poetics, and he posits O'Hara's and Mayer's work as successful to the degree that they advance that project. This is to say that in some ways Mayer's work was cast in a defensive position for a decade before her *Utopia* appeared, subject to Bernstein's translation of its aesthetics of the personal into the terms of Language. The 1980s breach was intense for Mayer: asked to describe Language poetry in an interview conducted not long after *Utopia* was published, Mayer responds, "I might get excoriated again if I say what I think," to which her interviewer replies, "Let's censor the manuscript and not the tape."[44] Mayer understands that the very fact that *Midwinter Day* might be said to be "about something" would read as a knowing transgression, jesting in the interview that it might make her seem in the eyes of the avant-garde "just like John Updike" (that is, quite mainstream). Rower responds, "In a way, *Midwinter Day* is certainly not 'about' anything, but in a sense it's about love and children and all that." Mayer's comeback is telling: "Isn't that okay?"[45]

This is in keeping with the many performances of shame (however serious) in the interview: when Mayer is asked about her "thing for Hawthorne," one of her great influences, she replies, "Should I be ashamed of it?" She then identifies Hawthorne as himself "ashamed of his obsession with the imaginary," perhaps a projection of her own poetic shame. She admits feeling "embarrassed" by her school journal entry naming only male "culture heroes." She references being "called . . . a 'failed experimentalist' because of [her] attempts to be clear" and says that in her community, the turn to (comparative) "clarity" in the 1970s "could be thought . . . a crime." At the same time, she admits that she was once herself "guilty of writing" in the "purist" (not clear) ways of Language writers.[46] In *Midwinter Day,* Mayer is "ashamed that death obsesses" her, and though she argues, "These apologies are what they call under control / I've no respect for their repetitious logic," she nevertheless indulges a string of self-conscious admissions of shame—about getting older, not keeping the house clean enough, seeking clarity in her writing, and finally, writing anything at all: "When I think each time I write a line / I know someone I know won't approve of it / I begin to wonder about my mother" (*MD,* 102–103).

Mayer's invocations of shame emphasize the abject status of one who transgresses community norms, and members of her community apparently needed to negotiate their attachments to Mayer after her "fall." Indeed, one suspects that Mayer's piece and Bernstein's response to it have contributed to Mayer's qualified place in (and even absence from) some histories of the American poetic avant-garde.[47] In *Total Syntax* (1984), Language poet and literary theorist Barrett Watten's seminal critical exploration of the politics and practices of Language writing, Watten argues that, while "the advantage of Mayer's techniques [in her late 1970s work] is their adherence to the quotidian . . . the 'permanent avant-garde' vaporizes, leading to more conventional roles. As actually happened—in the course of Mayer's later editing of United Artists, the stylistic opening-up returns all these techniques to 'the self.'" Watten criticizes Mayer as having turned away from what, in the mid-1980s, was still a passionate discussion among Language writers about the social roles that poetic texts could produce, affirm, and disrupt in their strategies for engaging readers. The "techniques" Watten mentions are workshop experiments that Mayer offered to her Poetry Project students (some published in $L=A=N=G=U=A=G=E$ 3 and the only work of Mayer's reproduced in *The L=A=N=G=U=A=G=E Book*, a selected volume of the journal's run edited by Bernstein and Bruce Andrews in 1984). To Watten's dismay, he regards these techniques as compromised by Mayer's autobiographical and self-representational turn in work of the late 1970s, clearly the most explicit source of Mayer's (and her work's) shame.[48]

The following Bruce Andrews comment from a 1979 radio interview of himself and Bernstein by Susan Howe should remind us that, from the perspective of those who aim at the "permanent avant-garde" that Watten invokes, to unconsciously reproduce "traditions of representation" that support "the notion of a sovereign self" was then (and is still for some) to perpetuate processes of social alienation:

> [Language] writing tends to try to undercut . . . the notion of a sovereign self and a sovereign subject as the center of meaning in a text—which I think again is not only a limited and limiting notion, but a notion that derives from the operation of an oppressive social system that we all are living under. To some extent we are living out society's alienating qualities without being encouraged to look at what these qualities are, to see how alienation is related to, say, traditions of representation in the arts or in writing, how all those things operate together.[49]

Thus, as will be obvious to those who are familiar with the Language agenda, to be a "failed experimentalist," as Mayer understood she had been dubbed, was to fail at more than taste or an aesthetic agenda: it was to fail at a revolutionary ethical, social agenda. Indeed, the 1984 breach strongly points to Mayer's rebellion in her late 1970s work as a risky, conscious transgression of discursive boundaries that her community had established (a view that challenges Maggie Nelson's claim that "speaking was never a problem for Mayer").[50] This makes the topic of lyric shame in her work importantly different from its place in Sexton and Bishop, whose work predates the high mark of poststructuralism and the Language critique. And it makes the feminist stakes of entertaining, with full knowledge of the avant-garde critique, the risk of exposing one's work to a lyric reading quite acute. In an undated letter to the poet Susan Howe, the Language writer Lyn Hejinian identifies the "problem" of poets' uses of "the domestic present" "as material" in work of the period, arguing that Mayer, for instance, "imagin[es] herself and Lewis [Warsh] as heroic." Nevertheless, Hejinian assures Howe (perhaps the greater admirer of Mayer), "[I have] pulled all her books off my shelf and been rereading them."[51] By "heroic," Hejinian seems to mean "exemplary" and "unique": she accuses Mayer of implicitly projecting an image of self as primary to all that surrounds it, and in the work. The poet and critic Nada Gordon, thinking through avant-garde criticisms of Mayer's work of the period, *defends* Mayer's work on much the same grounds: "Mayer's stance in her later work is to be the heroine of the personal in an increasingly objectified and objectifying world. . . . Her work becomes more determinedly subjective at the same time as it becomes more publicly accessible. This may be a viable way to rescue the problem of the lyric utterance."[52] What Gordon reads as a willing and salutary embrace of a heroic stance, Hejinian takes as a regrettable weakness of the work.[53]

But the notion that Mayer embraces a heroic logic of "the personal," or "lyric utterance," whether celebrated or lamented, depends on modes of lyric reading whose limits Mayer tests. Mayer's work takes on techniques established as shamefully personal and expressive, exploring her own desires and worries about being read lyrically as a distinctly feminist concern. She engages, rather than suppresses, the shame dynamics that surround that desire. In foregrounding and exaggerating the claim that her poems will "speak," very much in conscious rebellion against avant-garde permits, Mayer adopts and makes strange the idealized, abjected figure of speech, opening vital new problems for lyric readers.

Her later work thus helps to mark gender as it significantly complicates the history of lyric reading in the late twentieth century, seeing her caught between the antiexpressive Language agenda, the arguable heroics of male personalism (or personism) in Beat and (some) New York School writing, and a dawning feminist poetic consciousness about the limits of both stances. Many Language writers were also entertaining the consequences of prohibitions on legible representations for those poets who were historically silenced. Ron Silliman raised the issue in 1988 by asking whether "the spectrum of the marginal" groups might be forgiven for maintaining conventional notions of subjectivity: "Women, people of color, sexual minorities . . . have a manifest political need to have their stories told. That their writing should often appear much more conventional, with the notable difference as to whom is the subject of these conventions, illuminates the relationship between form and audience."[54] Rae Armantrout entertained that view skeptically ten years earlier when asked by Bernstein to respond to the question, "why don't women do language-oriented writing?" Her initial answer was "that women need to describe the conditions of their lives," which "entails representation."[55] But her move to disparage that thought as "obvious" and, ten years later, as "facile" suggests how powerful the antirepresentative, antisubjective position could be, despite the power that self-representation seemed to hold out for oppressed subjects.[56]

Mayer's work, on the other hand, questions the supposed origins of the clarity that Armantrout rejects and Silliman allows, catching us in our own lyric readings of work that knows its susceptibility to be shamed (or defended) as "lyric." In modes comparable to self-conscious admissions of frankly sexual material into public speech, Mayer's performances of pride, skepticism, and shame about making legible self-representations rebel against (male) Language authority.[57] The payoff is her illumination of the lyric-reading assumptions that allow a simultaneous abjection and idealization of the personal and expressive figure in avant-garde discourse.

"CAN I SAY THAT?" POETIC AUTHORITY
AND THE EXPRESSIVE FIGURE IN *MIDWINTER DAY*

Midwinter Day and other Mayer texts of the era rebel not only by courting more clarity but also by explicitly adopting and disturbing the expressive figure that Mayer knew had been at the heart of Language critique. One could invoke Robert Grenier's 1971 seminal essay "On Speech," which declares "I HATE SPEECH," tacitly obsessing over the prominence placed on speech in Charles Olson's influential "Projective Verse," an essay that defined both the historicization and course of avant-garde poetics in the United States before Language. Grenier's essay recasts William Carlos Williams and Robert Creeley as text-based (not speech-based) poets and, in general, addresses the desire that many in his circle shared: to maintain the New American legacy while still "proclaim[ing] an abhorrence of 'speech,'" in order to realize a denser, more opaque, language-centered poetry.[58] Grenier's essay is often cited, however tentatively, as seminal to the formation of a self-conscious Language aesthetic.[59]

Though more recent accounts of the history of Language-centered poetics have attempted a more subtle reading of Grenier's gesture (and its relation to varied poetics of the moment), it was meant to mark and was long read as heralding a radical "breach" (in Ron Silliman's words) definitive of a new era of writing; thus, it seems notable and pointed to find Mayer emphasizing the word "speak" (along with "tell" and "say," among other speech-based words) as well as the expressive trope in her work of the era.[60] At the midpoint of *Midwinter Day* (which is a six-part book of 119 pages), Mayer interrupts mostly left-justified lines with the scattered visual emphasis in these:

<blockquote>
I don't deny it
What but the impulse to move and speak
          Can change the world
Where should we move
    Who is this person speaking
Who am I speaking to
    To you whom I love,
      Can I say that?
(*MD*, 46)
</blockquote>

As Mayer knew, Language poets of the day aspired to "change the world" by denaturalizing and denouncing expressive conventions, which makes her accession/request for permission seem addressed not only to the singular loved "you" but also to a coterie of readers who believed that political reform entailed writing that was forged *against* speech. One need only look at a few titles from the table of contents for issue 9/10 of *L=A=N=G=U=A=G=E*, from October 1979, to see the idealization of writing as politics: "Writing the Wrong" by David Bromige, "Writing, Power and Activity" by Bruce Boone, and "Writing Social Work & Political Practice" by Bruce Andrews, to name a few.[61] Taken in this context, Mayer's question "What but the impulse to move and speak / Can change the world" reads as a direct transgression of Language politics.

But the question dissolves underlying assumptions of that politics—by raising the question of how we distinguish "speech" writing from "writing" writing, simultaneously offering and rescinding these speech-based expressive-emotive figures: "move," literalized by the line "Where should we move," implies a material location, suggesting how variously "to move" might be read (as opposed to heard) and foregrounding its artifice as a figure. The lines' invocation of a cohesive speaking subject is challenged by the questions "Who is this person speaking" and "Who am I speaking to." Mayer's lines both do and do not quite entertain an expressive position, revealing expectations for a speaker as an "impulse," something that Mayer understands as problematic, even shameful, but that she will nevertheless not "deny."

Clearly, Mayer was thinking about poetic reception both in and against the terms of antiexpressive discourse. Savvy yet skeptical, her work draws attention to speech as an empowerment that requires license and assent, as indicated in the lines' final appeal to an authoritative reader who has the power to permit or reject speech. An important historical context is the situation for women writers attempting to participate (in both writing and speech) in significantly male-dominated poetry circles at the time, a situation perhaps more bittersweet for women seeking visibility in politically progressive communities. For one example, a panel of Bay Area women poets and intellectuals addressed the question of how women's speech could be valued and devalued in poetic circles in a panel titled "Who Is Speaking?" in 1983. Lyn Hejinian's contribution addresses the situation in notably oblique, abstract terms, discussing the discursive limits that aesthetic communities can place on members' modes of participation. Hejinian discusses "key words or phrases that designate particular or general ideas of mutual concern and around which there is some shared excitement" (citing the Language keywords *ostranenie, parataxis,* and *the new sentence*")—pondering their discursive power both to define community and also to control its borders. The statement inexplicitly historicizes and problematizes some of the "who's in / who's out" rhetoric that enabled the Language community's rise to visibility, citing the "danger that such terms can become tyrannical—that they will circumscribe the community or that the power embedded in them is of the kind that some persons can wield over others." Hejinian specifically imagines keywords and other markers of discursive borders for their power to "edit the speaking of the community." It seems no accident that the piece, in a typically elliptical manner, then moves to consider a history of gender inequality as it, too, has constrained speech: "[Women's] speech is regarded as trivial, second-class, since it is held to originate not in the public world (of free men) but in the private and domestic sphere (maintained by women and servants). Because of this, it is also regarded as disgusting."[62]

Though the passage leaves ample room for interpretation and though Hejinian is careful to distinguish that "silencings [can] occur that are manifestations of a drama whose history is longer than that of any community," it reflects the then-heated and ongoing conversation among female writers affiliated with Language about limits on female visibility and power in certain public Language forums.[63] In letters from the period, for instance, Susan Howe and Hejinian frequently return to this issue, weighing their obligation to community against a literary history marked by suppression of female work.

This background suggests that when Mayer's work asks, "Can I say that?" it alludes not only to broadly historical tensions but also to specific tensions surrounding Language prohibitions on speech-based poetics, in effect asking not only to be "heard" (a broader feminist figure for political recognition) but also, "Can I invoke speech-based poetics here, or is that not allowed?" Barrett Watten has argued that Grenier's own antispeech gesture "refers importantly to political speech," which, he believed, in its "address to the historical moment, is inauthentic"; Grenier rebelled against the notion of the speech of a "collective subject."[64] It was this aspect of the Language position—not unrelated to Bernstein's view that if we have read it before (if it is familiar to us), it is "speech" and thus a form of cultural repetition—that Mayer struggled with and against.[65] Mayer extends something of the Bishop tradition, however (strategies that many male Language poets used as well), in experimenting with discourse and cliché to defamiliarize the familiar. Her strategies resemble Anne Sexton's exaggerations of conventional expressive tropes and norms of lyric reading, but in a way that we must understand as being differently self-conscious. There are *several dozen* instances of the word "say" in *Midwinter Day*, half of which are concentrated in the book's first twenty-six-page section. The request for permission recurs frequently in Mayer's work from the period—in *Studying Hunger Journals* and in some of the poems in the collection *Another Smashed Pinecone* (1998), which includes poems from the mid-1970s forward.[66]

If read as addressing the avant-garde audience that Mayer knew would be "moved" by the emphasis on "saying," "moving," and "speaking," such requests take on a productive complexity. To ask, "Can I say that?" both points to awareness of the limits of speech-based poetics and yet also raises the potential for a reader who is skeptical of that poetic to be "moved," whether to dismay or shame by the invocation of an abjected expressive aesthetic. Mayer creates the conditions for a (begrudging?) emotional response from readers who are ill disposed to be spoken to or "moved."

This somewhat impishly insistent and nuanced toying with expressive aesthetics is in keeping with Mayer's tendency to play, in *Midwinter Day* and *Poetry*, with the theoretical possibilities of foregrounding abjected "lyric" figures, revealing overlap between norms of lyric and antilyric reading:

> Stately you came to town in my opening dream
> Lately you've been showing up alot
> > I saw clearly
> You were staying in the mirror with me
> You walk in, the hills are green, I keep you warm
> Placed in this cold country in a town of mountains
> Replaced from that balmier city of yours near the sea
> . . . .
> I only wait in the lobby, in the bar
> > I write
> People say, "What is it?"
> I ask if I must tell all the rest
> For never, since I was born
> And for no man or woman I've ever met,
> I'll swear to that,
> Have there been such dreams as I had today,
> The 22nd day of December,
> Which, as I can now remember,
> I'll tell you all about, if I can
> > Can I say what I saw (*MD*, 1–2)

Mayer takes pains here to contrast writing and saying with visually emphasized phrases on right-justified lines: "I saw clearly," "I write," and

"Can I say what I saw." A sharp enjambment in lines 12–13 juxtaposes "I write" and "People say." Our awareness of that juxtaposition emphasizes "tell" in the next line. In foregrounding (and making strange) the common identification of writing with speaking (even as she asks permission to "say"), Mayer puts us in the position to recognize our own investments (or divestments) in her speech. This relates to the pleasurable trouble of thinking about *Midwinter Day* in its relationship—temporally and as a representative object—to the "day" it claims to represent: for if, as is stated in the back-cover copy, the book was "written on December 22, 1978," it can seem a real-time account of that day and, in this sense, to function with the impromptu and immediate qualities traditionally associated with lyric speech. Readers stumble over how to conceive of the work's composition, a confusion that Mayer has courted: in a 1989 Naropa University lecture on the book, she claims, "Nobody ever believes me when I tell them it was written in one day, but it almost was."[67] But when asked by Rower, "Did you actually write all of *Midwinter Day* in one day? Is this a trade secret?" Mayer explains that she took notes on her dreams in the morning and adds, "There were many other things I wrote in the course of the day. Like I noted down which books I was reading to the children and later I made synopses of them so I could include them in the poem. All those things were easy to do later and impossible to do in the course of . . . *I mean I never intended to just spend the day writing, though that would be interesting to try.*"[68]

The question as to whether the book *was* written in one day concerns what we imagine "writing" to be, involving fantasies about a realm of pure expressiveness that are contradicted by the obvious craft in the poems' deft repetitions and shapings. Indeed, so unlikely is it that the work was accomplished as an only lightly corrected draft of real-time writing composed over sixteen hours of a day spent caring for two small children (what Rower's question supposes), we may wonder what Mayer has come to represent for those who *admire* her later work. There is obviously an important difference between, on the one hand, the idea of the "time allotted to the work," as Hejinian describes it—"time [as it] predetermines the form of . . . *Midwinter Day*"—and the time allotted to the *making* of the work: to confuse the two is to confuse the author's lived life with the work itself, to imagine *Midwinter Day* as Wordsworthian "spontaneous overflow of powerful feelings," feeling speech into print.[69]

Mayer's stated aim to make a document of lived experience clearly crosses with fantasies about spontaneous expression with which she had been experimenting since *Memory* and *Moving*: "Let me tell you what I saw, listen to me," she writes, invoking the expectation for poetry to function as speech, even when it is "like a story" (*MD*, 2). And yet the deformation of experience by writing is *Midwinter Day*'s problem/project: it attempts to capture the dailiness of life without destroying its dailiness by abstracting and reshaping it overmuch, and it theorizes the failure. On page 4, the poem wonders, "What man or woman / Could this be involving," perhaps in reference to the dream,

> . . . so fleet it is indulging
> In not quite flying but dreaming, flaunting
> The short-lived continuity of a sound like hummingbirds
> What is a story
> Can I say that here
> Or should I wait till later whatever the question (*MD*, 4)

Questions about where and when to "say" something throughout emphasize and call into question the naturalness of speech, for even in "impromptu" speech, the poet entertains convention and decorum. Later in the section (now in formatted prose blocks), Mayer makes another such obviously artificial "real-time" gesture:

> I better hurry to accommodate family to see what's going to happen
>   with them today, every morning's the same dawning before it's
>   talked about or told like the dull man who wanted to tell the dream
>   he had of you a week ago, then he never said it, he just said it was
>   recurrent
>
> Doesn't everybody know everything or not, please let me know,
>   isn't the truth always the same, firm as a tree, is it an accident of
>   pose that I say what I say, can I look into the dream room and
>   then run away? (24)

Both paragraphs ponder what of "primary" material (experience, dreams) survives its "telling." Mayer writes with the course of the day but "plots" the family. The dailiness of "morning's . . . dawning" is always the "same" unless it is processed by language (a Lacanian notion), and Mayer longs to maintain the glimpse at the Lacanian "Real": "can I look into the dream room and then run away?" Her answer is to "tell you how each day is different," and we begin to see that the request for permission to "say that" involves earnest research into what would best keep the freshness of experience intact.

Part of the answer entails self-conscious exploration and problematization of lyric-reading conventions of the day—the very kind that would have to be in place to attribute a heroic posture to Mayer's work. Mayer's complex play with deixis, lyric presence, and the speaker figure foregrounds the instability of the work's "I" in an attempt to hew to the flow of experience perhaps. A group of lines begins, "Today I'm the present writer / At the present time the snow has come," and subsequent lines seem to comment on the readerly habit of demanding a personal presence from writing, which the poem has been both celebrated and shamed for (purportedly) attempting to convey:

> Now and then
> Just talking to talk or reading to read
> And exchanging great reading with others
> Someone says don't say sleep tight
> And don't let the bedbugs bite
> Now we'll never know
> If the dough I was kneading
> Was play-doh or cash, I don't do you?
> Just now people need Christmas money
> Sweet thick-skinned red and green peppers
> Gimme yours, nowadays that's not funny
> Now and again I always need you
> Don't be absurd, go back to sleep
>
> Come now (17)

Such passages make it difficult to see how Mayer returns experimental techniques to an uncritical project of self-enunciation or "conventional roles," as Watten supposed. Homophonic play with "knead" and "need" (and the pun on "dough") emphasizes the difference of language "talking to talk" and what is written to read, suggesting the openness of interpretation that written language allows. And hearing—the poem claims "we'll never know" which is which ("kneading" or "needing," presuming that we are the bourgeois audience who has heard the words, not read them), in fact, "we," the readers, read "the dough I was kneading" and do not mistake "knead" for "need." At the semantic level, however, dough and dough and dough are "equal": is this kneaded/needed dough "play" or real—how would we ever know? Does Mayer really need money? The book repeatedly suggests she does, but what would verify it? Sentences give us evidence of a life lived (the children need entertaining, the poet needs to buy dinner) and yet also remind us of all we do not know.

The effect is far from a "heroics" of self: self-report is emphasized as shaped by the impersonal forces of language, and we see how ambiguous are speech (or a life) isolated and seen out of its embedded contexts. In this, Mayer problematizes the primary technique at her disposal—the first-person singular. If readers are not sure which is which (life or art), oddly the "I" also "doesn't know." Mayer foregrounds the "I" as engendered anew by each context in which it appears (each phrase or sentence and each reading), so that the "I" who "kneads dough" is different from the "I" who asks, "do you?" The command (from whom?) to "go back to sleep" might be "said" to the one who "says don't say sleep tight" (a child? an avant-garde poet?), or it may be a lover (as could be suggested in the "Come now") or no one in particular or the reader (or no one at all). In failing to be clear (even when mostly so), Mayer provokes our awareness of our and the first-person subject's distance and differences from Mayer.

Given how closely such passages hew to techniques and aims of experimental avant-garde projects of the day, one wonders how Mayer came to represent (for a time) an abjected expressivism, except through the force of lyric readings. Not that such readings are not courted or their potential appeal acknowledged: in the penultimate page of part 1, as domestic urgency mounts (the Mayer character feels pressure to wake to the day of domestic tasks), so does the admission of real longing for personal expression. "There's something / I want to say, I don't know how to put it," the section begins, turning to a repetition of Richard Crashaw's "Out of Catullus" to "say" it:

> There's something
> I want to say, I don't know how to put it
>   Brightest Sun that dies today

> Lives again as blithe tomorrow
> But if we dark sons of sorrow (25)

After repeating several more of Crashaw's adapted Catullan lines, the poem apologizes, foregrounding the assertion of a subjective "I" as an experiment that cannot be reduced to "the expressive":

> Don't take what I say too seriously
> Or too lightly,
>   I'm sorry,
>   Nevermind
> I was just playing around, I'm trying to find
> What I guess I'd rather not know consciously
>
>   I'd like to know
> What kind of person I must be to be a poet
> I seem to wish to be you
>   Love is the same and does not keep that name
>   I keep that name and I am not the same
> You,
> Shakespeare, Edwin Denby and others, Catullus,
> I've nothing else to say, the anonymous
> Blue sky is gray, I love your being
> In my unresisting picture, all love seen
> All said is dented love's saluted image
> In the ending morning, nothing said is mean,
> Perhaps it's too long, I'm only learning
> Along with love's warning
> To invent a song
>   Then for the breath of words respect
>   Me for my dumb thoughts, speaking in effect
> This was my dream
> Now it is done. (26)

The lines are worth quoting at length for their extended play with norms of lyric reading, a performance that seeks to ward off potential shaming by a reader who might "take" them "too seriously." Take what too seriously? Is it the lines' exaggerated first-person stance—and the assertion of "say[ing]"—that requires apology? What, in fact, has "I" said but words of a poem (and really a poem of a poem, Crashaw's liberal translation of Catullus)—not properly a sign of a singular subjectivity at all? Does Mayer apologize for the invocation of Crashaw—a metonymy for traditional forms or for tradition? Is it that apostrophe itself requires apology?[70] Or, perhaps related, has the poet claimed too much for her self by invoking a male line of inheritance, mouthing Crashaw's (Catullan) words? Knowing Mayer's concerns about the status of women's license to "speak," how should we take this apology? The whole performance—the dip into traditional verse and the begging forgiveness for it—depends on an ironized personalism: a "speaking in effect" that nevertheless urges us not to take it straight (too "seriously"), in part (it would seem) out of concern for how it might be shamed.

Mayer's use of expressive conventions is rather complex then: for while she critiques lyric-reading assumptions, nevertheless, the pathos of her position and concern as a woman writer comes through urgently. While her first person cannot be taken as merely expressive, Mayer cannot treat the illusion of a self "too lightly" either: for the answer to the question of "what kind of person I must be to be a poet" could appear to be a male person. This is a concern that will shape the thoughts that pass through the book's day, as in the passages in part 4 that juxtapose small details about the day's activity with facts about female writers, many of whom were feminists and mothers. Here are two examples: "Clark hasn't taken off his coat and now he has to go. The bushel of apples has candy canes too and some honey and cheese. Anne Bradstreet had eight children, she lived in Boston around 1650 and the manuscript of her first book of poems was taken to England and published without her knowing anything about it" (62). And just after, "Lewis goes into his room to work. Someone said Harriet Beecher Stowe became quite crazy towards the end of her life and pretended she was selling matches on the street" (62). Later, a call to the children's nursery school is interrupted by a brief, matter-of-fact history of Margaret Fuller Ossoli's marriage, child, and bizarre death (68). Mayer makes these women writers' histories, often marked by intense suffering, coincident to those quotidian facts of the day, as if to suggest how consciousness of these histories structures the writer's day as much as making lunches and changing diapers do. Indeed, the text, which largely refuses narrative plot and strains lyric reading by including "everything" in the day, nevertheless returns to self-consciousness that Mayer will be judged by her peers for the choice to have children and move out of the city:

> At random we have visitors, usually all at once
> Some people don't seem to like the children
> And when they come to see us they ignore them
> As if the sentient children were as unintentional
> As our presence in ironic New England
>
>   Some say
> This place is too pretty or too clean, not Marxist
> Or Leninist or Maoist enough,
>   why live anywhere? (107)

Such passages suggest what Mayer's slightly later prose work, *The Desires of Mothers to Please Others in Letters* (1979–1980, published 1994), takes up explicitly: that avant-garde critique of "the personal," meant to undermine the notion of the sovereign self, might have felt untimely and of limited use for a woman writing in the late 1970s. *Midwinter Day* is stranded between needing two forms of license: seeking permission to exist from male masters—as had been true for writers such as Fuller or Stowe—it also must ask for permission from the (mostly male) avant-garde poets.

At the end of part 4, addressing a "you" whom we cannot identify and a love story (it seems) between the Mayer persona and an unspecified "you," Mayer writes, "If that is not a story then I who have so far listened so much and now am beginning to be able to say something, which is another story, am surprised" (79). The doubleness produced by syntactic and pronominal play is significant. On the one hand, cliché contaminates: "saying something" is contrasted to the passivity of listening, which is "another story," or a history of women's expression and the importance of claiming political "voice." On the other hand, however, the sentence critiques the very figure of speech as "true expression"—authentic and idiosyncratic—by positing "saying something" as (just) "another story." Mayer's sentence takes on, rather than undercuts or rejects, the potential identificatory pitfalls of expressive discourse. The result is a doubly exposed picture of her attitude toward the expressive. Exposed by the political concerns of her time and place, Mayer nevertheless double exposes the era's verbal icons by producing a text that cannot quite be (lyrically) read.[71]

Throughout Mayer's work of the late 1970s, she seems highly aware
of the lyric reader lying in wait, ready to critique her aesthetic choices
and, in a way that perhaps seemed paradoxical to her, to identify her
with them. In "I Imagine Things," from *The Golden Book of Words* (1978),
Mayer's proliferation of first-person enunciations seem both to rebel
against prohibitions to "speak of myself" and yet also to be *produced* by
that prohibition:

> It's a fine time to think it
> I've got other rhythms and rhyme, time to think it's made by you,
> made by me, what's the time I think it's a better time to sound
> it all out, I must have found it all out before, before I saw you,
> before I met you, I think this time I might know more than
> before, this is the first time I feel I know it at all or all of it, too
> many people call, I feel I'm not a good poet, I'm half a poet, I
> lose my poethood, I don't compose knowing enough, I don't go
> far enough away, I'm too close to myself, I don't lose myself
> enough, I must free the language more, I free it too much, and
> now it's lost, lost to you and others too, I wing it, I wonder
> about it, I indulge in it, I listen to every word, I sing and I
> wonder every time, am I doing it wrong, I swim and I flounder,
> I go and I wander, I see but I go under, and when I am simple
> it's too simple for you and when I am . . . . wait, now
> I see what others are doing, they're imposing a discipline and
> saying now I can't speak of myself anymore, I must describe the
> wall of bricks and the little limited vis[t]a I've here.[72]

The poet is visibly caught amid several (untenable) evaluations: between
too much control over composition and not enough; between freeing the
language too much or not enough; between clarity and the charge of simplicity. One senses that the list of her failures could go on and on. If what
this "I" fantasizes is the freedom to say "I," the vision is tempered by the
potential for judgment. Lyrically read, the poem seems to want to "speak
of" the self, but its perverse onrush of first-person rhetoric so exaggerates
speech and cliché that it nearly fails to express anything. We become
aware of overdetermined phrases: even the seemingly personal phrase "I
don't lose myself" can be read as about expressive abandon or modernist
impersonality or as the demotion of subjectivity achieved by avant-garde
antilyric techniques, which is to say it does not express much except ex-

pressiveness. The repetition of "I" sentences proliferates so many selfish concerns that the picture of the self is, finally, blurred. As Nada Gordon writes, this is a "fortress both of and for the self."[73]

Indeed, while Gordon reads this poem (and Mayer's late 1970s career generally) as driven by the "desire to please, not alienate the reader" and as sign of Mayer's stance as "the heroine of the personal," I would qualify that the poem performs the limits of the personal as it was constructed by lyric-reading and avant-garde antilyric discourse, exploring a shame dynamic produced by the disciplinary limits of those discourses.[74] Notice that it is only with the realization that there has been a "discipline" about self-enunciation imposed—"wait . . . they're imposing a discipline and saying now I can't speak of myself anymore, I must describe the wall of bricks"—that the barrage of self-indulgent anxious first-person "talk" stops.

At one level, the admonishment interrupts and disciplines the first-person rant, but at the same time, the prose block of ranting creates the very "bricks" in question, as though the admonishment against expressivity produces an expressive anxiety.[75] The poem goes on to imagine the mix of contradictory pressures enforced by the disciplinary prohibition on speaking: "where will I enter my plea to be at the same time different and forgiven, who will listen to me, and am I whole or am I all in pieces." To choose not to write about the self under pressure of a disciplinary judgment is, Mayer seems to know, to reinscribe the category of the self refused, for only an idealized self subjects itself to a paralyzing judgment. She goes on to wonder, if the pieces will "be riveted back to another, like the nervous doctor implied, how can I expect them to read all I've written" and then shifts, quite unexpectedly, to an address to a "you" who seems a child: "how can I ever continue to carry you, carry you, through every room, through every change of the light in the color" (*Golden*, n.p.).

Here, the burden of desiring one's corpus of writing to be read shifts quite suddenly to the fatigue of carrying one's (book? reader?) child room to room. The poem concludes by meditating on a "you" who might be the infant daughter, the reader, the book, or the self as muse: "again I take liberties with you because I think perhaps you don't even understand what I'm saying, who are you, are you my daughter or are you my whim, my own excuse for living, the person I read to, my actual mentor, the one who trusts and trims what I say. . . . you are looking too, we speak these words aloud, in the words that my mouth can form independently, I needlessly love you" (*Golden*, n.p.).

The poem is not content to ignore its desire to touch a reader who, in fact, may "speak" these words, and it seems to move past its anxiety over a prohibited expressive lyric mode ("I can't speak of myself anymore") by exploring text as an identificatory form of intersubjective engagement (and hopefully a nonidentificatory one). This is figured as a mother and daughter reading together: "we speak these words aloud" (as Mayer "spoke" Crashaw, and Crashaw, Catullus), but the words belong to each mouth "independently" and thus represent a manner in which mutuality can be "needless." In *Midwinter Day*, in part 2, reading aloud to one's child similarly suggests text that can "speak" without our having to invest in or identify (with) a speaker: "I say that chipmunk who can speak is learning to speak as you [Mayer's child] say you want to read a book which means look at it so you demand of me, say it" (*MD*, 30). Interested to maintain the difference between mother and daughter / writer and reader (those cross purposes where mother/text is thinking one thing and daughter/reader another, and vice versa), Mayer nevertheless enjoys the idea of text as a place of convergence—a form of intersubjectivity that need not (as Language discourse assumed) sign on to normative notions of the self or to ill uses of others.

Here, we arrive at an interesting problem. I have argued that Sexton's relaxation of standards of aesthetic control grotesque and explode lyric-reading conventions: excessive, sloppy self-report challenges the assumption that to write a poem is to speak in an ideal and sympathetic privacy. Uncontrol takes Sexton's work outside of what for both New Critical readers and the avant-garde might be held up as good lyric-reading practice. In this way, Sexton and Mayer seem kin: Mayer's excess of self-enunciation similarly thwarts a logic of control, constituting a refusal to arrange either for the "permanent avant-garde" (on the one hand) or the interpretive operations of a lyric reader (on the other).

But of course, it is easier to believe that Mayer knew she was taking a risk, turning away from the criteria of her community of readers and fellow writers by taking *on* the problems of representational art in order to take concerns about poetic access in a new direction. Explaining her attitude toward "clarity" in her interview with Rower, Mayer eddies around making a defense of "accessible" writing. Starting with a comment sympathetic to Language discourse, she says, "perhaps obfuscating poetry might land on new forms of clarity. . . . Other poets . . . often feel you're better off if you're not clear. Truly inaccessible poetry is and always has been celebrated in an academic way." She then goes on to say, however, "I always held out the hope that my poetry and other people's poetry would be read by everyone."[76] In the process, Mayer also explores the forms of identification and projection that accessibility risked.

"CONFUSIONS OF IDENTIFICATION IN LOVE": ADDRESS AND AUTHORSHIP IN *THE DESIRES OF MOTHERS TO PLEASE OTHERS IN LETTERS*

Charles Altieri describes post–World War II experimental art as marked by a "deep hatred of the gestures of making or interpreting meanings of any kind," given how making and interpreting meaning embroil one in "desires to be recognized that one cannot control."[77] One way to reiterate what I have been arguing so far is to say that Mayer's late 1970s work recasts the situation that Altieri describes, asking to what extent desires to be recognized necessitate making (or interpreting) easily consumable images of the kind experimental avant-gardes loathed. In Mayer's work's shift toward more reference, it engages the possibility that identificatory desires and processes and projections are endemic to social life (including writing, reading, childrearing, living in a community), something to be explored in multiple arenas. In a long passage from the middle of *Midwinter Day,* she considers the processes of estrangement and identification that enter into such desires.[78] Moving out of a long mapping of all the houses on the blocks surrounding her house, Mayer lingers on the "Shell-shocked war veterans / . . . in a house at the top of the Lenox Hill" who, she claims, are "alot like us," meaning Lewis and herself (*MD,* 50). Yet to counteract the claim of identity between her and the veterans' feelings of estrangement from the bourgeois inhabitants of the town, Mayer entertains a series of stories about shocking encounters with animals quite "other"—a lobster, a deer, a fox, and a raccoon—followed by a memory of a self-estranging game "I" played with her sister in childhood that flowers into a quick series of overdetermined uses of the word "her":

> And in the middle of the night in the room full of shadows
> I used to tell my sister
>   "I'm not me, I'm someone else!"

And then I would creep out of bed over to scare her
                                        We took turns
Going down to the cellar alone in the dark
                                                Hold my hand,
Let's cross the street, something about mothers all of them
I can't remember how I met her there's something inexorable about
    her
As if there were nothing completely new to offer or to render
As if whatever's new must be turned back and redone by force
Exactly the way we secretly know everything if you believe that
I do, I can hear the voice of another though I don't want to
In a voice I thought had been mine, now just rehearsing
To make the future the past in little steps like a baby leaps
To simulate walking at first and then forgets all about it
Only to remember to learn it faster later like she imitates
The movements of your lips not the sounds
                                        I swear I know it's only
The fantastic hedonistic narcissism
                                (Like the mother who said
The best thing is he looks just like me)
                                        Of having another self (51)

Mayer's drift—from the game of "not being me" through the dislocated
phrase "hold my hand" (to whom is this addressed?) to the move to sum
up "mothers, all of them" into one inexorable "her," to lip-reading and narcissistic projection—suggests memory's deforming power (and our tendency as readers) to condense people and times in overlapping identifications. Such deformations problematically and inevitably enter into
forms of what Mayer would call "love," including writing and reading.
But it would be difficult to read this as heroizing the self unless we read
the passage lyrically. The overdetermined "her" references myriad possible females in the poem—the aforementioned sister, Mayer's own
mother, female writers, Mayer's daughter (both invoked by the lines in
which "she imitates / the movements of your lips not the sounds")—
reiterating the poem's constant enticement to identify with its amor-
phous "you." This intersubjective sharing is literalized in the figure of
the child who learns to speak by mimicking the movements of her

mother's mouth, echoed by "the voice of another" that "I thought had been mine."

Many of Mayer's stand-alone poems of the period (collected in *The Golden Book of Words* and in *Poetry*) explore not unrelated difficulty of recognizing the distinctness of the other's presence without deforming it or projecting onto it. In "The Naive Tradition of Marie," from *Poetry*, desire to honor distinctness of persons does not assure one's ability to "recognize" the other as "separate":

As each is separate so I write alone to you as each is clearly there
And not three there as one each is not always raining or starting
   fires
As Kathy has turned off the t.v. so, but not, it is hard to recognize
   presence, her presence (*Poetry*, 104, Eclipse 108, ll. 1–3)

The poem elegizes Mayer's mother, Marie (the name, importantly, is her daughter's as well), but explores the difficulty of "recogniz[ing]" her "presence." Lack of punctuation and the similes create a grammatical slippage showing how quickly the distinctness of "I" and "you," self and other, can be lost: Mayer's poem self-consciously fails to distinguish the person it is trying to remember, a failure framed as generic confusion:

And I have memory, time-honored or time-horrored, perhaps of
   Marie
And this last elegy which I might confuse with eulogy or
   encomium
Is to her. And to all the hers that might replace her, I mean,
   become her
And that is, their suffering
And that is, there is nothing to say about it except unbearable,
   impenetrable weakness & design to die (*Poetry*, 104, Eclipse
   108, ll. 14–18)

Is this eulogy, elegy, or encomium? The confusion relates to the poem's stuttering, ongoing, almost obsessive nuancing of its relation to audience, address, and poetic "speech": is this an elegy only "to her," or is this addressed to "all the hers"—a Millean "ourselves"—who can identify with "her"? The fact that the poem foregrounds genres that tend to get subsumed by the supercategory "lyric" seems pointed, given the poem's ongoing concern with

writing and reading as these involve "speaking" or not. Eulogies are written
to be spoken, whereas encomia (historically a song tradition) tend now to be
written poems of praise. The eulogist literally speaks (to a group of mourn-
ers), whereas other "lyric" forms "speak" only metaphorically, such as elegy
in its apostrophe or addresses to one (absent) person in written form.

Awareness of the complex aspects of audience—constructed fantasy
readers, the pressure of coterie-determined literary conventions—marks
much of Mayer's work of the period. Confronting myriad concerns about
the potential shaming of her work, Mayer realized some of them as theorizations of the forms of connection that writing can foster and depend
on. In *Midwinter Day,* Mayer describes "desires to be recognized" by another as forms of introjection and projection:

> You think something like a book will change the world, don't you?
> . . . .
> Of all the people I know
> I sometimes think of Peggy, Nancy, Lewis, Grace, Ted and David
> As being my mother now but a mother is never another,
> She is still you, almost by rote
> There are certain dead writers
> Who are like mothers who are more like moths
> Coming to the light at night like friends (*MD,* 52–53)

Concerns about originality are imagined in terms of the identificatory
love between children and parents: the "rote" quality of our internalization of the mother (we learn her through imitation and repetition) can
resemble how we take in text. When the poem just before turns to the
sworn confession—"I swear I know it's only / The fantastic hedonistic
narcissism / . . . Of having another self" (51)—it exposes the blurred line
between the self one has in writing and the one produced by others reading, comparing both to identifications between children and parents. In
the lines that follow, the meditation drifts into a pregnant moment that is
knowingly cliché: "The amazing thing / Is if they didn't take so long to
grow up and live without us, / They'd never learn to love or even change /
Should I say all this? / I'm sure everybody knows it already" (52).

In Bernstein's response to Mayer's *Utopia,* his answer to the question
"should I say all this?" was no: he critiqued writing that repeats the already
known. And yet Mayer's almost obsessive thinking about conventions
and forms by which self can be made articulate makes it clear that even

her very moving autobiographical work is largely about forms and problems of self-enunciation: "Falling down is a transition I offer you," she writes in *Midwinter Day,* "I have a feeling I want to be adored, is poetry a luxury, I won't defend it, I'll change my tone of voice to share the rest but I won't end it" (88). For Mayer, as for many post-1945 writers, the embarrassing "luxury" of poetry entails the poet's potential narcissism, but her work also asks who bears responsibility for the image of a person that emerges, only here and there, in flickers, in these writings. This is the acute challenge Mayer raises in *The Desires of Mothers to Please Others in Letters,* the book-length epistolary poem that followed *Midwinter Day.*

At the level of form, the "letters" that make up Mayer's *Desires* are not quite letters: they contain no address headings, dates, or greetings. Many were published in literary journals, well before Mayer published the book as a whole, which suggests that she conceived them as "literary" texts. And yet the work insists, in its opening note, on the fact of its being "real" letters: "*The Desires of Mothers to Please Others in Letters* is a series of letters written but never sent to people living and dead during a nine-month period in 1979–80."[79] Hovering between the two kinds of "letters," *Desires* explores processes of readerly identification and desire through the figure of address. Full of veiled references to Mayer's coterie, the book seems usefully contextualized by biography—chiefly by her anxiety about her place in the world of avant-garde letters and about her choice to have a third child. "Are you mad at me," *Desires* asks of us or someone, worrying she has "gone too far." How "far" is too far toward a recognizable image? How disjunct need a poem be, how unconventional must a life be, to not displease others, given the shame that displeasure might produce?

And yet, as the ambiguity of the title shows, the book very much explores the problematic allure of imposing a biographical reading (such as mine) on mute, decontextualized language. *The Desires of Mothers to Please Others in Letters:* Is it that mothers, writing epistles, may wish to please others with those epistles? Or is it that motherly desires, conveyed in letters, will be pleasing? On the other hand, might mothers (such as Mayer) wish to please those others of letters—that is, of a literary culture (her avant-garde readers, perhaps)? Or do mothers wish to please others through their own literary arts? The ambiguity of how to read the title bespeaks the problem of how to read Mayer's *Desires.*

In the generic questions that the book foregrounds—What *has* Mayer written? To whom is it addressed?—Mayer could be said to explore (and question) conventions of lyric address. *Desires* is not a lyric, but the questions it raises around address help develop a picture of her work engaging and testing the primary assumptions of lyric readings. It is in this mode that Mayer's work most seems to insist that we turn the charge of shame for lyric practices toward questions about reading.

Invoking an epistolary form but not fulfilling its dictates, *Desires* wavers between addressing and not addressing its readers, inviting us to identify its "I" as Mayer yet denying us the ability to identify *with* her—to take her place (to mouth her words). On the whole, it is difficult not to read *Desires* as commentary on the world of "letters" in which Mayer moved—not to read in its veiling of addressees a mix of protection (both of herself and others) and an enticement for real, particular readers to stumble over whether and how the letters address or reference them. It would feel willful and awkward not to identify Mayer with the "I" of *Midwinter Day* or *Desires,* which is not true for me in reading Sexton or Bishop. And yet in the same moment, the veiled address of *Desires* renders it oddly closed and distanced. Consider the book's second "letter," "Public Lice," a visual pun on a Sharon Olds–type indecorous confession (*pubic* lice) that also suggests *public lies*—personal confessions that, made literary, "lie like truth."[80] The letter renders any reader but an intimate a voyeur of conflicts within Mayer's small, close-knit literary culture. "I" (whom we can barely resist identifying as Mayer) has been receiving "hate mail," inspired, we vaguely sense, by a rejected manuscript (Mayer was an editor). Finally, the context is veiled, and, poised as intimate strangers (the new friend who can listen in but cannot yet participate), our lyric-reading strategies are powerfully tested. Mayer's transcription of gossipy speech directed at her correspondent paradoxically emphasizes the acute difference between hearing and reading, recalling Emily Dickinson's claim that "A Pen has so many inflections and a Voice but one":[81]

> You wouldn't say I thought I liked bankers or bakers like you might say
> I don't like poets, I've heard people say that, but when what's-his-name
> asked me to be in that magazine and didn't ask Lewis it seemed like it

was all more trouble than the rag would ever be worth, strictly New Grub Street: I know there's always that question of his right to do this to allied people but I say if you're gonna be friends you have to forfeit a few of your rights to this nitwitted honesty which is so defiantly stupid and based on some peculiar personal sensationalism, I mean it wasn't my writing that was at stake or the stakes, the man had struck a bargain with himself. But this is all too boring and everyone is awful except you know who and a few others and a million ones. (*Desires*, 14)

The passage can be read as a mostly clear statement about arguing with a fellow poet. However, by rendering the context unclear (as well as underpunctuating it), Mayer emphasizes the inaccessibility of the intimacy we feel privy to. Because addressed to someone other than a Millean "ourselves" (as is suggested by references to situations we cannot follow), the letter trips us at "You wouldn't say": is it that "you" (in particular) would not say that she, Mayer, thought she liked bankers or bakers? Or is it what "you" (in particular) would not say? Or is this a general you? Language becomes literal and strange. However quickly we correct our sense of estrangement by reading "You wouldn't say" as an idiom indexing proper discursive behavior ("you" here serving as "one"), the stumble forces attention on the oddness and artifice of the discursive convention. How casually, I begin to think, does "you wouldn't say" ask that we fall into assent to what counts as normative speech.

In this, the letter resists the lyric-reading norm dictating the "bourgeois audience's" expectation to "listen," to be "alerted to levels of meaning," and then to "understand" (*Eruditio*, 38). Veiling gestures—"you know who" and "what's-his-name"—suppose the potential for a private utterance to arrive in the wrong hands. But because these are not quite letters, the gesture makes literal the idea of lyric's private publicity. In a blurb for the book on the back cover, Clark Coolidge called Mayer's *Desires* "secret letters . . . addressed to everyone," and indeed, Mayer broadens the figure of audience in an almost comically literal way: "everyone is awful except you know who and a few others and a million ones" (*Desires*, 14–15).

In this experiment with private publicity, Mayer invokes and tests lyric-reading assumptions about the ideally universal address of literary language. Letters addressed to everyone both invoke the nineteenth and twentieth centuries' idealization of poetry as a lyric intimacy with strangers so unproblematic that it can be figured as "feeling confessing itself to itself" and also challenge the figure. Though intended for publication, the letters insist on an addressee so particular or situations so specific (as in references to previous conversations) that we cannot quite identify with either subject position ("you" or "I"). Most readers are "others" to these letters: "It was such a great surprise to be talking to you last week that even though I can remember everything you said I can hardly bring to mind anything I might have mentioned to you except that we were happy we will not be you know where this summer" (29). Exaggerating the intimacy between reader and writer expected of the Confessional, the letters' assumptions become so visible that they collapse. As with many Frank O'Hara poems, we encounter proper names that we may know belong to members of her circle—"Lewis," "Grace," "Peggy," "Ted," and "Alice"— but that for most of us function as signs of intimacy whose particular meanings we cannot decode.

The effect of the work's mix of lyric and epistolary aims, then, is its insistence (by flagrant exclusion) on the inevitable power that particular literary cultures and audiences play on literary production and consumption, often suppressed in theories of lyric. The work refuses to be transmuted into a "literary" or "lyric" experience, if by these we mean overheard private thoughts supposed not to be meant for a particular listener but that nevertheless supposedly "speak" to all. Indeed, Mayer crosses the detachment of a reading subject who peeks into someone's literary "Letters" with an identified reader-subject who is meant to speak as the lyric I in "overhearing" lyric intimacies.

The poet Lucie Brock-Broido has suggested that the "epistle procession" is "that impure, irresistible form of prose which lies on top of poetry," a comment that invites us to think about how the epistolary figures in a twentieth-century revival of the vitality of the "you" that was suppressed through the codification of a Mill-like lyric theory.[82] As William Waters argues, for Mill (and later for the Romantics and Hegel), the focus in conceptions of lyric has been on the lyric I, the "consequence" of which, Waters argues, is that "address [is held to be] incidental to the real matter of a poem. Who (or what) gets addressed, when and how," has tended to be thought to say "little about the work's artistic or human concerns"; in those many theories of lyric address that have construed lyric as "overheard," "all a poem's hailings are equally void of effect and therefore essentially interchangeable." As Waters goes on to assert (using Northrop Frye's famous dictum "the poet, so to speak, turns his back on his listeners," as well as Jonathan Culler's views on lyric apostrophe), readings of lyric since Mill have tended to suppose that a poet "turns his back not just on his listeners but also on any differentiation of the entities he addresses (listening or not)."[83]

Mayer's awkward literalization of that situation in *The Desires of Mothers to Please Others in Letters* suggests her interest in the consequences that such a radical distancing or outright diminishment of the lyric "you" effects. Indeed, while literary critic Ann Keniston has argued that "postwar apostrophe is concerned . . . with . . . the often irreconcilable conflict between the desire for others to be made present and the essential solitude of the lyric speaker," Mayer reminds us that that the "I" in a poem was never really alone in the first place but was always already produced in awareness of or pressure from the social sphere—conventions and modes of discourse. What if the supposed solitude of poetry is not "essential" and its I no "speaker"? Keniston reads address in postwar poetry "enact[ing] and explor[ing] . . . a longing for a lyric mode that is . . . hopelessly out of date."[84] Yet Mayer's writing in *Desires* does not quite long in this way; by making the suppression of address a literal fact of her work, Mayer's *Desires* opens up possibilities for articulating aspects of "self" and personal experience in writing that do not have to do with isolation and sovereignty. It rather explores and problematizes the expectation that we should feel, or long to feel, intimate with, or even identical to, a text:

> I had been thinking for a long time I was supposed to write you something that would be telling all kinds of awful secrets, like the kinds of things about men, women and children you cannot even write or publish not because they are so awful but because if you wrote them then you would no longer be able to associate at all with any human beings, you would be shamed, oh I guess I could still hang around with my children they wouldn't know about it. (*Desires,* 18)

The slip from confessional paradigms ("telling awful secrets") to gossipy exposé, both of which entail potential shaming, along with the shift from a specific you (addressee) to a generalized you (one), emphasizes the social realm in which writing and reading occur. Mayer here reminds us that the very idea of lyric isolation that Keniston ever so slightly idealizes as "lost" (and that Mayer's coterie negatively idealized as shameful) depends on modes of reading and social forms of assent, processes Mayer wished to foreground and explore. Mayer turns the shame of poetry read as lyric back on us as readers, alerting us to, and helping us to explore, our own desire for the text to become identified with (shamefully or pleasurably) its author's life.

This is to say that *Desires* incites and plays with the allure of biographical readings and the inevitable problematics of literary identification, neither endorsing these (as lyric readings of the work might assume) nor outright rejecting them. In "A Bean of Mine," the potential shame of being identified with Wallace Stevens is raised:

> What does anybody know about anything if you'll forgive me, I remember so many people's opinions and of course their opinions of me, even of my hair. . . . It's trivial to tell everything when you're told nothing yet, you see it's just because I know nothing again and I feel like I never wrote a poem and I know I don't know how to write one and it will probably take fifteen years again to find out how and I don't think I could get away with not practicing at all in the meantime which will make me ashamed like a shy girl working in the 5 & 10. Lewis told me today about Wallace Stevens' fascism and racism. Nevertheless we can't say we never knew the guy worked for an insurance company and it was stupid to think he worked there more like Kafka. (*Desires,* 20)

By the late 1970s, Stevens had become a shameful identification for more than a few contemporary poets (though not for his work's expressiveness, as was true of the shame of Confessionals). Both Robert Hass, in print, and Susan Howe, anecdotally, have indicated that he is a shameful love for them, one whose associations with "luxury" and bad politics they feared becoming identified with.[85] In "A Bean of Mine," Lewis's "revelation" raises the question, how can one admire poems that were written by a supposed fascist, a racist, and an insurance man? What is the connection between Stevens's comments in letters and his poems? Do these connections expose us?

Mayer's performed shame over Stevens's bad politics is not quite straight when we consider it in light of her general skepticism about the logic (implicit in Lewis's comment) that would identify writing with author. That logic contradicts the Barthesian theory and anticonfessionalism that writers in and adjacent to her circles had (by the late 1970s) absorbed. In the odd "nevertheless," a retort to the "news," Mayer's persona seems ready, if not to defend Stevens, then to problematize the innocence that she and Lewis once supposedly had toward Stevens's vocational choices. In claiming, "Nevertheless, it was stupid to think [Stevens] worked [in insurance] like Kafka" (Kafka being another famous letter writer and insurance lawyer), Mayer raises the question, what were we once willing to ignore about the personal origins of Stevens writing, and for what reason? Mayer seems to suggest that Stevens's readers were willing to fantasize or invent an ideal manner in which Stevens-the-man worked in insurance, one in keeping with an idealized Stevens whose imagined person could authorize the pleasures that his poems produced. Mayer here glances at the complex, perhaps unconscious, identifications readers make, fantasize, or demand to make with an author's biography and their own projective fantasies about authorial identity.

The passage extends Mayer's research into the question asked in *Midwinter Day*: "What kind of person I must be to be a poet," a pressing one in part because of her community's views on her life choices (having a third child, writing personally) and their consequences for her poetry (*MD*, 26). Here, Mayer subtly draws her own shame at potentially never "practicing [poetry] at all" into comparison with Lewis's shame (or shaming) of Stevens's work as supposedly fascist and racist (possibilities made visible in his letters), both of which involve questions about the poet's other job—Stevens's as an insurance lawyer and Mayer's as a mother. Stevens functions as a metonymy for a cluster of related concerns about art, economic necessity (day jobs), and social pressure; Mayer also discusses her dread that a third child will necessitate her getting a job teaching, something she had never wanted to do.

It seems no accident that Stevens functions this way in *Desires:* Stevens's depressing, casual racism and comments on Mussolini had became visible through the relatively recently published selection of his *Collected Letters* (the first edition appeared in 1966). Holly Stevens had sold her father's archive in 1975, just a few years before Mayer wrote *Desires;* concerns about Stevens's politics had became increasingly important in the late 1970s and early 1980s, facts of his biography shaping the discourse around his canonical status. Asking whether Stevens's letters could shame his writing, Mayer then explores the possibility that, conversely, her aesthetic choices might shame her person.

Significantly, the passage takes on these issues by playing with modes of address, syntax, and person in writing. The poem's address is unspecified, which makes its "you" feel like a breach of the fourth wall—a strange address to us. I will quote at length, as the passage's drift and range of rhetoric is key to understanding its theorization of the lyric shame situation:

> I've got to tell you I often talk as if you were both me and you and a third person, another person too. I do this to subsume my desire to tell everything in confusion but as if it were public. . . . Maybe there is a way to write myself back to a revealing lack of syntax, do you think so? I believe it might be compared to trying to lose weight. Many people say it is impossible and I empathize most with the people who have to bear the weight but I can't stop believing that anything is possible, you see I have gotten myself back into that old thing about the perfection of states. . . . I see that my eyes reflect the light with too much time included like the curvature of the lens, I can't speak about the value of seeing this, I'm bug-eyed, beady-eyed, I'd give anything to be lyrical and to have good teeth, those eyes are accused of something, it's being annihilated by circumstances so we tell everything in the hope of returning like I'm having the chance to do I think, if only I had some cocaine or something like the guy's supposed to have all those people said I looked like. I do have an eye, I mean my eye is palpable, not like June or July, do I have to make rules for myself or others, against my own feelings that barely even time exists and a picture of a poet needs to have some interesting light. (21–22)

Here the "palpable" "eye" can be read as a lyric I that "talks" (even a confessional one: "I've got to tell you," "tell everything"), and there is something scathing and laughable about the fact that being "lyrical" results in "good teeth," an embarrassingly American form of poetic luxury. Such "eyes" (I's) are "accused of something," and Mayer's persona cannot "speak about the value of seeing" herself in a certain light. The language of the passage seems to ponder a mode of lyric address ("I've got to tell you I often talk as if you were both me and you and a third person, another person too") that approaches the conditions of self-address that, as in much modern lyric theory, is also universal. Mayer is riffing on the "rules for myself and others" about how to write poetry, making a verbal collage that lights on key phrases concerning narrativity, autobiographicality, and expression then circulating (as we see in Sexton's work of the era, as well) through poetic discourses.

Both Sexton and Mayer make more than a complex lyric-expressive subjectivity available, that is; their work reminds me how fraught it was to even be writing about "I's" or about the self in 1979. In Mayer's case, furthermore, is the potential shame of feeling, as the letter suggests, that one had lost control over the avant-garde convention of a "revealing lack of syntax." A "lack of syntax" helps produce the elliptical, fragmentary, fractured modernist surface informing Language poetics and was meant to work against conventions of subjective expression (supposed revelations of self). The paradox, Mayer's passage understands, was that to engage or not engage such syntactic disruption could be taken to *reveal* one's aesthetic-political affiliations. That Mayer compares the effort to reachieve a less-syntax-heavy line with the effort to "lose weight" suggests how gendered she found the particular shame of having put on the "weight" of narrative and the autobiographical in her poems. The *presence* of syntax exposes one to shame, as if one were a fat woman. Mayer empathizes with those who have to "bear the weight" (ostensibly, her readers), but she also identifies with the ashamed girl who cannot lose "the weight." Writing is the exercise "practice" that she needs to find her way back to suitably slender poems, so that she will not feel ashamed like "a shy girl working at the 5 & 10" (21).

Mayer's letter walks a razor's edge, imagining a reader who will judge the poem, exploring her identification with shameful poets, subjugated female workers, and abjected poetic tendencies. But the passage also suggests why women might not view connections between vocation, aesthetics, and identity as essential and necessary in the way that men, traditionally, have. As if remembering her daily life in the 1960s, Mayer writes,

> I was too forgetful of being a woman or a girl, which was lucky, except of course when I was at my job. I don't mean writing but the job I had typing for a company for $65 dollars a week in 1965 but I hate it when anyone mentions that year especially anybody who says in '65 I blah blah blah and then I met Olson and so on. I mean I am just talking here about my job as a typist at Barnes & Noble, I hope you'll ennoble me by forgiving me for remembering. It was better than being a floor-walker which I feel like tonight like if you wanted to be scared enough to please me as I'm scared enough to want to please you all the time,

then you might, what, take me to New Orleans but don't introduce me to Wallace Stevens down there and tell me traditional beauty is just this world and then forgive me my trespasses, not for thine is the kingdom and the power and the glory and so on for I wasn't brought up a Protestant, I can't remember the right end. (22)

The 1965 story that Mayer wants to be forgiven for narrating is of mere work, a day job as a typist, one that, we can assume, exposed her to a then-pervasive sexism that would have made it difficult to be "forgetful of being a woman or a girl." How could Mayer want to identify her self with that job (not writing but a typing job), which could not ennoble her, as the stories someone (implicitly male) could tell about his life in 1965? And yet, we can assume, this identification between activity and self was just what guided both the presumably male (and presumably avant-garde) storyteller—"blah blah blah and then I met [Charles] Olson and so on"— and the concern about Stevens's vocation and its potential to infect both his work and his readers. Mayer's "blah blah blah" shows us, by contrast, that such stories are generic and banal, undercutting their author-heroics.

With Charles Olson as the heroized author-figure, we are left with a question: is Mayer invoking Olson as a figure for the abjection of subjective poetics, or is she invoking his near-heroic status for many (male) avant-gardists of the late 1970s? It would be hard to decide without projecting onto the passage, of course.

Mayer's work seems most interesting to me, as below in "The Naive Tradition of Marie," for its research into the capacity for intimate and imploring "speech" (one thing we might mean by calling language "personal") to nevertheless deny us a ground of identification with it, or full access to it. The shortest and latest of Mayer's poems in *Poetry* often force the word "speak" on us, emphasizing the lyric reading convention that so many poets and readers have been taught to assume:

I have told you so much about myself
So share me, I am separate
As each is separate so I wrote alone to you as each is clarity
And share what I know generously
Cause I have learned it to have good aim
Cause I have learned it by sharing Marie's intense suffering, and
    her addiction
And now I speak of it

And it's to share with certain of you & I am sure I will learn more
Share that with me
And speak
And I will speak with you
As I spoke normally
To Marie ("Naive Tradition," *Poetry,* 105, Eclipse 109)

Mayer's under-punctuated, slippery syntax and run-on sentence structure, not to mention her plethora of underspecified pronouns, deny us the ability to identify with either the "I" or the "you" invoked who become "all the hers" and "certain of you"—those who suffer on account of "I" being there (or not), and so on. As in much of Sexton, the flaunted, exaggerated, and finally multiple speaker figure here invites us to recognize the lure to identify ourselves with an "I" that becomes too fluid and shapeless to accommodate the urge.

And yet the savvy seems hard won and not without pathos: if the poem operates on a sincere level (and I imagine it does), it is in researching a problematic identification with a parent whose life was full of pain:

In her addiction to die
In her design to morphine
In her place as my mother
. . . .
In her need for love I share
. . . .
In my youth which was her youth, I could not make the change
I didn't die with her (105, Eclipse 109)

Several of the collection's last poems (which Mayer has admitted she wrote very quickly the year the collection appeared) similarly exaggerate the first person with onrushes of "I" statements, made excessively expressive, as with her earlier, more Gertrude Steinian experiment in *Moving* (1971):

I will not walk into a wall, I will not even talk, rewind, whatever
    that means, I will change the record, I will look & see
I will stay the person that no one accepts as me
. . . .
I give [memory] the finger, I am not around, I am out sinking ships
No matter what reveals the endless stubbornness of my own soul

> I live with it, I make it new, I don't excite it, I endure its moments
>   of anarchy & take them in
> Not the people but the thought, strange to repeat it, stranger still,
>   to have said it at all
> I am being influenced. I am in thrall, I repeat myself still more
> I am the person thinking there is no one at the door.
> ("Nails Sock & Nobody Knows," *Poetry*, 111–112, Eclipse
>   115–116)

As if busting through the possible charges of hypostasis and reification that the Language critique of poetry (read as lyric) was then refining, Mayer's poem insists on the critical possibilities of exploring a lyric-reading inheritance, testing its outer limits, a trend that many poets since (the post-Language Flarfists, for instance) have continued.[86] I will close by looking at one of Mayer's more famous poems, "The Way to Keep Going in Antarctica" (1976), whose exaggerated expressivism (figured as a geographic outer limit) and self-address comment on Mayer's exploration of the critical possibilities of working with lyric-reading conventions in full awareness that to do so would open her work to a shame that cannot, so to speak, belong to it. The poem begins,

> Be strong Bernadette
> Nobody will ever know
> I came here for a reason
> Perhaps there is a life here
> Of not being afraid of your own heart beating
> Do not be afraid of your own heart beating
> Look at very small things with your eyes
> & stay warm
> Nothing outside can cure you but everything's outside
> (*Poetry*, 128, Eclipse 132)

Mayer tests our tendency to want to read this poem lyrically and literalize its speech as belonging to a person "here" before us: "I came here for a reason" comically literalizes the space of the page as the Antarctic place in which to "be brave" and seems to take on the shameful "drive . . . to meaningful statement" that Perloff imputed to Bishop's poems to exemplify mainstream lyric tendencies. Mayer's persona here takes comfort in the idea that, if some personal drive to mean motivates the coming "here," its origins will be safely lost (or misidentified). That is, Mayer refuses to stand for a psychic interiority: "everything's outside," after all, and the poem's "life" is conditioned by the refusal of the mortal heartbeat.

At one level, the poem invites us to read it as championing a brave return to the human presence in poetry, an isolating challenge comparable to that Douglas Mawson faced in his Antarctic expeditions, which Mayer references in the lines,

> I had written: "the man who sewed his soles back on his feet"
> And then I panicked most at the sound of what the wind could do

It is tempting to read this as an allegory for Mayer's difficult return to a poetry of the self:

> There is great shame for the world in knowing
> You may have gone this far

However, the poem keeps us at a distance even as it offers us confessional conventions:

> Until there is no more panic at the knowledge of your own real
>   existence
> & then only special childish laughter to be shown
> & no more lies no more
> Not to find you no
> More coming back & more returning
> Southern journey
> Small things & not my own debris
> Something to fight against

"Something to fight against" and "no more lies" are familiar because cliché, and a phrase such as "Southern journey," evocative of so much—the civil rights era, Alan Lomax's recordings of folk music, tourism—that the passage, already drawing on the heroic *topos* of the South Pole Antarctic expedition, evokes strong feelings while being overdetermined. As Mayer writes,

> & we are all very fluent about ourselves
> Our own ideas of food, a Wild sauce
> There's not much point in its being over: but we do not speak them:
> I had written: "the man who sewed his soles back on his feet"

And then I panicked most at the sound of what the wind could do
    to me
        if I crawled back to the house, two feet give no position, if
        the branches cracked over my head & their threatening me,
          if I
        covered my face with beer & sweated till you returned
    If I suffered what else could I do (128, Eclipse 132)

By the last three lines, our own fluency comes up against a surrealism of private reference that cannot support our identification: What is it to cover one's face with beer? What is "its," and this "them" that "we do not speak"? The chain of phrases linked by colons seems to promise some explanation. But way leads to way, and we cannot follow. What began as an expressive poem, practically bludgeoning us into identifying Bernadette Mayer with its "I," by the end reminds us that that image of "real existence" depends on "our own ideas," a "Wild sauce" for Mayer's written (not spoken) words. Mayer's self-projection onto Dawson's terrible ordeal (his frostbite was so advanced that he had to sew his foot soles, separated from his feet, back on to keep going) is perverse but human, pervasive in lyric readings, in adjudications of others' aesthetic choices, and in our fantasies about others and ourselves. If from Mayer's first poem in *Poetry,* "Corn Borer"—a disjunctive dictionary poem written in the 1960s that riffs on the words "corn borer"—to her last, "The Way to Keep Going in Antarctica," written in 1976, we see a great stylistic shift toward the personal; it is a shift informed, but not ashamed, by her earliest concrete experiments with syntax and antilyricism.

    The result is a poetics that explores processes of lyric reading rather than a naïve embrace of expressive principles. Throughout, I have been arguing that lyric reading projects a lyric subject and that antilyricism projects a shamed lyric subject onto its abjected others. Mayer's work not only does not quite deserve its lyric shame, but it may help us deconstruct its premises. Avant-garde antilyricism's refusal of the figure of expression and voice, meant to alert readers to the social nature of poetic reception, encouraged a mutual isolation of reader and writer, replicating in new terms the Millean figure of solitary confinement. Whereas in Millean lyric readings the isolated lyric reader falls into complete identity with the isolated lyric speaker, that is, much avant-garde antilyric theory assumes a text so open that it is safeguarded from producing, in textual space, a ground of identification. Mayer's work, by contrast, helps (me) to see how problematically and richly such processes define human experience. Her work investigates that space, rife with desire and narcissism and love and shame.

CHAPTER FOUR

Tired of Myself

The 1990s and the "Lyric Shame" Poem

America, you don't need poetry.
Could we not go back to the way things were:

. . . .

Before you and I were forced to speak?
—*Lynn Emanuel, from "Dream in Which I Meet Myself,"*
Noose and Hook *(2010)*

I look out the window and I am deep.
—*parody of lyric poetry, attributed to Bob Perelman*

ROBERT HASS'S 1996 poem "Interrupted Meditation" ends with its poet-persona's admission that he is "a little ashamed."[1] He is ashamed not of the failure of his marriage, nor of revealing in the poem painful and intimate details of his breakup with his wife. What ashames him, if only "a little," is his desire to move from meditation to epiphany: "I'm a little ashamed that I want to end this poem / singing, but I want to end this poem singing." The poem's self-conscious turn to singing around this line's steep enjambment comes as a surprise, especially in a poem that is full of more obviously shameful issues, including a friend's admission that he failed to act on behalf of Jewish neighbors during the Nazi invasion of his Hungarian city. The lines clarify that what this long and meandering poem meditates on is not so much the self but the ethics of engaging expressive poetics.

Hass's lines are echoed in several poems written by other "mainstream" poets around the same time. Gerald Stern's poet-speaker in "Hot Dog" admits, "I am a little / embarrassed; I would like not always to have to / be the one who sings." Another self-conscious poet-speaker, in Charles Wright's "Disjecta Membra," longs for negative capability as both cause and cure for expressive embarrassment: "If I could slide into a deep sleep, / I could say—to myself, without speaking—why my words embarrass me." Jorie Graham's "Pollock and Canvas," an *ars poetica* advocating a turn to process-oriented poetics, makes a refrain of the parenthetical phrase fragments "(without embarrassment. without shame)" across its second and third sections. And any number of poems from James Tate's 1990s work could be invoked to suggest how often Tate's poet-subject flogs himself for "the embarrassing heartache / of [his] latest aperçu," chiding himself for engaging an epiphanic, meditative mode. Hass's shame at "singing" is something of a motif, sign of a trend whereby established, "mainstream" writers explore embarrassment and shame over poetic practices identified with lyric and resulting in an abstract discourse about "expressive poetics."[2]

I am going to call the mode that these lines exemplify "the lyric shame poem," a mode informed by the lyric shame situation of the late twentieth century—when twentieth-century pedagogical idealizations of a lyric "tradition" reenter and redouble in the academy in negative form as avant-garde antilyricism. Hass's work marks one end of a range of later-twentieth-century poems that self-consciously posit lyric as a problematic identification (on the other end of this range would be Language poetry), showing us a "mainstream" version of a self-conscious, emergent critical-poetic discourse about lyric and lyric reading. Identifying this motif helps describe a pivotal moment in the history of contemporary poetics in the United States, adding to available accounts of poetic production and reception in the 1980s and 1990s.[3]

Hass's and others' confessions of the desire to engage poetic tendencies that they understand to be shamefully "lyric" suggests the pressure that poststructuralism and Language theory's critique of the sovereign subject exerted on poetic practice in the mainstream. It also bespeaks a broader trend of awareness (and self-conscious admission of that awareness) of the professional literary critic as audience for the contemporary lyric poem, a situation that begins with the installment of a boiled-down, pedagogical version of New Critical theories, whose emphasis was on closural poetry reading, in schools and universities in the post-1945 era. Along with a vaguely New Critical hermeneutic dominating the poetic culture of the day, we can also invoke the emergence of a more diffused, new "teacher-poet" culture and style of writing that Elizabeth Bishop associated with American high capitalism and its glib cultural tone of "slickness." This culture determined in large part how poets were trained, how they would work, what they would read, and how they would write and publish. By the 1990s, an academic-, MFA-, and PhD-heavy market for poetry books and journals had become the norm.[4]

No doubt, there are previous modern examples (or coterie situations) wherein we would find a metacritical awareness assert itself in poems, but starting in the 1990s in the United States, this trend accelerated to a far point, evident in Flarf and Conceptual projects (two forms of avant-garde poetics that became visible in the 2000s and where much debate about "lyric" now resides).[5] As I have been arguing, we can see early instances of metacritical awareness about lyric-reading norms emerging not only in Language projects from the 1970s but also in Sexton's emphasis on the "speaker," which she knew to be an important interpretive hermeneutic for New Critical professors. We could also look to Bishop's late poem "Santarem" (1976), whose speaking subject's conception of the confluence of two Brazilian rivers she flags as mediated by both New Critical and poststructural lyric-reading strategies (chiefly, the identification of tensions and binaries) and thus by her cognizance of an academic audience for the poem: "Even if one were tempted / to literary interpretations / such as: "life/death, right/wrong, male/female—such notions would have resolved, dissolved, straight off / in that watery, dazzling dialectic."[6]

An important prehistory to the most intense lyric shame moments of the 1990s would involve John Ashbery's work (and, as I will point out later, Jorie Graham's). Even since its earliest appearance, Ashbery's work has sought to manage the embarrassments of conventions associated with lyric in the twentieth century, as Lynn Keller points out in saying that Ashbery's "parodic versions of traditional motifs . . . and of traditional lyric forms" evidence "half-apologetic embarrassment."[7] In a review of Ashbery's late work for the *Boston Review,* James Longenbach sums up Ashbery's oeuvre in a way that locates that stance in an earlier American poetic: "Shyness, awkwardness, embarrassment: no poet has made these tones more available in poetry. And in doing so, Ashbery has reached back to what he thinks of as a golden age of American literature."[8] Longenbach historicizes Ashbery's attachment to that "golden age"—the late 1930s and 1940s and the work of Randall Jarrell, Delmore Schwartz, Paul Goodman, Jean Garrigue, Elizabeth Bishop, and W. H. Auden specifically—as invoking that era's "shyness, awkwardness, embarrassment" about *poesis*. This, Longenbach suggests, offered Ashbery an alternative to 1950s and 1960s American poetics:

> The grand stuff of literary history had happened while Ashbery was living in France—Ginsberg's *Howl,* Lowell's *Life Studies*—but Ashbery remained unmoved by it. When he returned to New York, American poetry seemed to him oppressively dour. And if it wasn't dour, it was hysterical. And if it managed to be playful, it seemed sanctimonious, tilting at the windmills of the establishment. The lost world of American poetry, the world of Ashbery's youth, seemed much more attractive.[9]

Longenbach's assessment allows that Ashbery did not need to write lyric shame poems in the 1990s as a response to the Language discourse because he had been writing them all along, a possibility obscured (as I have been arguing about Bishop and Sexton) by the polarizing critical terms available for thinking through post-1945 poetic production.[10] Ashbery experimented with concrete and disjunctive forms, resisting what Keller calls "traditional lyric" and the hermeneutics of New Critical reading. But he engaged this resistance through strategies of rhetorical play he learned from writers such as Bishop. Such rhetorical experiments do not mark a retreat from his supposedly more potent syntactic experiments, as Perloff has argued, but a different approach to exploring the embarrassments of "tradition."[11]

Ashbery's rhetorically inflected antilyric project (like that of the New York School, for instance) predicts the metacritical lyric shame poems of the late 1980s and 1990s. Metacritical self-consciousness is a mode that reaches full, almost stifling flowering in such poems as "The Lyric 'I' Drives to Pick Up Her Children from School: A Poem in the Postconfessional Mode" (2005), by Olena Kalytiak Davis. Davis's poem, which I will discuss at the end of this chapter, makes explicit references to a canon of academic lyric and antilyric theory both of the "mainstream" (M. H. Abrams and Helen Vendler) and avant-garde (Boris Tomashevsky and Marjorie Perloff), all, Davis's poem posits, oppressively definitive of the possible forms in which contemporary poets can take their autobiographical impulses.

ABRAMS TO PERLOFF

Hass flags his interrupted "meditation" as problematically expressive and as a source of interrupting self-consciousness. This is clear from the poem's beginning, and in ways that invoke both New Criticism–informed lyric discourses and specifically Perloff-inspired antilyric discourse. An antiexpressive statement interrupts the opening lines' meditation on place—a highly specific description of creek-side flora—just at the brink of a simile that would usher the poetic subject's presence into view:

> Little green involute fronds of fern at creekside,
> And sinewy clear water rushing over creekstone
> of the palest amber, veined with a darker gold.
> Thinnest lines of gold rivering through the amber
> like—ah, now we come to it. *We were not put on earth,*
> the old man said, . . .
>
> . . . *to express ourselves.* (*Sun,* 73)

Hass's first-person-plural pronoun ("ah, now we come to it") is pointed—teacherly and corrective. The singular "I" will go on to recall the longer conversation with the (nameless) old man, a Hungarian exile who bluntly criticizes conventional American expressive poetics as self-involved, self-important, and demonstrative of a culture of luxury. It is the memory of that exile's rebuke that, ostensibly, checks the drive to metaphor and deflates the poet's expressive, identificatory path, producing a "we." Hass here addresses other poets, readers of critical theory—a resolutely academic audience.

   In this poem's connection of simile making with problems of poetic of subjectivity, it feels apposite to Bishop's concern in the 1930s with a "tradition of likenesses" and the subjective stance that such a "tradition" could produce. More locally, however, the moment reflects the antiexpressive, anti-"meditative," and anti-"lyric" agenda that, by the mid-1990s, was moving out of the various, mostly closed circles of avant-garde community into a larger academic mainstream discourse on poetry in the United States. Thus, it is important to note how strongly Hass's poem begins showing itself both engaged (and also ashamed) by those conventions. For example, Hass's "I" confesses to shame at the poem's end, where, in 1996, conventions would dictate an epiphanic closure confirming the poet's commitment to "lyric" "singing." Hass's shame lines conform to the "lyric" expectations of the day in several ways, especially by interrupting what wants otherwise to be a shimmering epiphany-*cum*-symbolic-description:

> This morning I am pretending
> to be walking down the mountain in the heat.
> A vault of blue sky, traildust, the sweet medicinal
> scent of mountain grasses, and at trailside—
> I'm a little ashamed that I want to end this poem
> singing, but I want to end this poem singing—the wooly
> closed-down buds of the sunflower to which, in English,
> someone gave the name, sometime, of pearly everlasting. (*Sun,* 76)

It is the combination of fluid rhythm (nearly iambic pentameter), complex syntax, and the poem's claim for heightened perception or intense personal realization that codes these lines, in the critical idiom of the day, as lyric. Critical *disapprobation* of lyric, which had risen to a pitch in the two decades leading up to Hass's poem, focused on these lyric habits not merely as conventional and expected but as indicating and producing the poet's "privileged position," his or her control over meaning, and the limits of that subject position for the poem's potential readers.[12]

Hass's admission of shame is explicit, but the poem codes its awareness of the by-then-decades-old Language critique of "voice" poems and a purported expressive tradition in more subtle ways, as well. The "pearly everlasting" flower that Hass's poet-I wishes to praise is the *Anaphalis margaritacea,* a short-lived, white perennial in the sunflower family that "American Indians and colonists" used to treat everything from headaches to heart disease (echoed here perhaps by the "medicinal" smell of the grasses encountered). The medicine men of the Mohegans (a Connecticut Algonquin tribe) "even claimed that chewing everlasting made the user want to sing."[13] Perhaps this is the history that Hass's final lines take weird pains to elide or ignore—note in the last line "someone," "sometime." For all the poet's Williams-like efforts to render the flower concretely, it serves the poet's attempt to transcend the darker issues that the poem raises: what poetry might do in light of the horrors of the twentieth century; the individual's complicity with acts of genocide; and, at a more personal level, the failure of the poet's marriage. The everlasting reference also subtly inscribes (given its medicinal uses) the possibility that being moved to sing, like the longing for heaven, is habit-forming intoxication, escapism mistaken as engagement.

I mention this idea of intoxication because, by 1996, the conventions of meditative lyric were increasingly visible in negative form, treated as something one ought to give up, not unlike an addictive intoxicant (think opiate of the masses). The lyric shame poems I will discuss in this chapter—especially those of Hass and James Tate—foreground their I's self-consciousness about engaging a "meditative," "lyric" tradition commonly referred to in the shorthand as the "epiphany poem," a term coined by Perloff in the early 1970s and singled out by her and others subsequently not only for its ubiquity but for its "easy," "smarmy," and "self-important" qualities by subsequent writers. The poem often derided as exemplary of epiphany poems—William Stafford's "Traveling Through the Dark" (1965)—was singled out in the Language-centered journal the *Hills* in 1980; by the 1990s, the terms of that critique circulated widely, in large part through the visibility of Perloff's essays, among poetry readers and critics in the United States.[14]

This is to say that Hass's poem is very much of its moment. Literary historians cite the mid-to-late 1990s as the peak of a long and subtle process of the absorption of Language ideas into the academy, a process that Andrew Epstein argues started in the early 1980s with the appearance of a "Language sampler," edited by Charles Bernstein, in the *Paris Review* and Perloff's seminal 1984 account of Language politics-aesthetics in *American Poetry Review*.[15] By the 1990s, many of the first wave of Language writers had gained visibility through their or their collaborators' employment in university jobs and their works' accessibility in university publications, which, Epstein argues, some in avant-garde circles took as a betrayal of Language's early oppositional politics. If there was suspicion of Language's entry into the academy by members of the avant-garde, for those "mainstream" figures already installed in the university, "new" Language ideas were often met with reactionary hand-wringing.[16]

Hass, writing in Northern California, situated in a poetic culture that saw poets from both the "mainstream" and avant-garde mingle at such venues as the San Francisco State University Poetry Center, was ahead of the curve, but by 1996 (the year *Sun Under Wood* appeared), the Language critique of "lyric" had been so fully absorbed into the academy that Perloff's use of its oppositional lyric and antilyric terms that year to historicize the choices facing U.S. artists after modernism seemed rather natural. It became an "obsess[ion]" for the writer after modernism, she argued, as to "whether poetry should be lyric or collage, meditation or encyclopedia, the still moment or the jagged fragment."[17]

More explicitly than Hass, that is, Perloff negatively identifies "lyric" with "meditation," a choice that nevertheless maintains midcentury New Criticism–informed lyric theory, particularly the identification of lyric with a narrow corpus of English Romantic poetry. Indeed, in coining "epiphany poem" to identify a mode that she believes dominates from the 1970s forward and that extends a moribund lyric "tradition," and in invoking "meditation," Perloff and Hass reanimate terms deriving from M. H. Abrams's famous essay "Structure and Style in the Greater Romantic Lyric" (1965), which itself extends (with more historical nuance perhaps) the lyric theory of Reuben Brower and Cleanth Brooks.[18] The Millean assertion of lyric as meditation (spoken to no one or to the self) had of course been made by T. S. Eliot in *The Three Voices of Poetry*. Abrams's famous terms describing "the" Romantic lyric, are as follows:

> Some [Romantic lyrics] . . . approach the ode in having lyric magnitude and a serious subject, feeling fully meditated. They present a determinate speaker in a particularized, and usually a localized, outdoor setting, whom we overhear as he carries on, in a fluent vernacular which rises easily to a more formal speech, a sustained colloquy, sometimes with himself or with the outer scene, but more frequently with a silent human auditor, present or absent. The speaker begins with a description of the landscape; an aspect or change of aspect in the landscape evokes a varied but integral process of memory, thought, anticipation, and feeling which remains closely intervolved with the outer scene. In the course of this meditation the lyric speaker achieves an insight, faces up to a tragic loss, comes to a moral decision, or resolves an emotional problem. Often the poem rounds upon itself to end where it began, at the outer scene, but with an altered mood and deepened understanding which is the result of the intervening meditation.[19]

I quote at length because this portion of Abrams's essay is a hub around which many (anti)idealizations of "the lyric" as meditation cluster: the essay appeared as Hass was embarking on a PhD in English and as Perloff was completing hers, in the moment when poets associated with the concept of the "Deep Image," such as William Stafford and James Wright and Robert Bly, were first celebrated, and yet also in the moment when many Language writers and even so-called Confessional, "voice" poets were producing work that implicitly or explicitly tested Abrams's terms.

Writing in 1973, Perloff describes the major mode of (then) contemporary work in terms drawn straight out of Abrams's account of Romanticism: "a brief lyric in which contemplation of the external landscape suddenly gives way to insight into the world beyond."[20] By the later 1970s and early 1980s, her account of the meditative "epiphany poem" became increasingly oppositional; she animates these Abramsian terms to describe "lyric," "later modernism," "mainstream," and Romantic conventions, all terms informing oppositional Language experiments. Perloff clearly takes Abrams's account as an accurate description of lyric poetry, rather than as itself symptomatic of a critical moment in academia. Following Abrams's lead, as so many critics did, she confuses a critical paradigm for lyric reading (and later writing) with the quiddity of a tradition. The shame she attributes to certain poems held to carry on a moribund tradition is in fact the shame of lyric reading.[21]

Surveying Perloff's critical evolution through the figure of the "epiphany poem"—from descriptive to oppositional—indicates the charge of shame that conventional "lyric," whether construed as meditation, Deep Image, epiphany, or workshop poem, was charged with in the 1970s and after. Deeply influencing contemporary criticism, Perloff's account of the "epiphany poem" identifies it as a technique of the "logocentric universe," of Cartesian ideology, one that emphasizes the "centrality of persons" and is thus deeply out of tune with any politics concerned with intersubjectivity and community.[22] Seeds of this critique, which Perloff drew from her readings of Language writing (itself informed by Abrams's Millean terms), offered to a broad academic audience a version of lyric whose coherence depended on its abstract function as an antitype that has been influential and widely circulated. Craig Dworkin (a student of Perloff's) identifies the mainstream of poetic understanding in similar terms, as involving epiphany: "for many people, 'poetry' has come to mean simply a genre of writing that includes a small epiphany—a 'deep' thought or 'profound' insight or a bit of self-realization by an especially sensitive person."[23] The epiphanic lyric mode, in Dworkin's Perloffian-Abramsian terms, is a technique that enables the self-indulgent self-regard of the confessional American subject.[24] In the years surrounding the publication of Hass's *Sun* and Perloff's *Dance,* it has become more and more common to identify (and disparage) lyric using Abrams's terms, as poetry marked by an "impassioned or meditative poetic voice [and] determinate setting and/or occasion" and as "conventional poetic practice."[25] I rehearse this poetic-critical phenomenon to show that Hass cannot have evoked "meditation" as lyric "singing" in the mid-1990s without knowing that his Eliotic, Abramsian terms would also activate the Perloffian Language critique of them.

This is not to literalize the critique in the poem (which emerges from the character of the eastern European exile and nihilist) as singly located in Perloff or in Language poetry. For one, Hass clearly *is* exploring a "scenic mode," as Charles Altieri describes it, that *does* have a history and whose discontents might more confidently locate Hass in, rather than out of, a "lyric" meditative mode idealized as tradition by Abrams in the late 1950s and early 1960s. And yet the figure of the eastern European exile seems a pointed, if subtle, invocation of contemporary inflections of that tradition. As I have mentioned, that exile's own "time of shame" involves his failure to fight for Jews in hiding (perhaps in his Hungarian hometown) during the Nazi occupation in World War II. Hass lets us know that the exile is *not* Czeslaw Milosz, whose work Hass had translated; the exile in fact refuses the poet's invocation of Milosz as an answer to the impasse of writing poetry after World War II. Milosz's answer, "responsibility to being," and Hass's own admiration for it, represents a Williams-inspired, Keatsian-inflected answer to lyric-subjective discontent—devotion to concretion, particularity, and negative capability. The exile casts these as illusory because, finally, they are underwritten by privilege and evasive of the nothingness and death that exceed poetry of expression: "There is silence at the end," the exile complains, "and it doesn't explain, it doesn't even ask" (*Sun*, 75).

In marking the exile's critique not just as anti-Wordsworthian (as Keats's was) but also as tacitly anti-Keats and anti-Williams, Hass subtly invokes the more recent, avant-garde critique of lyric subjectivity, which identifies the abjected Romantic lyric with Keatsian, Emersonian *"Einfühlung"*—a subjective stance in which "nature always wears the colors of the spirit."[26] The exile's rejection of expression and voice metonymizes the more contemporary critique of lyric's purported soothing legibility and self-centeredness. The exile is a reader of Edmond Jabés, for instance, and his flagging of the poet's window view suggests that the American taste for "self-expression" is made possible by forms of leisure and privilege recalling Perloff's focus on the "speaker located in a specific place": "*Of course, here,* gesturing out the window, pines, ragged green / of a winter lawn, the bay, *you can express what you like, / enumerate the vegetation*" (*Sun,* 75, my emphasis).

Hass also takes pains to show how steeped the poet-I is in midcentury American conventions that Hass knew to have fallen out of favor in avant-garde poetics circles. When the Hungarian offers his Jabés-informed nihilistic mysticism to the poet as an (ironic?) "magic key" that will open "Anything, anything! But what?" the poet admits that he "found" himself unable to think of anything but "the failure of [his] marriage," then offered as a written snippet of confessional, narrative poetry, in the poem's last strophe. This metaconfessional moment leads to an epiphany so flatly voiced and weakly reprising of the Hungarian's view that one wonders if it admits Hass's own weariness with available poetic language and conventions: "I don't know what the key opens. I know we die, / and don't know what is at the end. We don't behave well. / And there are monsters out there" (76).[27] Whether intentionally or not, this flatness speaks (pardon the pun) to conventions of voice that Hass knew his poem would be read through and about which it feels "a little ashamed."

Hass's poem weaves together a range of possible poetic stances after World War II but as quickly unravels them. The inadequacy of a praise mode becomes associated with self-expression (and a derided lyric tradition), unseemly confessional melodrama, privilege, and cultural dominance. And yet the poet-I guiltily turns to these at the end of the poem, despite understanding that this mode implicates him in national and cultural shame, even at the level of the personal. Thus, "Interrupted Meditation" shows Hass's poet-I refusing to turn an understanding of the avant-garde critique of "lyric" into new formal "antilyric" practices: the poet chooses to foreground his poem as knowingly, ineluctably "mainstream lyric" (coded through singing, meditation, and epiphany) and to maintain these conventions, and their shame, in his own work. Reasserting the identification of poetry with lyric, it also marks it as shameful.

Hass's poem participates in a growing self-consciousness about midcentury lyric (reading) intensified by the Language/avant-garde critique of the epiphanic, meditative "voice" poem and its supposed lyric "tradition" and the version of subjectivity both were reputed to endorse. The fact that Hass's poem is "mainstream" (if by that we mean widely distributed and central to an economy of prizes, academic classrooms, reviewing, and MFA reading circuits) makes it difficult to decide what its attitude toward the critique is: oppositional terms would have us read it as defensive, only a "little" ashamed, because it profits from the tradition it knows is thought suspect. And yet it works, at least at a thematic level, with avant-garde discourses and in a way that shows how powerfully both lyric-reading and antilyric-reading strategies were shaping poetic practice.

Indeed, as was also true of many of the Language writers of Hass's generation, he was thinking about how to write his way out of midcentury conventions—specifically, "an autobiographical poetry that none of us could quite sit in comfortably after what modernism did to the assumption of a coherent self"—in light of the avant-garde turn to disjunctive technique. He not only was exposed to but carefully thought about Language writing, including that of Susan Howe and Ron Silliman; in one interview, he calls Silliman's claim that "the practice of mimetic art . . . is to repeat the lie of capitalist economics" "profound."[28]

Given this, "Interrupted Meditation's" self-conscious admission of shame and its particular way of paying homage to avant-garde discourses might be analogized to, and even perhaps be informed by, the *recusatio,* an ancient poetic motif believed to have originated with the Greek poet Callimachus and common in a great deal of Latin poetry of the Augustan and Flavian periods. The motif of the Latin *recusatio* was the poet's refusal "to comply with a request (real or imaginary) to write a certain type of poem," originally the epic or high-themed poem that the Emperor Augustus preferred over the more homely, personal lyric.[29] Common in the work of Ovid, Propertius, and Horace, the *recusatio* has been read as a strategy that would allow poets to go on writing lyric despite Augustus's preference for a grand style and epic themes. The motif, which, as Sander M. Goldberg puts it, often took the form of "false modesty" about the poet's supposed inability to approach his subject in a suitably grand manner, served as a form of respectful diffidence, as well as a defense (some scholars of the early Republican poets suggest) of the virtues of "private themes against imperial pressures and real or imagined critics."[30]

Taken as a sly reanimation of that motif, the suggestion in Hass's poem that the poet-persona is "a little ashamed" of wanting to "sing" draws our attention to late-twentieth-century concerns about what compels the poet's rhetoric, subject, and techniques. In Virgil's famous *recusatio* in his sixth Ecologue, the poet-figure apologizes to General Varus for writing pastoral lyric—"I only sing as bidden"—defending himself for failing to write of war and politics by invoking Apollo's authority to compel the song over that of Varus (a general to Emperor Augustus, whose pressure to dictate poetic tastes Virgil may have felt but chosen not to heed).[31] By contrast, and in the poem's larger context, when Hass's poet-I refuses to not "sing" (in effect, refuses to not write "lyric"), it reads as a comment on antilyric discourses then being institutionalized, with power to define poetic practice. If Virgil's failure to serve politics can be attributed to Apollo, Hass's failure to heed an antilyric pressure can find no outside sanction or forgiveness—it is an American poetic habit. Hass has to own his shame at failing to meet the imperative, which is an ethical one (thus the *shame*). Hass's poem allows us to connect the European immigrant's "time of shame" (his weak defense of the neighbors taken to camps) and the poet's own weak "shame" at singing, lending both political and ethical import to the question of whether or not to "sing" and also casting his choice to sing as a form of self-preservation, as the exile's choice may have been. In exposing the poem as only weakly ashamed by and resistant to the prohibition against lyric, Hass suggests both diffidence to and skepticism about the politics animating the avant-garde critique of "lyric."

Taken as a version of *recusatio*, the lyric shame motif makes visible a little-thought-about form of avant-garde discourse's institutionalization and absorption.[32] "Interrupted Meditation" is not comfortably described by currently available critical terms for determining avant-garde or lyric affiliation: it is not the hopeful marriage of lyric and antilyric in poems thought to be "hybrid," nor is it "post-avant," "post-Language," or naïvely School of Quietude. This suggests the value of lyric shame as a category by which to nuance our understanding of American poetics in the late twentieth century.[33] Most of the new terms for lyric after Language seem anxious to imagine either a happy fusion or a retrenchment of the oppositional terms. But such operations ill serve lyric shame poems, which clearly identify the expressive and personal as problems. That is, whereas in Cole Swensen's formulation of "hybrid" poems, some anodyne synthesis of "lyric" expression and "experiment" is achieved, yet reaffirms the supposed difference and the supposed "lyric" values of the "emotional spectra of lived experience" and the "expressive potential of poetry," Hass carries on with the conventions of the meditative, personal, expressive poem, foregrounding nevertheless the knowledge that they are thought shameful.[34] The effect is to straddle a divide, informed but unwilling, dubious about the critique of the meditative tradition but also not wanting to seem naïve to it. Hass announces both impasse and impulse, and in this, "Interrupted Meditation's" gestures to lyric are absolutely defined by its critical moment.[35]

REMEDITATIONS (IN AN EMERGENCY): ROBERT HASS'S *SUN UNDER WOOD* AND CHARLES WRIGHT'S "DISJECTA MEMBRA"

Since the first publication of Hass's work in the mid-1960s, it had taken on the conventions of what most critics would call a "meditative" mode that extended the post-1950s revival of conventions of the "conversation poem" that Abrams helped to cast as "the" Romantic tradition and that was strongly derided by Language practitioners.[36] Before Language critiqued the mode, and just at the moment that Abrams himself was identifying (with) it, Frank O'Hara seems to refuse it, in his 1957 poem "Meditations in an Emergency," in which O'Hara more or less mocks the expectation that the lyric poet must experience an implicitly heterosexualized, or classicized homosexual, indwelling communication with nature in order to realize himself:

> Even trees understand me! Good heavens, I lie under
> them, too, don't I? I'm just like a pile of leaves.
> However, I have never clogged myself with the
> praises of pastoral life, nor with nostalgia for an innocent past of
> perverted acts in pastures. No. One need never leave the
> confines of New York to get all the greenery one wishes—I can't
> even enjoy a blade of grass unless I know there's a subway
> handy . . . or some other sign that people do not totally *regret*
> life. It is more important to affirm the least sincere; the clouds
> get enough attention as it is and even they continue to pass. Do
> they know what they're missing? Uh huh.[37]

Though Hass is ambivalent about the mode, rather than sardonic, I borrow O'Hara's title for this section to raise the important prehistory to the specifically meditative lyric shame mode of 1990s poetry. I have been arguing that there was shame of lyric before there were lyric shame poems and before there was avant-garde antilyricism, all of which might be read as forms of response to trends in lyric reading. We should not be surprised to find Hass's concerns about "meditation" as a logic for reading prefigured not only, quite locally, in Perloff but also in O'Hara, given that the Brooks-Warren and Eliotic ideals for lyric reading, which register as concern in both Bishop's and Sexton's work, were framed through the language of "meditation" in Eliot's 1954 *Three Voices* essay. For educated readers, one connotation of O'Hara's references to meditation in his book and poem title might have been Eliot's "first voice" of poetry (given that the essay in question had recently appeared).

By the time Hass's *Sun Under Wood* was published, the terms "meditation" and "meditative" had been so thoroughly absorbed into literary-academic culture that they had become ubiquitous and, in the process, abstracted. The jacket copy for Hass's book identifies it as "at once, intensely sensual, meditative, and shot through with sharp humor," and several reviewers note how strongly the meditative features in the collection.[38] If a contemporary reader were curious to clarify the meaning of that much-used literary term in 1995, however, he or she would find it only dimly defined, if at all, in a range of literary dictionaries, including *The Princeton Encyclopedia of Poetry and Poetics*. Whereas O'Hara was resisting a set of literary authorities somewhat more local, contemporary, and vivid, Eliotic and Abramsian assumptions more pervasively, if subtly, inform the lyric-reading culture that marks Hass's antilyric moment.

Thus, "Interrupted Meditation" is not the only poem from his 1996 *Sun Under Wood* that dramatizes an unwillingness to refuse conventions of lyric meditative poetry as defined by 1990s antilyric critique. This fact helps distinguish these 1990s poems from Hass's career-long tendency to define himself against poststructuralism, as in poems from the 1979 collection *Praise,* such as "Meditation at Lagunitas" or "Picking Blackberries with a Friend Who Has Been Reading Jacques Lacan," which tip their hand to poststructuralism in lighthearted dismissals of its doubts about referential language and in favor of the pleasure of experience. *Sun Under Wood,* by contrast, is marked throughout by lyric shame gestures that take their poststructural lessons more seriously.

According to the Perloff-Abrams terms, many of the collection's twenty poems, most of them long-lined, enjambed free verse, would qualify as first-person meditations set in a distinct landscape. For instance, in "Dragonflies Mating," the Abramsian conventions of the "lyric" meditation are evident in such lines as "Thinking about that story just now, early morning heat, / first day in the mountains, I remembered stories about sick Indians / and—in the same thought—standing on the free throw line" (*Sun,* 8). The poem reflects on several scenes at once, circling back to memories and reflections that are gathered together under the sign of the poet's consciousness and experience.

The poem's relationship to the conventions of the "epiphany poem" are mixed. Despite the poem's somewhat muddled narrative and its situation of the self in terms of history, it maintains its commitment to exploring a single subject's point of view. It is at first unclear what collects sections 1 and 2; section 1 begins with abstract musing about "the people who lived here before us," and section 2 zeros in to a scene of Berkeley linguist Jaime de Angulo talking, in 1934, to a "Channel Island Indian / in a Santa Barbara bar" about various native cosmologies (6). By section 3, which locates the poet in a particular place and time (with the previously quoted line in which the poet-I is "thinking about that story just now"), the conventions of a meditative free-verse poem set in. The poem's turns pressure the illusion of coherence and temporal continuity that a more continual first-person meditation would produce, with sections 4 and 5 moving to first-person plural and second person, respectively. However, we are returned in the last section to a first-person meditation, evidenced by the poet located and thinking.

While compared to today's standards for narrative disjunction, self-consciousness, and irony, the poem seems not to stray too far from convention, for at least one of the collection's contemporary and major reviewers (Michael Hofmann in the *New York Times,* in 1997), the poem's shifts through its sections seemed a sign of the collection's overall frustrating resistance to maintaining expressive conventions. Hofmann calls "Dragonflies Mating" a sequence that "never adds up," and his discomfort with the collection confirms that the lyric shame trend produced what for many 1990s mainstream readers was a disturbing level of poetic self-consciousness. Focusing on the collection's self-consciousness about engaging poetic conventions, Hofmann finds the "conventional, 'fourth wall' illusionism of poetry . . . under continual assault."[39]

Here we might remember that this assault is exactly what, several years earlier, Bernstein had described as the "antiabsorptive" tendency waged against the nineteenth-century lyric conventions derived from readings of Mill. Despite Hofmann's apparent distaste for such self-consciousness, in many ways his is one of the stronger readings of Hass's collection—one of few that register the poems' embarrassment and even shame at uses of the meditative conventions of the day. Hofmann's catalogue of Hass's "strategies of invalidation" and refusals of the "well-made poem" suggests the use of then-radical (from the vantage point of the mainstream press in particular) techniques that other reviewers downplay or evade: endings "come out of nowhere," and there are "goofy, campy refrain[s]," ironic

gestures to traditional verse forms, self-conscious admissions of the conventions that produced the poem, and so on. Hofmann can only conclude
that Hass's chafing against conventions (Hofmann calls them "restraints")
indicates an expression of midcareer lassitude or depression: "The poems
are scapegoats; he takes out his feelings of 'self-hatred and remorse' on
them instead of bringing them to expression in the writing."[40]

However, Hass's frame for the collection rather suggests a critically informed, pointed discomfort with the very expressive conventions with
which Hofmann wants to, and cannot, read the collection: negativity is
provoked in part by available forms of knowing or producing a self in poetry.
For instance, the collection's opener, "Happiness," disrupts the "real-time"
trope expected in meditative verse by meditating on the genesis of the very
meditative account of "happiness" we are reading (thus calling its contrivance into view; 3–4). The last poem is "Interrupted Meditation," which (as
I have discussed) identifies the impulse to go from meditation to singing
(the epiphanic) with shame. Between these doubt-laden bookends, Hass
offers two poems that foreground their use of meditative conventions—
"Layover" and "Iowa City: Early April"—each of which is, in effect, written
again in a companion poem. "Iowa City: Early April" for instance, is represented by "A Note on 'Iowa City: Early April,'" the second poem acting
as a supplement or revision of the "original."

The resulting pairs of poems suggest the metacritical consciousness I
see as common to the lyric shame mode: they announce a recognition that
someone specific may read and find these meditations wanting and thus
flag Hass's desire to think through the critique of the meditative epiphany
poem that was then increasingly sounded by the American critical avant-
garde. Hass's choice to reimagine and challenge meditative conventions
decentralizes the primacy of meditative "voice," pointing to its production
in and as technique and exposing the authority of the meditative poem,
thus putting it into question.

The first of these pairs, "Layover" and "Notes on 'Layover,'" are dif-
ferentiated by form: "Layover," a poem lineated in three sections, strongly
suggesting the conventional meditative poems of the day and in the collection (and leading us to expect a conventional meditative poem); "Notes
on 'Layover,'" a prose poem in seven prose blocks. If lightly infused by
the politics informing Language writing, each also clearly depends on the
"epiphany" conventions that Perloff and others had critiqued. "Layover"
locates the poet and elicits expectation of an epiphany in its conventional

layout, but it does not realize one, even stringently limiting the intrusions of "I's" own experience into what is described. The poetic eye/I strives to function as a way station (like a layover itself), where unrelated phenomena and people are gathered as if by chance. The poem moves from an image of workers on the Anchorage Airport tarmac hauling luggage, "hard at what must be / half the world's work, loading and unloading" (25) to Bishop-like attempts (as in her 1930s Williams-inspired "Florida") at neutral descriptions of the airport buildings:

> The colonizer's
> usual prefab, low-roofed storage sheds in the distance
> pale beige and curiously hopeful in their upright verticals
> like boys in an army, or like the spruce and hemlock forest
> on low hillsides beyond them. And beyond those, half seen
> in the haze, range after range of snowy mountains
> in the valleys of which—moose feeding along the frozen streams,
> snow foxes hunting ptarmigan in the brilliant whiteness—
> no human could survive for very long, and which it is the
>   imagination's
> intensest, least possible longing to inhabit. (26, ll. 11–21)

Though in "range after range of snowy mountains" we hear Wallace Stevens, too, it is Bishop who most informs these lines, especially her stances of lyric impersonality. As with Bishop's poems of the revised Wordsworthian meditative sort ("At the Fishhouses," for instance), Hass's shows an unwillingness to privilege the self, evident in the passive "half seen" and the general, reportorial tone. The poem never turns (as would have been expected in an epiphany poem) to the poet's personal associations or memories. Rather, it quietly ends by invoking the specters of race and class (describing Indian faces and a man on the airstrip "waving his black, / monstrously gloved hands at someone") without quite turning these to a "larger" purpose. The closing image is of a community assembled by travel and subject to "the stale air, breathed and breathed, we have been sharing" (26). Invoking only the descriptive foreepiphany expected of the meditative poem, "Layover" refuses to make sense of the diversity of images of people and things except through the logic of travel and, as the synecdoches in a news report suggest ("Iraq has agreed. Russia has promised"), as subjects of state power.

Is the logic of personal lyric epiphany the "stale air" that Hass's poem refuses? Whatever our reading, Hass's rewrite of the poem in "Notes on

'Layover'" destabilizes several critical assumptions that attach to the meditative mode at the time of his poem's publication: chiefly, that meditative poems are "spoken" and offer a mimesis of "real-time" inner speech.[41] Each section in "Notes on 'Layover'" reviews what "Layover" has imaged, structured by long sentences that begin, "I could have said," imagining what "Layover" could have "said"—or, in serving as a rewriting, written—differently. The rewriting demonstrates the contingency of poetic form, allowing us to see this self-effacing refusal of epiphanic and meditative convention as itself a convention, intensifying the Bishopian alertness to the forces of convention and discourse on poetic subjectivities. It also challenges Cleanth Brooks's argument, in "The Heresy of Paraphrase," against interpretive resaying of the well-wrought poem in light of the poem's supposed achievement of an ideal structure, inseparable from content.[42] Hass's poem asks us to see another possibility, foregrounding forms and their consumptions as artificial and asking us to imagine this artifice as inseparable from poetic content.

Furthermore, because we are left to guess about Hass's attitude toward the questions that the new form of the poem raises (does the poet prefer the impersonal eye of "Layover" or the more personal and confessional "I" of "Notes"?), the concept of epiphany is evacuated by being foregrounded as conventional. Foregrounding how else the scene could have been written shakes the link between chosen poetic modes, authorial identity, and ethics that arguments about "the politics of form" and mode (even if only vaguely or tacitly) circle around. Is Hass's a Bishopian meditative mode, opposed to the egotistical sublime, or is this "I" asserting an almost perverse power to control the poem and penetrate the unknown other through acts of imagination and projection? "Notes on 'Layover'" serves as the notebook that produced "Layover," offering the details that a Bishop meditation might excise in order to achieve its air of impersonality. From "Notes on 'Layover,'" we learn things about the "objectively" viewed characters in "Layover" that no fellow traveling stranger could know, including the fact that the woman with the baby has an ovarian cyst and is filling out insurance paperwork; she is the wife of a technician in the army. We also learn what has been in the poet's mind but suppressed in the version of experience that "Layover" offered of the time: "watching the men unload the luggage, I was thinking of [the woman's] body, and then of her underwear. Pretty, not very expensive, neatly folded for the journey." The begrudging "I could have said" suggests a rebellion against the imperative not to impose the self; the poet does end up saying what he "could have said" (and perhaps should not have) and threatens to cast the scene's realism in fictional light. Whatever ethical character is implied by one mode is undone by the other, unsettling the identification of author with form or genre as a stable index of ethics.

All this is mediated through an invisible reader (as opposed to listener) poised to adjudicate these works in the lyric/critical terms of the day. In the pairing "Iowa City: Early April" and "A Note on 'Iowa City: Early April,'" that idiom is "the backyard epiphany mode" (a critical evolution of Perloff's term that finds the conventional epiphany located too often in a backyard setting), to which Hass shows a mixed, self-conscious commitment.[43] In "Iowa City: Early April," the poet is at work, reflecting on the morning spent observing backyard fauna (typical of the derided "backyard" mode), but it leads to an antiepiphany. The poem indicates its cognizance of critiques of narrative form, moving in long lines and eleven variable verse paragraphs (some as short as one long sentence) with a largely paratactic logic of accretion; nine of the eleven verse paragraphs present a description of flora or fauna beginning with "And." The poem's beginning demonstrates the loose logical structure:

> This morning a cat—bright orange—pawing at the one patch of
>   new grass in the sand- and tanbark-colored leaves.
> And last night the sapphire of the raccoon's eyes in the beam of the
>   flashlight.
> He was climbing a tree beside the house, trying to get onto the
>   porch, I think, for a wad of oatmeal (32)

Again, we are in a Bishopian self-conscious lyric mode; "and, and, and" evokes the Williams of mere presentation, but "I think" (as with Bishop's "The Bight") breaks in to admit a point of view. In the fifth verse paragraph, that "hands-off" stance nearly collapses when a description of a "doe and two yearlings" elicits a memory, midline, of the poet's dream about a doe walking into the house while he "was writing at the kitchen table" (33). However, the poem refuses the Deep Image epiphany that an avant-garde reader might expect; it makes a point of moving from a description of the dream not to a reading of its meaning or the feelings it produces but rather to another verse paragraph of unrelated description beginning "And." In the dream, the deer has entered the kitchen,

> And snatched a slice of apple, and stood, and then quietened, and
>   to my surprise did not leave again.
> And those little captains, the chickadees, swift to the feeder and
>   swift away. (33)

After this brief descriptive image, predicted only by the contiguity of two images of feeding, the poem then moves through several similarly discon-nected strophes before it gets to its muted, almost anti-, epiphany:

> All this life going on about my life, or living a life about all this life
>   going on,
> Being a creature, whatever my drama of the moment, at the edge of
>   the raccoon's world—
> He froze in my flashlight beam and looked down, no affect, just
>   looked (35)

Hass's epiphany reports something we assume the poet already understood—the ineluctable difference between human creatures and their objects of interest in the natural world. This is pointedly not the heroic mother skunk at the end of Robert Lowell's "Skunk Hour," made epiphanic emblem of the poet's self-state. Our interests and those of the animal world are "en-tirely apart," and this leads the poet to philosophic talk about subjectivity:

> And as for my experience of myself, it comes and goes, I'm not sure
>   it's any one thing, as my experience of these creatures is not,
> And I know I am often too far from it or too near, glad to be rid of
>   it which is why it was such a happiness,
> The bright orange of the cat, and the first pool of green grass-leaves
>   in early April, and the birdsong—that orange and that green not
>   colors you'd set next to one another in the human scheme. (35)

The poem fulfills its original logic with the return to the image of the cat and, as if to fully demonstrate the poet's eagerness to be rid of his experi-ence of himself, ends on a stark, one-line paratactic note:

> And the crows' calls, even before you open your eyes, at sunup. (35)

Though the poem fulfills the expectations for the "backyard epiphany" poem (privileging, at last, the self), it does so in alertness to the critical environment in which it will be read. The poem evidently wants to fore-ground the poet's refusal to gain his (and, by metonymy, the human's) insights and self-knowledge through nature (especially the perhaps Stafford-inspired dream doe, the lone female among the many animals in the poem), even as it offers this refusal as a kind of epiphany.

It is a mixed relationship to the convention, then, because, of course, the heroizing of human experience through the figure of nature was the much-derided, signature move of a conventional backyard epiphany mode whose supposed Romantic origins had come under staunch attack in arguments informing and informed by Perloff's. If, in "Iowa City: Early April," it is a happiness to lose the self, such self-erasure still must occur *through* a metaphoric or analogic relationship to the figure of nature, however inscrutable nature seems to be. Thus, Hass's poem is guiltily steeped in its purported tradition, self-conscious about its origins and their critical consequences. The fact that he then rewrites the poem in "A Note on 'Iowa City: Early April,'" again (as in "Notes on 'Layover'") pointing to the artifice and contingency of the "experience" on offer, further suggests this self-consciousness about the meditative conventions engaged.

As a point of contrast, consider the poem often referenced as epito-mizing the mode: again, Stafford's frequently anthologized "Traveling Through the Dark" (1963), to which Hass's doe seems to allude.[44] Stafford's speaking subject in "Traveling Through the Dark" earns his mo-ment of epiphany through the figure of a wounded, pregnant doe, becom-ing confident—in mulling over whether to let her die slowly or to roll her off the road where he finds her into a river—that he can "hear the wilder-ness listen" and asserting that it is the poet's charge and place to "th[ink]" hard for us all."[45] Nature becomes a symbol of formless chaos, and the "thinking hard" an emblem for poetry; the poet-subject will manage for "us all" in part by rendering the deer a carefully plotted moral emblem. By contrast, both of Hass's "Iowa City" poems self-consciously attempt to forfeit such claims. Hass aligns himself with the critique of such poems as Stafford's, advanced so influentially by Perloff, which saw the mainstream, canonical "lyric" poet-subject as marked by its problematic confidence to "use[] metaphor to characterize what he perceives" and an unsettling assur-ance that he "knows . . . what he sees when he looks out the window."[46]

The quotes come from Perloff's account of the "lyric subject" in Charles Wright's poem "Disjecta Membra" (like Hass's poem, first published in 1996), which makes her case that the canonical "lyric subject" that Wright's poem purportedly exemplifies is paradigmatically "Romantic" not because of its "expressivity or subjectivity as such" but because of the high level of "authority ascribed to the speaking voice" (432). Perloff wishes to suggest that Language poems are not indistinct examples of the posthuman but in fact evidence a great variety of possible authorial "signatures" (413). Their autobiographical subjects, however, do refuse the kinds of "authority" traditionally claimed by "lyric subjects" (432). Remembering Bishop's Williams-inspired concern about a "tradition of likenesses," Perloff, very similarly, sees this authority asserted by acts of mimesis: through "confident" use of metaphor and the poet's claim, through the aegis of metaphor, over what he describes. "Nature always wears the colors of the spirit" in this specifically Keatsian Romanticism, Perloff argues, and she finds the unabashed employment of it as characteristic of the autobiographical subjects in "mainstream" poems, as opposed to the autobiographical subjects in Language poems (433).[47]

However, it is worth entertaining other possibilities for how to place Wright's poem, and its subject, in relation to its purported tradition. What if Wright, like Hass, was already engaging the terms of the Perloffian-Language critique? After all, she had identified and begun to critique the epiphanic, meditative mode over twenty years prior to both the writing of these poems and also her "lyric subject" essay. All emerge from the same midcentury lyric-reading culture that defined these terms in the first place.

Another possibility is that, like Bishop (whom both poets invoke), Wright and Hass had found ways other than the disjunctive methods that Perloff and Language writers prefer to explore and critique lyric-reading assumptions and the lyric subject they produced. Indeed, by showing their poems flinching from their own epiphanic inclinations, and the forms of subjectivity these produce, they unsettle the very ground on which we might think it valid to identify a poet with his or her words. "Disjecta Membra," like so many of Wright's poems explicitly a "back-yard" meditation, admits to the embarrassments and shame of the poet's self-projection and importance, singling out Rainer Maria Rilke as a poet who recognized the shame of poetry even as he carried on with it. (Hass nearly makes this move himself in *Sun Under Wood,* by having the "I" admit, in "Regalia for a Black Hat Dancer," that in the period after his divorce, he "rag[ed] against Rilke"; *Sun,* 49.)[48] The first word of the first line of Wright's poem dramatizes the poet looking for himself in the "Backyard," which is "a mirror of personality, / unworldly and self-effacing" (*Black Zodiac,* 3).[49] Yet this is done with self-consciousness about the conventional setting, through whose conventions, the poem suggests, "The onlooker sees himself in, / a monk among the oak trees," commenting,

> How silly, the way we place ourselves— . . . .
> For our regard; how always the objects we draw out
> To show ourselves to effect
> (The chiaroscuro of character we yearn for)
> Find us a shade untrue and a shade untied.
> Bad looking glass, bad things. (71)

The poem admits several times the groundlessness of the self-revelatory speech it nevertheless knows it cannot quite purge, including any attempt to realize it through other means (here, "ease in the natural world"; 83). In its second section, the I's embarrassment about its own inclination to *speak* through nature is informed by the ineluctability of the figure of speaking that would help to "say" it:

> If I could slide into a deep sleep,
> I could say—to myself, without speaking—why my words
>   embarrass me.

> Nothing regenerates us, or shapes us again from the dust.
> Nothing whispers our name in the night.
> Still we must praise you, nothing,
> still we must call to you. (75)

Wright here cleverly refuses the in-feeling, "correspondent breeze" that Abrams identified with the major poems of Samuel Taylor Coleridge and other Romantic poets.[50] Though Perloff finds the poem illustrative of the (Abramsian) Romantic lyric "paradigm"—"an observer located in a particular place" revived by nature, and a metaphorical network "wholly consistent and of a piece" ("Language Poetry," 432)—Wright's poem also undercuts those tropes and shifts in and out of descriptions mixing disparate temporal frames. Its many sections, assembled as fragments (as the title suggests), disrupt the illusion of a real-time epiphanic experience that some of its smaller sections dramatize. This is not to say that it is not metaphor making or representational or referential (or that many of Wright's poems do not undercut or foreground their investments in meditation); there is no doubt that Wright is not a Language-centered writer. However, the poem

suggests a less unselfconscious approach to this topos and trope than Perloff's reading prepares us to see. It represents a mixed, even vexed taking on
of conventions of backyard meditation and lyric reading and could be said
to turn to its Buddhist perspective in order to address the problem of the
Romantic and Deep Image inheritance that Perloff disparages.[51] The poet
admits a longing "to be at ease in the natural world," and yet the epiphany
that would attempt that reconciliation is hardly a confident access that
enlarges the self but rather something longed for, lost, recommenced, somewhat with the mindless ongoingness of time itself. Perloff is correct that the
poem dramatizes the poet's "emptying out" and yet, I would add, finally
frames it as impotent. If it invites our identification of a distinct subject
through lyric-reading conventions, nevertheless Wright takes pains to make
that subject visible as shamed, or ashamed, to assert its existence. This suggests a shared set of concerns between Wright and the avant-garde position
that Perloff advocates about the authority of the speaking subject.

In fact, acknowledging the shame of "lyric" became a motif for many
"mainstream" poets writing in the mid-to-late 1990s. It is telling that,
in a 2003 essay on American "meditative" poets, poet-critic Richard Lyons
takes a jab at conventions of the "discursive" meditative mode by calling it
marked by the "usual group flagellation." He marvels, in light of those
conventions, over the fact that Jon Anderson's meditative work escapes this
fate by being "not ashamed, not embarrassed, and not self-congratulatory."[52]
To corroborate, we could point to earlier-quoted lines from Gerald Stern's
"Hot Dog," whose quasi-"backyard" meditation (the very long poem is set
in the city) is compelled, in a manner stunningly like Hass's and Wright's
(and published within a year of these), to admit its shame (here "embarrassment") at "singing":

> I get frenzied,
> especially in the morning, the sprinkler has already
> been there and the brushes bare scarred the cement,
> though who am I to be a bird at that hour
> or some kind of walking plant, a six-foot daisy,
> a truly great delphinium? I am a little
> embarrassed; I would like not always to have to
> be the one who sings, the one who does it
> for others since they stand there dumb and dazed
> or smiling like cuckoos. I would just as soon

breathe quietly at my kitchen table or at a twenty-four-hour
  cafe . . .
      . . . Ridiculous panting.
Ridiculous even talking (*Odd Mercy,* 78)

Stern's poems had earlier addressed the embarrassment of poeticism.[53] But
the invocation of "singing" in the 1990s poem feels more pointedly about
the ethics of taking on a specifically "lyric" tradition, flanked as it is by
Stern's numerous gestures to Greater Romantic Lyric poetic emblems.
Though the poem's most explicit debts are to the Romanticism of Walt
Whitman's *Song of Myself,* it also can be read as exaggerating the "conversation poems" mode of Coleridge, which operated with and against expectations for the poet's autobiography that Wordsworth's *The Prelude* established. In seventeen long, talky sections, the poem works as a poet's
autobiography that manically meditates (by circling back several times to
the figure of a homeless woman named Hot Dog) on the poet's obligations
to self and society. Stern's poem returns almost obsessively to Romantic
tropes—wind and breath and birds—making it difficult not to read the
embarrassment of singing in light of a moment when many people in the
poetry world felt the pressure to identify their place in a schema of "lyric"
and "antilyric," whether defensively, begrudgingly, or confidently.

Of course, vexed, embarrassed, and ashamed "lyric" assertions had
been available in the work of established, contemporary poets writing
before the 1990s, especially that of Jorie Graham and John Ashbery (as
I stated earlier, as early as the 1950s), both of whose attempts to theorize
contemporary poetics through experimental practices led them to explore, in quite different modalities, the potential embarrassments of "traditional" *poesis.* Significantly, each poet has proved problematic for advocates of a strict division between avant-garde and mainstream, antilyric
and lyric, such as Perloff, who worried in 1998, for instance, that the
mainstream academic appeal of Ashbery's work was "normalizing John
Ashbery," the title of her essay on the subject. In 2002, she explains the
popularity of Graham's work (through a reading of the poem "Evolution")
in terms that are clearly "lyric" epithets: it is "just familiar enough to hit a
responsive chord" despite "calculated difficulty"; is "a neo-Romantic, lyric
meditation"; and is mimetic of a "thought process that culminates," for
Perloff, in an all-too-conventional, closed realization (read epiphany?).
Perloff concedes that "Evolution" "testifies at every turn to its author's

awareness of the Language movement," but Perloff wants to keep Graham and Language apart because of Graham's disinterest in taking "dislocation and discontinuity to the extremes of [Rae] Armantrout or Bruce Andrews, of Charles Bernstein or Clark Coolidge."[54]

Though I agree with Perloff that Graham is not a Language writer, it is worth wondering why we would frame Graham or Ashbery in the oppositional rhetoric of the poetry wars. Graham and Ashbery fall outside that situation's compelling terms: Graham's concerns have long been Continental philosophical questions about epistemology and materialism. Ashbery's interest in French surrealism and Gertrude Stein dates to the 1950s, thus predating the schema that Perloff employs, and he reanimates nineteenth-century techniques and forms somewhat outside either mainstream or avant-garde canons of technique in the 1970s. Both slip through the usual oppositional net because neither, for different reasons, had engaged and wrestled with the Confessional and Deep Image inheritances that concerned both Language poets and also Wright and Hass. In the absence of such wrestling, neither Graham nor Ashbery seems to have felt compelled to align his practices strongly with a particular school or poetics. Indeed, Ashbery repeatedly rejects the call to do so.[55]

In some ways, then, Graham's and Ashbery's already-much-discussed works stand outside this chapter's concerns because each was engaged (along with the 1970s American poetic avant-garde) by postmodernist movements that sought to work "against interpretation" (to invoke Susan Sontag), rather than by oppositionality as such. I will turn briefly to each poet's 1990s work, however, to show the Bishop-like qualities in small instances of lyric shame in that work.[56]

WITHOUT SHAME

Graham explores the connection between specific "lyric" strategies and their shame most explicitly in her long poem "Pollock and Canvas," from *The End of Beauty* (1987). Stephen Burt argues that this phase of Graham's career (in which her second and third collections were published) enabled a critical exchange between Language discourse and mainstream poetics.[57] This may be because it marks Graham's self-conscious break from the short, enjambed line that dominated her first two collections and marks her alignment of her own techniques—long lines of loose syntax separated by numbers, for instance, in "Pollock and Canvas"—with modernist experimenters such as Jackson Pollock. In an interview with Thomas Gardner, Graham reflects on the choice to extend her line and push against tight formal structures and closure that she associates with "imperialisms of all kinds," a view that aligns with the Language-inspired view that experimental techniques effect an ethically superior politics.[58]

In "Pollock and Canvas," artistic desires to possess objects of one's attention are shameful but can be tempered by certain disjunctive, "new" forms. The parenthetical phrase fragments "(without embarrassment. without shame)" recur across the second and third sections of the poem; as a motif, they describe and perform the relief that taking on nonnarrative, nonlinear, interrupting, and nonclosural forms can offer from shame. They also gloss the figure of Pollock at work and the poetics of his drip practice, enacting and championing a poetics of process over product, one that attempts a formal relinquishing of an aesthetic (which the poem loosely associates, as Graham does in the aforementioned interview, with Western political and social structures) of closure, consequence, and acquisitive desires of all kinds. In section 2, when instances of the phrase "without embarrassment. without shame" first appear, they gloss the proximate lines (which also recur), "Oh but we wanted to paint what is not beauty, how can one paint what is / not beauty," suggesting that to "paint what is . . . beauty" is another source of embarrassment and shame—what Pollock's practice and Graham's long poem about it will both address and redress (*End of Beauty*, 81–89). The phrases recur in section 3 in a context suggesting mimetic practice and "story" (narrative closure) as other sources of embarrassment, akin to the pursuit of "beauty" in art:

> . . . . . The moment
> a figure appears on the canvas, she said,
> the story begins, the story begins the error sets in,
> the error the boredom, she said, the story talking louder
> than the paint, she said, the boredom the hurry, she said
> (without embarrassment, without shame)
> (and you must learn to feel shape as simply shape whispered the
> wind, not as description not as reminiscence not as what
>
> it will become) (89)

Rejecting narrative structures and "description" as what wrest the what-ness of experience out of the flow of time, these lines constellate with the work of Lyn Hejinian, who articulates a similar aesthetic in a range of work, including such talks-essays from the 1980s as "The Person and De-scription" and "The Rejection of Closure."[59] Such moments in Graham also, as in Hass, recall Bishop's concerns about mimesis and its problem-atic and embarrassing implications—that "tradition of likeness" Bishop saw Williams trying to "escape." And we should note that Graham, per-forming the impasse (what Bishop seems to have learned from Williams), chooses to narrate the renunciation of narrative ("she said"). Indeed, Gra-ham has said that what she shares with Bishop is a desire to "suffer[] the limits of description" in order to show "what leaks in between attempts" to capture things in words, concerns that she believes, for her and for Bishop, to be "essential issues."[60] Thus, though their "music" is not simi-lar, Graham sees both preoccupied with the limits of description, part of what made Graham's work (to Burt and others) seem to bridge avant-garde and mainstream concerns, continuing, I would add, a tradition that includes Bishop.

Ashbery also claims Bishop as part of his tradition, as other critics have noted, and identifies their sharing the same "quandary" about capturing the odd and difficult relationship between an "outer reality" and an "in-ner, private reality," quoting her lines from "Rainy Season, Sub-Tropics" to accentuate the point: "For neither is clearer / nor a different color / than the other."[61] For Ashbery, the mode of exploring the shame of poetry (as I argue is also true for Bishop) tends to be rhetorical and discursive; it is a way of working against lyric-reading assumptions underexplored in con-temporary critical accounts of American poetics as divided between lyric and antilyric.

The poem "Vaucanson," from *April Galleons* (1987), offers one explicit later instance in which Ashbery's work engages the embarrassment of a poetic-expressive endeavor through rhetorical and discursive experiment, situating the poet writing alone in a room:

> It was snowing as he wrote.
> In the gray room he felt relaxed and singular,
> But no one, of course, ever trusts these moods.[62]

If the writer is self-conscious, what he mistrusts is writing undertaken as the leavings of an exemplary, heroic self, for these are the potential terms of shame that accompany the poet's desire to "give a dimension / To life, when life is precisely that dimension." The deflation (here by abstraction) of the urge to assert one's poetic specialness is the Ashberian hallmark:

> We are creatures, therefore we walk and talk
> And people come up to us, or listen
> And then move away.
>
> Music fills the spaces
> Where figures are pulled to the edges,
> And it can only say something.

For Ashbery, poetry is ashamed by the claim that it should attest to the singularity of a subject whose experience should (paradoxically) function as representative. And yet much of his work (as Bishop's did) attends to the discomforts of dwelling (tentatively, embarrassedly) in that situation:

> But if one were to invent being a child again
> It might just come close enough to being a living relic
> To save this thing, save it from embarrassment
> By ringing down the curtain,
>
> And for a few seconds no one would notice.
> The ending would seem perfect.
> No feelings to dismay,
> No tragic sleep to wake from in a fit
> Of passionate guilt, only the warm sunlight
> That slides easily down shoulders
> To the soft, melting heart. (*April Galleons*, 25)

What is different of course is that Ashbery critiques that situation, rather than enacting it. If this is an elaborate figure that tries to image the poem saved from the meditative poetic subject's shame, it is self-dissolving; Ashbery is expert at showing how quickly the thought of something genuine turns to a sardonic cringe: that "soft, melting heart" sounds a little too much like an advertisement for candy, as with many of his admissions of anxiety about lyric as distinctly feminized. What produces the feeling of shame is often what has pleased one; many of Ashbery's poems capture the real time of the poem's turn away from tropes and trails leading to the old pleasures of a problematically feminized poetry.[63] In "And *Ut Pictura Poesis* Is Her Name" (1977), Ashbery bifurcates a potential lyric subject

into a distant "I" who counsels the silent, writerly "you" about how to
proceed with "your poem-painting." Such a split subject marks Ashbery's
particular mode of engaging an abjected poetic "tradition" as well as ambivalence about aligning himself too stringently with an "other tradition"
that depends on a fantasy of "clearing" past discourses away. This stance
toward the problem of affiliation with avant-garde antilyricism proved influential for such writers as James Tate and, later, Dean Young.

That Ashbery's poem participates specifically in a critique of tradition
as "lyric" is available in his title and first line, whose Ruskinesque use of
the phrase "Ut Pictura Poesis" indicates, specifically, an expressive art.
"You can't say it that way any more," the poem begins, not just referencing
the limits of the pursuit of beauty and perceptual mimesis but quickly addressing the limitations and exhaustion of a meditative-expressive mode.
Indeed, the poem is quickly diverted from its refusal of beauty onto a
meditative and confessional track, describing what one "bothered about
beauty" must now do with the poem:

> You can't say it that way any more.
> Bothered about beauty you have to
> Come out into the open, into a clearing
> And rest. Certainly whatever funny happens to you
> Is OK. To demand more than this would be strange
> Of you, you who have so many lovers,
> People who look up to you and are willing
> To do things for you, but you think
> It's not right, that if they really knew you . . .
> So much for self-analysis. Now,
> About what to put in your poem-painting:
> Flowers are always nice, particularly delphinium.
> Names of boys you once knew and their sleds,
> Skyrockets are good—do they still exist?
> There are a lot of other things of the same quality
> As those I've mentioned.[64]

Whatever the resolve to move away from beauty and "come out into the
open," the poem's rhetoric quickly morphs, almost against the poem's
will, into a rather tedious and self-absorbed confessional train of spontaneous "self-analysis." Ashbery shows the conventions of self-expression to
be exhausted, neurotic, and yet almost ineluctable—a discursive mask

that the poem cannot help but don. A discourse shift at "Now" reasserts aesthetic questions, yet the poem is too exhausted—a caricatured sentimental "voice"—suggesting the difficulties of actually making "the clearing" from tradition and convention that is at first sought. In a way more exaggerated than in Hass's "Interrupted Meditation," Ashbery tries on several postwar poetic stances here, all of which fail to realize an authenticity. In this, the poem takes on an agency severed from a person. In Ashbery's sharp foregrounding of discourses and rhetoric of the personal, his work, like Bernadette Mayer's, marks an early exploration of the difficulty of wanting to "write like Tennyson but make it new," for the figure of the feeling person is, in effect, written out. Like Bishop, and Williams before them both, Ashbery explores the situation of being steeped in modes of lyric whose premises one knows have been rendered embarrassing. And as Vernon Shetley implies, he refuses not just lyric but, in his peculiar form of rhetorical difficulty, the forms of lyric reading that New Critics employed to render modernism more legible.[65]

JAMES TATE: "THE EMBARRASSING HEARTACHE OF MY LATEST APERÇU"

The particular critically aware strain of Ashbery's work discussed in the preceding section informs James Tate's practice, and the curiosity of Tate's acceptance by the critical and publishing establishment presents an interesting angle on the situation of lyric and antilyric in the later twentieth century. Especially as Tate gained wide success, his poems were taken as "contemporary" in ways that, for all their "language-liveliness" (as Amy Gerstler put it in her review of the 1994 *Worshipful Company of Fletchers*), could nevertheless see the poet safely identified as "meditative" and comparable to Eliot (as said Julian Moynahan in the *New York Times* in 1972), even "sentimental" and "uplift[ing]" (as Adam Kirsch put it in the 1990s).[66] Gerstler compares Tate to Ashbery but finds Tate, happily, "less distant" and "not . . . soul-less." Earlier, Moynahan took Tate's meditations to provide an antidote to "sick" Confessionalism.[67] Gerstler's and Kirsch's later assessments of Tate's work's "not being soul-less" and managing "uplift" reveal a fear of the "death of the subject" that marked much anxious critical response to an increasingly institutional avant-garde antiexpressive poetic in the years surrounding the publication of *Worshipful Company of Fletchers*. As Perloff notes and fears about Ashbery's work, in the 1990s, Tate's was read as a lighter, less disjunctive version of some of Language poetry's experiments with the foregrounding of text, a critique of the self, and what we could call the estrangement of poetic language. Andrew Zawacki emphasizes Tate's refusal of the poetics of self-exploration as generational, citing an interview in which Tate argues, "I really feel when I read a lot of poets that they're most obsessed with presenting their viewpoints as individuals. . . . I don't feel that protective or retentive about—myself. I'd like to destroy that selfhood."[68] One could argue that Tate, not unlike Ashbery, Graham, and, to a lesser extent, Hass, brought to a broader poetry-reading public the news about poststructuralist critiques of the rational subject that Language poets had been exploring already for two decades.

Yet it is important to specify that, in suggesting that his project is to destroy the self, Tate shows a vexed closeness to the Deep Image agenda against which Language practice in part defined itself and, insofar as he shows us a different way out of that agenda from that provided by Language-centered practices, helps to variegate our picture of post-1970s American poetic practices. Indeed, in his way of playing out the lyric shame of the 1970s, Tate also extends concerns about poetic subjectivity that were present, I have argued, in the work of poets (such as Bishop) not only who do not tend to get included among the historical avant-garde but who, in the lyric/antilyric logic, are singled out as inspiring its oppositional rhetoric.

If in Bishop we heard the sound of discourse disturbing supposedly "lyric" conventions—the socialness of language complicating the claim that poetry expresses the feeling self's idiosyncrasy and inimitable originality—then Tate (like Ashbery) overdetermines discourse almost to the point of its making no sense at all, so that one strains to hear anything but the sound of scare quotes or the intonations of a radio advertisement. In this, Tate is like Ashbery and yet very unlike Hass, for we rarely doubt that Hass communicates with us as anything but a poet-persona very closely related to himself, willing us to understand that persona, however self-consciously. Bishop can be read as pointing the way toward both sets of practice.

But the particular culture of postmodern American life and letters qualifies the difference of Ashbery, Tate, and Hass from that which fostered Bishop's concerns about lyric subjectivity in the 1930s and midcentury and which shaped the rhetorical, discursive experiments by which she played these out. If Bishop found herself at the cusp of a turn toward the personal in American poetics, these poets find themselves steeped in its premises. Thus, it seems no accident that, at numerous points, all three later male poets, writing in the mid-1990s, foreground the backyard setting in poems of self-conscious "personal" expression in such a way that indicates a much more explicitly metapoetic, critically self-aware agenda about the personal than we find in Bishop or Sexton. This marks a tendency at work in the larger poetic culture of the 1970s and after, in which, among other things, the feedback loop between poems and their professional, critical readings grows swifter and shorter.

Yet Tate's 1970s poems, with their own version of lyric shame, challenge the suggestion that "mainstream" writers realize the shame of lyric through a Language-centered discourse of antiexpressive lyricism. Tate's 1970s poems often present the self as an unruly animal or as something pathetic, perhaps Tate's way of negotiating conventional meditative poetics in the light of postsubjective theory. By contrast, Tate's first and award-winning book, *The Lost Pilot* (1967), allowed his even-then-surrealistic notes to be read autobiographically: defamiliarizing pain and suffering explained by Tate's father's death in World War II (he was an air force pilot who died shortly after Tate's birth). In the collections that followed, little mitigates the sense that Tate is mocking the expressive expectations animating lyric readings and writings, and there are even glimmers of doubt about the expressive in *The Lost Pilot,* as in "The Book of Lies," in which the reader function is invoked in an aggressive and unnerving way: "I'd like to have a word / with you. Could we be alone / for a minute? I have been lying / until now. Do you believe // I believe myself?"[69] Beginning with the 1970 collection *Oblivion Ha-Ha,* if a Tate poem registers the conventional meditative-descriptive mode of the day, it quickly departs into a surrealism that undermines it, suggesting the leisured mentality underwriting meditation bespeaks a kind of monstrous privilege, as in "It's Not the Heat So Much as the Humidity": "Only a dish of blueberries could pull me / out of this lingering funk. / I'm tired of taking the kids down / to watch the riot, no longer impressed / with fancy electrical nets, sick / of supersonic nightsticks" (*SP,* 58).

In "Dear Reader," the poet admits that he half hates the reader (who has got the poet's "identification papers"), and it feels that way throughout Tate's many collections. Tate's readers are invited to feel the shame of the lyric situation in which identification with a speaker is expected but, the poem seems to know, constitutes a loathsome reduction of subjectivity. In *Absences* (1972), "Teaching the Ape to Write Poems," here reproduced in full, expresses acute disdain for the abstract ideal of a poet-subject:

> They didn't have much trouble
> teaching the ape to write poems:
> first they strapped him into the chair,
> then tied the pencil around his hand
> (the paper had already been nailed down).
> Then Dr. Bluespire leaned over his shoulder
> and whispered into his ear:
> "You look like a god sitting there.
> Why don't you try writing something?" (*SP*, 122)

Tate's skepticism (even disdain) for the very generic expectation he invokes—poems as inflated self-expression coded male—makes it tempting to wonder why he bothers so often to write in the first person and to invoke the most ashamed version of lyric (meditative poetry) and to frame the whole poetic endeavor as a form of narcissism and embarrassing self-importance. In this, he also gives to the reader a sense of complicity with a moribund mode.

That Tate is doing so at the same time as Language writers are but not from within their community is important. As Language writers were, Tate was working out his relationship to a set of midcentury, homosocial, hypermasculine lyric inheritances that were less determinative for Ashbery's earlier practice. Tate is self-conscious, if not always explicit, about his work's vexed relation to the soft surrealism of the Deep Image poets, themselves the object of Language critique. The male personal poem of the 1980s and 1990s was inclined, indeed, against a "lyric egotism" attributed to Confessional writing, which had been attractively but problematically repurposed in the "quiet but luminous" forms of self-realization that the Deep Imagist soft-surrealist poets such as William Stafford, James Wright, Robert Bly, and Donald Hall had written in the 1960s and 1970s.[70] Hass and Charles Wright thus turned to American Buddhist/Emersonian strains in combination with surrealism—seeking that "emptying out" that Perloff assigns to Wright. Tate's poems, though also inheritors of that Deep Image surrealism, rather takes jabs at the vague Buddhism of his peers. The 1972 "First Lesson," for instance, proceeds as a failed sit-meditation, sardonically foregrounding the fact of its writtenness as problematic to the meditative mode's claim to mimic mind in action.[71] "Heatstroke," from *Riven Doggeries* (1979), begins in the backyard as a first-person confessional self-examination that stalls at line 3:

> I always have many flowers—
> my neighbor gives them to me.
> I seem not to have the strength
> to go on with my confession. (*SP*, 166)

It is as if the very convention of a meditative confession has wearied the poem off its course before it can gain any momentum. This figures the poem in the tenacious, autonomous grip of a convention supposed to be freeing and authentic, highlighting the subject's weariness or embarrassment at the poem's inability to either surpass or sustain that mode with any energy. "With a Child All Day" (also from *Riven Doggeries*), which is ostensibly committed to self-reflection about the experience of being "with a child all day," breaks down at the line, "Why this embarrassed despair, this recoiling?" (*SP*, 170). The subjective-expressive mode in Tate often unravels into a language game, the soliloquy undercut by humor almost before it has begun, as in "Rooster":

> Tomorrow, since I have so few,
> and Tomorrow, less dramatically,
> and Tomorrow any number of times. (*SP*, 168)

Tate's subject here, as elsewhere, is "renouncing," and what is renounced are conventions and traditions of self-enunciation (here, the soliloquy) that the poet inhabits only sardonically. This marks Tate's aesthetic as informed by the surrealism and humor of his great mentor Ashbery (and with second-generation New York School writing) but also marks its difference from these. In Ashbery, that inhabitation is still often tinged with longing, almost as if he inhabits an abandoned structure, animating it as a ghostly presence, however resigned to its loss.[72] And Tate is much closer to the metonymic word play of certain Language and post-Language poets (Charles Bernstein or Bruce Andrew come to mind) than to that of Hass or Jorie Graham, who maintained a seriousness of purpose that Tate rarely seems to share (and even seems to mock).

By the 1990s, Tate inhabits the conventions of the subjective-expressive poem (the "lyric") in such a way that belies how intensely self-consciously

"lyric" performances were subject to (even constituted by) forms of embarrassment, derision, and shame. Indeed, about a dozen of the forty-
eight poems in *Worshipful Company of Fletchers* indicate their moment
with gestures to the backyard setting and epiphany mode that Perloff
had identified in the 1970s and that, by the 1980s and 1990s, was synonymous with the problems of the "lyric" of "mainstream" conventionality. Nine in that set place a markedly or ironically meditative speaker in a
specific outdoor setting.[73] Perhaps this is why Ashbery, in his judge's citation for Tate's Tanning Prize in 1995, identifies Tate's work with the backyard: "Tate, born in Kansas City, landed in New England where he has
developed a homegrown variety of Surrealism almost in his own backyard, which figures frequently in his poetry."[74] Ashbery is quoting the title
of Tate's poem "In My Own Backyard," which, Ashbery must have
known, draws on and critiques Hass's and Wright's own self-conscious
references to the backyard setting and the peculiar form of power—
domesticated down from Wordsworthian heights, a form of cultural
isolation—that it afforded the poet to realize himself.[75] Indeed, as the emphatic *"own* backyard" suggests, the setting sees Tate reflect on the peculiar mix of limitation and privilege marking the suburban, American, male
poetic imaginary.

Ashbery makes it seem as though the "backyard" setting is consistent
through all of Tate's work, and yet before publishing *Worshipful Company
of Fletchers,* very few of Tate's poems had been set in the backyard. It is in
that mid-1990s collection that Tate explores the setting and trope extensively. One wonders to what extent Tate's morphing of the harder surrealism with the backyard meditative mode comments on the trope's ubiquity
in the literary culture of the day, the ashamed meditative setting now
associated both with Abrams's lyric "tradition" and also with the avant-
garde critique of post-Romantic Deep Image and workshop poems.
Where, in fact, had the mode originated? "In My Own Backyard" leads
us into this problem. Tate's subject both trundles along in the backyard
mode and has also internalized attacks on the idea of a unified subject
that were still then, at least for the mainstream poetry world, somewhat
"new": the act of self-enunciation—supposed to be distinguishing—is not
just fraught and outdated (thus the subject is being put "out to pasture")
but corrupted by discourse ("touched, as they say") and ashamed, self-
loathing, even violent. The poem begins,

I've seen fox, deer, wild turkey, pheasant, skunk,

snakes, moles, guinea hens. I've thrown a boomerang
that never came back.[76]

Slight surrealisms (the missing boomerang threatening to knock us out,
for instance) gradually indicate this poem's difference from a more
"straight" invocation of the epiphanic meditative mode in a Hass or
Wright poem:

There's an old weathered chicken coop full
of empty paint cans, a homemade wooden wheelbarrel

Beyond that is an ersatz compost heap—I'm not consciously
composting anything. (68)

As with both Hass's and Wright's self-conscious meditations, Tate's poem
foregrounds the only paratactic connection between things and, as with
Hass's, raises conventional expectations for epiphany only to refuse them.
Tate's "I" is "not . . . / composting anything" on purpose, not composing
a transformative experience or end product of any kind. But whereas in
Hass and Wright antiepiphany is a way to refuse a problematic lyric inheritance while still enacting a drama of self-realization, the critique in
Tate's poem cuts deeper, suggesting the very project of self-realization to
be problematically bound up in ideals of private property. The subject
formations that private property promise—a selfhood made visible by
privileged experiences of isolation, for instance—here get crossed with the
freedom of (self-)expression, reiterating the Language critique of canonical, expressive lyric as based on "alienating processes of social atomiza-
tion," indeed, one chief form of that process.[77]
    As the poet "walks "the property line" out "along the vacant field /
where local kids played softball forty years ago— / the pitcher's rubber is
still in place," we find that the details are just a little off—would a vacant
suburban field once used for children's games remain undeveloped and
untouched after forty years? The use of "rubber," though accurate as a
term, invokes more idiomatically the prophylactic that, in the next verse
paragraph, the poet-I seems to be "inspecting . . . in the grass." By now,
the poem has primed us for how this bucolic setting turns weird or even
queer: "but I am a little daft, touched, as they say, / a little on my way

out to pasture" (69). With such terms as "softball," "pitch," "rubber," and "touched" taking on the whiff of sexuality, the particulars of the poem's swerve toward surrealism begin to suggest divergence from the "straight" narrative poem; walking the vacant field becomes an overdetermined trope (familiar in too many directions), something seeding a longing for closure that it resists. Thus, the "property line" we are limning is both the individual's yard and the limits of lyric proper. The slight surrealism prepares us somewhat for the backyard setting's promise of a tiny epiphany turned suddenly to a deeply sardonic moment of violence directed at the "self":

> I grab my throat and wrestle me to the ground.
> "There, there," I say, "lighten up ol' boy."
> "It's a free country, it's your own backyard."
> I listen intently: sky and daisies burlesque each other,
>
> bivouacked between worlds. (69)

Taken as Tate's comment on the canonical poem of the day, "In My Own Backyard" darkly emphasizes the meditative mode's self-importance by literalizing "lyric" self-regard as possible to sustain only as a form of violence. The poem goes a step beyond Hass's performance of mild shame at desiring, and yet feeling self-conscious about desiring, the canonical comforts of the self-exploratory modern meditative poem. What emerges is a sense of the poet's deep discomfort and paranoia—a violent, even "crippling" self-consciousness about proceeding in a conventional, meditative poetic stance, itself implicated with violence of a kind. In the preceding stanza, Tate's "I" seems on the brink of entering into a fairly expected, bemused introspection about age or a nostalgically rendered personal and national, specifically male, childhood. And yet, just before the self-attack, though alone, the poet-figure as backyard wanderer feels watched, as if the subject's very claims to solitude depended on the unacknowledged presence of a critical other.

The specter of Mill enters here, given that what watches and judges the poet is himself, literalized as a monstrous double. This renders the poet's move to forgive himself ("there, there")—in effect, the move in both Hass's and Wright's lyric shame poems, too—both a sign of the conventional meditative stance and also a figure for the acute self-consciousness about normative modes of lyric reading and conventions of lyric writing summed up by the epithet "New Criticism" and assigned to "lyric." One

suspects that, for writers of Tate's generation, this self-consciousness became even more pronounced in light of the negative, antilyric forms of
reading for a lyric speaker in ever-wider circulation. The complexity of
thinking through the origins of the lyric's shame (is it attributable to a
genre, to a mode of critical reading?) is suggested by the fact that we cannot know exactly whether the advice from one aspect of the self—"It's a
free country, it's your own backyard"—comes from the "I" who has wrestled "me" to the ground or the I-me who is now on the ground. What
does the throttling self hope to achieve—to silence the throttled one?
There are several ways we might read the scene: is this the throttled self's
retort to the throttling, attacking self? Or does it extend the attack, as if
to say, you need not go on analyzing yourself—after all, it is your own
backyard? Either way, the poem articulates the double vision of lyric
shame that, by the 1990s, many poets even slightly self-conscious about
working in self-expressive or meditative modes would be susceptible to.
Indeed, lyric shame, a conventional "self-flagellation," as Lyons put it, can
seem to be the affective form that poetic subjectivity takes for many poets
of this generation. Thus, the poet figure is left listening "intently," though
it is not clear to what: what follows is rather a visual image of sky "bur-
lesqued" by daisies and daisies by sky. Because the meaning of this image
does *not* interpret or unify the whole poem, it suggests the poem's final
refusal to seed its own interpretability, reiterating the largely sardonic
view on "lyric" that the piece as a whole presents.

Though "In My Own Backyard" is the most obvious of the group, the
collection repeatedly stages its lyric shame in terms of the backyard epiphany mode. In "The Great Root System," the Keatsian, lyric analogy of poet
to bird is reduced to nearly comic outlines and ultimately rejected:

> When the birds talk, I answer.
> When they are hungry, I need feed.
> They desire to propagate, I do too.
> But the story ends here, it goes
> nowhere. It's just too early
> in the morning to think anything through. (*Worshipful,* 15)

The poem keeps lowering the curtain on peripatetic mental travel, in effect wearied of the conventions that drive it. Meditation falters because
the thinking "has completely exhausted" the poet (16), and where we expect an epiphany, we get the abstract idea of one:

My own humanity has overwhelmed me,
it has nearly defeated me, the me who was
trying to rise up. It—that is, my own
humanity—seethed up when I least wanted it. (16)

If there is an undoing that seems cathartic here (the poem ends with an image of birds scattering), it is such a sudden uprising that it seems to undercut the poem's mock attempt to transcend into epiphany. Pronoun confusion renders the self as double at first (as in "In My Own Backyard) and then as an "it." Similarly, "A Manual of Enlargement," set in the backyard with "a pet squirrel / watching all of this" (a nod perhaps to Lowell) attempts to enlarge but always deflates—a series of antiepiphanies: from "I saw green!" to "It's really nice this time" (*Worshipful,* 19). As with many of Tate's poems, feeling is clipped or clamped at the very instant it might have been expressed; indeed, irony in Tate usually serves an antiexpressive agenda. Instead, everything is "just fine," the poem's assurance also its undoing: "What little meditation I had / was gone in a puff" (20).

In short, if these are "interrupted meditations" (à la Hass), they advance without Hass's desire and longing in play and are unlike the meditations on emptying out or nothingness in poets such as Mark Strand or Charles (or James) Wright or Hass or Wallace Stevens. In Tate, the death of the subject is more like a beheading that nevertheless leaves some vestigial idea of the self flailing, the verbal wake of self-analysis trailing behind it. We get a strong sense of the autonomous power of convention to carry on even without the poem's good faith in it. When it does seem that the poet has an expressive agenda, it is always already embarrassed or ashamed. In "The Nitrogen Cycle," the poet who "would stagger out into the yard" when military planes would fly too low, encounters a "Snake person" who walks out of the forest. The muse/haunting may be Ashbery:

"My name," he finally replied,
"is Mr. Ashby. Please address me
by that name or I will embarrass you
by telling you a beautiful story." (*Worshipful,* 36)

If the I-poet figure in Tate's poems from this collection is looking for something, he is destined not to have it, except in a perverse and isolated fantasy of connection that can only fleetingly admit a hunger for poetic expression that can never quite occur.

In *Shroud of the Gnome* (1997), the collection that followed *The Worshipful Company of Fletchers* (appearing at the peak of the "poetry wars"), Tate's "Of Two or Three Minds" explores its self-consciousness about lyric meditation by showing self-scrutiny becoming baroque, almost filigreeing out of sight:

> With all my knickknack injuries
> and curiosity detours
> and the embarrassing heartache
> of my latest aperçu,
> one would think I would have something
> better to do than what I actually do
> when I do what I actually do do.[78]

The comical mix of the Cole Porter–esque mad-cap and childish defecatory humor in those last lines offers answers—variegation of tone and humor—to the embarrassment of cherishing one's "latest aperçu." It is precisely sensitive "poeticism" as personal insight that avant-garde critics such as Dworkin and Perloff had held to account and, arguably, held up to shame—the idea that poetry demands "sincere emotional expression of especially sensitive individuals" inclined to inner research and must focus on "a profound thought or small epiphany."[79] Though Perloff first launched such definitions of canonical lyric in the 1970s, these particular quotations are from 2011 and 2012, nearly a decade after the publication of Tate's poem. The poem thus indicates and announces an impasse we seem not to have gotten beyond: after denouncing a poetics of expressive sensitivity and meditative self-indulgence, the poem admits, "I am always telling myself that / with no discernible effect as yet. / And yet I am always telling myself that" (*Shroud*, 38). It is a little unclear what "that" is: Is it the specialness of his own sensitivity that the poet repeats? Or is it the admonishment to do something *more* than articulate one's latest aperçu? Either way, the poet anguishes until an admonishing voice interrupts, calling him "Mr. Odium-on-the-halfshell" and arguing,

> but there is a world out there
> and it thinks precious little of you
> and your suppurating, crinkled noggin.
> I am bifurcating from you now.
> I am on my own, a virginal spinster (38)

Here, the poet's self-directed dismay results in his (brief) fracture into himself and a Poetess figure—a virginal spinster that recalls popular conceptions of such earlier "lyric" figures as Emily Dickinson or Emily Brontë and becomes an antidote for (and prefigure of?) the unbearable, odious, implicitly male "lyric" subject of neurotic self-searching.[80]

Here, as elsewhere, Tate draws attention to the implicit gendering of "the lyric subject" as male, implicit also in Bishop's claim that she writes as a "minor female Wordsworth" and explicit in Mayer's concerns about antilyricism.[81] Tate's bifurcated, admonishing, critically savvy, and ashamed lyric subject highlights the often less-than-trenchant treatment of gender in other male poets of his generation (such as Hass and Wright): Tate exposes questions about gender that circle around the question of either taking on or rejecting "the" lyric subject. Is the lyric inheritance masculinist, even hypermasculine, and if so, in what senses? His 1990 poem "Crimes against the Lyric," for instance, perpetrates the "crime" of failing to cohere its series of poetic statements around the figure of its female protagonist. If this is a "Portrait d'Une Femme," "she" fails to function as a symbol of either the poet's mind or the world *he* strives to bring to order. The metaphoric resonances that would lead to interpretive closure remain just out of reach:

> She throws her ragdoll to within earshot
> of a viola and, miles downstream,
> a gramophone loses power.
> There is a cooing from the mountaintop.
> Bees have been struck by lightning.
> A looking-glass is hurled down in self-defense.
> The multitudinousness of the world
> stops her from having one clean thought.[82]

The dashed looking-glass refuses mimesis of mind or self, and the figure of voice gets dispersed through the landscape, not stabilized by the poet or by the poem's female object. As Mark Ford writes of Tate's poems in general, his "characters and properties continually escape the control of his authority and refuse to be defined by his needs," and we could also emphasize how this escape occurs through female, or feminized, figures.[83] Related is the tendency for Tate's backyard meditators and their critics to be pointedly, problematically male, a figure doubled and ruptured in the act of both critiquing and reinstating the masculinist scene of self-discovery that was common to much "major" poetry of the American midcentury. As Michael Davidson has argued, in Beat and Deep Image poetry, male poetic self-discoveries, what Davidson calls "greater sensitivity or vision," are "purchased at the expense of women, even when her gender (as in more recent men's movement rhetoric) is invoked as a positive value."[84]

Tate's poems seem savvy to Davidson's critique: "Of Two or Three Minds" suggests that both the Poetess and the hypermasculine lyric figures are vicarious, abstract identifications, one no more authentic than another, though poets take these roles on to enact or mimic authentic self-discovery. In the poem, the virginal spinster agrees to act as the subservient partner to the sensitive male poet, and in the process, the critique of male poetic hubris gets reduced to a "fit of ill temper." The poem suggests that this "bifurcating" is finally no more successful than the problematic donning of the sensitive, backyard, male poet role (remembering this chapter's epigraph): "I stand by the kitchen window / for what seems like an eternity, / but in point of fact was probably thirty seconds" (*Shroud,* 39). It is a quietly bitter ending, in which both the one who critiques male poeticism and the one who tries for a more "authentic" poeticism (the virginal spinster) are comically thin: the critique concedes that the (male) poet is a "Lover of stillness, lover of silence, / dreamer of small, fuzzy things, / king of the armchair cowboys," reasserting the hypermasculine figure who delights in his "latest aperçu" (38).

Tate's 1997 poem shows how strongly gender factors into late-twentieth-century experiments with the shame of "lyric"—both in response to "lyric" abstracted, since the eighteenth century, as the genre of overabundant affect (read feminine) and to its redrawing, in the mid-to-late twentieth century, as the authentic site of homosocial, hypermasculine self-actualization.[85] In both cases, the gender trouble that attends the reading (and shaming) of poetry as lyric expresses "lyric" as a critical abstraction. For what person (of what gender) should be associated with "the lyric I" or its shame?[86] The sometime bitterness of Tate's poems seems a self-conscious reflection of the broader realization among poets of Tate's generation that writing personal lyric, even in a Deep Image, surrealist, or Confessional mode, might not assure a subject position in league with feminist ideals, nor (by attending to the thingly and local) would it counter the masculinist assumptions about universalism or objectivism marking Eliotic New Critical and Imagist modernist poetic modes. Rather, male and female poets alike found "lyric" implicated in a broader (implicitly male) politics to which they did not consciously subscribe. If it is unclear whether Tate is embarrassed because he is either too male or too female (as a window-gazing poet), it may be because lyric is itself an abstract, detachable identification. The lyric shame poem of the 1990s leads to poems in the 2000s that are ever more self-conscious about gender as it has played into twentieth-century critical constructions of "lyric" all along.

"WHY IS I STILL HERE?": RECENT VERSIONS OF THE LYRIC SHAME POEM

Sensibility to the missing person at the heart of "the lyric I" is one object of interest that emerges as the critique of "the lyric I" is fully absorbed and adopted by academic poets in the 2000s. For many younger poets writing then, self-consciousness about "traditional" poetic subjectivity and poetry technique understood as praxis become givens, and a postsubjective stance becomes de rigueur in some poetic communities. Not quite lyric shame poems, then, the most recent examples of the motif tend to explore, and are sometimes perceived to ironize, the critical pressure to write a post-subjective poem, as well as the resulting problems of the phantom subject who haunts the postsubjective contemporary American scene. Such poems only murkily distinguish themselves from Silliman's (murky) account of the post-avant. For instance, whereas the poet Lynn Emanuel writes whole collections that theorize postpersonal poetry, only one poem, the quite recent "I Tried to Flatter Myself into Extinction," from part 3 of her collection *Noose and Hook* (2010), extends the lyric shame motif, riffing, as it does, on what results from the pressure (on whom? on what?) to write a postsubjective poem:

> I tried to flatter myself into extinction; tried to bury alive in a landslide of disparagement ego and subjectivity and the first person singular pronoun. I ran identity to ground with the dogs of irony; I tried to kill, bury, burn, embalm, and erase the outlines of me, mummify myself in the damp wrappings of surrealism, sever and rearrange me with Stein's cubisms, break, buy, bribe, drive a stake through me; tried to whip to death the whole frumpish horse-and-buggy, essentialist, runs-in-the-blood notion I had of who "I" was. . . . So what is I still doing here? Why is I having to keep its eye peeled? Its eye on the ball? Trying to

steer by some dim star, that small, raw planet of self-loathing ham-
mered into the night ahead? Why is I hauled forth over this choppy
terrain like a tug on the rough boulevards of a black river? And by
whom?[87]

Emanuel's poem recognizes the entrenchment of subjective thinking even
(perhaps especially) in the attempt to dispense with it. The conundrum
here is not exactly like Hass's; after all, Hass's persona is still somewhat
committed to what Emmanuel's argues it wants to give up. Emmanuel is
without Hass's or Graham's vaguely anguished seriousness. The poem
takes Tate's apparent savvy with the postsubjective tropes and imperatives
at hand further, performing the lyric shame impasse with an even-more-
practiced version of exhaustion than occurred in the surrealistic disruption in Tate's late poems. Yet Hass, Emmanuel, and Tate are arguably in
the same universe, and like Tate's, Emmanuel's poems gesture to the gender confusion of the phantom "lyric" person-figure—here subtly coded as
both a Romantic male explorer and also a "frumpy" nineteenth-century
woman. The "I" keeps getting produced by the linguistic tropes that
would kill it, and yet these are all stock characters trotted out in her verbal
exercise.

For the American writer Olena Kalytiak Davis, in her long poem "The
Lyric 'I' Drives to Pick Up Her Children from School: A Poem in the
Postconfessional Mode" (2005), the postsubjective, postconfessional moment is also specifically steeped in a problematically gendered critique of
"lyric" as meditation, which brings her poem into a direct line with much
of the work I have considered.[88] Playing on Rimbaud's "Je est un autre"
and parodying, as Ira Sadoff puts it, the poststructuralist "tenet that the
'I' is socially constructed," Davis's approximately 135-line-long poem is
composed of sentences that mix the first-person pronoun with third-
person verbs, as in the opening lines:[89]

> "i" has not found, started, finished "i's" morning poem,
> the poem "i" was writing about "i" having sex with the man "i"
>   left her husband for
> the night before or maybe just this morning. (99)

Gender is foregrounded by the oddness of writing as "the lyric I" and
yet being explicitly female. At first, it seems that Davis means to critique
the fact that the universal "I" of the supposed lyric tradition is tacitly

male. Thus, to write a "lyric" as a female is to lose one's sex, as the "lyric i's poem" (some twenty-seven lines written in "straight" first person, without scare quotes or the tense experiment) seems to suggest:

SEX

i lost my sex/poem!
how did it go?
i know it was called

SEX

something about my bosky acres,
my unshrubb'd down
'bout all being tight and yare (99)

As here, with the reference to Ceres's lines from *The Tempest,* the poem is notably, comically bogged down in a (male) tradition, repeatedly making editorial comments alluding to a male, Western canon of works that "i" fears she should emulate—Ovid's *Metamorphosis,* Shakespeare's *The Tempest,* and William Butler Yeats's "Among School Children," among others (including the criticism of Allen Grossman, one of the chief articulators of a transhistorical "lyric" tradition).[90] In other words, Davis's poem critiques (at first) the writing of unselfconscious, first-person poetry (and seems to use "lyric," unselfconsciously, to stand for that here), which would be to agree to be or to feel pressured to be "tacitly" male. One writes a "lyric" and loses one's sex, if "one" is female.

And yet, when the poem resumes its "real-time" action, returning to the postsubjective "i" in scare quotes, the gesture grows ridiculous:

"i" notices it is almost time to pick up her children from school!
"i" realizes she has gotten nowhere, nowhere near it, much less
    inside it, wasted another morning, can't fucking write a poem to
    save "i's" life, oh well,
"i" is, at least, "working".
"i" pulls on her tight jeans, her big boots, her puffy parka.
"i" remote starts her car.
"i's" car is a 1995 red toyota 4-runner with racing stripe that
    doesn't have enough power for "i".
"i's" car stereo also doesn't have enough power for "i".

"i" drives cross town listening to dylan, who has plenty of power
    for "i".
"i" wonders how why dylan isn't "i's" man.
"i" gets some looks from some lesser men, some in better, more
    powerful trucks, even though "i's" dirty dirty-blonde hair is
    covered by a woolen cap.
"i" feels the power of being a single mom in a red truck.
"i" knows it is not enough power. (100)

Davis uses both the conventions of autobiographical poetry and also the
techniques that would critique them (that "i" in scare quotes), which makes
hers a lyric shame poem; it recognizes the shame of an uncritical use of
the "lyric i" while also proceeding as an autobiographical poem informed
by ideals of "lyric" subjectivity. The comedy of this double vision, of this
overtly critical use of both the conventions of autobiographical meditation
and its postmodern critique, is most keen when Davis's lines describe "the
lyric i" engaged in mundane activities. "Remote starting" the car, putting
on one's "puffy jacket"—these details are so mundane, consumerist, and
generic as to poke fun at the critical undermining of the first-person subject that scare quotes intend; since there is no claim for the "i's" uniqueness
or grandiosity here to start with, the deflation and distancing feel comically
hyperbolic, dutiful convention more than critique. Davis may agree that
we cannot write autobiographically post-Language without feeling that
we assume the self-importance attributed to such poets as Robert Lowell,
and yet she persists. (Davis seems here to extend and problematize Donald Antin's line, "if robert lowell is a poet, I don't want to be a poet.")[91]

This is to say that, whereas for Sadoff, Davis's use of "i" in quotation
marks is explained by the idea that "the lyric speaker experiences no unity
but a set of contradictions," I find the poem rather more ambivalent about
"the lyric 'i'" as a (negative) epithet or anti-ideal thought to describe,
qualify, interpret, discover, or police poets' relationships to any number of
supposedly "traditional" poetic choices or supposedly experimental ethical achievements.[92] In New Criticism–informed pedagogies of the midcentury and after, the ideal of an impersonal, speaking subject served as
an interpretive lens by which some works could be credited with the
achievement of "significant emotion" and suitably complex, if unified, responses to "situations." In antilyric readings (many by critics also trained

to read with the New Criticism–informed lyric-reading models), "the lyric i" is, likewise, an interpretive lens, though one differently geared: as with readings for a "speaker" performed by "New Critical" interpretations, readings for a "lyric I" also seek to fix a poem's tone or attitude. The point of reading for such an "I" is to corroborate what is already believed to be true of the Confessional, the "Romantic tradition," and so on—their purportedly expressive mission.

Most of the ambivalence toward "the lyric I" in Davis's poem is focused around questions of gender and how gender has informed debates about the "lyric" subject (sometimes inexplicitly or, worse, as a shadow presence). Thus, in quoting a famous Whitman line from "Song of Myself" in the line, "'i' thinks 'i am the man, i suffered, i was there,'" Davis at one level invokes the problematic, overreaching "power" that "the lyric I," especially by avant-garde detractors, has been thought to have—its ability to assume, even consume, the other (100). Whereas Whitman invoked the representative self's power as positive, Davis's line raises the skepticism that later generations of poets feel toward "lyric" power.

But at another level, the poem also complicates that (by now unsurprising) skeptical wisdom by turning to the (perhaps no more surprising) countercritical claim that the *prohibition* against lyric—particularly against legible autobiographical poems—can serve antifeminist, and even misogynistic, agendas. Crossing the critical reading of the abstract "lyric I's" "power" with the "power" of an actual single mother (whom we are invited, anyway, to imagine is Davis herself) in a red truck (a social-sexual "power" and an image that may suggest an only limited socioeconomic "power," too) does more than critique Whitman's fantasy of unlimited imaginative range or Lowell's self-importance and does more than raise the crossed agendas of feminism and radical disjunctive technique that Mayer explored in the late 1970s. For the poem, from here, goes on to remind us that the critical savvy that drives and dictates the terms of a radically antisubjective poetics that will explode the assumptions of "the lyric I" (whether through disjunctive techniques or Conceptual experiments) is itself conventional and originates in academic critical prerogatives and licenses coded as male.

Note that, as the car-ride meditation on writing as a woman goes forward, Davis cites a range of canonized academic texts that are critical touchstones for scholars thinking through questions about "the personal," "the lyric I," the Confessional, and the reputation of the "meditative" poem: a 1970 essay by Perloff on Lowell and "the confessional," M. H. Abrams's "Structure and Style in the Greater Romantic Lyric" (also referenced in the Perloff essay), David Yezzi's "Confessional Poetry and the Artifice of Honesty" (a 1998 essay from the *New Criterion*), and, quoted within Yezzi's essay, M. L. Rosenthal's review of Allen Ginsberg's *Howl and Other Poems*. These texts are central to teachers and students of contemporary poetics in the United States, particularly those who think about the status of "lyric" (or expressive poetry) in contemporary poetics and "the personal" (as I do).

In Davis's way of invoking this critical inheritance, she foregrounds hypermasculine rhetoric that runs through not only the poetry under discussion but also the criticism of that poetry since the American midcentury. Indeed, her poem raises unremarked gender complications that do not neatly locate themselves on either side of the lyric/antilyric, expressive/antiexpressive fence. Though "i" may be writing a poem whose ostensible subject is the lyric and SEX, Davis seems to be writing a poem about gender in the critical discourse on "the lyric I":

> "i" gives, well, has given, good head.
> "i" takes it like a man.
> "i" thinks there should be a new "new sexualized and radicalized
>   poetry of the self",
> "i" knows the "single-minded frenzy of a raving madman" but,
> "i" mostly keeps her head.
> "i" remembers that "as long ago as 1925, boris tomashevsky,
>   a leading russian formalist critic, observed that the
>   'autobiographical poem' is one that mythologizes the poet's life
>   in accordance with the conventions of his time. it relates not
>   what has occurred but what should have occurred, presenting an
>   idealized image of the poet as representative of his literary
>   school" (101)

Up to this point, with her invocation of Rosenthal's reading of Ginsberg's *Howl* ("new sexualized and radicalized poetry of the self"), we feel we are watching Davis attempt to identify herself, as "the lyric i," with an idealized, hypermasculine (even when overtly homosexual) "lyric i," one broadly celebrated as ushering in lyric's new (hypermasculine) potential at midcentury. Davis's "i" may not want to align herself with Ginsberg's expressive frenzy, but she nevertheless tells us she "takes it like a man." To

complicate matters, in the next lines it seems that Perloff (from whom the
Tomashevsky quote comes) is also a man:

> "i" wants to be a man like marjorie perloff, helen hennessy vendler,
> boris tomashevsky.
> "i" thinks, on the other hand, "i mean i like in art when the artist
> doesn't know what he knows in general; he only knows what he
> knows specifically" (101)

These lines align the "lyric I," *critiques* of "the lyric I" and of the Confessional, and perhaps the whole critical climate in the United States with
machismo. They certainly suggest that a masculinist perspective informs
poetic discourse across the divide of the poetry wars (as is suggested by
calling both Perloff and Helen Vendler "a man").[93] Davis seems to feel
steeped in an oppressively male tradition put forth by Vendler and, more
surprisingly, by Perloff, whose references to Tomashevsky's reading of the
autobiographical poem (again, in a 1970 article on Lowell and the Confessional) Davis's 'i" has clearly taken in but also feels as a rebuke to "take
it like a man."

Take what? we may ask. Criticism, it would seem. Both the turn from
Tomashevsky to Perloff and Davis's response to the shame surrounding
the personal, autobiographical lyric are quite subtle; the poem tentatively
advocates an alternative position, adapted from an interview comment
made by Fairfield Porter: "i mean i like in art when the artist doesn't know
what he knows in general; he only knows what he knows specifically."[94]
This is to say that Davis's "i" seems to want to justify using the "i" without wanting to be thought to be indulging "the lyric i" per se. The position is one that finds "i" embarrassed, even ashamed:

> "i" just wishes "i" could talk more smarter theory, no
> "i" just wishes "i" could write more smarter poems, no
> "i" thinks "WHY I AM A POET AND NOT A . . ."
> "i" thinks "KALYTIAK DAVIS PAINTS A PICTURE" (101)

The poem here refers us to an appropriated (misquoted) version of Frank
O'Hara's poem title ("Why I Am Not a Painter") and to Thomas B. Hess's
canonical 1953 review essay for *ArtNews,* "De Kooning Paints a Picture,"
which did much to define readings of de Kooning's work in the twenty
years after it first appeared, heroizing the artist's existentialism and process-
oriented working methods. Both the Hess and the O'Hara references

invoke the historical avant-garde, specifically New York "schools" of painting and poetry (mostly by men) and the interest of many of the artists affiliated with these in process, irony, and antitraditional spontaneity and
improvisation, which figure as antidotes to canonical late-modernist and
midcentury formalist poetry. Appropriating these alternatives, Davis also
turns to new use something of the ambition and self-promotional brio of
both O'Hara and de Kooning throughout their careers.

Davis's appropriation of the O'Hara title, however, may ironize her relationship to what David Lehman calls O'Hara's "nervy self-celebration,"
for it is clear that this "i" does not feel so unswervingly confident to assert
either herself or her methods as O'Hara's poet-I's seem ready to do.[95] It is
unclear whether, in appropriating Hess, Davis means to reference the critic's bold promotional energy in writing the de Kooning article about the
controversial show in which *Woman I* debuted (the article appeared before
the show opened); or de Kooning's work's ambiguity; or his midcentury
fame; or the charges of misogyny leveled at his complex, disturbing female figure in the multilayered "action" painting *Woman I.* Does Davis
wish to align herself with what Jed Perl has called de Kooning's "howl of
giddy frustration" in *Woman I,* directed at the impasse that faced artists
interested in the handmade in an era of high capitalism, which had become the sign of an exhausted romantic individualism?[96] Perhaps Davis
means to invoke the consequences of de Kooning's midcentury fame—a
decline in his critical reputation as an avant-garde painter.[97] In the 1970s
and 1980s, de Kooning came to be thought of as the "salon" painter
against whom later avant-gardes set their agendas. Could Davis be aligning herself with de Kooning's own vexed relationship to the critical
avant-garde?[98]

Finally, the interpretive point of the Hess / de Kooning reference remains just out of reach, multilayered and steeped in complexities (not
unlike de Kooning's picture). In 1968, Hess figured de Kooning's process
in painting as a "system for studying an infinitely variable number of prob-
abilities" and celebrated the resulting ambiguity of de Kooning's paintings by asserting that "[de Kooning] refuses any conclusion that would
close the argument."[99] In many ways, Davis's poem also refuses interpretive closure. If nothing else, however, we are led to see how not only "i's"
anxiety but its/her very existence is predicated on and assembled out
of received editorial comments, other (mostly male) texts, potentially
shaming critical expectations, and possible editorial and anthological

destinations for her work. Notice that she references not de Kooning's painting but an article about it—one that powerfully determined the work's later fortunes and its avant-garde status and that has come to serve as shorthand for both de Kooning's rise and fall.

Indeed, given the poem's seeming anxieties about the critical views that inform "lyric" practice (and its antilyric and avant-garde other), its turn to Abrams, at this point, is quite revealing. The poem asserts, " 'i' wishes she could remember Abrams's definition of the structure of the greater romantic lyric" and then quotes it exactly, which insists that we read the poem in light of a "lyric" meditative tradition and in light of Abrams's particular version of lyric history, which so centrally informs, as negative example, Perloff's (new) lyric agenda. If the relationship of Davis's poem to this tradition is mixed, it is not exactly a reconciling "hybrid" of lyric and postmodern or lyric and antilyric. Davis's poem explores the ashamed self-consciousness that, among other things, literary-critical awareness thrusts on a poet of her generation. Finally, the poem cannot quite be held to advocate any single position: the meditative, lyric, and its antilyric mirror image are this "i's" inherited tradition, and she receives both as male dominated and dictatorial. At the poem's close, "i" (and Davis) seem to throw up her hands about the confused subject position advised by the postconfessional mode:

> "i" has fucked with the facts so "you" think she's robert lowell. *(but whoever saw a girl like robert lowell?)*
> "i" doesn't care if "you", silent human auditor, present or absent, never heard of, could give a flying fuck about, robert lowell.
> (103)

We may at first hesitate over the source of "silent human auditor, present or absent": is it Wordsworth, or Vendler, or is it Mill, or is it Perloff (deriding the lyric)? It turns out to be Abrams, but I fantasize that Davis enjoys its echoey bounce back and forth across the lyric and antilyric divide, articulating the shared space in which both reside.

In referencing several canonical critical articles without attribution, Davis pulls the curtain on the poetry reading-writing-critical culture and its increasing self-sameness—that "you" that renders her lyric "i" legible as "good" or "bad." If Mill had struggled to imagine (and Abrams had insisted on) the presence of a universalized "ourselves," unseen but always perfectly addressed by the successful Romantic lyric, Davis's poem turns the spotlight on the particular social and cultural condition of today's "you," shining the light on the reading culture that defines the likely "you" of her work, as well as how its "i" will be judged and interpreted, even in the act of denying that her poem's "i" cares about it.

The poem thus identifies its addressee (and most likely its reader) with someone who, he or she may regret, is quite a bit like me (and, I assume, you, dear reader): one versed in the texts Davis cites and one quite aware of the debates about Lowell, lyric, subjectivity, the Confessional, and so on that the poem invokes. This is a step beyond Sexton's exaggerating exposure of the lyric-reading paradigms she knew would define her poem's reception, but it marks a far point extending out from the same set of critical problems. For Davis, the not "giv[ing] a flying fuck" is belated, willful, and only half insincere: chances are that those who bother to register the poem's references have reading practices defined by these debates, as Davis herself shows us is true, too, of her writing practices.

The overall effect of the poem is, for me, a hybrid *not* of lyric and anti-lyric but of critical and poetic. It serves as an autobiographical account of a twenty-first-century poet's working through her vexed reception of lyric-reading practices (including their antilyric mode as "poetry wars" about tradition and poetic subjectivity) that have dominated critical discourses on poetics in academia since the 1940s. While on the one hand Davis critiques the implicitly male, Romantic subject (now referred to in short-hand with the phrase "the lyric i"), on the other, she finds it living on in available "postconfessional," ironic practices. But most significantly, for me, the poem performs all this with a strong, even oppressed recognition that its possible horizons are defined by critical intervention in the first place: midcentury critical definitions of lyric, including both Perloff's and Vendler's. One might then say that Davis both maintains and evacuates the position of "the lyric i"—suggesting, as Lynn Emanuel does, how inescapably it structures both critical and poetic responses (as aligned as ever) to the very idea of what constitutes a poem.[100] This, finally, seems to place the lyric shame poem into the light of late-twentieth- and twenty-first century art made out of capitalism: art so aware of the situations of its production and consumption, so late capitalist, that it cannot look away from them, let alone entertain a fourth wall enabling its privacy or distinction. The university setting from which Davis's poem emerges also suggests what a different moment poets of her generation are in from the one in which Mayer was living in the late 1970s. Though there are myriad university-trained poets who are not writing lyric shame poems, the lyric shame poem testifies to the dominance of the university system in shaping and accrediting poets and to literary-critical debates born of New Critical pedagogical discourse and its antilyric other to mediate the very idea of the personal, both in readings of older texts (as I explored in my chapters on Bishop and Sexton) and also in the production of new texts.

Afterword

I AM RELUCTANT to attempt a summing up; my wish is for others to shape this book's meanings and to push its thinking along. I would like, however, to share a few of the many questions left unanswered while writing this book and to point to other quite contemporary poetic sites, aside from those I've identified, where the thread of lyric shame runs, or where the concept might prove useful.

This book kept having to re-realize the constant, problematic lure, in thinking about the trajectory of the contemporary American poetics it charts, to mistake diffuse, general literary critical ideas with the eccentric, specific texts and "movements" that are only parts of their origination. Informing this difficulty is the diversification of American poetries and the expansion of American universities after World War II. On the one hand, we see competing, often politically or ethically inflected aesthetic proving grounds proliferate, and on the other, we see a university reading and writing culture establish the terms by which most poetry is funded. This double character is reflected in the language of countercultural "schools" and "movements"—Confessional, New York School, Black Arts, Language poets, Conceptual writing, and so on—that render the field either teachable or marketable and overtidied. Acts of criticism and scholarship of contemporary poetry are often urgently if messily bound up in forms of advocacy or defense, with "the field's" visibility depending on bitter anthology wars and competing accounts of the most vital and ethical contemporary "lines." The poet D. A. Powell, one of eight poets asked to write a poetic manifesto for *Poetry* magazine in February 2009, refused the very group-making premise in play: "Maybe it's peculiar to our time, in which actual schools (academies) proliferate and spawn, that we're seeing so much *centrism*. What we need is more *eccentrism.* Who isn't tired of the contemporary qua contemporary? Who isn't bored by innovation for innovation's sake?"[1] Powell's longing for a poetry culture defined by noninnovative eccentricity seems paradoxical but makes sense in the context of the aesthetic turf wars and binary logics structuring them, as here discussed. Furthermore, Powell's consensus-making address—"who isn't"—flags once radical innovations driven by lyric shame as new norms and tries to hail into being a "we" marked by weariness at critical pressures (however politically sound, however illusory, however sourceless) to nonconform.

Other of the manifesto writers in Powell's company similarly perform lyric shame as a cheeky weariness of their own hyperawareness of only vaguely-sourced critical pressures. The first four lines of Joshua Mehigan's twenty-three-lined, enumerated "The Final Manifesto" humorously thrust on us a vague sense of paranoia, a fear of a shaming identification that describes the fantasy (and sometimes the reality) of entering spaces of contemporary academic poetry culture in the United States:

1. We see you.
2. We know who you are.
3. Your ideas are worthless.
4. Your aesthetic is stupid.
5. Your "technique" is a welter of narcissism, superstition, and habit.[2]

"Superstition" draws us back to Bishop's feeling shamed in the 1930s by a fantasized Freudian critic who would regard her pleasures in the correspondences of rhyme and plot to be neurotic and childish. (A. E. Stallings's "Presto Manifesto!" reprises that fear by asserting rhyme as "nothing to be ashamed of.")[3] "Narcissism" might seem to invoke a charge against "the lyric I." However, Mehigan's poem-manifesto is more like the 1970s Bishop of "Five Flights Up," savvy about how mobile the shame identification can be. What is fascinating to me, indeed, is how quickly my own shame rushes to fill his abstract second-person subject and its derided, underspecified "aesthetic," and this tendency is part of the critical interpolative process that I have sought to explore in this book.

The "lyric" and "antilyric" abstractions that I have explored here may mean something important to everyone, but they do so by dint of being open to projection. The "lyric" abstraction draws on aspects of critical theory drawn from writings associated with the "New Criticism" that were overcirculated, dulled, and naturalized into tokens of pedagogic culture—eccentricities made central. One can feel that a similar fate (if not on the same scale) may await ideas abstracted as "Language poetry." Perhaps this is an inevitable process, but it asks for careful tracings of routes by which critical epistemologies become established in institutional channels, including, lately, the increasingly institutional blogs and websites run by the Poetry Foundation and the Academy of American Poets. The speed with which contemporary online culture circulates these tokens can feel overwhelming. At one far end of this train of thought is my sense that all a critic can ever do (really well) is read texts by situating him- or herself and the text in the most "relational," self-conscious, and particular terms, as conegotiators of historically complex matrices. Here I mean to invoke relational psychology's proposal that analysts and patients collaborate in producing the patient's account of him- or herself, a model (at least metaphorically speaking) whose uses for contemporary criticism I find intriguing.

Related questions about how processes of identification and projection relate to modes of reading are central to the issues this book raises, and yet I am still searching for just the theorist or discourse to corroborate and refine my sense of how these play in my and other lyric readings. Questions about how identificatory and projective aspects of lyric shame would play in debates about identity politics and contemporary poetics fascinate me but this book was not prepared to take them on. For one small example, we could consider the late Amiri Baraka's railing against the personal, expressive aesthetics that he saw informing work in the *Norton Anthology of Contemporary African American Poetry* and that he not so subtly shames as classist ignorance and arrogance. He takes to task Norton editor Charles Henry Rowell's emphasis on the idea that contemporary African American poets have renounced a call (one integral to the Black Arts Movement Baraka helped launch) for explicitly group-identified, political writing in favor of works that, in Rowell's words, "bear witness to the interior landscape of their own individual selves or examine the private or personal worlds of invented personae and, therefore, of human beings living in our modern and postmodern worlds."[4]

Though Baraka does not say as much, Rowell's distinction between politics and (paradoxically) generalized and "individual selves" reiterates an outdated binary (difficult to sustain even for Mill, certainly problematized by such metadiscursive Baraka poems as "Hymn to Lanie Poo") that seeks to keep writing devoted to the "individual" distinct from the social, and thus reiterates a passé lyricizing mode.[5] However, Baraka's essay, Rowell's introduction, and the histories of oppression and identity politics informing them raise questions: How would lyric shame figure in an assessment of African American poetics in the postwar period, not least for those writing out of collective experiences that so obviously and visibly problematize and exceed conceptions of "the" autobiographical or lyric subject, or "an" "American Poetry." Furthermore, how would the concept of lyric shame bear on the history and institutional culture of interpreting and canonizing African American poetry and poetics? More broadly, questions about authorial identity, identification, and the legibility of nonwhite "lyric" subjects would add significant dimension to my account of lyric shame, dimension I would pursue in readings of poems by Gwendolyn Brooks, Baraka, Audre Lorde, Li-Young Lee, Mei-Mei Berssenbrugge, Claudia Rankine, John Yao, Evie Shockley, and Terrance Hayes, to name a few. In Rowell's formulation, the personal ("lyric") subject contrasts with a collective, representative, but marginalized subject aligned with urgent political concerns. To engage this problematic schema among nonwhite, undocumented, and non-American writers, would no doubt shift and complicate the logics of this book and its sense of lyric shame. Here I wish to acknowledge Dorothy Wang's recent charge that the field of American poetics has perpetuated a marginalization of nonwhite writers as "secondary" to the field's major interests.[6] Wang's powerful call for a paradigm shift has profound implications. At the same time, the perhaps overwhelming nondiversity of the lyric shame articulators I've engaged here is not quite an accident, as the beginnings of the lyric shame situation I seek to historicize are in fact located in forms of entitlement bound up with histories of minority oppression and white privilege. Among such forms of entitlement are Mill's and Eliot's assumption of the poet's warrant to speak and expectation to be broadly relevant to and understood by "all."

This privilege finds a strange new life, however, in the assumption that poetry by nonwhite, disabled, and female subjects (those once denied such privilege) can or should be read as naïvely lyrical. Multimedia performance poet and disability studies theorist Petra Kuppers points to the continued shaming of "the personal" and the doctrinal "policing" of its supposed intrusion on poetry in disability studies circles, citing Patrick Durgin's lyric-shame-laced dismissive summary of several disability poetry texts for advancing "a neo-romantic poetics of commiseration, tempered by a preponderance of confessionalist and essentialist attention to authorial 'voice.' "[7] Kuppers points to the historical association of these derided terms with "those marked by (gendered, raced, classed, or other) specificity, those that are non-neutral," a fact that (disturbingly) undergirds the poetic community's tendency to posit "confessional" as "the other" to experimental poetries. Kuppers proposes that we "look under the hood of the term" "confessional" to find its resonances and positive connotations, especially for those who face cultural invisibility.[8] From my perspective, that work is rendered both more possible and, in a way, less necessary as we begin to recognize the pressure that critical acts exert to produce the abstract, negative (and implicitly white) "confessional" subject. This in turn will allow us to imagine more ways in which texts can be thought to enable critical forms of "social analysis," as Kuppers herself says.

Kuppers's essay is one in a group produced in honor of the "Shape of the I" conference at the University of Boulder in 2012. Organizers Julie Carr and John-Michael Rivera, both poet-scholars, identify the inspiration for the essays and the conference as the "anxieties about what constitutes subjective agency" and about the "value we place on the individual subject" in the post-poststructural period. They point out that conference participants reprised a "tension playing out" in many fields, including contemporary poetry, between identity politics' privileging of the subjective experience of the individual and the lyric shame view that "first persons . . . recall Romanticism's investments" in subject positions that "many believe we have, or should have, outgrown. And yet, writers continue to represent the 'I,' even as they do so in heavily ironized ways."[9]

Carr and Rivera's closing sentence suggests a common conundrum: a being attached (Mehigan's "habit"?) to a way of making meaning that is too abstract and fluid to actually have "a" shape: I. It is no surprise that Carr's blog entry at the Academy of American Poetics website about the conference is called "Shame and 'The Shape of the 'I,' " in which she openly reflects on "the strictures against the revealing of the self that (in some realms of poetry) have not yet been lifted, that continue to be reinscribed." Reminiscent of Bishop's savvy about early modernism's longing to "escape," Carr writes, "The effacement of the I: is it an ethics or a sham? Or a result of shame?" Carr then invokes Eve Kosofksy Sedgwick, interested, as I have been, in "the productive nature of shame."[10] In Carr's

version," "the self" recognizes its borders in defensive awareness of needing
to protect itself. I would shift her terms by saying that, in the moment a
subject feels ashamed, he or she becomes aware of "the self" as a social
contract in the first place. Shame, in this sense, need not be a bad thing.
The intensely social and contingent lives we are all already living are what
lyric shame helps call to mind.

Indeed, the poet Rachel Zucker, to whom Carr alludes and whose own
work makes frequent allusion to Bernadette Mayer's, has argued for the
importantly social possibilities of "Confessionalism" and "Autobiographicality" in contemporary poetry by redrawing the lyric figure of poetic
mutual isolation in Mill—adjacent solitary confinements—as an image
of a poet who makes "direct eye contact" with his or her audience and "is
aware of the audience and doesn't pretend otherwise." Interestingly, her
redefinition of "Confessionalistic" poetry (her preferred mode) returns us,
alas, with some lyric shame shunted onto "Romantic poetry," to something not unlike the "significant emotion" and the transpersonal universalism of Eliot: Confessionalistic poetry "transcends the personal . . . not
because it is embarrassed by the particulars, and the personal" but in service to "larger subjects."[11] Similarly, Cate Marvin is quite savvy, in her
October 2013 contribution to an online "Poets' Roundtable on Person
and Persona" to argue that "we have spoiled the brilliant work of the confessional poets by mucking about in their private lives to the extent that
we can no longer read their poems with imagination," but concludes with
hopes for "a new New Criticism" that, in my view, reanimates the trope of
the lyric poem as a message in a bottle, with writer and reader in "connection over and outside of time, as faithful as the constellations upon which
we rely for symbol and direction."[12]

Finally, quite near to the concerns of this book is the recent wave of
reassertions of "lyric" that has followed defensively upon the canonization of Conceptual and "unoriginal" poetry inclined "against expression."[13] Myriad calls for a reprisal of lyric constitute a counterreaction formation to aspects of the antilyric reading concerns that I have discussed
here. One such example is poet-blogger Sina Queyras's call for poets to
bring back lyric through the writing of "New Lyric Manifestos," a call
whose wording shows that "lyric" is still an idea both greatly overdetermined and yet firmly identified with the pedagogical history that I have
here invoked. After wearily listing familiar "calls" of lyric and antilyric
camps ("calls" for the death of poetry, of lyric, of Conceptualism, and so

on), she writes, "We want, damn it, we want what we want. And what we appear to want is poetry that retains that y as in lyric poetry. We want a speaking subject, or we want to be spoken directly to. We want Kenny [Goldsmith] to speak more than we want to read what Kenny prints out of the Internet."[14] Whether or not Queyras is sincere, her poetic group "call," overdetermined by oppositional poetic debates informed by New Critical lyric reading, is symptomatic of the lyric shame situation that I have described. That I cannot tell how sincere her call (on my behalf) is feels symptomatic of that situation, too. By the logic of the binary she both aligns with and refuses, a poet on first-name basis with "Kenny" Goldsmith (the principal advocate of antiexpressive poetry) should not advocate for a "lyric" that will "speak" to her, right?

If Queyras is playing on my (our) lyric shame here, it seems in keeping with what I see as the mode's latest form, and where my own thoughts will tend next—to that dizzying hyperawareness of a critical process grown less and less distinct from the poetic "products" it would once have received for "us." The poems and prose of Zucker, Carr, Queyras, Marvin, Maureen McClane, Haryette Mullen, Nathaniel Mackey, Ben Lerner, along with those of Davis, Emmanuel, and Paul I discussed form only a partial list of sites for further exploration of this self-conscious critical hyperawareness. Many of the conference essays that Carr and Rivera print show the anxiety about the politics of the first-person lyric subject's subjectivity shifting onto the critical subject's purported objectivity, a process that has informed much Language-centered writing, particularly that of Hejinian and Craig Dworkin, for some time, and that we could find in the writing of Anne Carson as well. For me, the potent contemporary hybrid is not a hybrid of "lyric" and "Language" but of poetry and criticism, one that eschews the conventions by which critics have, historically, assumed to offer objective, authoritative knowledge. And here I end.

Notes

INTRODUCTION

1. Elizabeth Bishop, "Five Flights Up," in *Bishop: Poems, Prose, Letters,* ed. Robert Giroux and Lloyd Schwartz (New York: Library of America, 2008), 171.

2. Eve Kosofsky Sedgwick, "Queer Performativity: Henry James's *The Art of the Novel,*" *GLQ: A Journal of Lesbian and Gay Studies* 1, no. 1 (1993): 1–16. One way to gloss this quote is by noting that "guilt" does not have a cognate grammatical form. We never say, "Guilt on you!"

3. Eve Kosofsky Sedgwick, *Touching Feeling: Affect, Pedagogy, Queer Performativity* (Durham, NC: Duke University Press, 2003), 62.

4. "Lyric reading" is a term I take from Virginia Jackson, who draws it in part from Paul de Man. Jackson sketches out a theory and history of lyric reading in *Dickinson's Misery: A Theory of Lyric Reading* (Princeton, NJ: Princeton University Press, 2005) and in "Lyric," in *The Princeton Encyclopedia of Poetry and Poetics,* ed. Roland Greene, Stephen Cushman, Clare Cavanagh, Jahan Ramazani, and Paul Rouzer, 4th ed. (Princeton, NJ: Princeton University Press, 2012), 826–834. The term serves as shorthand for two ideas: first, the idea that lyric is not a transhistorical *genre* but a reading strategy. Poems are read in a way that ascribes to them qualities we associate with the abstract concept "lyric." Thus, the term also flags a history whereby a set of interpretive practices became identified as lyric and then projected back onto poems of earlier eras. Jackson maintains that New Critical pedagogy helped "forge a model of all poems as essentially lyric." This model and way of reading both "influenced the way poems were written" and, she asserts, "remains the normative model for the production and reception of most poetry." See Jackson, "Lyric," 826–834.

5. The phrase "canon of taste" comes from Ron Silliman, Carla Harryman, Lyn Hejinian, Steve Benson, Bob Perelman, and Barrett Watten, "Aesthetic Tendency and the Politics of Poetry: A Manifesto," *Social Text* 19–20 (1988): 262. For these writers, the expressive mode of "lyric" produces and defines a canon of taste. Recent theorists of lyric, writing after poststructuralism, have also argued persuasively

that the expressive model was initially pedagogical but became normative. As Jackson argues in her essay on "lyric" in the *Princeton Encyclopedia,* that pedagogic model "became a way of reading that, in turn, influenced the way poems were written, and it remains the normative model for the production and reception of most poetry." Jackson, "Lyric," 833.

6. Edward Hirsch, *How to Read a Poem and Fall in Love with Poetry* (New York: Harcourt, 1999), 1, 6.

7. Cleanth Brooks and Robert Penn Warren, *Understanding Poetry,* 3rd ed. (New York: Holt, Reinhart, 1960), 367.

8. Scott Newman, *Ballad Collection, Lyric, and the Canon: The Call of the Popular from the Restoration to the New Criticism* (Philadelphia: University of Pennsylvania Press, 2007), 209. See ibid., chapter 5, "Reading as Remembering and the Subject of Lyric," which discusses New Critical uses of children's ballads to initiate readers into lyric reading (185–228).

9. "Ambient shame" is a term of Lucas de Lima's that I borrow and repurpose here. See "Ambient Shame, Power & the Voracious 'I': Coeur de Lion vs. Paula Deen," *Montevidayo,* October 30, 2011, http://www.montevidayo.com/?p=2109. *Montevidayo* is a poetics blog that de Lima writes with poet Joyelle McSweeney.

10. Sina Queyras, "New Lyric Manifestoes," *Lemon Hound* (blog), August 1, 2013, http://lemonhound.com/2013/08/01/new-lyric-manifestos/. For differences between early modern and modern ideas of "lyric," see Jackson "Lyric," 827.

11. Helen Vendler, "The Friendship of Cal and Elizabeth," *New York Review of Books,* November 20, 2008, http://www.nybooks.com/articles/archives/2008/nov/20/the-friendship-of-cal-and-elizabeth/?pagination=false.

12. See W. H. Race, "Recusatio," in *Princeton Encyclopedia of Poetry and Poetics,* 4th ed., 1150–1151. For a word on the conventional aspects of Augustan *recusatio,* see also Karl Galinski, *Ovid's Metamorphosis: An Introduction to the Basic Aspects* (Berkeley: University of California Press, 1975), 214.

13. Georgia Brown, *Redefining Elizabethan Literature* (Cambridge: Cambridge University Press, 2004), 181. Jackson argues (via Roland Greene) that lyric in the sixteenth and seventeenth centuries was in fact "one of many poetic varieties" but often cast as "the least important, the most occasional and ephemeral kind of poetry," and thus an object of defense. Jackson, "Lyric," 827.

14. Anne Janowitz, *Lyric and Labour in the Romantic Tradition* (Cambridge: Cambridge University Press, 1996), 7–8.

15. Jackson, *Dickinson's Misery,* 6.

16. Paul, born in 1972, received an MFA at the Iowa Writers' Workshop and has been widely published in highly visible poetry journals that attest to the broad diffusion of once-marginal avant-garde aesthetics. These journals—*Fence, Boston Review,* and *Iowa Review* (just to name a few)—have long been "open" to avant-garde aesthetics but have never needed to construct their identity in opposition to a "mainstream." Paul has won notable awards: his first collection was selected by the poet Brenda Hillman for

award/publication, and his second collection won the Associated Writing Program's Donald Hall Award in 2009. "Anybody Can Write a Poem," which is the opening poem in that second collection, *The Animals All Are Gathering* (Pittsburgh: University of Pittsburgh Press, 2010), 1–2, is also published on the Academy of American Poets website: http://www.poets.org/viewmedia.php/prmMID/21434 (accessed May 28, 2013).

17. Russell Bittner, "Poet's Corner: An Interview with Bradley Paul," *Long Story Short: An Ezine for Writers,* n.d., http://lssarchives.homestead.com/poetscorner-bradleypaul.html (accessed March 13, 2012). The "deep distress" is from Wordsworth's "Elegiac Stanzas Suggested by a Picture of Peele Castle, in a storm, Painted by Sir George Beaumont" (1807), *The Poems: Volume I,* ed. John O. Hayden (New York: Penguin Books, 1990), 695.

18. The terms are not always "lyric" and "antilyric" but are versions of these (as with "School of Quietude" and "post-avant") that have evolved from antilyric discourses.

19. That once the woman is spoken for, her face becomes drowned "ragged pulp" textualizes her, inducting her into a long-perpetuated trope of dead women in poetry. We could invoke Poe's famous claim that "the death . . . of a beautiful woman is, unquestionably, the most poetical topic in the world." Edgar Allen Poe, "The Philosophy of Composition" (1846), in *Literary Theory and Criticism,* ed. Leonard Cassuto (Mineola, NY: Dover Publications, 1999), 105. Adrienne Rich's invocation of the trope to critique patriarchal power in "Diving into the Wreck" (1972) also seems apposite here. "Diving into the Wreck," in *Diving into the Wreck: Poems 1971–1972* (New York: W. W. Norton, 1973), 22–24. Paul's poem may be read as fearing the association of a lyric-expressive urge as a form of damaging appropriation—implicitly male and, perhaps, white.

20. Charles Bernstein, "Artifice and Absorption," in *A Poetics* (Cambridge, MA: Harvard University Press, 1992), especially 18–26. Subsequent page references to this source will be given parenthetically in the text.

21. Chiefly, I am thinking of Brooks and Warren's identification of poetry with communicative expression of a dramatized "speaker" through whose figure the poem's meanings should resolve into unity. See Brooks and Warren, introduction to *Understanding Poetry.*

22. In a related but more complex critique of my poststructural reading, feminist critics have raised concerns about the timing of poststructuralism's evacuation of the humanist subject—about the "deconstructing, dismissing, or displacing the notion of the rational subject at the very historical moment when women are beginning to have access to the use of discourse, power, and pleasure." Rosi Braidotti, *Nomadic Subjects: Embodiment and Difference in Contemporary Feminist Theory,* 2nd ed. (New York: Columbia University Press, 2011), 267.

23. One complicating factor is the context of Paul's interview with Bittner. *Long Story Short,* the online magazine in which Paul's interview with Bittner appears, is popular for many working writers but does not quite fall into even the mainstream

of literary publishing. The journal arranges its archives by genres of work, fore-grounding their relationship to a self-consciously "popular" market: among genres it advertises are "Soldiers' Stories," "Critters," "The Way It Was," and "WWII Memoirs." It champions "sincerity" and autobiographical stories to such an extent that one won-ders how much the print context for the interview conditioned the terms by which Paul frames his work.

24. Silliman et al., "Aesthetic Tendency," 267.

25. Ibid., 262.

26. Craig Dworkin, "Language Poetry," in *Greenwood Encyclopedia of American Poets and Poetry,* ed. Jeffrey Gray, James McCorkle, and Mary McAleer Balkun (New York: Greenwood, 2006), 880–883.

27. Sianne Ngai, *Ugly Feelings* (Cambridge, MA: Harvard University Press, 2005), 306.

28. Ibid. Ngai's point is another matter: the redundancy that results from how strongly avant-garde poetry and theory, which developed in the same historical tra-jectory, "speak to each other" and the sense of belatedness that results for critics (308–312).

29. Sedgwick, *Touching Feeling,* 116. Sedgwick is writing with Adam Frank.

30. Helen Merrell Lynd, "The Nature of Shame," in *Guilt and Shame,* ed. Her-bert Morris (Belmont, CA: Wadsworth, 1971), 166; first published in *On Shame and the Search for Identity* (London: Routledge, 1958).

31. Sedgwick, *Touching Feeling,* 64.

32. Jackson, "Lyric," 833.

33. For a recent defense of thinking generically about lyric, even in light of Jackson's theory of lyric reading, see Jonathan Culler, "Lyric, History, Genre," *New Literary History* 40 (2009): 879–899.

34. I would not be the first to worry about invoking "avant-garde" and "Language poetics" too broadly. One could describe varied avant-garde modes, even within the narrowed field of contemporary American poetics, and the term "Language poetry" problematically implies unity of purpose, character, and texture across what is a diverse set of practices and modes of theoretical intervention, including "lyric" critique. For a good account of the "historical conflict" between the Language "ten-dency and its name," see Barrett Watten, "The Secret History of the Equal Sign," *Poetics Today* 20, no. 4 (Winter 1999): 581–627. See also Marjorie Perloff's article "Language Poetry and the Lyric Subject: Ron Silliman's Albany, Susan Howe's Buffalo," *Critical Inquiry* 25, no. 3 (1999): 405–434, for one very helpful discus-sion of the specific texture of two different "Language" poetic turns away from a "romantic paradigm" that emphasizes the *authority* ascribed to the speaking voice" (Howe's and Silliman's). For Perloff, neither indicates a rejection of "expres-sivity" and "subjectivity" per se (432–433). At the same time, by grouping these diverse practices as similarly geared against a "romantic paradigm," Perloff justifies my generalizing the "avant-garde" and "Language" critique: she also generalizes by

arguing that this de-authorization of the speaking voice is what motivated "the theo-retical discourse of Language manifestos in the first place" (433).

35. For a discussion of how this process of institutionalization from countercul-ture to academic classroom occurred, see Andrew Epstein's "Verse vs. Verse: The Language Poets Are Taking over the Academy, but Will Success Destroy Their Integrity?," *Lingua Franca,* September 2000, 45–54.

36. Silliman et al., "Aesthetic Tendency," 262, 264.

37. Here we could point broadly to the rise of MFA programs in the United States as helping to produce new pressures on conventions in the United States. See Mark McGurl's *The Program Era: Postwar Fiction and the Rise of Creative Writing* (Cambridge, MA: Harvard University Press, 2009), for a not unrelated history of the intimacy between fiction writing and schooling in the United States and the effects of academic patronage on questions of style and taste.

38. Jackson, "Lyric," 833.

39. For a discussion of the canonical pressures that text produced at midcen-tury, see Alan Golding, *From Outlaw to Classic: Canons in American Poetry* (Madi-son: University of Wisconsin Press, 1995), especially chapter 3.

40. Brooks and Warren, *Understanding Poetry,* 14–15, 20. They also assert that the failure to interpret the poem's "value" (which turns out to be its particular "po-etic" qualities) is undertaken out of "embarrassment." For the reader loathe to inter-pret, "he would probably be embarrassed if we asked him what held these things together [in a poem], making it a *poem* rather than simply a collection of pleasing items" (14–15).

41. William Kurtz Wimsatt and Cleanth Brooks, *Literary Criticism: A Short History* (New York: Knopf, 1957), 691.

42. Scott Brewster, *Lyric,* New Critical Idiom (New York: Routledge, 2009), 38. Subsequent page references to this source will be given parenthetically in the text.

43. Silliman et al., "Aesthetic Tendency," 265, 274.

44. John Stuart Mill, "Thoughts on Poetry and Its Varieties" (1833, rev. 1859), in *Dissertations and Discussions Political, Philosophical, and Historical,* vol. 1 (New York: Holt, 1874), 97.

45. Silliman et al., "Aesthetic Tendency," 266–267.

46. Ibid., 266.

47. Ibid., 268.

48. Ibid., 262–264.

49. Hank Lazer, *Opposing Poetries,* 2 vols. (Evanston, IL: Northwestern Univer-sity Press, 1996).

50. Ron Silliman, "Wednesday, July 7, 2010," *Silliman's Blog,* July 7, 2010, http://ronsilliman.blogspot.com/2010/07/i-know-whenever-i-use-phrase-school-of.html. See also the entry describing differences between "post-avant" and "School of Qui-etude": "Monday, January 5, 2004," *Silliman's Blog,* January 5, 2004, http://ronsilliman .blogspot.com/2004/01/on-new-years-eve-philadelphia-inquirer.html.

51. Ron Silliman, "Sunday, September 2, 2007," *Silliman's Blog,* September 2, 2007, http://ronsilliman.blogspot.com/2007/09/america-s-first-poet-laureate-joseph .html.

52. Ron Silliman, "Monday, January 5, 2004," *Silliman's Blog,* January 5, 2004, http://ronsilliman.blogspot.com/2004/01/on-new-years-eve-philadelphia-inquirer .html.

53. Ron Silliman, "Saturday, June 15, 2003," *Silliman's Blog,* June 15, 2003, http:// ronsilliman.blogspot.com/2003_06_08_archive.html.

54. Cole Swensen and David St. John, eds., *American Hybrid: A Norton Anthology of New Poetry* (New York: Norton, 2009). Swensen wishes the "hybrid" in question to be between techniques often attributed to mainstream "lyric" (such as "narrative" and the "expressive potential of language") and innovation.

55. Mlinko makes this comment in a vitriolic blog exchange between herself and the late Reginald Shepherd, which sees the poets hurl epithets at each other and in which Mlinko suggests that Shepherd ought to stop before he "embarrasses himself." Reginald Shepherd, "Who You Callin' 'Post-Avant'?," *Harriet* (blog), February 6, 2008, http://www.poetryfoundation.org/harriet/2008/02/who-you-callin-post -avant/.

56. So impassioned, and numerous and therefore onerous, did they become, in fact, that Silliman closed the comments option in 2010 (in the process destroying the previous eight years of commentary, provoking intensely cathected commentary about both the choice and the blog that was forced to unfold on other blog threads).

57. Ron Silliman, "Monday, January 5, 2004," *Silliman's Blog,* January 5, 2004, http://ronsilliman.blogspot.com/2004/01/on-new-years-eve-philadelphia-inquirer .html.

58. Ron Silliman, "Wednesday, July 7, 2010," *Silliman's Blog,* July 7, 2010, http:// ronsilliman.blogspot.com/2010/07/i-know-whenever-i-use-phrase-school-of.html.

59. Daisy Fried, quoted in Ron Silliman, "Tuesday, December 3, 2002," *Silliman's Blog,* December 3, 2002, http://ronsilliman.blogspot.com/2002_12_01_archive .html.

60. For discussions about aspects of the "self-concept" and how shame factors into self-image, see chapter 1 of Michael Lewis's *Shame: The Exposed Self* (New York: Simon and Schuster, 1995).

61. Christopher Honey, "A Reason to Push the 'School of Quietude' Meme," *The Coffee Philosopher* (blog), September 3, 2010, http://coffeephilosopher.wordpress .com/2010/09/03/a-reason-to-push-the-school-of-quietude-meme/.

62. Café Press once carried a T-shirt with Silliman's image accompanied by the sentence, "Obey Ron." Poet-blogger Greg Rappleye imagines Silliman as Sauron, anticipating battle with Reginald Shepherd in a post entitled "Dark Clouds Over Mordor," in *Sonnets at 4 A.M.* (blog), Wednesday, January 10, 2007, http://sonnetsa t4am.blogspot.com/2007/01/dark-clouds-over-mordor.html. Silliman, true to the Café Press T-shirt, comments on Rappleye's blog post two days later, in "Friday,

January 12, 2007," *Silliman's Blog*, January 12, 2007, http://ronsilliman.blogspot
.com/2007/01/in-webnote-that-he-calls-dark-clouds_12.html.

63. I take Daisy Fried's epistolary exchange with Silliman to exemplify one such
halfhearted yet vexed engagement of the SoQ label and its politics.

64. Reginald Shepherd, "Some Thoughts on Online Discourse," *Reginald
Shepherd's Blog*, June 6, 2007, http://reginaldshepherd.blogspot.com/2007/06
/some-thoughts-on-online-discourse.html ("petty viciousness"); Shepherd "Who You
Callin' 'Post-Avant'?" ("post-avant").

65. Stephen Burt, "Smokes, by Susan Wheeler," review, *Boston Review* 23 no. 3
(Summer 1998), http://www.bostonreview.net/BR23.3/burt.html. See also Burt,
"The Elliptical Poets," *American Letters and Commentary #11: Elliptical Poets: new
school or new spin* (1999), reprinted in *Close Calls with Nonsense: Reading New Poetry*
(St. Paul, MN: Graywolf Press, 2009), 346.

66. Craig Dworkin and Kenneth Goldsmith, eds., *Against Expression: An Anthology of Conceptual Writing* (Evanston, IL: Northwestern University Press, 2011).

67. "Poetry Debates and Manifestos," Academy of American Poets website,
http://www.poets.org/page.php/prmID/201 (accessed October 31, 2012).

68. I do not wish to exaggerate the visibility and canonicity of Language discourse in the academy. No doubt there are many people in MFA or PhD programs
who are only dimly aware of Language aesthetics. Access to avant-garde titles is
limited, even in well-funded academic libraries. However, I would hazard that for
many people who generate poetic discourse in the academy, the shifts engendered by
Language poetics and the post-Language debates about "expression" are significant
and ongoing.

69. Sedgwick, *Touching Feeling*, 64. Jameson, *The Political Unconscious: Narrative as a Socially Symbolic Act* (Ithaca, NY: Cornell University Press, 1981).

70. Jeff Elison and Susan Harter, "Humiliation: Causes, Correlates, and Consequences," in *The Self-Conscious Emotions: Theory and Research*, ed. Jessica L. Tracy,
Richard W. Robins, and June Price Tangney (New York: Guilford Press, 2007),
313.

71. Jessica L. Tracy and Richard W. Robins, "The Self in Self-Conscious Emotions: A Cognitive Appraisal Approach," in Tracy, Robins, and Tangney, *Self-Conscious
Emotions*, 6.

72. Jeff Elison and Susan Harter, "Humiliation," 314.

73. Brian Lickel, Toni Schmader, and Marija Spanovic, "Group-Conscious
Emotions: The Implication of Others' Wrongdoings," in Tracy, Robins, and Tangney, *Self-Conscious Emotions*, 356.

74. Apposite here is Jonathan Culler's sense of apostrophe (and thus lyric) as
embarrassing. For Culler, apostrophe is embarrassing primarily because it bespeaks a
poetic pretension to embody a tradition. However, I would argue that for Culler, it is
little more than embarrassing and not quite shameful; in any case, its embarrassments are not his primary subject in the essay on apostrophe. Culler, "Apostrophe,"

in *The Pursuit of Signs: Semiotics, Literature, Deconstruction* (1981; repr., Ithaca, NY: Cornell University Press, 2002), 135–154.

75. Erika Meitner, interview by Brian Bodeur, *How a Poem Happens* (blog), December 17, 2010, http://howapoemhappens.blogspot.com/2010/12/erika-meitner .html. Bodeur has collected hundreds of interviews and often includes the question about whether the poet's poem is a narrative poem, suggesting the centrality of "narrative" to current poetic discourses.

76. Paul Gilbert, "The Evolution of Shame as a Marker for Relationship Security: A Biopsychosocial Approach," in Tracy, Robins, and Tangney, *Self-Conscious Emotions,* 284.

77. Jeffrey Stuewig and June Price Tangney, "Shame and Guilt in Antisocial and Risky Behaviors," in Tracy, Robins, and Tangney, *Self-Conscious Emotions,* 372.

78. Ibid.

79. Gerhart Piers and Milton B. Singer, "Shame" (1953), in Morris, *Guilt and Shame,* 147.

80. Charles Ashbach, "Persecutory Objects, Guilt, and Shame," in *Self-Hatred in Psychoanalysis: Detoxifying the Persecutory Object,* ed. Jill Savege Scharff and Stanley A. Tsigounis (Hove, UK: Brunner-Routledge, 2003), 77.

81. Sedgwick, *Touching Feeling,* 37.

82. Lynd, "Nature of Shame," 166.

83. Though Language writers have identified the Confessional to be the precursor to the "voice" poem, my point here is more that the shaming of the Confessional was perpetuated, as my Sexton chapter will argue, by establishment figures into whose lyric-reading schemata her work would not quite fit.

84. Sedgwick's exploration of Tomkins's theories of shame led to her groundbreaking work on queer resistance, identity, and performativity, work that has been helpful in thinking about a range of political questions involving identity politics and political correctness. See chapter 1 of *Touching Feeling.* See also an earlier version, "Queer Performativity."

85. David M. Halperin and Valerie Traub, "Beyond Gay Pride," in *Gay Shame,* ed. David M. Halperin and Valerie Traub (Chicago: University of Chicago Press, 2009), 5.

86. See especially the introduction to Heather Love's *Feeling Backward: Loss and the Politics of Queer History* (Cambridge, MA: Harvard University Press, 2007).

87. Ruth Leys, *From Guilt to Shame: Auschwitz and After* (Princeton, NJ: Princeton University Press, 2009), 124; Ngai, *Ugly Feelings.* Anthropologists of the mid-twentieth century, led in part by Margaret Mead (1937) and Ruth Benedict's (1946) work on Japanese culture focused heavily on the idea that the West was a "guilt culture" and the East a "shame culture," under the view that whereas "shame cultures" regulate members' behaviors via external sanctions, members of "guilt cultures" internalize sanctions. This is a view that has been revised from a variety of positions and disciplines. See Harald G. Wallbott and Klaus R. Scherer, "Cultural

Determinants in Experiencing Shame and Guilt," in *Self-Conscious Emotions: The Psychology of Shame, Guilt, Embarrassment, and Pride,* ed. June Price Tangney and Kurt W. Fischer (New York: Guilford, 1995), 467–468, for a discussion of psychoanalytic understandings of the role of ego-ideal and superego in differentiating shame and guilt. More recently, psychologists have called for cross-cultural evaluations of shame and guilt in order to consider the ways that these models reflect "a view of the self that pervades many individualistic cultural contexts, including the United States." Ying Wong and Jeanne Tsai, "Cultural Models of Shame and Guilt," in Tracy, Robins, and Tangney, *Self-Conscious Emotions,* 209–223. Cultural psychologists, operating on the premise that culture and psyche "make each other up," focus on whether the social context in which shame occurs fosters and implements a view of the self as independent or interdependent with others and have been interested to evaluate the different ways in which cultures construct the experience of self-conscious emotions such as shame. Evolutionary anthropologists have focused on the possibility of shame as a "human propensity," as Daniel M. T. Fessler puts it, "differentially masked or elaborated" by different cultures. Fessler, "Shame in Two Cultures: Implications for Evolutionary Approaches," *Journal of Cognition and Culture* 4, no. 2 (2004): 207–262.

88. Brown, *Redefining Elizabethan Literature,* 15.

89. Christopher Nealon speculates that guilt is "a powerful structure of feeling in American political life" that has "posed problems for the left," congealing in "the idea that it is a betrayal to think against the system—a betrayal against one's friends, one's community, one's art." Transposing that situation "into an academic setting," Nealon wonders if the resistance on the part of aesthetically left critics (such as Perloff and Charles Altieri) to consider the "matter of capital" in their accounts of late- and postmodernism, may involve the fear that in thinking so abstractly, the "critic forsakes daily life" or "becomes arrogant." I do not wish to make Nealon's point less subtle than it is, but he seems to suggest that this guilt structure has produced a situation in which the academic left loses its force. I am interested in how the shame dynamics surrounding questions about lyric, the subject's agency, the self, and where it does and does not belong contribute to such a situation. Nealon, *The Matter of Capital: Poetry and Crisis in the American Century* (Cambridge, MA: Harvard University Press, 2011), 7.

90. Gilbert, "Evolution of Shame," 289.

91. The association between Romantic expressive aesthetics and the Confessional was forged by the first critics to use the term and probably tells us a great deal about how Romanticism (and lyric) was construed in the late 1950s through and into the early 1970s. See M. L. Rosenthal, "Poetry as Confession," *Nation,* September 19, 1959; reprinted in *Our Life in Poetry: Selected Essays and Reviews* (New York: Persea Books, 1991). See also A. Alvarez, *The Savage God: A Study of Suicide* (New York: Norton, 1971), 275–276. See also C. B. Cox and A. R. Jones, "After the Tranquilized Fifties, Notes on Sylvia Plath and James Baldwin," *Critical Quarterly* 6

(Summer 1964): 99–100. Even in reappraisals of the Confessional, recent scholars have nevertheless been willing to maintain the problematic association between Romantic poetry and expressive aesthetics. Even Jo Gill, who most helpfully updates our understanding of Anne Sexton's work (and, in the process, of what the Confessional might come to signify), shunts the bad lyric reputation of Sexton's and others' work—chiefly the idea that expression in confessional poems was "apparently natural, organic and inadvertent"—onto the "Romanticism" in whose debt critics have, she believes, wrongly placed the Confessional. Gill argues that the Confessional is more "skeptical, knowing and inquisitive about the status" of authenticity, referentiality, and expression than it has been credited with being and also savvier "about the processes by which these are established and understood." Gill, "Anne Sexton and Confessional Poetics," *Review of English Studies* 55, no. 220 (2004): 425–445. See also Mark Jeffreys, "Ideologies of the Lyric: A Problem of Genre in Contemporary Anglophone Poetics," *PMLA* 110, no. 2 (March 1995): 185.

92. Rosenthal, "Poetry as Confession."

93. See A. Alvarez, "Sylvia Plath: A Memoir," in *The Savage God: A Study of Suicide* (London: Weidenfeld and Nicolson, 1971), 214–228.

94. Mill, "Thoughts on Poetry and Its Varieties," 97. Unless otherwise specified, subsequent page references to this source refer to this version of the essay (cited in note 44) and will be given parenthetically in the text.

95. William Wordsworth, "Preface to the Second Edition of Several of the Foregoing Poems Published, with an Additional Volume, Under the Title of 'Lyrical Ballads,'" in *The Poetical Works of Wordsworth*, ed. Thomas Hutchinson, new edition 1936, rev. Ernest Selincourt, (London: Oxford University Press, 1950), 735.

96. Susan B. Rosenbaum's recent study of Romantic and post-1945 Anglophone poetic cultures details how difficult it has been, in modern history, to think about "sincerity" and theatricality, poetry and the marketplace, in any other than oppositional terms. See Rosenbaum, *Professing Sincerity: Modern Lyric Poetry, Commercial Culture, and the Crisis in Reading* (Charlottesville: University of Virginia Press, 2007).

97. John Stuart Mill, "Thoughts on Poetry and Its Varieties" (1833), in *The Collected Works of John Stuart Mill*, vol. 1, *Autobiography and Literary Essays*, ed. John M. Robson and Jack Stillinger (Toronto: University of Toronto Press, 1981), 350. This source prints the original essay, which Mill later revised. Accessed online at http://oll .libertyfund.org/title/242/7740 (December 3, 2012).

98. Deborah Nelson, *Pursuing Privacy in Cold War America* (New York: Columbia University Press, 2002), 45.

99. Northrop Frye, *The Anatomy of Criticism* (Princeton, NJ: Princeton University Press, 1957), 250; Helen Vendler, *The Given and the Made: Strategies of Poetic Redefinition* (Cambridge, MA: Harvard University Press, 1995), x–xi; Hirsch, *How to Read a Poem*, 4.

100. In fact, so parallel are reader and writer/text in Vendler's conception of lyric that she chooses to distinguish it from poems in which another consciousness or "voice"—"clearly not [the reader] himself"—seems to be overheard, a mode she prefers to call dramatic monologue (*Given and the Made*, xi).

101. For a trenchant discussion of this question, see Nealon's chapter "'Language' in Spicer and After," in *The Matter of Capital*.

102. Tiffany Atkinson, "Black and White and Re(a)d All Over: The Poetics of Embarrassment," in *The Writer in the Academy: Creative Interfrictions*, ed. Richard Marggraf Turley (Cambridge, UK: D. S. Brewer, 2011), 121–122.

103. Michael Warner, *The Trouble with Normal: Sex, Politics, and the Ethics of Queer Life* (New York: Free Press, 1999), 3.

104. Sedgwick "Queer Performativity," 3, quoted in Douglas Crimp, "Mario Montez, For Shame," in Halperin and Traub, *Gay Shame*, 71. I have Crimp to thank for the move from Warner to Sedgwick.

105. Halperin and Traub, introduction to *Gay Shame*, 23.

106. Elizabeth Bishop, "Unsuperstitious Dr. Williams," Elizabeth Bishop Papers, Vassar College Library Special Collections, box 54, folder 4.

107. Bishop is described to be "our greatest and most beloved poet" on the dust jacket of *Edgar Allan Poe & The Juke-Box: Uncollected Poems, Drafts, and Fragments*, ed. Alice Quinn (New York: Farrar, Straus and Giroux, 2006). About what other American poet would we say this? Why such strong identifications with Bishop's person?

108. Mutlu Konuk Blasing's recent arguments about Sexton and typewriters also assert the antinaturalizing aspects of Sexton's interest in the typewriter, though Blasing does so in a larger framework of claims made for lyric that is understood, at times, abstractly. "In this medium, in this mediation, the 'I' she produces can only be a displacement, a symptom of the original split that allows its inscription. The typewriter protects from bodily depths and keeps the dissociation in view: 'I never write by hand,' she says, it's 'so ugly—like my adolescence'" (188), in "Anne Sexton, "'The Typo,'" in *Lyric Poetry: The Pain and the Pleasure of Words* (Princeton, NJ: Princeton University Press, 2009), 178–198.

I. YOU OUGHT TO BE ASHAMED (BUT AREN'T): ELIZABETH BISHOP AND THE SUBJECT OF LYRIC

1. Elizabeth Bishop, "The Art of Poetry No. 27," interview by Elizabeth Spires, June 28, 1978, *Paris Review* 80 (1981), http://www.theparisreview.org/interviews/3229/the-art-of-poetry-no-27-elizabeth-bishop.

2. Brett C. Millier, *Elizabeth Bishop: Life and the Memory of It* (Berkeley: University of California Press, 1993), 135.

3. The Byronic figure appears as a metonymy for one problematic version of poetic endeavor in a draft of (another) abandoned essay, on W. H. Auden's poetics,

"The Mechanics of Pretense" (1937), available in the Vassar archive and only recently published in draft form in *Edgar Allan Poe and the Jukebox,* ed. Alice Quinn (New York: Farrar, Straus and Giroux, 2007), and in "In Prison" (1939), in Bishop's *The Collected Prose* (New York: Farrar, Straus and Giroux, 1984).

4. "Egotistical sublime" appears in Keats's letter to Richard Woodhouse from October 27, 1818. In John Keats, *Selected Letters,* ed. Robert Gittings and John Mee (New York: Oxford University Press, 2002), 147–148. Walter Jackson Bate discusses Hazlitt's Shakespeare and Milton lecture and its relevance to Keats's thinking about "negative capability" in *John Keats* (Cambridge, MA: Harvard University Press, 1965), 259–261. See also Walter Kalaidjian, "'The Pardon of Speech': The Psychoanalysis of Modern American Poetry," in *The Oxford Handbook of Modern and Contemporary American Poetry,* ed. Cary Nelson (New York: Oxford University Press, 2012), 425–460, especially 441.

5. M.L. Rosenthal's influential readings of midcentury poetry in the United States reasserted the "Wordsworthian" version of Romanticism to describe the "confessional" mode, calling it "one culmination of the Romantic and modern tendency to place the liberal Self more and more at the center of the poem." Rosenthal, *The New Poets: American and British Poetry since World War II* (New York: Oxford University Press, 1967), 27.

6. W.K. Wimsatt and Monroe Beardsley, *The Verbal Icon: Studies in the Meaning of Poetry* (Lexington: University Press of Kentucky, 1954), 5; Cleanth Brooks and Robert Penn Warren, *Understanding Poetry: An Anthology for College Students* (New York: Holt, 1938).

7. See J. Hillis Miller's "The Poets of Reality," in *Poets of Reality: Six Twentieth-Century Writers* (Cambridge, MA: Harvard University Press, 1965), 1–13, and Albert Gelpi's "Stevens and Williams: The Epistemology of Modernism," in *Wallace Stevens: The Poetics of Modernism,* ed. Albert Gelpi (Cambridge: Cambridge University Press, 1990), 3–23.

8. For a rundown of such positions, see Thomas Travisano on modesty in Bishop: "'The Flicker of Impudence: Delicacy and Indelicacy in the Art of Elizabeth Bishop," in *Elizabeth Bishop: The Geography of Gender,* ed. Marilyn May Lombardi (Charlottesville: University of Virginia Press, 1993), 111–125.

9. Examples include Marilyn May Lombardi, *The Body and Song* (Carbondale: Southern Illinois University Press, 1995), especially 44–46; Victoria Harrison, *Elizabeth Bishop's Poetics of Intimacy* (New York: Cambridge University Press) 1993; and Susan McCabe, *Elizabeth Bishop: Her Poetics of Loss* (University Park: Penn State University Press, 1994), 100–101, which reads Bishop's "covert" passions implied and repressed in her work.

10. Elizabeth Bishop, "At the Fishhouses," in *Poems, Prose, and Letters,* ed. Robert Giroux and Lloyd Schwartz (New York: Library of America, 2008), 50. Subsequent page references to this volume will be given parenthetically in the text as *PPL.*

11. Marjorie Perloff, *21st-Century Modernism: The "New" Poetics* (Malden, MA: Blackwell Publishers, 2002), 25. "Normalizing John Ashbery," *Jacket* 2 (January 1998), http://jacketmagazine.com/02/perloff02.html. O'Hara's comments about Lowell's poem appear in Edward Lucie-Smith, "An Interview with Frank O'Hara," *Standing Still and Walking in New York,* ed. Donald Allen (San Francisco: Grey Fox, 1975), 13, and were first published in abbreviated form in *Studio International,* September 1966. Ann Hartman discusses the comment as a charge of contrivance in "Confessional Counterpublics in Frank O'Hara and Allen Ginsberg," *Journal of Modern Literature* 28, no. 4 (Summer 2005): 40–56.

12. Perloff, "Normalizing John Ashbery." See also Perloff's "Language Poetry and the Lyric Subject: Ron Silliman's Albany, Susan Howe's Buffalo," *Critical Inquiry* 25, no. 3 (1999): 405–434. For over a decade, Bishop critics have attempted to refuse the charge that Bishop is a narrowly expressive poet. For a recent example, see Lesley Wheeler's case for reading Bishop and others outside the logic of a "false binary of expressive (and authentic subject speaks through transparent language) versus experimental (the poem concerns itself with its own processes and the linguistic medium)," in Wheeler, *The Poetics of Enclosure: American Women Poets from Dickinson to Dove* (Knoxville, TN: University of Tennessee Press, 2002), 4. An early example of resistance driven by lyric shame is Langdon Hammer's claim that Bishop's work challenges "the stereotypical subject of contemporary lyric autobiography" and "the expressive self prized in American poetry since mid-century," in "The New Elizabeth Bishop," *Yale Review* (Winter 1993): 148–149. Nevertheless, I've cited recent antiexpressive avant-garde readings of Bishop's work that attempt to reinstall a naively expressive Bishop, drawing on premises that, I contend, demand rethinking. Indeed, even some critics intent to show Bishop's "I" as decentered nevertheless displace lyric shame from her poems onto Wordsworthian Romanticism. Charles J. Rzepka offers an account of this critical tendency in "Elizabeth Bishop and the Wordsworth of Lyrical Ballads: Sentimentalism, Straw Men, and Misprision," in "The 'Honourable Characteristic of Poetry': Two Hundred Years of Lyrical Ballads," *Romantic Circles* (November 1999), http://www.rc.umd.edu/praxis/lyrical/rzepka /bishop.html.

13. Bonnie Costello, "Elizabeth Bishop's Impersonal Personal," *ALH* 15, no. 2 (2003): 337.

14. Ibid., 340, my emphasis.

15. Ibid., 342.

16. Indeed, some of what I argue is previewed in sometimes-defensive readings of Bishop by James Longenbach and Mutlu Konuk Blasing, each of whom argues that midcentury and late century non-avant-garde poets call into question subjective perceptual authority and logocentrism, almost as the avant-gardes are said to do. That both they and Hammer are writing in the 1990s, as avant-garde lyric theory enters the mainstream, is no accident—as I discuss at length in my last chapter. See Longenbach's opening chapters, "What Was Postmodern Poetry?" and "Elizabeth

Bishop's Bramble Bushes," in *Modern Poetry after Modernism* (New York: Oxford University Press, 1997), 3–33; and Blasing's "Introduction: Poetry after Modernism" and "Elizabeth Bishop: '*Repeat, Repeat, Repeat; Revise, Revise, Revise,*'" in *Politics and Form in Postmodern Poetry: O'Hara, Bishop, Ashbery, and Merrill* (New York: Cambridge University Press, 1995).

17. Helen Vendler, "Life Studies: *The Collected Prose of Elizabeth Bishop*," *New York Review of Books,* February 16, 1984, 128, http://www.nybooks.com/articles /archives/1984/feb/16/life-studies/.

18. Perloff, "Normalizing John Ashbery."

19. Marjorie Perloff, *21st-Century Modernism: The "New" Poetics* (Malden, MA: Blackwell, 2002), 10. Perloff, "A Conversation with Marjorie Perloff," interview by Hélène Aji and Antoine Cazé, May 26, 2007, Marjorie Perloff's website, http:// marjorieperloff.com/interviews/aji-caze-interview/.

20. Rae Armantrout, "Feminist Poetics and the Meaning of Clarity," in *Artifice and Indeterminacy: An Anthology of New Poetics,* ed. Christopher Beach (Tuscaloosa: University of Alabama Press, 1998), 288.

21. Ron Silliman, "Monday, November 14, 2005," *Silliman's Blog,* November 14, 2005, http://ronsilliman.blogspot.com/2005/11/within-history-of-school-of quietude.html.

22. In Ruben Brower's *The Fields of Light: An Experiment in Critical Reading* (New York: Oxford University Press, 1951), which, along with Brooks and Warren's *Understanding Poetry,* institutionalized the idea of a lyric speaker model, Brower argued for the importance of tone as a critical tool: "Our whole aim in analysis of tone is to delineate the exact speaking voice in every poem we read, but we can succeed only by attending to the special, often minute language signs by which the poet fixes the tone for us" (29).

23. Elizabeth Bishop, "Unsuperstitious Dr. Williams" (partial draft), Elizabeth Bishop Papers, Vassar College Library Special Collections, box 54, folder 4.

24. Perloff, *21st-Century Modernism,* 114.

25. Ibid., 119. Perloff is quoting the concluding line of Eliot's 1917 poem "The Love Song of J. Alfred Prufrock," in *The Complete Poems and Plays* (New York: Harcourt Brace, 1950), 7.

26. This story is recounted by Harriet Tompkins Thomas in "New York, Europe and Key West, 1934–1940)," in *Remembering Elizabeth Bishop: An Oral Biography,* by Gary Fountain and Peter Brazeau (Amherst: University of Massachusetts Press, 1994), 65–66.

27. Bishop, "Unsuperstitious Dr. Williams," my emphasis.

28. Brett C. Millier reports in *Elizabeth Bishop* (118) that Bishop was reading Freud in 1940. See also Jonathan Ellis, *Art and Memory in the Work of Elizabeth Bishop* (Burlington, VT: Ashgate, 2006), 58. The Williams review draft is undated in the archives but, in its apparent intent to serve as a review of *In the Money,* probably dates from the same year (1940).

29. Bishop, "Unsuperstitious Dr. Williams."

30. In 1938, Winifred Bryher had suggested that Bishop try Freudian analysis. Bishop declined. Her explanation to Marianne Moore that "everything I have read about [psychoanalysis] has made me think that psychologists misinterpret and very much underestimate all the workings of ART!" suggests the comment to be psychoanalytically informed. Elizabeth Bishop to Marianne Moore, September 7, 1937, in Elizabeth Bishop, *One Art: Letters,* ed. Robert Giroux (New York: Farrar, Straus and Giroux, 1994), 63.

31. Thomas Scheff argues that Freud regards shame (Scham) as a childish emotion in "modern societies," attributing it only to "children, women, and savages"; the mature individual or society is liberated by refusing this repressive affect. Scheff argues that recently, theorists have become interested in the shame of shame, indeed, in a taboo on shame in English-speaking societies that Freud's turn to drive theory produced, and not just for American psychologists. For Freud, guilt was the mature emotion, a theme expanded and systematized by the American anthropologist Ruth Benedict, for instance, whose work of the 1930s and 1940s distinguished between traditional shame and modern guilt cultures. See Thomas J. Scheff, "Shame in Self and Society," *Symbolic Interaction* 26, no. 2 (May 2003): 251, http://onlinelibrary .wiley.com/doi/10.1525/si.2003.26.2.239/full. In "The Interpretation of Dreams," Freud famously compares childhood to the unashamed situation of mankind in Eden, "till a moment arrived when shame and anxiety awoke, expulsion followed, and sexual life and the tasks of cultural activity began" (1900). By comparison, in *Civilization and Its Discontents* (1930; repr., New York: Norton, 1989), Freud refers to guilt (Schuld) over a dozen times yet only mentions shame (Scham) once, attributing it to early man upon his first standing and exposing his genitals (54 n.). See June Price Tangney and Rhonda L. Dearing, *Shame and Guilt* (New York: Guilford Press, 2002), 113–119, for a brief history of Freud's abandonment of the notion of shame after 1905 and the resurgence of interest in the concept among psychologists.

32. Sir Philip Sidney, "Defence of Poesie" (1595), in *The Prose Words of Sir Philip Sidney,* ed. Albert Feuillerat (Cambridge: Cambridge University Press, 1968), 30.

33. John Malcolm Brinnin, *William Carlos Williams* (Minneapolis: University of Minnesota Press, 1964), 5.

34. Quoted in Stephen Burt and David Mikics, introduction to *The Art of the Sonnet,* ed. Stephen Burt and David Mikics (Cambridge, MA: Harvard University Press, 2010), 21.

35. Laura (Riding) Jackson, "Poet: A Lying Word," in *Collected Poems* (New York: Random House, 1937), 237.

36. Brooks and Warren, *Understanding Poetry,* 343. Although it is not clear when, it is clear that Bishop read Brooks's 1939 *Modern Poetry and the Tradition* (1939), among others, as a letter to Robert Lowell from 1948 indicates. See Bishop to Lowell, September 11, 1948, in *Words in Air: The Complete Correspondence of Robert*

Lowell and Elizabeth Bishop, ed. Thomas Travisano and Saskia Hamilton (New York: Farrar, Straus and Giroux, 2008), 61–62, including the editors' note.

37. Milton Cohen, *Beleaguered Poets and Leftist Critics: Stevens, Cummings, Frost, and Williams in the 1930s* (Tuscaloosa: University of Alabama Press, 2010). Subsequent page references to this source will be given parenthetically in the text.

38. Cohen picked up the Herbst quotation from David Madden's introduction to the volume of essays he edited, *Proletarian Writers of the Thirties,* ed. David Madden (Carbondale, IL: Southern Illinois University Press, 1968), xxvii. The source of the quote, Madden tells us, was a letter Herbst wrote him declining an invitation to contribute to the volume of essays (xv).

39. Quoted in Cary Nelson, *Repression and Recovery: Modern American Poetry and the Politics of Cultural Memory, 1910–1945* (Madison: University of Wisconsin Press, 1989), 182. The statement appears on the back flap of the book jacket of *Genevieve Taggard: Collected Poems, 1918–1938* (New York: Harper, 1938). See Joseph Harrington, *Poetry and the Public: The Social Form of Modern U.S. Poetics* (Middleton, CT: Wesleyan University Press, 2002), for how such responses countervail the dominant tendency in academia (in the wake of high modernism) to construct poetry as a genre distinct from public life. See especially his introduction, 1–20. For a quite recent account fleshing out a picture of popular poetics obscured by the high/low and public/private distinctions that took hold in the 1930s, see Mike Chasar, *Everyday Reading: Poetry and Popular Culture in Modern America* (New York: Columbia University Press, 2012).

40. William Carlos Williams, "A 1 Pound Stein," *The Rocking Horse* 2 (Spring 1935): 3, reprinted in *Selected Essays* (New York: Random House, 1954), 162.

41. See Gillian White, "Readerly Contingency in Bishop's Journals and Early Prose," *Twentieth-Century Literature* 44, no. 3 (Fall 2009): 322–356.

42. Nelson, *Repression and Recovery,* 179.

43. See Ian Copestake, *The Ethics of William Carlos Williams's Poetry* (New York: Camden House, 2010), 3; Tom Orange, "William Carlos Williams Between Image and Object," in *William Carlos Williams and the Language of Poetry,* ed. Burton Hatlen and Demetres P. Tryphonopoulos (Orono, ME: National Poetry Foundation, 2002), 139; Hank Lazer, *Opposing Poetries,* vol. 2, *Readings* (Evanston, IL: Northwestern University Press, 1996), 17; and George Hartley, *Textual Politics of Language Poetry* (Bloomington: Indiana University Press, 1989), 2, for just a handful of examples.

44. A number of recent books have taken up the ethics of Objectivist and experimental modernist work. See Tim Woods's *The Poetics of the Limit: Ethics and Politics in Modern and Contemporary American Poetry* (New York: Palgrave, 2002), John Wrighton's *Ethics and Politics in Modern American Poetry* (New York: Routledge, 2010), and Grant Matthew Jenkins's *Poetic Obligation: Ethics in American Experimental Poetry after 1945* (Iowa City: University of Iowa Press, 2008).

45. Charles Olson, "Projective Verse" (1950), in *Collected Prose* (Berkeley: University of California Press, 1997), 247; Albert Gelpi, *A Coherent Splendor: The Ameri-*

can Poetic Renaissance, 1910–1950 (New York: Cambridge University Press, 1987), 87; Patrick Moore, "William Carlos Williams and the Modernist Attack on Logical Syntax," *ELH* 53, no. 4 (Winter 1986): 902–904; Miller, *Poets,* 8. See also Perloff's contrast of Eliot's "symboliste mode" with Williams's ethically superior ametaphoric use of "particulars" in *Kora in Hell,* in *The Poetics of Indeterminacy: Rimbaud to Cage* (Princeton, NJ: Princeton University Press, 1981), 117.

46. William Carlos Williams, "This Florida," in *The Collected Poems of William Carlos Williams,* vol. 1, *1909–1939,* ed. A. Walton Litz and Christopher MacGowan (New York: New Directions, 1991), 361. Subsequent page references to this volume will be given parenthetically in the text as *CP1.*

47. And in 1954, in "The Desert Music," Williams admits to "an agony of self-realization / bound into a whole / by that which surrounds us. / I cannot escape / I cannot vomit it up / Only the poem!" In *The Collected Poems of William Carlos Williams,* vol. 2, *1939–1962,* ed. Christopher MacGowan (New York: New Directions, 1991), 275. Subsequent page references to this volume will be given parenthetically in the text as *CP2.*

48. Perloff, *21st-Century Modernism,* 25; and Perloff, "Language Poetry," 462.

49. For discussions of Bishop's left political leanings and concerns about writing what many critics saw as apolitical poetry in the 1930s, see James Longenbach, "Elizabeth Bishop's Social Conscience," *ELH* 62, no. 2 (Summer 1995): 467–486; and Betsy Erkkila, "Elizabeth Bishop, Modernism, and the Left," *ALH* 8, no. 2 (1996): 284–310.

50. See especially the 1930s prose fables "In Prison" (1939), and Bishop, "The Sea and Its Shore" (1937) in *The Collected Prose* (New York: Farrar, Straus and Giroux, 1984).

51. Bishop to Moore, February 19, 1940, in *One Art,* 88.

52. See especially Blasing, *Politics and Form in Postmodern Poetry,* whose chapter on Bishop in many ways matches my own thinking about her work: "If the textual meaning of personal experience can only be a shared meaning, it must appeal to a tradition or history of what constitutes meaning within a given discursive framework" (96).

53. Perloff, "Normalizing John Ashbery."

54. Sigmund Freud, *Totem and Taboo: Some Points of Agreement between the Mental Lives of Savages and Neurotics,* ed. James Strachey (London: Routledge and Kegan Paul, 1950). Subsequent page references to this source will be given parenthetically in the text.

55. Elizabeth Bishop, "Dimensions for a Novel," Bishop Papers, box 70, folder 9.

56. Ibid.

57. Bishop, "Unsuperstitious Dr. Williams." Freud identifies art as where the "omnipotence of thought" persists for modern subjects, who compare artists to "magicians." Artists accomplish desires "just as though it were something real" (*Totem,* 113). In "Dimensions," Bishop twists Freud's point, defending the omnipotence of thought in life, not art.

58. The review's ironic tone suggests that Bishop bristled over the persistent trend among avant-garde writers to present their works' break with traditional forms as "maturity" or progress. Williams's (and Pound's) insistence that art should work toward more accurate, naturalistic representation of reality "subscribes," in Mutlu Konuk Blasing's words, "to a progressive model of literary change as a continuing liberation from, or a repeated series of breaks with, the forces of tradition" (*Politics and Form in Postmodern Poetry,* 2). Blasing points out that the "plot of this politicized scenario of liberation turns on . . . [novel, disjunctive] poetic techniques," which avant-garde modernists align with the "scientific, objective, and presentational" and thus with "truth-value" (2–3). Williams's rhetoric about old forms being "ritualistic" makes the point. Blasing does not quite historicize these critical phenomena, but her argument is compelling.

59. One thinks also of Freud's *Civilization and Its Discontents* (1930; repr., New York: Norton, 1989). Further evidence that poets took Freud's work as a directive lies in Wallace Stevens's comment, in "The Noble Rider and the Sound of Words" (1941), that Freud had "cut poetry's throat" by asking that we "surrender to . . . the cruelty of reality" and "do without the consolation of what he calls the religious illusion." In Stevens, *Collected Poetry and Prose* (New York: Literary Classics of the United States, 1997), 651.

60. Bonnie Costello argues that, however Bishop might have appreciated Williams's "objectivism," she does not imitate it, a claim that my reading of "Florida" challenges. In *Elizabeth Bishop: Questions of Mastery* (Cambridge, MA: Harvard University Press, 1991), 23.

61. Comparable to Bishop's "Florida" is Williams's "Morning" (1938), whose movement from detail to detail is remarkably like Bishop's. See Williams, *CP1,* 459. Both poems describe what appear to be groups of representative objects: in the Williams poem, "houses," "benches," "cobbles," "car rails," "fruit trees," "pulley lines," and so on.

62. Almost all her other poems are structured around a third-person collective narrator (a "we") or an explicit or implied first-person singular "I," or else they work like fables, presenting their readers a character to observe—"The Gentleman of Shallot" or "The Man-Moth." Even the two poems that are like "Florida" in suppressing a narrative perspective—"Large, Bad Picture" and "Wading at Wellfleet"—take a didactic tone, which "Florida" does not.

63. Brooks and Warren, *Understanding Poetry,* 20.

64. "Hermetic inwardness" from Millier, *Elizabeth Bishop,* 85; "stick to the facts" from Jeredith Merrin, *An Enabling Humility: Marianne Moore, Elizabeth Bishop, and the Uses of Tradition* (New Brunswick, NJ: Rutgers University Press, 1990). See also, somewhat contradicting my earlier cited claim of hers, Costello, *Elizabeth Bishop,* 100. For Costello, the "sense of figurativeness remains" because the poem is "about how the imagination responds to temporality," and while she reads the buzzards as "surrogates of the poet-beholder," she reads the poem's agenda as

fundamentally expressive: "the poet longs to find a voice in nature, a buried spirit to predict the end of nature." This Costello reads as an ambivalent troping of "spiritual presence" (102).

65. See McCabe, *Elizabeth Bishop,* 40. See also Jacqueline Vaught Brogan, "Elizabeth Bishop: Perversity as Voice," in Lombardi, *Elizabeth Bishop,* 175–195.

66. It is important to stress that the poem need not be read (thus) as mourning the passage of time and nostalgic in longing for a transcendent spiritual presence (as Costello and other have read it). See Costello, *Elizabeth Bishop,* 102. In Bishop's correspondence with Anne Stevenson of 1963, Bishop firmly corrects Stevenson's suggestion that her poems express a "loss of the religion Emily Dickinson had," as Stevenson believed: "[The loss] is not religious. I have never been religious in any formal way and I am not a believer." Elizabeth Bishop, *Prose,* ed. Lloyd Schwartz (New York: Farrar, Straus and Giroux, 2011), 406, 415.

67. Elizabeth Bishop, "Now I'm adjusted to reality," Bishop Papers, box 76, folder 1. A note at the bottom of the draft indicates that Bishop had drawn the scenario from a psychological case study from Helene Deutsch's *The Psychology of Women,* 2 vols. (New York: Allyn and Bacon, 1943–1945).

68. Bishop, "Now I'm adjusted to reality."

69. Bishop, "Dimensions for a Novel."

70. Stuart Hall, "Foucault: Power, Knowledge, and Discourse" (1997), in *Discourse Theory and Practice: A Reader,* ed. Margaret Wetherell, Stephanie Taylor, and Simeon J. Yates (Thousand Oaks, CA: Sage, 2001), 72.

71. Elizabeth Bishop, draft of "The Bight," Bishop Papers, box 56, folder 11.

72. Draft materials in Bishop's archives suggest that Bishop would sometimes revise poems in the midst of writing them, adding a replacement line or word without crossing out the previous one. In *Edgar Allan Poe,* see transcribed drafts of "Young Man in the Park," (96–97), "Something I've Meant to Write About for 30 Years" (137–138), and "Inventory" (143).

73. Charles Darwin, "Natural Selection" (1861), in *The Origin of Species by Means of Natural Selection, or, The Preservation of Favored Races in the Struggle of Life* (New York: Modern Library, 1993), 109.

74. Apposite here is Wallace Stevens's critical jab, in "Rubbings of Reality," embedded in the comment that Williams's poems belong in a world we could "suddenly remake" "on the basis of our own intelligence," seen "clearly" and "represented without faintness or obscurity." Stevens compares the "clarity" of Williams's vision to Communism and to Puritanism. In *Collected Poetry and Prose,* 815–816.

75. Williams, "Charles Sheeler–Paintings-Drawings-Photographs" (1939), in *Selected Essays,* 233.

76. John Keats, "Ode to a Nightingale," in *The Works of John Keats: With an Introduction and Bibliography* (New York: Wordsworth Editions, 1994), 218–220.

77. Robert Pinsky, *The Situation of Poetry: Contemporary Poetry and Its Traditions* (Princeton, NJ: Princeton University Press, 1976), 58.

78. For one of many interesting examples of statements in line with this view, see Rae Armantrout's early talk and poetic exchange, "On Poetic Silence," in *Collected Prose* (San Diego, CA: Singing Horse, 2007), 21–37.

79. The poem "Seascape" (1941) can be read as inverse companion to "Florida," for exaggeratedly figuring likeness making as a form of projective subjectivity.

80. See Bishop, "Art of Poetry No. 27."

81. Bishop, letter to "Miss Pierson" (identity unknown), May 28, 1975, in *One Art,* 596. Bishop's claim about talking is preceded by resistance to poetic trends we might associate with New Critical poetic culture: the tendency for "young poets . . . to try to tie everything up neatly in 2 or 3 beautiful last lines," and for poets to read "too much about poetry," 596. For the history of institutionalization of New Critical ideas, see Alan Golding, *From Outlaw to Classic: Canons in American Poetry* (Madison: University of Wisconsin Press, 1995). For a polemic on the primacy of "voice" in American poetics, see Jed Rasula, *American Poetry Wax Museum: Reality Effects, 1940–1990* (Urbana, IL: National Council of Teachers of English, 1996), especially chapter 1. For the emphasis on speaker and expression in the New Critical institutionalization, see Virginia Jackson, *Dickinson's Misery: A Theory of Lyric Reading* (Princeton, NJ: Princeton University Press, 2005), especially chapter 3. See Lesley Wheeler's *Voicing American Poetry: Sound and Performance from the 1920s to the Present* (Ithaca, NY: Cornell University Press, 2008) for a history of the 1950s shift in poetry performance culture from a focus on recitation and performance to one on the "authentic poet-performer," an argument that helps us see how "voice" begins to be so strongly associated with authentic presence in the soundscape of American poetry performance (see the introduction, especially page 12).

82. Jacqueline Vaught Brogan argues similarly about Bishop in her "Elizabeth Bishop: Perversity as Voice": "For all her apparent reticence, Bishop uses her own lyrics . . . to expose the lyric voice itself, with its implicit and traditional associations with authenticity, originality, and authority, as a manifestation of a traditionally dominant (and dominating) phallic poetics" (176). For all Vaught Brogan does here, I do not see Bishop arguing against the logocentric or the "phallocentric belief in that 'constructive faculty' that 'orders' chaos into meaning" (177). Nor does it seem right to assign, as Vaught Brogan does, the "authentic, spoken voice" to Wordsworthian lyricism (175, 178–179). Rather, I see Bishop's work pushing against a picture of subjectivity that depends on expression as its mark of success. Vaught Brogan demands we see Bishop's poems as triumphant "feminist expression" (183) projected against a tradition of male appropriation of the female voice and figure.

83. Rasula, *American Poetry Wax Museum,* 42. Rasula places the "compulsion today . . . to homogenize the proliferation of voices—and internalize the police"— and the "hypnotic" "lure of the carceral voice" in a postwar context but does not explicitly address the New Critical pedagogy's particular part to play in that compulsion (43).

84. Peter Middleton, *Distant Reading: Performance, Readership, and Consumption in Contemporary Poetry* (Tuscaloosa: University of Alabama Press, 2005), 10–11.

85. John Ashbery, "Soonest Mended," in *The Double Dream of Spring* (New York: Ecco, 1976), 17–19. In a May 1988 interview with John Trantner for the Australian Broadcasting Corporation, Ashbery called it his "One Size Fits All Confessional Poem." A transcript of the interview was published in *Jacket* 2 (1998), http://jacketmagazine.com/02/jaiv1988.html.

86. Bishop to Lowell, letter dated by Bishop "About two weeks later" with editors' dating of October 1960, in *Words in Air,* 344. Subsequent page references to this volume will be given parenthetically in the text as *WIA.*

87. Bishop's attitude toward mainstream 1950s and 1960s poetics ought to help push back against the assessments by such writers as Ron Silliman and Charles Bernstein that Bishop is a key figure of a stilted, midcentury "mainstream," a paragon of "official verse culture" or "School of Quietude." Again, see Silliman's blog entry on Bishop's place in the midcentury from November 14, 2005: "Monday, November 14, 2005."

88. Robert Lowell, "The Art of Poetry No. 3," interview by Fred Seidel, *Paris Review* 25 (Winter–Spring 1961), http://www.parisreview.com/viewinterview.php/prmMID/4664.

89. There is some critical disagreement as to what Klee painting Bishop here references. Travisano and Hamilton consider it to be *Mask of Fear* from 1932, from the permanent collection at the Museum of Modern Art. See *Words in Air,* 364, note 4. Peggy Samuels, in her "Elizabeth Bishop and Paul Klee," *Modernism/Modernity* 14, no. 3 (September 2007): 543–568, instead identifies the painting as *Fear (Angst)* from 1934. I suspect Samuels is correct, though I disagree with her sense that what Bishop discovers there is a "quiet, private voice" (550), a claim that depends on a public/private binary that Bishop's late 1950s work seems determined—in an effort to realize the "space" and "modesty" that interest Samuels as well—to problematize. However, Samuels's reading of the ontology that such an aesthetic might imply brings our views in line. See page 561 in specific.

90. Bishop dates the letter as July 27, 1960, but indicates her uncertainty of the actual date. Given that she says it was Friday, the actual date would be July 29, 1960.

91. See Harrison, *Elizabeth Bishop's Poetics of Intimacy,* 32.

92. See Perloff's essay "A Step Away from Them: Poetry 1956," in *Poetry on and off the Page: Essays for Emergent Occasions* (Evanston: Northwestern University Press, 1998), 83–115.

93. In line with my reading of "space" is Blasing's reading of "Brazil, January 1, 1502." Blasing proposes that that poem "*leaves the reader room*" to question the poet's "rhetoric and representation" (in a poem that wonders broadly about the ethics of representation), and she concludes, "The poem tells its story by emphasizing the mediation of its own figuration" (*Politics and Form in Postmodern Poetry,* 89, my emphasis). Blasing does not historicize the phenomenon, however.

94. Michael Davidson, "'Skewed by Design': From Act to Speech Act in Language Writing," in Beach, *Artifice and Indeterminacy*, 74.

95. Evidence that "Somebody loves us all" evokes one of the most powerful phrases mobilized by evangelical discourse might be found in many places but is certainly testified to by the Baptist hymn "Somebody Loves You: 'Tis Jesus," which Bishop might have encountered while living in Great Village, Nova Scotia. See *The New Evangel: Songs People Sing for All Religious Gatherings*, ed. and comp. Robert R. Coleman (Boston: American Baptist Publication Society, 1911), http://www.archive.org/stream/newevangel00colegoog/newevangel00colegoog_djvu.txt.

96. For a brief sampling, see Robert Dale Parker in *The Unbeliever: The Poetry of Elizabeth Bishop* (Urbana: University of Illinois Press, 1988), 25, 27; and Costello, *Elizabeth Bishop*, 37–39. Timothy Morris's suggestion, made in specific about "At the Fishhouses," that the "dialogic" qualities in Bishop make her work difficult to place generically, is instructive here. See Morris, *Becoming Canonical in American Poetry* (Urbana: University of Illinois Press, 1995); and Renée R. Curry, *White Women Writing White: H.D., Elizabeth Bishop, Sylvia Plath, and Whiteness* (Westport, CT: Greenwood, 2000), 114–115.

97. See *Oxford English Dictionary*, 3rd ed., s.v. "monkey suit," which shows both meanings: http://www.oed.com/view/Entry/253108?redirectedFrom=monkey-suit#eid.

98. Costello, "Elizabeth Bishop's Impersonal Personal," 341.

99. Again, Blasing realizes something similar when she says that Bishop's poems "emphasize the mediation of [their] own figuration" (*Politics and Form in Postmodern Poetry*, 89).

100. See, for instance, John Ashbery's "The Bungalows" (1967): "How does it feel to be outside and inside at the same time?" from *The Double Dream of Spring* (New York: Ecco Press, 1976), 71.

101. See Bishop to Lowell, May 19, 1960, in *WIA*, 327.

102. See, for instance, Bishop, *Words in Air*, letters from March 1, 1961 (355), December 11, 1964, in which Ashley Brown's being "literary" seems to indicate his literary professionalism (563–564), and from September 20, 1972, where Frank Bidart's being "literary" suggests the potential provincialism of American exceptionalism (726).

103. Margaret Dickie, "Race and Class in Elizabeth Bishop's Poetry," *Yearbook of English Studies* 24 (1994): 53.

104. Ibid., 89.

105. Countee Cullen, "Incident," in *Color* (New York: Harper, 1925); reprinted in *My Soul's High Song: The Collected Writings of Countee Cullen, Voice of the Harlem Renaissance*, ed. Gerald Lyn Early (New York: Doubleday, 1991), 90.

106. Rachel Blau DuPlessis, *Genders, Races, and Religious Cultures in Modern American Poetry, 1908–1934* (Cambridge: Cambridge University Press, 2001), 17.

107. Gwendolyn Brooks, "a song in the front yard," in *A Street in Bronzeville* (New York: Harper, 1945); reprinted in Brooks, *Blacks* (1987; repr., Chicago: Third World, 2000), 28.

108. Elizabeth Bishop, "Review of *Annie Allen* by Gwendolyn Brooks," *United States Quarterly Book List* 6 (March 1950), 21, reprinted in Elizabeth Bishop, *Prose,* ed. Lloyd Schwartz, 260.

109. Virginia Jackson, "Lyric," (833) in *Princeton Encyclopedia of Poetry and Poetics,* ed. Roland Greene, Stephen Cushman, Clare Cavanagh, Jahan Ramazani, and Paul Rouzer, 4th ed. (Princeton, NJ: Princeton University Press, 2012), 826–834.

2. SOMETHING FOR SOMEONE: ANNE SEXTON, INTERPRETATION, AND THE SHAME OF THE CONFESSIONAL

1. Ron Silliman contrasts Sexton's "drunken nursery rhymes" with a more taut avant-garde masochism marking the "true confessionalism" of Robert Kelly and Birgit Kempker's collaborative work *Shame/Schaum: A Collaboration* (New York: McPherson, 2005). Ron Silliman, "Joanne Kygers Night Palace Wasn't Only," *Silliman's Blog,* January 30, 2006, http://ronsilliman.blogspot.com/2006/01/joanne-kygers-night-palace-wasnt-only.html.

2. Elizabeth Bishop, *Edgar Allan Poe & The Juke-Box: Uncollected Poems, Drafts, and Fragments,* ed. Alice Quinn (New York: Farrar, Straus and Giroux, 2006), dust jacket. For a rundown of criticism hostile to Sexton, see the opening pages of Jo Gill's "Textual Confessions: Narcissism in Anne Sexton's Early Poetry," *Twentieth-Century Literature* 50, no. 1 (2004): 59–87. See also Linda Wagner-Martin's "Introduction: Anne Sexton, Poet," in *Critical Essays on Anne Sexton,* ed. Linda Wagner-Martin (Boston: G. K. Hall, 1989). Even J. D. McClatchy, ostensibly a fan, qualifies his interest in Sexton in his introduction to *Anne Sexton: The Artist and Her Critics,* ed. J. D. McClatchy (Bloomington: Indiana University Press, 1978), viii.

3. Robert Lowell, "Anne Sexton," in McClatchy, *Anne Sexton,* 71. Lowell's statement is difficult to date. It appears in 1978, after his death, one of several "Reflections" solicited by McClatchy, it seems, appearing in this collection of Sexton criticism. At what point it was written between Sexton's death in 1974 and Lowell's in 1977 is unclear. Maxine Kumin refers to the statement as a "terse eulogy" in the foreword to Sexton's *Complete Poems* (Boston: Houghton Mifflin, 1981), xx. I cannot confirm that Lowell attended Sexton's memorial.

4. I am referring to Lowell's *Life Studies* (New York: Farrar, Straus, and Cudahy, 1959). M. L. Rosenthal coined the term "confessional" in "Poetry as Confession," *Nation* 189 (September 19, 1959): 154–155; reprinted in *The Critical Response to Robert Lowell,* ed. Stephen Gould Axelrod (Westport, CT: Greenwood, 1999), 64–68.

5. Marjorie Perloff, "The Blank Now," *New Republic,* July 7 and 14, 1973, 24.

6. T. S. Eliot, "Tradition and the Individual Talent" (1919, *Egoist*), reprinted in *Selected Prose of T. S. Eliot,* ed. Frank Kermode (New York: Harcourt, 1975), 37–44 (my emphasis). Subsequent page references to the Kermode volume will be given parenthetically in the text as *SP*.

7. Several New Critics referred to the results in terms of the lyric's "drama" or "dramatic" qualities—often meaning a processing of ideas or the personal or irony, an achievement that makes the poem objective, for general use. For a few examples, see T. S. Eliot, "A Dialogue on Dramatic Poetry" (1928), in *Selected Essays* (New York: Harcourt Brace, 1932), 38; Yvor Winters, *The Anatomy of Nonsense* (Norfolk, CT: New Directions, 1943), 13. See also Cleanth Brooks and Robert Penn Warren, *Understanding Poetry,* 3rd ed. (New York: Holt, Reinhart, 1960), 20. See also Brooks and W. K. Wimsatt's discussion of Eliot, in which their and Eliot's ideas about the importance of "the dramatic character of poetry" become one, in *Literary Criticism: A Short History* (New York: Knopf, 1957), 673–676. Helen Vendler invokes an intrinsic quality of poetic "analysis" (analyzability?) in a way that seems similar to me, in *The Given and the Made: Strategies of Poetic Redefinition* (Cambridge, MA: Harvard University Press, 1995), 90.

8. Brooks and Wimsatt, *Literary Criticism,* 675.

9. Golding cites Robert Creeley's 1973 remembrance in his "Introduction" to the Penguin *Selected Whitman* that, in the 1940s, to like Whitman, considered "naively affirmative," was in "bad taste"; Robert Duncan's view was that "people would be embarrassed about" Whitman, whose work was thought to be insufficiently complex to support New Critical readings of it. Quoted in Alan C. Golding, *From Outlaw to Classic: Canons in American Poetry* (Madison: University of Wisconsin Press, 1995), 92–93. Creeley, "Introduction to Penguin *Selected Whitman*" (1973), reprinted in *The Collected Essays of Robert Creeley* (Berkeley: University of California Press, 1989), 4, 3. Golding cites page 67 of Ekbert Faas's, *Young Robert Duncan: Portrait of the Poet as a Homosexual in Society* (Santa Barbara, CA: Black Sparrow Press, 1963) as the source of the Duncan quotation, but seemingly in error.

10. Allen Tate to R.L., December 3, 1957 (Houghton Library), quoted in Ian Hamilton, *Robert Lowell: A Biography* (New York: Random House, 1982), 237.

11. Quoted in Diane Middlebrook, "'I Tapped My Own Head': The Apprenticeship of Anne Sexton," in *Coming to Light: American Women Poets in the Twentieth Century,* ed. Diane Middlebrook and Marilyn Yalom (Ann Arbor: University of Michigan Press, 1985), 203. Middlebrook's source is the correspondence of Anne Sexon with John Holmes, February 11, 1959 (misdated by Sexton 1958), in Anne Sexton Archive, Humanities Research Center, University of Texas, Austin.

12. By 1960, as Herbert F. Tucker reminds us, lyric reading for a speaker had "advanced from advice to prescription"—to a pedagogical norm or, as Tucker puts it, a near compulsory "march[ing of] readers past the author of a poem to its dramatic speaker." Tucker, "Dramatic Monologue and the Overhearing of Lyric," in *Lyric Poetry: Beyond New Criticism,* ed. Chavina Hosek and Patricia Parker (Ithaca, NY: Cornell University Press, 1985), 240.

13. John Stuart Mill, "Thoughts on Poetry and Its Varieties" (1833, rev. 1859), in *Dissertations and Discussions Political, Philosophical, and Historical,* vol. 1 (New York: Holt, 1874), 97.

14. Ibid., 93.

15. In a different reprinted version of Mill's essay, the phrase is "human heart" rather than "human emotion." See Mill, "What Is Poetry?," (1833) in *Early Essays: John Stuart Mill,* ed. G. W. M. Gibbs (London: George Bell & Sons, 1897), 204. However, both editions—the Henry Holt and the George Bell—cite the source of their text as the *Monthly Repository,* 1833.

16. Adrienne Rich, "In Those Years," in *Dark Fields of the Republic* (New York: Norton, 1995); reprinted in *After Confession: Poetry as Autobiography,* ed. Kate Sontag and David Graham (St. Paul, MN: Graywolf, 2001), 333.

17. Ibid.

18. Michael Davidson, "Philosophy and Theory in US Modern Poetry," in *A Concise Companion to Twentieth-Century American Poetry,* ed. Stephen Freedman (Hoboken, NJ: Wiley, 2008), 246.

19. Edward Hirsch, *How to Read a Poem and Fall in Love with Poetry* (New York: Harcourt 1999), 6; Ron Silliman, Carla Harryman, Lyn Hejinian, Steve Benson, Bob Perelman, and Barrett Watten, "Aesthetic Tendency and the Politics of Poetry: A Manifesto," *Social Text* 19–20 (Fall 1988): 264.

20. David Orr, "The Personal," in *Beautiful and Pointless: A Guide to Modern Poetry* (New York: HarperCollins, 2011), 14–16. Orr invokes Erving Goffman's idea of "role segregation" to suggest that the friction between a public persona and a private individual leads to "embarrassment" (18–19).

21. Quoted in Diane Wood Middlebrook, *Anne Sexton: A Biography* (New York: Vintage Books, 1992), 201. Middlebrook's source is a letter from Sexton to Dr. Orne written July 20, 1963, among Dr. Orne's files. See also Mutlu Konuk Blasing, *Lyric Poetry: The Pain and the Pleasure of Words* (Princeton, NJ: Princeton University Press, 2007), 180.

22. Quoted in Middlebrook, *Anne Sexton,* 62. Middlebrook's source is the notes Sexton typed to Dr. Orne during a research leave in which they stopped appointments. It dates from April 29, 1958, and was among his files. See also an interview with Sexton by Barbara Kevles, in *Writers at Work: The Paris Review Interviews,* 4th series, ed. George Plimpton (New York: Viking, 1976), 422.

23. Quoted in Middlebrook, *Anne Sexton,* 82. Middlebrook calls this a letter, but also "typed notes," as above. It dates from September 29, 1958, and is counted among Dr. Orne's papers. Middlebrook reads the RATS–STAR notes or letter as showing that Sexton understood that "the feel of reality is only one of the tricky effects words achieve just by being arranged in certain ways. . . . The poem's 'I' is real because it has become visible in the medium of print and circulated among those who are positioned to recognize it" (83).

24. Written in 1957–1958, the poem was first published in the *Christian Science Monitor,* July 28, 1958.

25. Anne Sexton, "The Reading," in *Anne Sexton: A Self-Portrait in Letters*, ed. Linda Gray Sexton and Loring Conant, Jr. (New York: Houghton Mifflin, 1977), 30. Subsequent page references to this volume will be given parenthetically in the text as *Letters*.

26. For episodes in the public poetry-reading culture in the twentieth-century United States, see the work of Lesley Wheeler, who argues that the fusion of an older model of poetry performance as theater (undertaken by a performer of a text, not necessarily the author) with a newer model of poetry performance as a spectacle of authorial personality became increasingly the norm after World War II and under specifically academic institutional pressures. Wheeler, *Voicing American Poetry: Sound and Performance from the 1920s to the Present* (Ithaca, NY: Cornell University Press, 2008), 130–146. See also Peter Middleton's *Distant Reading: Performance, Readership, and Consumption in Contemporary Poetry* (Tuscaloosa: University of Alabama Press, 2008), chapter 3.

27. See Wheeler, introduction to *Voicing American Poetry*.

28. Virginia Jackson, *Dickinson's Misery: A Theory of Lyric Reading* (Princeton, NJ: Princeton University Press, 2005), 132.

29. Vernon Shetley, *After the Death of Poetry: Poet and Audience in Contemporary America* (Durham, NC: Duke University Press, 1993), 111.

30. Sexton, a student of Lowell, would have been exposed to a host of New Critical views on tone.

31. See Philip MacGowan, introduction to *Anne Sexton and Middle-Generation Poetry: The Geography of Grief* (Westport, CT: Greenwood, 2004), especially page 5. See also Blasing's chapter on Sexton in *Lyric Poetry*. Dawn M. Skorczewski proposes that, in Sexton's therapy, she anticipated the "postmodern" or "intersubjective" turn in contemporary analytic thought in the United States, an awareness that "the analyst participates in the construction of his patient's story." Skorczewski, *Anne Sexton's Secrets: The Therapy Tapes of Anne Sexton* (New York: CRC, 2012), 87.

32. Gill, "Textual Confessions," 68, 62. The most compelling rereadings of Sexton come from Gill, in her several, formidable essays on Sexton, including "Textual Confessions"; and "Anne Sexton and Confessional Poetics," *Review of English Studies* 55, no. 3 (2004): 425–445.

33. Gill, "Textual Confessions," 62.

34. Anne Sexton, "Said the Poet to the Analyst," in *The Complete Poems* (Boston: Houghton Mifflin, 1981), 12–13. Subsequent page references to this volume will be given parenthetically in the text as *CP*.

35. John Stuart Mill, "Thoughts on Poetry and Its Varieties" (1833), in *The Collected Works of John Stuart Mill*, vol. 1, *Autobiography and Literary Essays*, ed. John M. Robson and Jack Stillinger (Toronto: University of Toronto Press, 1981), 350.

36. Sexton may have been following Lowell's suit here; in *Life Studies*, fifteen out of nineteen poems (some dramatic monologues but many first-person lyric) employ ellipses.

37. Jenny Chamarette, "Flesh, Folds and Texturality: Thinking Visual Ellipsis via Merleau-Ponty, Hélène Cixous and Robert Frank," *Paragraph* 30, no. 2 (July 2007): 36.

38. Indeed six out of the ten opening poems in *To Bedlam* foreground text or address or deemphasize voice, speaker, and dramatic setting: "You, Doctor Martin" has a centered text with radical enjambments. "Kind Sir: These Woods" is an epistolary poem. "Music Swims Back to Me" foregrounds address and the mediating presences of memory, text, and radios on the "experiences" described; the apostrophized, dead Elizabeth in "Elizabeth Gone" *responds* (atypical for lyric of the day); "Some Foreign Letters" stages an exchange with a "you" (a dead older aunt) through third-party letters of the aunt, taken nevertheless by "I" "as if these foreign postmarks were meant for me." The poem foregrounds the situation of approaching writing as a space in which we act "as if" the poem/letter/history/story were "meant for me"; "Said the Poet to the Analyst," discussed earlier, foregrounds textuality and emphasizes the poem's speech as intersubjectively determined. Anne Sexton, *To Bedlam and Part Way Back* (Boston: Houghton Mifflin, 1960), reprinted in *CP*, 1–42. Unless otherwise specified, subsequent page references refer to the *CP* edition.

39. Anne Sexton, "The Letting Down of the Hair," *Atlantic Monthly*, March 1972, 40–43.

40. Ibid., 41.

41. Ibid., 42.

42. Ibid., my emphasis.

43. Sexton, *To Bedlam* (1960), dust jacket. See also Elizabeth Bishop to Robert Lowell, May 19, 1960 in *Words in Air: The Complete Correspondence of Robert Lowell and Elizabeth Bishop*, ed. Thomas Travisano and Saskia Hamilton (New York: Farrar, Straus and Giroux, 2008), 327.

44. Sexton, *To Bedlam* (1960), dust jacket. Sexton may also have wanted, like Lowell, to stand apart from her poems, given the negative press she was receiving at the time, a desire to seem less "personal" and thereby more serious.

45. Sexton, "Letting Down," 42. Susan B. Rosenbaum explores "anxieties about the commercial nature of sincerity" in British Romantic and post-1945 U.S. poetry in ways that are relevant to my discussion, particularly in her claim, which draws on claims in Thomas Travisano's *Midcentury Quartet,* that "a 'confessional culture' has overdetermined the reading of lyric poetry." Rosenbaum, *Professing Sincerity: Modern Lyric Poetry, Commercial Culture, and the Crisis in Reading* (Charlottesville: University of Virginia Press, 2007), 7, 237; Travisano, *Midcentury Quartet: Bishop, Lowell, Jarrell, Berryman, and the Making of a Postmodern Aesthetic* (Charlottesville: University of Virginia Press, 1999).

46. In a strange double bluff, the subject of "The Letting Down of the Hair" receives a letter from a friend who discovers Christ and writes, "P.S. . . . I've even discovered what your hair means. It is a parable for the life of the poet." The Rapunzel figure asks, "Am I like a poet? I mean to ask her about that" (42). The moment

seems to anticipate our own desire to resolve this writing into a parable about Sexton's biography.

47. James Dickey, "Review of *To Bedlam and Part Way Back*" (1961), reprinted in *Anne Sexton: Telling the Tale*, ed. Steven E. Colburn (Ann Arbor: University of Michigan Press, 1988), 63–64.

48. Helen Vendler, *Invisible Listeners: Lyric Intimacy in Herbert, Whitman, and Ashbery* (Princeton, NJ: Princeton University Press, 2005).

49. Peggy Rizza, "Another Side of this Life: Women as Poets" in *American Poetry Since 1960: Some Critical Perspectives*, ed. Robert B. Shaw (Cheadle, UK: Carcanet Press, 1973), 174 (my emphasis). See also Charles Gullans, "Review of Live or Die" (1970), in which Gullans expresses something very similar and calls the poems "not poems at all"; reprinted in Colburn, *Anne Sexton*, 148–149.

50. Mill, "Thoughts on Poetry" (1859), 97.

51. Gerald Graff identifies Reuben Brower's *The Fields of Light: An Experiment in Critical Reading* (New York: Oxford University Press, 1951) as "probably the first major work of the New Criticism that explicated poems without an accompanying cultural thesis." Graff (1987) *Professing Literature: An Institutional History*, Twentieth Anniversary Edition (1978; repr. Chicago: University of Chicago Press, 2007), 150. Brower boiled down and disseminated the work of John Crowe Ransom, Wimsatt, and Brooks as a set of pedagogical norms in the 1950s.

52. Northrop Frye, *The Anatomy of Criticism* (Princeton, NJ: Princeton University Press, 1957), 250.

53. Charles Bernstein, "Artifice of Absorption" (1987), reprinted in *A Poetics* (Cambridge, MA: Harvard University Press, 1992), 31.

54. Orr, *Beautiful and Pointless*, 19.

55. Ibid., 30.

56. It must be the case that Sexton's reading performances came to define her name and the critical fate of her written work. Or, rather, her public image, as carefully crafted as any poem, came to supplant her work as its supposed interpretive key. And yet, as Sexton wrote in a letter of July 21, 1970, to John Mood, a professor/fan who invited Sexton to read before his college community in the late 1960s, her readings, down to even the "little introductory notes, [were] . . . not in the least spontaneous"; they were, in fact, highly stylized. Sexton read a draft of Mood's *Chicago Review* article reflecting on and describing that reading and asked him to remove references to what he took to be her spontaneous "little introductory notes," since he had misunderstood their entirely scripted nature. Anne Sexton, "Letter to John Mood, July 21, 1970," Harry Ransom Humanities Research Center. Correspondence 23:2. Quoted in Ashley Ray, "In Search of an Accident of Hope—The Live or Die Life of Anne Sexton," *University of Texas at Austin Undergraduate Research Journal* 3 (Spring 2004): 43. Mood's eventual published piece not only failed to make the change Sexton requested, it touted the seeming vulnerability and spontaneity of Sexton's introductory patter as the authentic mark of her real self: "a softly intense intro-

duction of her ownmost being" (116). John J. Mood, " 'A Bird Full of Bones': Anne Sexton: A Visit and a Reading," *Chicago Review* 23–24 (1972): 107–123.

57. William Waters, *Poetry's Touch: On Lyric Address* (Ithaca, NY: Cornell University Press, 2003), 3.

58. Mary Kinzie, *A Poet's Guide to Poetry* (Chicago: University of Chicago Press, 1999), 57.

59. Lawrence Lerner, "What Is Confessional Poetry?," *Critical Quarterly* 29, no. 2 (1987): 54; Kinzie, *Poet's Guide to Poetry*, 57. Paul Lacey's reading of "You, Dr. Martin" as "about power . . . explored by acting out rights of mastery" also takes the broken form of the poem (not unconvincingly) as mimesis of personal experience. Lacey, "The Sacrament of Confession," in Colburn, *Anne Sexton*, 224.

60. This is also true of the second poem in Sexton's first collection, "Kind Sir: These Woods"—an epistolary address, we should note (not typical of the day), in which all the voices of the poem are inhuman.

61. Sexton, *To Bedlam* (1960), dust jacket.

62. There are still other ways to identify Sexton with her poem's jarring surface: choosing not to identify Sexton with the madness or expressive feeling of enjambment but rather with the control that such contrivance requires, we nevertheless still identify the poem with Sexton's intentional hand. That tendency may explain why readers hostile to Sexton and the Confessional make an exception for some of her early work, which tends rather to cohere around a set of interrelated images.

63. Diane Wood Middlebrook, "Anne Sexton," in *Dictionary of Literary Biography*, vol. 169, *American Poets since World War II: Fifth Series*, ed. Joseph Conte (Detroit: Gale Research, 1996), 245.

64. Mill, "Thoughts on Poetry" (1859), 97.

65. Rosenbaum, *Professing Sincerity*, 6.

66. Jackson, *Dickinson's Misery*, 3; Mill, "Thoughts on Poetry" (1859), 97.

67. Jane Hedley, *I Made You to Find Me: The Coming of Age of the Woman Poet and the Politics of Poetic Address* (Columbus: Ohio State University Press, 2009), 3–4.

68. Brower, *Fields of Light*, 29. Subsequent page references to this source will be given parenthetically in the text.

69. Jacob and Wilhelm Grimm, "The Golden Key" (no. 200) in *The Grimm Brothers' Children's and Household Tales*, ed. and trans. D. L. Ashliman, http://www.pitt.edu/~dash/grimmtales.html.

70. Tales that work as feminist allegory include "White Snake," "Snow White and the Seven Dwarves," "Rumpelstiltskin," "Godfather Death," "Rapunzel," "Cinderella," "Hansel and Gretel," and "Briar Rose."

71. See in particular "Red Riding Hood," which asks (and refuses to answer) "where's the moral" (*CP*, 268).

72. Joyce Carol Oates, "Anne Sexton: Self-Portriat in Poetry and Letters" (review) in *The Profane Art: Essays and Reviews* (New York: Dutton, 1983), 177, 176.

73. Patricia Meyer Spacks, "45 Mercy Street" (review), *New York Times Book Review* (May 30, 1976), 6. Reprinted in McClatchy, *Anne Sexton*, 186.

74. Vendler, *Given and the Made*, 90. Similarly, Charles Gullans found Sexton's collection *Live or Die* to be embarrassing and irritating because it is "raw material for the understanding." Gullans, "Review of *Live or Die*" (1966), in Colburn, *Anne Sexton*, 148.

75. As Rosenbaum argues about poetry in the English Romantic and post-1945 American periods, "anxieties about the 'extravagant' nature of feeling were noticeably heightened around commercial culture and have tended to center on women" (*Professing Sincerity*, 6).

76. Alicia Ostriker, *Stealing the Language: The Emergence of Women's Poetry in America* (Boston: Beacon, 1986), 486, 162.

77. Ron Silliman, "Introduction: Language, Realism, Poetry." *In the American Tree*, ed. Ron Silliman (Orono, ME: National Poetry Foundation, 1986), xx.

78. Lyn Hejinian, "The Person and Description," in *The Language of Inquiry* (Berkeley: University of California Press, 2000), 202.

79. Abigail Child, "Melodrama and Montage: On Nicole Brossard / Hannah Weiner," in *This Is Called Moving: A Critical Poetics of Film* (Tuscaloosa: University of Alabama Press, 2005), 24.

80. This challenges Rosenbaum's view that for both post-Romantic and post-1945 writers, "built into the textual promise of sincerity was its opacity—the necessity of artifice, fiction, and theatricality" (*Professing Sincerity*, 5). Instead, Sexton flaunts that promise.

81. Frank O'Hara, "Personism: A Manifesto" (1959), in *The New American Poetry, 1945–1960*, ed. Donald Allen (New York: Grove, 1960); reprinted in *An Anthology of New York Poets*, ed. Ron Padgett and David Shapiro (New York: Random House, 1970), xxxi–xxxiv.

82. David Haven Blake, "Public Dreams: Berryman, Celebrity, and the Culture of Confession," *ALH* 13, no. 4 (2001): 719–720.

83. Ibid., 720. See Rosenbaum's introduction to *Professing Sincerity*.

84. Anne Sexton, "All God's Children Need Radios," originally printed as "A Small Journal," *Ms.* 2, no. 5 (November 1973): 60–63, 107, reprinted as retitled in *No Evil Star: Selected Essays, Interviews, and Prose*, ed. Steven E. Colburn (Ann Arbor: University of Michigan Press, 1985), 23–32. The circumstances of the retitling of the piece by Sexton are unclear to me. It is notable that in its *Ms.* form, the "journal" is illustrated with clip art that, in an almost exaggeratedly decorative way, presents the piece as a personal diary, deemphasizing the piece's interest in how "the personal" is mediated. Subsequent page references to this source will be given parenthetically in the text as *NE*.

85. Quoted in Middlebrook, *Anne Sexton*, 359. The mixed generic destiny may justify analogies with avant-garde antilyric experiments. Ron Silliman distinguishes avant-garde prose poetry from "the dramatic monologues and surreal short stories that characterize other recent prose writing by American poets," but it seems fair to

consider *All God's Children* as smudging the line: its indirections are, if to a lesser degree, not unlike the autobiographical, anticonfessional strategies in such works as Lyn Hejinian's *My Life,* Bernadette Mayer's *The Desires of Mothers to Please Others in Letters* (written not long after Sexton's piece), the early narrative experiments of Carla Harryman, and the "autobiographical" works of Bob Perelman. See Silliman, "Introduction: Language, Realism, Poetry," *In the American Tree,* xix.

86. Roland Barthes, "The Death of the Author" (1968), in *Image-Music-Text* (New York: Macmillan, 1978), 146.

87. An anonymous reader suggests that this may be Dimitri Oblensky's translation of "Remembrance" in *The Penguin Book of Russian Verse,* ed. Oblensky (New York: Penguin, 1962), 98. The date suggests the possibility, though if so, it is slightly misquoted. It may be a different translation of Pushkin.

88. In Yukio Mishima's 1951 novel *Forbidden Colors,* translated into English in 1968 by Alfred H. Marks, we find the sentence in slightly different form: "The unhappiness of other people when viewed through a window is more beautiful than when viewed from within." Mishima, *Forbidden Colors,* trans. Marks (1968; repr., New York: Knopf, 1999), 80.

89. T. S. Eliot, *The Three Voices of Poetry.* Published for The National Book League (New York: Cambridge University Press, 1955), 16.

90. Vendler, *Given and the Made,* 50. Vendler also asserts that "the purpose of lyric, as a genre, is to represent an inner life in such a manner that it is assumable by others" (xi).

91. Paul De Man, "Anthropomorphism and Trope in Lyric," in *The Rhetoric of Romanticism* (New York: Columbia University Press, 1984), 262.

92. Vendler, *Given and the Made,* 30.

93. Ibid., 49–50.

94. Craig Dworkin, "Parting with Description," in *American Women Poets in the 21st Century: Where Lyric Meets Language,* ed. Claudia Rankine and Juliana Spahr (Middletown, CT: Wesleyan University Press, 2002), 243. Juliana Spahr, a noted avant-garde poet and coeditor of the volume in which Dworkin's essay appeared, frames the volume as dealing with changes to the "lyric" after Language: "after modernism [lyric] has gotten its bad name for being traditional, for being romantic in the derisive sense." Spahr, introduction to Rankine and Spahr, *American Women Poets,* 1. We should here recall the multiple author manifesto by Silliman, Hejinian, and other Language writers, which calls the canonical "voice" poem of the 1970s and 1980s "genetically" related to "the confessional."

95. Silliman et al., "Aesthetic Tendency," 264, 265.

96. Lyn Hejinian, "The Rejection of Closure" (1983), in *Language of Inquiry,* 43.

97. Ibid., 40–41.

98. Hejinian, "Language and 'Paradise'" (1984) in *Language of Inquiry,* 75, 74. For Hejinian, it seems, no confession can be "true" because of the confession's narrative aspiration to conquer time and interpretive contingencies (74–75).

99. De Man reads Baudelaire's "Correspondences" and "Obsession" to figure and illustrate lyric pedagogy. He makes the connection between lyric and intelligibility clear when he argues, "'Obsession' translates 'Correspondences' into intelligibility, the least one can hope for in a successful reading." For De Man, the pairing functions as a "model for the uneasy combination of funereal monumentality with paranoid fear that characterizes the hermeneutics and the pedagogy of lyric poetry" ("Anthropomorphism and Trope," 259). Jerome McGann offers a celebratory description of Language writing in the 1980s in terms that are specifically *antilyric,* as "writing . . . conceived as something that must be done *rather than as something that is to be interpreted.*" McGann, "Contemporary Poetry: Alternate Routes," *Critical Inquiry* 13, no. 3 (Spring 1987): 636 (my emphasis). Douglas Barbour identifies "anti-lyrics" as "lyrics written against the conventional concepts of lyric" (7) (a tautology that brings home the often self-consuming quality of debates about lyric), which he identifies, quoting Robert Kroetsch, with "'ferocious principles of closure,'" (24) specifying antilyric tendencies as pitched against hermeneutic interpretation and clarity. Barbour, "Lyric/Anti-lyric: Some Notes about a Concept," in *Lyric/Anti-Lyric: Essays on Contemporary Poetry,* The Writer as Critic VII., gen. ed. Smaro Kamboureli (Edmonton: Ne West), 7–32. Robert Kroetsch, "Fore Play and Entrance: The Contemporary Canadian Long Poem," (1983) in *The Lovely Treachery of Words: Essays Selected and New* (Oxford: Oxford University Press, 1989), 117–134, 118.

100. Charles Bernstein, "Stray Straws and Straw Men," in *Content's Dream: Essays, 1975–1984* (Evanston, IL: Northwestern University Press, 2001), 44.

101. Jackson, "Lyric," *Princeton Encyclopedia of Poetry and Poetics,* ed. Roland Greene, Stephen Cushman, Clare Cavanagh, Jahan Ramazani, and Paul Rouzer, 4th ed. (Princeton, NJ: Princeton University Press, 2012), 833.

102. Rae Armantrout, "Feminist Poetics and the Meaning of Clarity," in *Artifice and Indeterminacy: An Anthology of New Poetics,* ed. Christopher Beach (Tuscaloosa: University of Alabama Press, 1998), 288–290.

103. Ibid., 295–296.

104. Edward Lucie-Smith, "An Interview with Frank O'Hara" (1966). in Frank O'Hara, *Standing Still and Walking in New York,* ed., Donald Allen (Berkeley, CA: Grey Fox, 1983), 4.

105. Anne Hartman, "Confessional Counterpublics in Frank O'Hara and Allen Ginsberg," *Journal of Modern Literature* 28, no. 4 (2005): 40.

106. Vendler, *Given and the Made,* 50, 57.

107. Armantrout, "Feminist Poetics," 288–290; Bernstein, "Stray Straws," 44; Hejinian, "Rejection of Closure," 41; O'Hara, "Personism."

108. McGann, "Contemporary Poetry," 636.

109. John Ashbery, "Review of Ted Berrigan's *The Sonnets,*" in *Selected Prose,* ed. Eugene Richie (Ann Arbor: University of Michigan Press, 2005), 117–119.

110. One interesting example of this contradiction is Marjorie Perloff's reading of "The Love Song of J. Alfred Prufrock" first as a quintessentially closed "Symboliste" text, in the early 1980s, and then as (contradicting the earlier view) a paragon of avant-garde openness, in 2001. See Perloff, " 'Lines Converging and Crossing': The 'French' Decade of Williams Carlos Williams," in *The Poetics of Indeterminacy: Rimbaud to Cage* (Princeton, NJ: Princeton University Press, 1981), 109–154, especially p. 114; and Perloff, "Avant-Garde Eliot," in *21st-Century Modernism: The "New" Poetics* (Malden, MA: Blackwell, 2002), 7–43.

111. Ashbery, "Review," 119.

112. See Gill, "Textual Confessions," 73, for an inventory of "critical consensus about the importance of the poem as an expression of Sexton's [confessional] poetics." Gill argues that it is not a "defense of what confession reveals" but an "exemplification of how it functions."

113. " 'Personism' means the *illusion* of intimate talk between an 'I' and a 'you' (or sometimes 'we,' 'he,' 'they,' or 'one,') giving us the sense that we are eavesdropping on an ongoing conversation, that we are *present*." Marjorie Perloff, *Frank O'Hara: Poet among Painters* (Chicago: University of Chicago Press, 1998), 26–27.

114. Another poem that does this, even more pointedly, is "What's That" (1960; *CP*, 25).

115. For a few examples of the Language critique, see Bernstein's essays in *Content's Dream*, "Stray Straws" and "Thought's Measure," especially 77–82. See also Robert Grenier, "On Speech" (1971), in Silliman, *In the American Tree*, 477–478. See also Silliman et al., "Aesthetic Tendency," especially 264–265, in which the mode in question is said to be "genetically related to early examples of the confessional voice poem." See also Lee Bartlett's summary of the lyric conventions against which Language-centered writers identified their goals, in "What Is 'Language Poetry'?," *Critical Inquiry* 12 (1986): 741–752. Bartlett cites Bob Perelman's seminal lecture "The First Person," about the "voice poem" and the trope of "finding one's voice" 743. Perelman, "The First Person," *Hills* 6–7 (Spring 1980): 156.

116. Andrew Osborn, "Difficulty," in *The Princeton Encyclopedia of Poetry and Poetics,* ed. Roland Greene, Stephen Cushman, Clare Cavanagh, Jahan Ramazani, and Paul Rouzer, 4th ed. (Princeton, NJ: Princeton University Press, 2012), 364.

117. Shetley, *After the Death of Poetry,* 104.

118. Jerome McGann, *The Point Is to Change It: Poetry and Criticism in the Continuing Present* (Tuscaloosa: University of Alabama Press, 2007), 97.

119. Gill, "Textual Confessions," 72.

120. Ron Silliman, *The New Sentence* (New York: Roof, 1987), 181.

121. Here I diverge from Deborah Nelson, who notes the poem's experiment with processes of readerly identification but assumes nevertheless (and relying heavily on biographical context) that Sexton means to clearly "tell" us and John (at the same time) that what he fears is identifying with a woman. Nelson, *Pursuing Privacy*

in Cold War America (New York: Columbia University Press, 2002), 105. Gill's argument is much closer to mine but takes the piece allegorically as a defense of narcissism in terms that seem, in moments, overliteralized: "Sexton's poem presents a fundamentally narcissistic moment of crisis in the subject's sense of self and her relation to the external world" ("Textual Confessions," 79). Indeed Gill continues by arguing "this is *laid bare* for contemplation by both speaker and reader" (ibid., my emphasis).

122. In interviews with Patricia Marx (1965) and with Alfred Poulin and William Heyen (1973), Sexton disavows the assumption that she truth tells. To Poulin and Heyen, she says, "I mean it's a difficult label, 'confessional,' because I'll often confess to things that never happened." In Anne Sexton, *No Evil Star: Selected Essays, Interviews, and Prose,* ed. Steven E. Colburn (Ann Arbor: University of Michigan Press, 1985), 75 (Marx), 133–134 (Poulin and Heyen).

123. In a recent blog post, Barrett Watten revises his earlier "skepticism" about "any kind of confessionalism," raising the possibility that decades of the Confessional's construction as the "bad lyric" has limited our understanding of the potential critical value of works that have fallen under the name. Reading Plath's work in light of Jacqueline Rose's reception of it in *The Haunting of Sylvia Plath,* Watten can newly imagine a Plath who is "anything but expressive of feminist anger or a confession of intimate secrets." He finds in her work a "public dimension of the presentation of the self," or Plath's self-consciousness of the public culture (as Rose puts it, that mix of "war, consumerism, photography, and religion") that conditioned the vogue of "personal expressive" and "confessional" lyric she wrote in the 1960s. Watten calls for others to see Plath in terms of the "cultural logics that produced *The New American Poets*— . . . a revision that . . . gets us past the avant-garde/mainstream, or post-avant/School of Quietude, faultline that has troubled our thinking on poetry for so long." Watten, "Entry 6: Sylvia Plath's Collage," *BarrettWatten.net*, January 16, 2010, http://barrettwatten.net/texts/entry-06-sylvia-plaths-50s-collage/2010/01/; Rose, *The Haunting of Sylvia Plath* (Cambridge, MA: Harvard University Press, 1992).

124. Robert Lowell, "Skunk Hour" (1959), in *Life Studies and For the Union Dead* (New York: Macmillan, 2006), 95. Subsequent page references to this source will be given parenthetically in the text as *LS.*

125. Ann Keniston, *Overheard Voices: Address and Subjectivity in Postmodern American Poetry* (New York: Routledge, 2006), 22. Keniston's historicist approach to postmodern lyric on the question of address is admirable, and her introduction to *Overheard Voices* has been helpful in corroborating my sense of the importance of Mill's lyric theory, and the assumptions about address that it raises, for midcentury poets. I quite agree with her sense that many postmodern poets thematize a "pathos" attending "the intertextual problem of relying on a figure [apostrophe] linked with a lyric tradition that seems obsolete" through the figure of address, which produced "intensity, awkwardness, and embarrassment" in "yearning for something unobtain-

able" (22). But I do not agree, and find awkward in her argument, the assumption of an abstract category of lyric for which she assumes an "essential isolation." I shift the terms by focusing on the poetic embarrassments of working within obsolete lyric-reading conventions, rather than on the embarrassment of failing to achieve "essential lyric" conditions.

126. Sexton referred to her therapist of the time as Dr. Z.

127. Bernstein, "Stray Straws," 45.

128. Ibid., 40–41.

3. "SPEAKING IN EFFECT": IDENTIFYING (WITH) BERNADETTE MAYER'S SHAMED EXPRESSIVE PRACTICE

1. Bernadette Mayer, *Midwinter Day* (1978; repr., New York: New Directions, 1999), 43 (epigraph), 111. Subsequent page references to this source will be given parenthetically in the text as *MD.*

2. John Ashbery, Frank O'Hara, and Barbara Guest are of the "first generation" of "New York School," an ambivalent identification, though not because abject, as "Confessional" might be. See Ashbery's "New York School of Poets" (1968), in *Selected Prose,* ed. Eugene Richie (Ann Arbor: University of Michigan Press, 2004), 113–115.

3. Mayer's reference in the epigraph to Elizabeth Bishop in *The Desires of Mothers to Please Others in Letters* (1979–1980; repr., West Stockbridge, MA: Hard Press, 1994) is similarly surprising, and because Mayer suppresses the addressee of the letter, we can only fantasize which avant-garde poet friend of Mayer's would have called Bishop's work "great" in 1979.

4. For useful canonical histories of the oppositional cast of much Language-oriented work, see George Hartley, *Textual Politics and the Language Poets* (Bloomington: Indiana University Press, 1989); Ronald Silliman, introduction, "Language, Realism, Poetry," to *In the American Tree,* ed. Ronald Silliman (Orono, ME: National Poetry Foundation, 1986); Douglas Messerli, introduction to *"Language" Poetries,* ed. Douglas Messerli (New York: New Directions, 1987); Hank Lazer, *Opposing Poetries,* 2 vols. (Evanston, IL: Northwestern University Press, 1996), especially vol. 1; Silliman, *The New Sentence* (New York: Roof, 1987); the collaborative essay by Silliman, Carla Harryman, Lyn Hejinian, Steve Benson, Bob Perelman, and Barrett Watten, "Aesthetic Tendency and the Politics of Poetry: A Manifesto," *Social Text* 19–20 (1988): 261–275; Marjorie Perloff, *The Dance of the Intellect: Studies in the Poetry of the Pound Tradition* (Cambridge: Cambridge University Press, 1985); Perloff, *Radical Artifice: Writing Poetry in the Age of Media* (Chicago: University of Chicago Press, 1991); Perloff, *Wittgenstein's Ladder: Poetic Language and the Strangeness of the Ordinary* (Chicago: University of Chicago Press, 1996).

5. Peter Baker, *Obdurate Brilliance: Exteriority and the Modern Long Poem* (Gainesville: University of Florida Press, 1991), 1. Lynn Keller refers to Mayer

briefly as among those "process-based experimentalist" poets (including Lyn He-jinian, Joan Retallack, and Rae Armantrout) who "wrote *against* the conventions of expressive lyric" that appealed to more mainstream writers. Keller, *Forms of Expansion: Recent Long Poems by Women* (Chicago: University of Chicago Press, 1997), 18.

6. Mayer, *Desires of Mothers*; Mayer, *The Golden Book of Words* (Lenox, MA: Angel Hair Books, 1978).

7. Bernadette Mayer, "Lives of the Poets: One of America's Greatest Living Writers Remains on the Outside Looking Out," interview by Adam Fitzgerald, Poetry Foundation website, April 4, 2011, http://www.poetryfoundation.org/article /241398.

8. Bernadette Mayer, interview by Ann Rower (October 18, 1984), *Bench Press Series on Art* (New York: Bench Press, 1985), 6.

9. Both Ann Vickery, in *Leaving Lines of Gender: A Feminist Genealogy of Language Writing* (Wesleyan, CT: Wesleyan University Press, 2000), and Maggie Nelson, in *Women, the New York School, and Other True Abstractions* (Iowa City: University of Iowa Press, 2007), devote substantial sections of their feminist histo-ries of New York School and Language avant-gardes to Mayer, but it is notable that neither Lynn Keller, nor Rachel Blau DuPlessis, in writing about Language and experimental aesthetics and feminism, deals with Mayer's work except in passing reference. Lynn Keller refers to Mayer briefly as among those "process-based experi-mentalist" poets (including Lyn Hejinian, Joan Retallack, and Rae Armantrout) who "wrote *against* the conventions of expressive lyric" that appealed to more main-stream writers. While partly true, this underserves Mayer's struggles with taking on the personal and her work's struggle with the lyric-reading assumptions informing the antilyric, oppositional mode. In Keller, *Forms of Expansion,* 18. Rachel Blau DuPlessis briefly mentions Mayer's *Midwinter Day* in *The Pink Guitar: Writing as Feminist Practice* (New York: Routledge, 1990), 211. In *Blue Studios,* DuPlessis mentions Mayer twice, once to imagine how, if it had been read more widely in the 1980s, Mayer's work (among others) might have affected critical views on lyric apostrophe, and once as a writer "skeptical of feminism." In DuPlessis, *Blue Studios: Poetry and Its Cultural Work* (Tuscaloosa, AL: University of Alabama Press, 2006), 263–264, note 3; 259.

10. Ann Vickery, *Leaving Lines of Gender,* 151.

11. Bernadette Mayer, "Experiments," reprinted in *The L=A=N=G=U=A=G=E Book,* ed. Bruce Andrews and Charles Bernstein (Carbondale: Southern Illinois University, 1984), 83; also in Silliman, *In the American Tree,* 534.

12. Daniel Kane, *All Poets Welcome: The Lower East Side Poetry Scene in the 1960s* (Berkeley: Berkeley University Press, 2003), 188. According to Kane, these workshops were "to play a part in the theoretical and critical work promoted in the later 1970s through magazines including *L=A=N=G=U=A=G=E*" (188).

13. In *Leaving Lines of Gender,* Ann Vickery investigates Mayer's being one of few women singled out for publication in both New York School and Language journals. See pages 152–158 especially. See also Maggie Nelson, especially pages 102–104, on Mayer's centrality to avant-garde practice in New York. Jerome McGann argues for Mayer's centrality to the formation of Language practice, in "Contemporary Poetry, Alternate Routes," *Critical Inquiry* 13, no. 3 (Spring 1987): 624–647.

14. Kane, *All Poets Welcome,* 189.

15. See McGann, "Contemporary Poetry." See also Vickery's discussion of Mayer's treatment in Language circles in *Leaving Lines of Gender,* 150–166.

16. Nelson considers Mayer's debts to and differences from Stein (*Women, the New York School,* 108–116).

17. Mayer, *Ceremony Latin* (1964) (New York: Angel Hair, 1975) facsimile at Eclipse Archive, University of Utah, http://eclipsearchive.org/projects/CEREMONY /html/contents.html, image 004. Subsequent page references to this source will be given parenthetically in the text as *CL,* with "Eclipse" specifying that the number given is the image number in the Eclipse Archives.

18. Bernadette Mayer, *Unnatural Acts* (self-published, 1972). The St. Mark's Poetry Project released a volume of the work, edited by Mayer and Ed Friedman, in 1972.

19. Libbie Rifkin, "'My Little World Goes on St. Marks Place': Anne Waldman, Bernadette Mayer and the Gender of an Avant-Garde Institution," *Jacket* 7 (April 1999), http://jacketmagazine.com/07/rifkin07.html.

20. Mayer, *STORY* (New York: 0–9 Books, 1968), facsimile at Eclipse Archive, http://eclipsearchive.org/projects/STORY/html/contents.html. Subsequent references to this source will be given parenthetically in the text. In some cases, Mayer's texts are numbered, but the image number in the Eclipse Archive differs.

21. Mayer, interview by Rower, 17.

22. Mayer reviewed Hejinian's *MY LIFE* in "Mayer on Hejinian," *L=A=N=G=U=A=G=E* 13 (December 1980), facsimile at Eclipse Archive, http:// eclipsearchive.org/projects/LANGUAGEn13/, images 016–017. In praising the book's autobiographical tactics, she shows the two authors' debts to each other: "it's knotted and knitted and it's completed. . . . there is something almost wishfully neat about it, childlike & apt, which is like the idea of courting & denying autobiography & becoming an I-character in a book."

23. Bernadette Mayer, *Poetry* (New York: Kulchur Foundation, 1976), 9, facsimile at Eclipse Archive, http://eclipsearchive.org/projects/POETRY/html/contents .html, image 013. Subsequent references to this source will be given parenthetically in the text, with both the page number in the original edition and the Eclipse image number.

24. "Bernadette Mayer, telephone interview by [Daniel Kane], November 6, 1998," in Kane, *All Poets Welcome,* 190–191 (see 269, note 12 for reference and more of interview).

25. Vickery, *Leaving Lines of Gender,* 151. See also Peter Baker, "Bernadette Mayer," in *Dictionary of Literary Biography,* vol. 165, *American Poets Since World War II: Fourth Series,* ed. Joseph Conte (Detroit, MI: Gale Research, 1996), 165–172.

26. Baker, "Bernadette Mayer," 168.

27. See Mayer, interview by Rower, 4, and interview by Ken Jordan, "The Colors of Consonance," *Poetry Project Newsletter* 146 (1992): 5–9.

28. Jordan, "Colors of Consonance," 8.

29. For audio files of Mayer's Naropa class describing her process and reasons for undertaking the exhibit, see "Bernadette Mayer Class on Memory, 1978," Archive Project, Naropa University, http://www.archive.org/details/Bernadette_Mayer _class_on_memory__78P084.

30. Rubinfine's preface can be read in light of the midcentury trend for publishers and authors to frame confessional writing in psychoanalytic contexts, as born under emotional pressure. It also participates in the trend for scandalously "personal" writing to be prefaced by an authority figure: Allen Ginsberg's *Howl and Other Poems* (San Francisco: City Lights, 1956) with an introduction by William Carlos Williams, Sylvia Plath's *Ariel* (New York: Harper and Row, 1966) with a foreword by Robert Lowell. Anne Sexton's *To Bedlam and Part Way Back* (Boston: Houghton Mifflin, 1960) was marketed as an account of her time in an asylum, as I discussed previously.

31. Bernadette Mayer, *Memory* (Plainfield, VT: North Atlantic Books, 1975), facsimile at Eclipse Archive, http://eclipsearchive.org/projects/MEMORY/memory .html, image 004. Subsequent references to this source are given parenthetically in the text and refer to Eclipse image numbers.

32. Bernadette Mayer, *Studying Hunger Journals* (1975) (Barrytown, NY: Station Hill Press, 2011), 2.

33. Douglas Messerli, "Anatomy of Self," *L=A=N=G=U=A=G=E* 7 (March 1979), facsimile at Eclipse Archive, http://eclipsearchive.org/projects/LANGUAGEn7/, image 009; Mayer, *Eruditio Ex Memoria* (Lenox, MA: Angel Hair Books, 1977), facsimile at Eclipse Archive, http://eclipsearchive.org/projects/ERUDITIO/html /contents.html. Subsequent references to both of these sources will be given parenthetically in the text.

34. That Mayer's work gestures to the confessional is not quite a new claim: Messerli takes *Eruditio* as "a sharing" and a "personal history" and calls it a "true confession" crossed with "anatomy" ("Anatomy of Self," Eclipse Archive 011, 009, 011). Messerli may well have an Augustinian tradition in mind, however.

35. In this argument and throughout, I am trying to problematize the trend in Mayer criticism to claim for her later work a more "traditional" and "traditional lyric" status. See Nelson, *Women, the New York School,* 108; and Baker, "Bernadette Mayer," 168, in which Baker associates the Language view of Mayer's late 1970s work as a "departure, even a betrayal of the movement" with the fact that it took on

"traditional conventions of poetry" he associates with a more "personal style of expression" (168).

36. Bernadette Mayer, *Moving* (New York: Angel Hair, 1971), facsimile at Eclipse Archive, http://eclipsearchive.org/projects/MOVING/html/contents.html, image 001. Subsequent references to this source are given parenthetically in the text and refer to the Eclipse image number.

37. Mayer, *Golden Book*, n.p.

38. Bernadette Mayer, *Utopia* (New York: United Artists Books, 1984). Subsequent page references to this source are given parenthetically in the text. The book exists in at least one earlier edition, hand-typed and with individual covers, less complete than this edition.

39. To Rower, Mayer identifies the "Homage" as being "about the language poets" (Mayer, interview by Rower, 5) and indicates that Bernstein's "The Only Utopia Is in a Now" was written as a reply. Bernstein's piece is reprinted in *The Sophist* (Los Angeles: Sun & Moon, 1987).

40. Mayer's piece can seem willfully naïve to the "textual politics" informing Language technique, which, it is clear, she was not. In her interview with Rower, Rower asks her to explain Language. Mayer hesitates, worries about "excoriation" for her "opinions," and then attempts an answer: "But how does one put this. It's an attempt to write a kind of poetry that makes use of language in an almost scientific manner and tries to create new combinations of thought. Well, that's not right but it's an experiment in that sense. And also tries to abdicate all of the properties of the old language that have gotten us all into political, emotional, and literal trouble. The political trouble is real apparent. The emotional trouble is debatable because once you abdicate emotion in your writing where are you left? But happily, all the rules are broken like at the beach and you can't not have emotion in poetry and the language poets might argue that they never said you could" (9).

41. Charles Bernstein, "The Only Utopia Is in a Now," in *The Sophist* (Los Angeles: Sun & Moon, 1987), 35.

42. The charge would appear to predate the writing/publishing of *Utopia*, as Mayer references it in a passage from the earlier *Midwinter Day* (64).

43. Charles Bernstein, "Stray Straws and Straw Men" (1976, 1977), in *Content's Dream: Essays, 1975–1984* (Evanston, IL: Northwestern University Press, 2001), 41.

44. Mayer, interview by Rower, 5.

45. Ibid., 8.

46. Ibid., 18, 5, 3, 8.

47. Mayer's part in the genesis of Bernstein's "The Only Utopia Is in a Now," for instance, goes unmentioned in two accounts of it: in Lazer's *Opposing Poetries*, vol. 2, *Readings*, 14–15, and perhaps more surprisingly, given the subject of the book, in Norman Finkelstein's *The Utopian Moment in Contemporary American Poetry* (Lewisburg, PA: Bucknell University Press, 1993), 114–116. The omission is not Bernstein's, given that he credits Mayer's *Utopia* in the acknowledgments of *The Sophist*.

48. Barrett Watten, *Total Syntax* (Carbondale: Southern Illinois University Press, 1984), 56–57.

49. Bruce Andrews, "The Pacifica Interview," *L=A=N=G=U=A=G=E*, supplement 3 (October 1981), facsimile at the Eclipse Archive, 029. http://eclipsearchive .org/projects/LANGUAGEsupp3/.

50. Nelson, *Women, the New York School*, 117.

51. Lyn Hejinian to Susan Howe, n.d., ms. 201, box 1, folder 9, Mandeville Special Collections, University of California, San Diego. It seems possible, given Hejinian's reference in the letter to the "current pompous LANGUAGE question re. capitalism and writing," that the letter is from 1979; the October 1979 special double issue of *L=A=N=G=U=A=G=E*, nos. 9–10, titled "The Politics of Poetry," included several contributions concerning capitalism and language and the arts. Susan Howe had interviewed Mayer on her Pacifica Radio program in April 1979; available at PennSound: http://www.writing.upenn.edu/pennsound/x/Howe-Pacifica .php.

52. Nada Gordon, "Introduction," *Form's Life: An Exploration of the Work of Bernadette Mayer* (originally a master's thesis, University of California, Berkeley, 1986), in *readme*, issue 3, ed. Gary Sullivan (Summer 2000). This is important scholarship, not least in representing one of the earliest critical overviews of Mayer's early career. The thesis has been published online: http://home.jps.net/~nada/mayer1 .htm. The cited section is here: http://home.jps.net/~nada/mayer9.

53. What Gordon means by "subjective" is not entirely clear, and matters to how we read the comment. I take it she means influenced by personal feelings, but one could imagine her suggesting something more like ambiguous (open to interpretation), which would align Mayer's project with a poet like O'Hara.

54. Ron Silliman, "Poetry and the Politics of the Subject: A Bay Area Sampler," *Socialist Review* 18, no. 3 (1988): 63. The issue of the place of "lyric, voice, and audience" and the gendering of American experimental writing is taken up by Linda Kinnahan, in " 'Look for the Doing Words': Carol Ann Duffy and Questions of Convention," in *Contemporary British Poetry: Essays on Theory and Criticism,* ed. James Acheson and Romana Huk (Albany: SUNY Press, 1996), 245–268. Kinnahan argues that the "condemnation of the lyric voice by Language poets almost automatically marginalizes [a woman writer's] experiments with the lyric" (247). Vickery takes Kinnahan's arguments—along with Ellen Friedman and Miriam Fuchs's anthology *Breaking the Sequence: Women's Experimental Fiction* (Princeton, NJ: Princeton University Press, 1989)—as important efforts to address problems of women's place in experimental canons but argues that such works do not explore the process of "engender[ing] . . . the canon" (*Leaving Lines of Gender,* 42). I would add that the idealization of lyric as voice raises the question of how rejected "lyric" norms might always already be feminized and shameful.

55. Rae Armantrout, "Why Don't Women Do Language-Oriented Writing?," *L=A=N=G=U=A=G=E* 1 (February 1978): 025, facsimile at Eclipse Archive: http://

eclipsearchive.org/projects/LANGUAGEn1/pictures/025.html. The essay was written at Bernstein's request. The later assessment of her answer as "facile" comes in
Armantrout, "Feminist Poetics and the Meaning of Clarity," in *Artifice and Indeterminacy: An Anthology of New Poetics,* ed. Christopher Beach (Tuscaloosa: University
of Alabama Press, 1998), 287. In that essay, Armantrout cites the same passage of
Silliman as I cite earlier in the text.

56. For Armantrout and other Language-oriented writers, clarity results from
narrative coherence, a problematic conventional technical habit. So ubiquitously is
narrative invoked as the definitive tendency of mainstream poetry in the late 1970s
that George Hartley, thinking broadly about Language poetry's aesthetic-politic,
sums up a range of rejected techniques with the phrase "narrative assumptions" (*Textual Politics,* xii).

57. It is worth specifying that Mayer never expresses shame or hesitates to
explore—often graphically—sexuality, in contrast to her frequent mention of the
shame of claiming traditions of "lyric" and "traditional" writers. See her conversation with Rower about male and female genitalia (Mayer, interview by Rower,
10–11).

58. Robert Grenier, "On Speech," *This* 1 (1971): n.p., available as "Robert Grenier:
Selected Essays from *This* 1," at Eclipse Archive: http://eclipsearchive.org/projects
/SPEECH/html/contents.html, images 0006–0007.

59. See Barrett Watten, *The Constructivist Moment: From Material Text to
Cultural Poetics* (Middletown, CT: Wesleyan University Press, 2003), 127–129, 279.
See also Bob Perelman, *The Marginalization of Poetry: Language Writing and Literary
History* (Princeton, NJ: Princeton University Press, 1996), 38–44.

60. Ron Silliman, "Introduction: Language, Realism, Poetry," in *In the American Tree,* ed. Ron Silliman (Orono, ME: National Poetry Foundation, 2007), xvii.

61. This and all issues of *L=A=N=G=U=A=G=E* are available at the Eclipse
Archive: http://eclipsearchive.org/projects/LANGUAGE/language.html.

62. Lyn Hejinian, "Who Is Speaking" (1983), revised and reprinted in *The Language of Inquiry* (Berkeley: University of California Press, 2000), 36.

63. Hejinian and Howe debated the subject of Perelman's anthology of the poetics talks given at his loft in Berkeley in the late 1970s. According to Vickery, Howe
criticized the paucity of women's writings represented in the anthology, to which
Hejinian objected that "the men" were not "ignoring" the women here; the problem
was "that women are extremely hesitant to pose their opinions; and that is a problem
with roots in the past far more than it is rooted in present conditions" (*Leaving Lines
of Gender,* 122). Howe's response implies her belief that the men in their group might
still be (however subtly) responsible for silencings: "Do you really feel it is the fault of
the various women who like Fanny [Howe] sit down and have [others] read their
words . . . or like you—for whatever reason decide your own should not be published, or like me, hide behind fragments of ideas rather than stating them[?]"
(quoted in ibid., 122).

64. Watten, *Constructivist Moment,* 279, 281.

65. One argument for seeing the avant-garde as a masculine preserve situated against women and mass culture is found in Nancy Armstrong's claim that "literary and cultural criticism has shown that, however strange and various, the formal innovations associated with modernism worked toward the single end of distinguishing authentic artistic expression from art which made itself accessible to ordinary consumers." Armstrong, "Modernism's Iconophobia and What It Did to Gender," *Modernism/Modernity* 5, no. 2 (1998): 47.

66. Bernadette Mayer, *Another Smashed Pinecone* (Brooklyn, NY: United Artist Books, 1998). See also Bernadette Mayer, *Scarlet Tanager* (New York: New Directions, 2005). For Nelson's reading of these gestures as both drawing on and rebellious against "the standard goals of analysis," see *Women, the New York School,* 113–114.

67. Bernadette Mayer, "From: A Lecture at Naropa Institute, 1989" in *Disembodied Poetics: Annals of the Jack Kerouac School,* ed. Anne Waldman and Andrew Schelling (Albuquerque: University of New Mexico Press, 1994), 100–101.

68. Mayer, interview by Rower, 16, my emphasis.

69. Hejinian, *Language of Inquiry,* 46; Wordsworth, "Preface to Lyrical Ballads" (1801–1802), in *Lyrical Ballads and Other Poems,* by Samuel Taylor Coleridge and William Wordsworth, ed. Martin Scofield (Hertfordshire, UK: Wordsworth Editions, 2003), 8, 21.

70. See Jonathan Culler on the embarrassment of apostrophe as a sign of feeling and mark of tradition, in "Apostrophe" (1977), in *The Pursuit of Signs: Semiotics, Literature, Deconstruction* (Ithaca, NY: Cornell University Press, 2003), 135–154.

71. Major, now canonical works of Hejinian, Watten, Silliman, and Bernstein suggest that one link among "Language-centered" writers is to assume that texts that show narrative clarity deserve to be read lyrically. Whether in Hejinian's attention to the advantages of the "synchronous" text, Watten's attention to syntax (and his rejection of Mayer's work for its return to the self), or Bernstein's attention in "Stray Straws" to "flowing syntax," the tendency has been to assume that critique happens through parataxis. For obvious reasons, this has bearing on the ways in which Language might read Bishop, Sexton, and Mayer, as well as a host of Victorian and Romantic texts (some of whose strategies Mayer, Bishop, and Sexton could be said to reanimate). See Hejinian "Two Stein Talks" (1985), in *The Language of Inquiry,* 83–130, especially 116–117.

72. Mayer, *Golden Book,* n.p. Subsequent references to this source will be cited parenthetically in the text.

73. Nada Gordon, "The Golden Book of Words" (1986), in *Form's Life,* printed in *readme,* issue 4 (Spring/Summer 2001), http://home.jps.net/~nada/mayer9.htm.

74. Ibid.

75. For a slightly different view of Mayer's "loggorhea" and her relationship to audience, see Nelson, *Women, the New York School,* 119–122.

76. Mayer, interview by Rower, 4.

77. Charles Altieri, "Contingency as Compositional Principle in Fifties Poetics," in *The Scene of My Selves: New Work on New York School Writers,* ed. Terrence Diggory and Stephen Paul Miller (Orono, ME: National Poetry Foundation, 2001), 377. Altieri's article is a compelling explanation of the turn from "heroizing existentialist melodrama" in post-1945 American poetry and painting thought to mark the era and be epitomized by Robert Lowell.

78. With identification, I invoke the broad psychoanalytic concept first theorized by Sigmund Freud and developed over the course of his career. For an overview of texts in which he explores the concept, see "Identification," in *The Freud Encyclopedia: Theory, Therapy, and Culture,* ed. Edward Erwin (New York: Routledge, 2003), 272–273.

79. Mayer, *Desires of Mothers,* 4. Subsequent page references to this source will be given parenthetically in the text.

80. The phrase comes from David Yezzi, "Confessional Poetry and the Artifice of Honesty," *New Criterion* 16 (June 1998): 14.

81. Emily Dickinson, August 1876 to Thomas Higginson letter 470 in *The Letters of Emily Dickinson,* ed. Thomas Herbert Johnson and Theodora Ward (Cambridge, MA: Harvard University Press, 1986), 559.

82. Lucie Brock-Broido, "A Preamble to *The Master Letters,*" in *The Master Letters: Poems* (New York: Knopf, 2005), vii.

83. William Waters, *Poetry's Touch: On Lyric Address* (Ithaca, NY: Cornell University Press, 2003), 3. Northrop Frye, *Anatomy of Criticism: Four Essays* (Princeton, NJ: Princeton University Press, 1957), 250. Jonathan Culler, "Apostrophe," in *The Pursuit of Signs* (Ithaca, NY: Cornell University Press, 1981), 135–184.

84. Ann Keniston, *Overheard Voices: Address and Subjectivity in Postmodern American Poetry* (New York: Routledge, 2006), 4.

85. Robert Hass, "Wallace Stevens," *Threepenny Review* 50 (Summer 1992), 6. Reprinted as "Wallace Stevens in the World," in *What Light Can Do: Essays on Art, Imagination, and the Natural World* (New York: Ecco Press, 2012). Quoted in Liesl Olson, "Robert Hass's Guilt or the Weight of Wallace Stevens," *American Poetry Review* 36, no. 5 (September–October 2007): 39. Susan Howe made the point about Stevens during a question-and-answer session at the Wallace Stevens conference at the University of Connecticut in 2004.

86. For an introduction to Flarf, a serio-comic, heavily ironic, poetic "movement" that originated in 2000, one might begin with Charles Bernstein, ed., "Flarf Files" (August 2003), a collection of Flarf-related materials available at the *Electronic Poetry Center* website, http://epc.buffalo.edu/authors/bernstein/syllabi/readings/flarf .html. For a series of blog posts distinguishing (sometimes with what seems mock animosity) Conceptual from Flarf "movements," see Kenneth Goldsmith, "Flarf is Dionysus. Conceptual Writing is Apollo," *Poetry,* July/August 2009, http://www .poetryfoundation.org/poetrymagazine/article/237176; Drew Gardener, "Why Flarf

is Better Than Conceptualism," reposted in Edwin Torres, "I'll steal your poets like
I sole your bike," *Harriet* (blog), April 2010, http://www.poetryfoundation.org/harriet
/2010/04/ill-steal-your-poets-like-i-stole-your-bike/; and Vanessa Place, "Why Conceptualism is Better than Flarf," originally a talk, transcribed in Sina Queyras, "Flarf is a
one trick pony that thinks a unicorn is another kind of horse," *Harriet* (blog), http://
www.poetryfoundation.org/harriet/2010/04/flarf-is-a-one-trick-pony-that-thinks-a
-unicorn-is-another-kind-of-horse/. See also Brian M. Reed's book tracing the emergence of Conceptual writing and Flarf, *Nobody's Business: Twenty-First Century
Avant-Garde Poetics* (Ithaca, NY: Cornell University Press, 2013).

4. TIRED OF MYSELF: THE 1990S AND THE "LYRIC SHAME" POEM

1. Robert Hass, "Interrupted Meditation," in *Sun Under Wood* (Hopewell, NJ:
Ecco, 1997), 73. Subsequent page references to this volume will be given parctheti-
cally in the text as *Sun*. Epigraph attributed to Bob Perelman by Dodie Bellamy in
"The Cheese Stands Alone," in *Academonia* (San Francisco: Krupskaya, 2006), 115.

2. Gerald Stern, "Hot Dog," in *Odd Mercy* (New York: Norton, 1995), 78;
Charles Wright, "Disjecta Membra" (1996) in *Black Zodiac* (New York: Farrar, Straus
and Giroux, 1997), 75; Jorie Graham, "Pollock and Canvas," in *The End of Beauty*
(New York: Ecco, 1987), 84, 89; James Tate, in *Shroud of the Gnome* (Hopewell, NJ:
Ecco, 1997), 38. Subsequent page references to all these works will be given paren-
thetically in the text.

3. For another account of 1980s poetic production, see Roger Gilbert, "Tex-
tured Information: Politics, Pleasure, and Poetry in the Eighties," *Contemporary Literature* 33, no. 2 (Summer 1992): 243–274.

4. For a recent history of MFA programs and their effects on postwar writing
(primarily fiction), see Mark McGurl, *The Program Era: Postwar Fiction and the Rise
of Creative Writing* (Cambridge, MA: Harvard University Press, 2009), especially
chapter 2. See also Vernon Shetley, *After the Death of Poetry: Poet and Audience in
Contemporary America* (Durham, NC: Duke University Press, 1993), which describes the "institutionally produced audience" of New Critical pedagogy (12); see
esp. 12–21 and 103–109, in which Shetley argues for the New Critical culture's pressure on audience and reading practices. Shetley applies Charles Altieri's binary
scheme of lucid and lyric discursive modes (which Altieri employs in his *Self and
Sensibility in Contemporary Poetry* [Cambridge: Cambridge University Press, 1984])
to describe a split between PhD and MFA cultures (assigning to MFAs the lyric and
to PhDs the lucid). Clearly, I think differently: that New Critical modes of reading
persist as antitype for would-be advocates of "lucidity" begins to show the limits of
that particular binary.

5. For a comprehensive and trenchant account of both movements and their
relation to each other, see Brian M. Reed, *Nobody's Business: Twenty-First Century
Avant-Garde Poetics* (Ithaca, NY: Cornell University Press, 2013).

6. Elizabeth Bishop, "Santarem" (1976) in *Poems, Prose, and Letters,* ed. Robert Giroux and Lloyd Schwartz (New York: Library of America, 2008), 175–176.

7. Lynn Keller, *Remaking It New: Contemporary American Poetry and the Modernist Tradition* (Cambridge: Cambridge University Press, 1987), 36.

8. James Longenbach, "Poetry Is Poetry: On John Ashbery," *Boston Review,* July 1, 2005, http://bostonreview.net/poetry/poetry-poetry.

9. Ibid. Longenbach refers us, with "golden age," to a statement Ashbery made about Robert Duncan, in which Ashbery suggests that what was attractive was the "tone" of that "fine, touching" work—a blend of English and French Surrealism and "American plain directness." In Ashbery, "Introduction to a Reading by Robert Duncan" (1967) in *Selected Prose,* ed. Eugene Richie (Ann Arbor: University of Michigan Press, 2004), 93.

10. The appeal of Ashbery's nondisjunctive experiments to readers and critics in the mainstream has rendered them problematic and shameful to some avant-garde readers. See Marjorie Perloff's "Normalizing John Ashbery" (*Jacket* 2 [1998], http://jacketmagazine.com/02/perloff02.html, whose title suggests Perloff's larger thesis: the legibility of some of Ashbery's less disjunctive poems has made him seem to confirm "traditional" and mainstream lyric values, thus "normalizing" him.

11. Ibid.

12. Bob Perelman, "The First Person," *Hills* 6–7 (1980), reprinted in *Hills* 3–8 (1983): 156.

13. Jack Sanders, *The Secrets of Wildflowers: A Delightful Feast of Little-Known Facts, Folklore, and History* (Guilford, CT: Lyons, 2003), 63–64.

14. Perelman, Robert Grenier, Jeanne Lance, Tom Mandel, and Ron Silliman discussed the poem in the previously cited *Hills* 6–7. Perelman finds it "all persona in the wrong sense" (156); the poem offers readers a conventional, "reassuring, soothing sense of self" coincident with commodity culture (161). Silliman focuses on its poeticism: "you hear language being used 'poetically,' like the car purring, it comes across in a really smarmy way" (162).

15. Andrew Epstein, "Verse vs. Verse: The Language Poets Are Taking Over the Academy, but Will Success Destroy Their Integrity?," *Lingua Franca,* September 2000, 45–54.

16. One example might be Tom Clark's "Stalin as Linguist," which appeared in *Poetry Flash,* July 1985, reprinted in *Partisan Review* 54, no. 2 (1987): 299–304. Fear of the Language writers' power as a group with an agenda also informs James Brook's short piece, in which he fantasizes a "language school" whose leader, Barrett Watten, he compares to Ronald Reagan as an "authoritarian personality." Brook, "Political Poetry and Formalist Avant-Gardes: Four Viewpoints," in *City Lights Review 1,* ed. Lawrence Ferlinghetti and Nancy J. Peters (San Francisco: City Lights Books, 1987).

17. Perloff's essay originally appeared in 1982, but she uses it as an introduction of sorts to her 1996 book on "poets in the Pound tradition," *The Dance of the Intellect:*

Studies in the Poetry of the Pound Tradition (Cambridge: Cambridge University Press, 1985), 23.

18. The murky keyword status of "meditative" lyric is confirmed, perhaps paradoxically, by the fact that the term is not defined in the last three editions of *The Princeton Encyclopedia of Poetry and Poetics.*

19. M. H. Abrams, "Structure and Style in the Greater Romantic Lyric," in *Correspondent Breeze: Essays on English Romanticism* (New York: Norton, 1984), 77.

20. Marjorie Perloff, "Poetry Chronicle, 1970–71," *Contemporary Literature* 14, no. 1 (Winter 1973): 128. In this article, and in the following two articles, Perloff coins and articulates the conventions of the epiphany poem. Perloff, "The Two Poetries: The Postwar Lyric in Britain and America," *Contemporary Literature* 18, no. 3 (Summer 1977): 263–278; and Perloff, "From Image to Action: The Return of Story in Postmodern Poetry," *Contemporary Literature* 23, no. 4 (Autumn 1982): 411–427. Though the following source does not mention the "epiphany poem," Perloff's terms in describing the "Romantic paradigm" against which Language reacted are the same here: "Language Poetry and the Lyric Subject: Ron Silliman's Albany, Susan Howe's Buffalo," *Critical Inquiry* 25, no. 3 (Spring 1999): 405–434.

21. Abrams's accounts of the Greater Romantic Lyric and meditative modes, Perloff's description of the "epiphany" poem, and descriptions of Deep Image poetry all share the idea that the poet-speaker is located—dramatically situated—poised to reflect, usually on a natural scene. Describing Bly's later work, Kevin Bushell writes, "The poet meditates upon a particular object, allowing the plenum of sensual detail to stimulate the imagination and produce a series a playful associative leaps, often leading to some sort of discovery or revelation. Many of Bly's object poems turn spiritual and surreal near their close." Bushell, "Leaping into the Unknown: The Poetics of Robert Bly's Deep Image," Modern American Poetry Site, n.d., http://www.english.illinois.edu/maps/poets/a_f/bly/bushell.html. Michel Delville writes of the Deep Image poem that it "usually delivers a moment of mystical enlightenment rooted in the poet's observation of concrete surroundings." Delville, *The American Prose Poem: Poetic Form and the Boundaries of Genre* (Gainesville: University Press of Florida, 1998), 165.

22. Perloff, "From Image to Action," 427.

23. Craig Dworkin, "Craig Dworkin Interview," by Jared Wells, in *Spratt's Medium* (blog), August 2011, http://sprattsmedium.blogspot.com/2011/08/craig-dworkin-interview.html.

24. Craig Dworkin, "The Fate of Echo," in *Against Expression: An Anthology of Conceptual Writing,* ed. Craig Dworkin and Kenneth Goldsmith (Evanston, IL: Northwestern University Press, 2011), xliii.

25. Michael Golston, "Mobilizing Forms: Lyric, Scrolling Device, and Assembly Lines in P. Inman's 'nimr,'" in *New Definitions of Lyric: Theory, Technology, and Culture,* ed. Mark Jeffreys (New York: Routledge, 1998), 3.

26. Indeed, in "Language Poetry," Perloff makes clear that a Keatsian, Stevensian Romanticism is what marks the epiphany mode of such mainstream writers as Louise Glück and Charles Wright (432–433).

27. Several critics have noted the flatness of these lines. See Tony Hoagland, "The Three Tenors: Glück, Hass, Pinsky and the Deployment of Talent," *American Poetry Review* 32, no. 4 (July–August 2003): 37–42.

28. Robert Hass, "An Interview with Robert Hass," by Thomas Gardner, in *Regions of Unlikeness: Explaining Contemporary Poetry* (Lincoln: University of Nebraska Press, 1999), 166–167.

29. Ruurd R. Nauta, "The *Recusatio* in Flavian Poetry," in *Flavian Poetry*, ed. Ruurd R. Nauta, J. J. L. Smolenaars, and H. J. Van Dam (Boston: Brill, 2005), 21, 25–26.

30. Goldberg, "Early Republican Epic," in *A Companion to Ancient Epic*, ed. John Miles Foley (Malden, MA: Blackwell, 2005), 429. J. P. Sullivan, *Propertius: A Critical Introduction* (Cambridge: Cambridge University Press, 2010), 127.

31. See Goldberg, "Early Republican," from whose translation and reading of the sixth *Ecologue* I draw. See also Nauta, "The *Recusatio*," 25–26.

32. Indeed, the very tenor of a blog like Ron Silliman's assumes still a kind of us-versus-them rhetoric that such poems as Hass's betray. This is not to say that I am advocating Hass's poem as a sign of a successful "hybrid" or "third way." It is precisely the uneasy admission of its own absorption of certain tropes associated with lyric that renders it an interesting prehistorical example to the critical urge to assert hybridization of so-called mainstream or School of Quietude and avant-garde principles.

33. While some of Stephen Burt's description of "Elliptical" poets (a term he coined) might fit Hass—"they have read (most of them) Stein's heirs, and the 'language writers,' and have chosen to do otherwise"—his claim in a later article, that "they [Elliptical poets] want to challenge their readers, violate decorum, surprise or explode assumptions about what belongs in a poem, or what matters in life, and to do so while meeting traditional lyric goals," rests on an idea of lyric that Hass foregrounds as shameful. Nevertheless, Hass does not tend to "swerve" in the ways Burt identifies. See Burt, "*Smokes,* by Susan Wheeler" (review), *Boston Review* 23, no. 3 (Summer 1998), http://new.bostonreview.net/BR23.3/burt.html; and the later article "The Elliptical Poets" (1999), in *Close Calls with Nonsense: Reading New Poetry* (St. Paul, MN: Graywolf, 2009), 346.

34. Cole Swensen coins the term "hybrid" for an anthology of poems she reads as "honoring the avant-garde mandate to renew the forms and expand the boundaries of poetry—thereby increasing the expressive potential of language itself—while also remaining committed to the emotional spectra of lived experience." It is thus a category that maintains a commitment to the expressive and personal that are centrally in question for the avant-garde, the shame of which is foregrounded by lyric shame poems. Swensen, introduction to *American Hybrid: A Norton*

Anthology of New Poetry, ed. Cole Swensen and David St. John (New York: Norton, 2009), xxi.

35. By contrast, we could point to poems from Hass's 1979 collection *Praise,* such as "Meditation at Lagunitas" or "Picking Blackberries with a Friend Who Has Been Reading Jacques Lacan," that tip their hand to poststructuralism only or even (as in the second) dismiss its doubts about language in favor, it seems, of "experience." Hass, *Praise* (New York: Ecco, 1979), 4–5, 36.

36. As Robert Archambeau indicates in his study of Yvor Winters's influence on a generation of poets who studied at Stanford, it is also very much the late-midcentury mode of other of Winters's students, such as Robert Pinsky. Archambeau, *Laureates and Heretics: Six Careers in American Poetry* (Norte Dame, IN: Notre Dame University Press, 2010).

37. Frank O'Hara, "Meditations in an Emergency," in *Meditations in an Emergency* (1957; repr., New York: Grove, 1967), 38.

38. See Andrew Rathman, review of *Sun Under Wood,* by Robert Hass, *Chicago Review* 43 (Winter 1997): 106–111, which complains of the collection's "current dilemma" about "singing" but praises "Interrupted Meditation" for handling that dilemma well. See also Wes Davis's review of Hass's *Time and Materials* in *Parnassus* 31, nos. 1–2 (2009): 275–308, which reads "Interrupted Meditation" as a "defense of lyric"; whereas Michael Hofmann's review of *Sun Under Wood* in the *New York Times* worries that "Interrupted Meditation" shows Hass turning, out of boredom, from the virtues of the "well-made poem." Hofmann, "At the Center of Things," in "Books," April 27, 1997, http://www.nytimes.com/books/97/04/27/reviews/970427 .27hofmant.html?_r=4. All these reviewers place Hass's work in a "meditative" context that goes undefined.

39. Hofmann, "At the Center of Things."

40. Ibid.

41. Richard Lyons would disagree with this: he says that meditative poems are always "conscious of [themselves] as a 'made thing.'" Lyons, "A Loose Net: Some Meditative American Poets," in *Planet on the Table: Poets on the Reading Life,* ed. Sharon Bryan and William Olsen (Louisville, KY: Sarabande Books, 2003), 218.

42. See Cleanth Brooks, "The Heresy of Paraphrase," in *The Well-Wrought Urn* (New York: Houghton, Mifflin, Harcourt, 1947). Brooks argues that we ought not think of form as external, warning against conceiving of "'form' in the conventional sense . . . as a kind of envelope which 'contains' the 'content.' The structure obviously is everywhere conditioned by the nature of the material that goes into the poem. The nature of the material sets the problem to be solved, and the solution is the ordering of the material" (194).

43. "Backyard epiphany" became a term by the late 1990s to invoke the tired, problematic conventions of United States contemporary verse. See Robert Archambeau, "John Peck: Modernist after Modernism" (review), *Notre Dame Review* 11 (Winter 2001), 165.

44. For a brief sampling of avant-garde responses to William Stafford's "Traveling Through the Dark," see the Modern American Poetry website for snippets of criticism on the poem: http://www.english.illinois.edu/maps/poets/s_z/stafford/dark.htm, including snippets of the printed critical conversation about the poem between Robert Grenier, Bob Perelman, Ron Silliman, and Jeanne Lance in *Hills* 6–7.

45. William Stafford, "Traveling Through the Dark," in *Traveling Through the Dark* (New York: Harper and Row, 1962), 11

46. Perloff, "Language Poetry," 423. Subsequent page references to this source will be given parenthetically in text.

47. Perloff argued the same using a Denise Levertov poem in her response to *New Definitions of Lyric,* published with that collection of essays. Perloff, "A Response," in Jeffreys, *New Definitions,* 243–253.

48. Liesl Olsen also recognizes that Hass's sense of shame as a poet is one he would associate with a Rilkean sublimity: she writes of "Interrupted Meditation," "To flee in song (the impulse is Rilkean) and to feel shame: the ambivalence of Hass's ending is characteristic." Olsen, "Robert Hass's Guilt or the Weight of Wallace Stevens," *American Poetry Review,* September 1, 2007, 37–45.

49. So commonly does the backyard setting appear in Wright's poetry that Willard Spiegelman sums up his work with the epithet "Backyard Metaphysician." Spiegelman, "Landscape and Identity: Charles Wright's Backyard Metaphysics," *Southern Review* 40, no. 1 (Winter 2004): 172–196.

50. Abrams, "The Correspondent Breeze: A Romantic Metaphor," in *Correspondent Breeze,* 24–43.

51. Another, perhaps even more explicit referencing of avant-garde aesthetics (a mix of embrace and refusal) occurs in Wright's poem "Envoi," which appeared with "Disjecta Membra" and several poems titled "Meditation . . ." in the collection *Black Zodiac* (1997).

52. Lyons, "Loose Net," 223. In Anderson's tenure at the University of Arizona, the poet whom Lyons calls unusually unashamed taught a range of poets who continued in a meditative tradition, including Tony Hoagland and the late Agha Shahed Ali. Over the course of Lyons's essay, he identifies three kinds of meditative poets: "talkers" (who include such poets as James Wright and would include Hass, though Lyons does not discuss him), "performers" (where he places Robert Lowell and Adrienne Rich), and "visual artists" (where he puts Elizabeth Bishop, Wallace Stevens, and Charles Wright). Nevertheless, he assigns to all a "discursive" quality.

53. In Stern's *Early Collected Poems, 1965–1992* (New York: Norton, 2010), see especially "Stepping Out of Poetry" (112), "The Shirt Poem" (170–172), and "Someone Will Do It for Me" (520–522).

54. Marjorie Perloff, *Differentials: Poetry, Poetics, Pedagogy* (Tuscaloosa: University of Alabama Press, 2004), 256.

322NOTES TO PAGES 236–239

55. One of many examples is Ashbery's refusal to align himself with "The New York School," even in the act of describing it. See Ashbery, "The New York School of Poets," in *Selected Prose*, 113–116.

56. "Against Interpretation" (1964) in *Against Interpretation: And Other Essays* (New York: Picador, 1966), 3–14.

57. Stephen Burt, "Close Calls with Nonsense: How to Read, and Perhaps Enjoy, Very New Poetry," in the *Believer*, May 2004, http://www.believermag.com/issues /200405/?read=article_burt, reprinted in *Close Calls with Nonsense*, 5–22. For another view on Graham's contested status as a bridge figure in the late 1990s, see Charles Molesworth, "Jorie Graham: Living in the World," *Salmagundi* 120 (1998): 276–284.

58. Jorie Graham, "An Interview with Jorie Graham," in Gardner, *Regions of Unlikeness*, 221.

59. Both essays appear in Hejinian, *The Language of Inquiry* (Berkeley: University of California Press, 2000).

60. Jorie Graham, "An Interview with Jorie Graham," in Gardner, *Regions of Unlikeness*, 230–231.

61. Quoted in Ashbery, "Throughout Is This Quality of Thingness: Elizabeth Bishop," in *Selected Prose*, 121. John Shoptaw discusses Bishop's influences on Ashbery throughout *On the Outside Looking Out: John Ashbery's Poetry* (Cambridge, MA: Harvard University Press, 1994). In an interview with Mark Ford, Ashbery names Bishop and Marianne Moore as the two greatest influences on the poems in his *Some Trees*. See Mark Ford, "Mont D'Espoir or Mount Despair: Early Bishop, Early Ashbery, and the French," *PN Review* 23, no. 4 (March–April 1997), reprinted in *Poetry and the Sense of Panic: Critical Essays on Elizabeth Bishop and John Ashbery*, ed. Lionel Kelly (Atlanta: Rodopi, 2000), 9–27. See also Terrance Diggory's recent *Encyclopedia of the New York School Poets* (New York: Infobase, 2010), 60, which reads Bishop as an influence on Ashbery's practice and locates her in the near vicinity of the New York School. See also Thomas Travisano, *Elizabeth Bishop: Her Artistic Development* (Charlottesville: University of Virginia Press, 1988), 98; Luke Carson, "John Ashbery's Elizabeth Bishop," *Twentieth-Century Literature* 54, no. 4 (Winter 2008): 448–471; and Thomas Gardner, "Bishop and Ashbery: Two Ways Out of Stevens," in *Wallace Stevens Journal* 19, no. 2 (Fall 1995): 201. This entire issue of the *Wallace Stevens Journal* concentrates on crosscurrents between the two poets.

62. John Ashbery, "Vaucanson," in *April Galleons* (New York: Viking, 1987), 25. Subsequent page references to this volume will be given parenthetically in the text.

63. David Sweet's "'And *Ut Pictura Poesis* Is Her Name': John Ashbery, the Plastic Arts, and the Avant-Garde" (*Comparative Literature* 50, no. 4 [Autumn 1998]: 316–332) considers a range of Ashbery's work from the period to be thinking through its "ambivalence about being avant-garde in the wake of the Avant-Garde" (322). Sweet is referring of course to the historical avant-garde as it emerged in the plastic arts in the late 1950s.

64. John Ashbery, "And *Ut Pictura Poesis* is Her Name," in *Houseboat Days* (New York: Viking Press, 1977), 45–46.

65. Shetley, *After the Death of Poetry*, 111; "Write like Tennyson" is quoted in "Parallel Lines," a profile of Ashbery in *The Guardian*, by Nicholas Wroe, Friday, April 22, 2005. http://www.theguardian.com/books/2005/apr/23/featuresreviews.guardianreview13.

66. Amy Gerstler, "Lively Language," *Los Angeles Times*, November 27, 1994, http://articles.latimes.com/1994-11-27/books/bk-1809_1_james-tate; Julian Moynahan, "Review of *Absences*," *New York Times*, November 12, 1972, 109; Adam Kirsch, "Stop Making Sense," review of *Shroud of the Gnome*, *New York Times*, April 26, 1998, http://www.nytimes.com/books/98/04/26/reviews/980426.26kirscht.html.

67. Gerstler, "Lively Language"; Moynahan, "Review of *Absences*."

68. Andrew Zawacki, "Present and Unaccounted For: James Tate and Mimetology," in *On James Tate*, ed. Brian Henry (Ann Arbor: University of Michigan Press, 2004), 33–54.

69. James Tate, "The Book of Lies," in *Selected Poems* (Middletown, CT: Wesleyan University Press, 1991), 4. Subsequent page references to this volume will be given parenthetically in the text as *SP*.

70. Ashbery had been working with surrealism all along. The phrase "quiet but luminous" comes from Dana Gioia's assessment of the Deep Image movement in "James Tate and American Surrealism," *Denver Quarterly* 33, no. 3 (Fall 1998): 77, reprinted in revised form in *Disappearing Ink: Poetry at the End of Print Culture* (St. Paul, MN: Graywolf, 2004), 252.

71. James Tate, "First Lesson," in *Absences* (Pittsburgh: Carnegie Mellon University Press, 1990), 11.

72. For more on Ashbery and abandoned structures, see Marit MacArthur, *The American Landscape in the Poetry of Frost, Bishop, and Ashbery: The House Abandoned* (New York: Palgrave Macmillan, 2008).

73. These poems include "The Great Root System," "A Manual of Enlargement," "More Late, Less the Same," "Becoming a Scout," "The Nitrogen Cycle," "From an Island," "In My Own Backyard," "Summer, Maine Coast," and "The Worshipful Company of Fletchers." Several others seem to promise a kind of meditative, natural, descriptive, and self-expressive mode that will follow from their titles and, flagrantly, fail to deliver: "Back to Nature" and "Color in the Garden," for instance. As such, one might say that Tate gestures here to a Wordsworthian tradition, which is not true of his earlier collections. The fact that this gesture to conventionality occurs in the late 1980s and early 1990s poems suggests even more strongly that Tate's work thinks through the lens of contemporary critiques.

74. John Ashbery, "John Ashbery on James Tate," Academy of American Poetry website, n.d., http://www.poets.org/viewmedia.php/prmMID/15760.

75. Most of the poems in the first section of Wright's *Chickamauga* are set in the poet's backyard, meditations on landscape taken up "after reading." Wright, *Chickamauga: Poems* (New York: Farrar, Straus and Giroux, 1995), 3–21. Another important

ur-text of the mode, however totally unashamed and unself-conscious about its "stand[ing] on top" of the nature it emblematizes, is, of course, Robert Lowell's "Skunk Hour" (1959), in *Life Studies and For the Union Dead* (New York: Macmillan, 2006), 94–95.

76. James Tate, "In My Own Backyard," in *Worshipful Company of Fletchers* (New York: Ecco, 1994), 68. Subsequent page references to this volume will be given parenthetically in the text.

77. Ron Silliman, Carla Harryman, Lyn Hejinian, Steve Benson, Bob Perelman, and Barrett Watten, "Aesthetic Tendency and the Politics of Poetry: A Manifesto," *Social Text* 19–20 (1988): 273.

78. James Tate, "Of Two or Three Minds," *Shroud of the Gnome* (New York: HarperCollins, 1997), 66. Subsequent page references to this volume will be given parenthetically in text.

79. Dworkin, "The Fate of Echo," xliii; Marjorie Perloff, "Poetry on the Brink: Reinventing the Lyric," *Boston Review,* May–June 2012, http://www.bostonreview.net/forum/poetry-brink.

80. The idea that the figure of the Poetess has always been about the missing person at the heart of supposed poetic expression, and a cipher for readerly desire, is available in a range of recent work on the Poetess tradition. For a general account, including a useful list of secondary resources on the concept of a "Poetess tradition," see Yopie Prins, "Poetess," in *The Princeton Encyclopedia of Poetry and Poetics,* ed. Roland Greene, Stephen Cushman, Clare Cavanagh, Jahan Ramazani, and Paul Rouzer, 4th ed. (Princeton, NJ: Princeton University Press, 2012), 1051–1054. For a broad account of that tradition, see Virginia Jackson, "Poetry as Poetess," in *The Cambridge Companion to Nineteenth-Century American Poetry,* ed. Kerry Larson (Cambridge: Cambridge University Press, 2012), 54–75.

81. Elizabeth Bishop to Robert Lowell, July 11, 1951, in *Words in Air: The Complete Correspondence of Robert Lowell and Elizabeth Bishop,* ed. Thomas Travisano and Saskia Hamilton (New York: Farrar, Straus and Giroux, 2008), 122.

82. James Tate, "Crimes Against Lyric," in *Distance from Loved Ones* (Hanover, NH: University Press of New England for Wesleyan University Press, 1990), 46.

83. Mark Ford, "Distance from Loved Ones," in Henry, *On James Tate,* 111. Lee Upton suggests something similar about the first-person "characters" in Tate's poems, who "fail at proper self-writing. They post in comic opposition to representations of self-aware, self-consistent, and responsible authority," a "demasculinizing of male characters" that "boldly counters patriarchal posturings of expertise." I would add that it is a specifically lyric interpretive expertise that Tate refuses and that would have both secured an image of self-awareness inclined to be interpretable and served as the "proper self-writing." Upton, "The Master of the Masterless: James Tate and the Pleasures of Error," in Henry, *On James Tate,* 57.

84. Michael Davidson, *Guys Like Us: Citing Masculinity in Cold War Poetics* (Chicago: University of Chicago Press, 2003), 30.

85. See Scott Brewster, *Lyric,* New Critical Idiom (New York: Routledge, 2009), 9, for claims about the trend, since the eighteenth century, for lyric to be gendered as "feminine" and understood as in need of defense by masculinization.

86. An interesting project in this regard is the book *Scham/Shame: A Collaboration* (Kingston, NY: McPherson, 2005), by Robert Kelly (once associated with the Deep Image poets but more recently with the American West Coast avant-garde) and Birgit Kempker, a noted German poet and essayist. The book was written, at Kempker's invitation, as a series of email exchanges by the two poets (who did not know each other personally). Kempker wrote in German and Kelly in English, and their original texts appear on right-hand pages; on left-hand pages, each poet translates the other's work into his or her own language. The cover photo presents half of Kempker's face on the left and half of Kelly's on the right. The work is punctuated throughout with comments (often by Kelly) about the shame of reading, of mimesis, and of having a self.

87. Lynn Emanuel, "I Tried to Flatter Myself into Extinction," in *Noose and Hook* (Pittsburgh: University of Pittsburgh Press, 2010), 45.

88. Olena Kalytiak Davis, "The Lyric 'I' Drives to Pick Up Her Children from School: A Poem in the Postconfessional Mode," *Fence* 8, nos. 1–2 (2005): 99–103, reprinted in *The Poem She Didn't Write, and Other Poems* (Port Townsend, WA: Copper Canyon, 2014). Subsequent page references to this poem refer to the *Fence* version and will be given parenthetically in the text.

89. Ira Sadoff, "Olena Kalytiak Davis Revising Tradition: The Retro-New," in *History Matters: Contemporary Poetry on the Margins of American Culture* (Iowa City: University of Iowa Press, 2009), 202. The poem's line count is difficult to determine because some lines are indented, as if too long for the page trim. However, some lines are indented as if they are prose blocks. In these cases, the very premise of lines is so strained that it is hard to know how (or whether) to count.

90. Grossman's text of note in lyric theory is "Summa Lyrica: A Primer of the Common Places in Speculative Poetics," in section 2 of *The Sighted Singer: Two Works on Poetry for Readers and Writers,* by Allen Grossman and Mark Halliday (Baltimore: Johns Hopkins University Press, 1992).

91. The line is from the 1972 collection of Antin's improvised "talk poems," *Talking* (1972) (New York: Dalkey Archive Press, 2001). It is quoted in Gilbert Sorrentino's review, "David Antin Talking," first published as "Review of *Talking at the Boundaries,* by David Antin" in the *New York Times Book Review,* November 28, 1976, reprinted in Sorrentino, *Something Said* (New York: Dalkey Archive, 1984), 197.

92. Sadoff, "Olena Kalytiak Davis," 203.

93. Lowell's presence in the poem suggests how limited these distinctions can be when thought through the lens of gender. Lowell famously, if subtly, gendered poetics of the midcentury in terms of "raw" and "cooked," and yet he complicated his own place within those categories: he admits that he "cooked" his raw material;

writes his famous, supposed "confessional" work at several moments from a female perspective (for example, in " 'To Speak of Woe That Is in Marriage,' " in *Life Studies*, 93; and explores his sense of identification with a Poetess tradition.

94. Quoted in "Oral History Interview with Fairfield Porter," by Paul Cummings, June 6, 1968, Archives of American Art, Smithsonian Institution. Davis makes a slight change in quoting Porter, who said, "I mean, I like in art when the artist doesn't know what he knows in general; he only knows what he knows specifically. And what he knows in general or what can be known in general becomes apparent later on by what he has had to put down. That is to me the most interesting art form. It expresses that. In other words you are not in control of nature quite; you are part of nature." Davis makes it "i mean i like in art."

95. David Lehman, *The Last Avant-Garde: The Making of the New York School of Poets* (New York: Doubleday, 1998), 343.

96. Jed Perl, *New Art City: Manhattan at Mid-Century* (New York: Knopf, 2005), 120.

97. Clement Greenberg famously dismissed de Kooning's work: "De Kooning has won quicker and wider acceptance in this country than any of the other original 'abstract expressionists'; his need to include the past as well as to forestall the future seems to reassure a lot of people who still find Pollock incomprehensible." Greenberg, " 'American-Type' Painting" (1955), in *Art and Culture: Critical Essays* (Boston: Beacon, 1961), 214. An earlier version appeared in *Partisan Review* in 1955. I offer the quotation for how it can seem relevant to Kalytiak's situation as someone who feels uncomfortable about her own relationship to tradition and its future in poetry.

98. See Susan F. Lake, *Willem de Kooning: The Artist's Materials* (Los Angeles: Getty Conservation Institute, 2010), 16–19, for a discussion of de Kooning's critical reception over the course of his career and beyond.

99. Thomas B. Hess, *Willem de Kooning* (New York: Museum of Modern Art, 1968), 16.

100. Here, one might invoke Sianne Ngai's chapter on "paranoia" and the belatedness of the critic of feminist avant-garde work experiences, in *Ugly Feelings* (Cambridge, MA: Harvard University Press, 2005), 304–317 especially.

AFTERWORD

1. D.A. Powell. "Annie Get Your Gun," *Poetry*, February 2009, http://www .poetryfoundation.org/poetrymagazine/article/182839.

2. Joshua Mehigan, "The Final Manifesto," *Poetry*, February 2009, http:// www.poetryfoundation.org/poetrymagazine/article/182835.

3. A.E. Stallings, "Presto Manifesto!," *Poetry*, February 2009, http://www .poetryfoundation.org/poetrymagazine/article/182841.

4. Quoted in Amiri Baraka, "A Post-Racial Anthology? *Angles of Ascent: A Norton Anthology of Contemporary African American Poetry*" (review), *Poetry,* May 1, 2013, http://www.poetryfoundation.org/poetrymagazine/article/245846.

5. LeRoi Jones (Imamu Amiri Baraka), "Hymn for Lanie Poo," in *Preface to a Twenty-Volume Suicide Note* (New York: Totem Press for Corinth Books, 1961), 6–12.

6. Dorothy J. Wang, *Thinking Its Presence: Form, Race, and Subjectivity in Contemporary Asian American Poetry* (Paolo Alto, CA: Stanford University Press, 2013).

7. Quoted in Petra Kuppers, "Poetry-ing: Feminist Disability Aesthetics and Poetry Communities," *English Language Notes* 49, no. 2 (Fall–Winter 2011): 73.

8. Ibid., 75.

9. Julie Carr and John-Michel Rivera, "The Shape of the I: A Poetics of Form," *English Language Notes* 49, no. 2 (Fall–Winter 2011): 3.

10. Julie Carr, "Shame and 'The Shape of the I," Poetry Foundation website, April 12, 2012, http://www.poetryfoundation.org/harriet/2012/04/shame-and-the-shape-of-the-i/.

11. Rachel Zucker, "Confessionalography: A GNAT (Grossly Non-Academic Talk) on 'I' in Poetry," Academy of American Poets website, n.d., http://www.poets.org/viewmedia.php/prmMID/5948#sthash.rDgbnDv7.dpuf. Another Zucker piece informed by and interesting in light of lyric shame is "a homespun of questions pulled over a loom of gender and race with the voices of ancestral (mostly living) women speaking in the lacunae," written for a panel called "The Need to Speak: Writing the Political Poem" at the Association of Writing Programs conference in 2012. It was published in *Evening Will Come* 25 (January 2013), http://www.thevolta.org/ewc25-rzucker-p1.html.

12. Cate Marvin and Amy King, "Poets' Roundtable on Person and Persona, Part 2," October 21, 2013, *Los Angeles Review of Books,* http://lareviewofbooks.org/essay/poets-roundtable-on-person-and-persona-part-2.

13. See Dworkin and Goldsmith, eds. *Against Expression: An Anthology of Conceptual Writing* (Evanston, IL: Northwestern University Press, 2011); see also Kenneth Goldsmith, *Uncreative Writing: Managing Language in the Digital Age* (New York: Columbia University Press, 2013), and Marjorie Perloff, *Unoriginal Genius: Poetry by Other means in the New Century* (Chicago: Chicago University Press, 2010).

14. Sina Queyras, "New Lyric Manifestoes," *Lemon Hound* (blog), August 1, 2013, http://lemonhound.com/2013/08/01/new-lyric-manifestos/. See also poet-scholar Rachel Galvin's 2013 "Lyric Backlash," an essay in the *Boston Review* written in response to Calvin Bedient's defense, in a previous *Boston Review* issue, of the "lyric" and "lyrical expression" "against Conceptualism." Galvin suggests that lyric shame can adhere even to experimental projects such as Kenneth Goldsmith's Conceptual writing, accused (Galvin cites) by Matvei Yankelvich of an "embarrassing

indulgence in left-over Romantic assumptions of authorial intent." Quoted in Galvin "Lyric Backlash: Thoughts on the Oulipo and César Vallejo in Response to Calvin Bedient's Complaint," in *Boston Review,* February 11, 2014, http://www .bostonreview.net/poetry/rachel-galvin-lyric-backlash. Calvin Bedient, "Against Conceptualism: Defending the Poetry of Affect," in *Boston Review,* July 24, 2013, http://www.bostonreview.net/poetry/against-conceptualism. An early draft of Galvin's essay helped me to remember that, even in the attempt to repurpose "lyric" away from its expressive associations poet Juliana Spahr performs her lyric shame. In Spahr, *This Connection of Everyone With Lungs* (Berkeley, CA: University of California Press, 2005), 13.

Acknowledgments

My thanks go first to Lindsay Waters, whose probing questions helped me enlarge this book's aims and whose vote of confidence still means a great deal to me, even as it strikes me as quite lucky. Shanshan Wang ably escorted the manuscript through the publishing process, with wit, grace, and a fine eye for detail. Several anonymous readers of the manuscript offered the detailed and generous responses and suggestions one dreams of, and I am hugely grateful for them. Akiva Gottlieb and Polly Rosenswaike helped with various stages of manuscript preparation, and Kimberly Giambattisto and Andrew Katz provided expert copyediting. All have my sincere and humble thanks.

This book was conceived and written at the University of Michigan, and many of its driving concerns were tested in several rounds of a seminar on contemporary American poetry and "the personal" I offered to advanced undergraduate and graduate students in Michigan's Department of English. Many of those seminar conversations have found their way into these pages. I have also been lucky to encounter the collective and individual wisdom of those in the Department of English, and to benefit from its many forms of support, including leave time to write and funds to prepare the manuscript. Jane Johnson and Karly Mitchell need special mention here for their professionalism and wisdom in managing department affairs. Department funds also allowed for a manuscript workshop, run by Theresa Tinkle, wherein I received heroically detailed, probing, and helpful suggestions on the book's first draft from Andrew Epstein, and from my esteemed colleagues, Kerry Larson and Marjorie Levinson. Larry Goldstein deserves special mention for his contributions to that workshop, and for his support in general. Alice Tsay and Megan Sweeney took remarkably fine notes at the meeting.

If I have failed to realize all that those first, careful readers imagined for the draft, I have learned a great deal from their responses, which will influence my future thinking, reading, and research agenda. And then there are warm thanks due to those who attended the manuscript workshop, and for conversations long and short, and for various kinds of support from people too numerous to list in full. I feel fortunate to have had these from all these people, though no doubt the list could be longer still: Michael Byers, Gregg Crane, Rachel Feder, Jonathan Freedman, Linda Gregerson, Zeynep Gürsel, Julia Hansen, Leslie Hinkson, Susan Hutton, Hui-Hui Hu, Van Jordan, Toshiaki Komura, Petra Kuppers, Khaled Mattawa, Steven Mankouche, Caroline Miller (who first inspired my interest in Mayer's work), Abigail Murray, Julie Orringer, Benjamin Paloff, David Porter, Rebecca Porte, Michael Schoenfeldt, Megan Sweeney, Theresa Tinkle, Valerie Traub, Cody Walker, Jennifer Wenzel, John Whittier-Ferguson, Patsy Yaeger, and Andrea Zemgulys.

Sean Silver and Tina Lupton read parts of this book (sometimes on short notice), and were my fourth floor mates and my West Side neighbors at the loneliest moment of its composition; I am grateful for (and miss) our conversations and camaraderie. Scotti Parrish's questions about my research helped me to rearticulate it in earnest, and I am grateful for her thoughtful support over the years. For her friendship and wise counsel, Adela Pinch has my deep gratitude and admiration, as for her beautifully comprehensive reading of the book as it neared completion, which helped me to see it more clearly through the trees. I also feel extremely fortunate to have been able to share in conversation with Yopie Prins, who talked with me about every stage of the conception and writing of *Lyric Shame,* and who generously read many of its pages more than once. For her exemplary generosity and wisdom as a mentor, and for her willingness to share in her brilliant thinking and deep knowledge of poetics and lyric theory, my gratitude and admiration run too deep for (adequate) words.

While my Credits officially acknowledge those publishers who granted me permission to reproduce parts of poems in this book, I wish here to express my thanks to Bernadette Mayer for the thrill of answering my telephone call and for giving her kind and generous permission to quote from her work. Sincere thanks also to Bradley Paul and Olena Kalytiak Davis for generously allowing me to reproduce their work.

My thanks are due, too, to Angus Cleghorn, Bethany Hicok, Thomas Travisano, and University of Virginia Press for publishing an essay of mine where I first explored ideas of Bishop's concept of "space" in art. Reena Sastri and Marit MacArthur deserve thanks for helping along early versions of ideas that appear in Chapter 1 and Chapter 4. Though the textual evidence is scant, my thinking on the poetics of contingency while a student at Princeton University laid important groundwork for this work. My thanks to Princeton friends, mentors, and colleagues with whom I thought about poetry and reading and who helped enliven that process—Michelle Clayton, Bryn Canner, Barry McCrea, Jason Baskin, James Richardson, Maria DiBattista, Stuart Burrows, Rachel Galvin, and Jeff Dolven, to name a few—all of whom I miss. Esther Schor, Douglas Mao, and Michael Wood advised my work there, and to them I owe a debt of gratitude for teaching me how to research and to think, and for their mentorship. I was lucky to have Michael Wood's shrewd eye on this book, too, and he should know it was he who first noticed that my work at Princeton kept circling around the concept of shame. Once upon a time, Mary Kinzie taught me to recognize the strange, mute powers of poems on the page; I still read in ways shaped by her formidable example. Rhoda and Benjamin Lewis want recognition and gratitude here, too, for early exemplifying the joys of (nonacademic) intellectual inquiry to me, and for their nearly lifelong friendship, love, and support. Thinking I did with the late Stephen A. Mitchell, and with Carol Wachs, touches every page of this book. I salute, with gratitude, his memory. She has my enduring gratitude.

I dedicate *Lyric Shame* to my family. My parents, Reid and Laird White, have made this work possible with myriad forms of support, including unwavering encouragement, love, and their good example. Meg and Jim Woolard have offered their love and care consistently and at crucial moments recently. My sister, Emilie White, is my favorite and longest-standing interlocutor about books, and her daughter, Madeline Tate, is one of my newest.

Jamie Woolard has heard out and shared in countless iterations of the ideas in this book, lending his subtle eye and ear to drafts and conversations. Without his love and encouragement, as well as his heroic partnership in caring for our children, Henry and Lilah, they or I or this book would surely have foundered. Henry and Lilah, who in the time it has taken me to write this book have grown into budding readers (and even writers) in their own right, cheered me on before they knew what they were cheering. They are my joy and my inspiration, and I thank them, and Jamie, with all my heart.

Credits

OLENA KALYTIAK DAVIS

Excerpt from *The Poem She Didn't Write, and Other Poems*. Copyright © 2014 by Olena Kalytiak Davis. Reprinted with the permission of The Permissions Company, Inc. on behalf of Copper Canyon Press, www.coppercanyonpress.org.

LYNN EMANUEL

Excerpts from "Hello, Mallarmé" and "I tried to flatter myself into extinction" from *Noose and Hook,* by Lynn Emanuel, © 2010. Reprinted by permission of the University of Pittsburgh Press.

ROBERT HASS

Excerpts from "Interrupted Meditation," "Layover," "Iowa City: Early April," "Notes on 'Layover'" from *Sun Under Wood: New Poems* by ROBERT HASS. Copyright © 1996 by Robert Hass. Reprinted by permission of HarperCollins Publishers.

ROBERT LOWELL

Excerpt from "Skunk Hour" from *Collected Poems* by Robert Lowell. Copyright © 2003 by Harriet Lowell and Sheridan Lowell. Reprinted by permission of Farrar, Straus and Giroux, LLC.

BERNADETTE MAYER

Bernadette Mayer was very kind in giving her permission to quote excerpts from her writing.
Excerpts from Bernadette Mayer, *Midwinter Day* copyright © 1982 by Bernadette Mayer. Reprinted by permission of New Directions Publishing Corp.

BRADLEY PAUL

"Anybody Can Write a Poem" from *The Animals All Are Gathering,* by Bradley Paul, copyright © 2010. Reprinted by permission of the University of Pittsburgh Press.

ANNE SEXTON

Excerpt from "All God's Children Need Radios," reprinted by permission of SLL/Sterling Lord Literistic, Inc. Copyright © by Anne Sexton.

Excerpt from "The Reading," reprinted by permission of SLL/Sterling Lord Literistic, Inc. Copyright © 1977 by Anne Sexton.

"Said the Poet to the Analyst," from *To Bedlam and Part Way Back* by Anne Sexton. Copyright © 1960 by Anne Sexton, © renewed 1988 by Linda G. Sexton.

JAMES TATE

WILLIAM CARLOS WILLIAMS

Index